CCNA Guide to
Cisco Networking,
Second Edition

Kurt Hudson
Kelly Caudle
Kelly Cannon

THOMSON

™

COURSE TECHNOLOGY

Australia • Canada • Mexico • Singapore • Spain • United Kingdom • United States

THOMSON
COURSE TECHNOLOGY

CCNA Guide to Cisco Networking, Second Edition

is published by Course Technology.

Associate Publisher:
Steve Elliot

Acquisitions Editor:
William Pitkin, III

Product Manager:
Amy M. Lyon

Developmental Editor:
Dave George

Production Editor:
Brooke Albright

Technical Editor:
John Bosco

Senior Manufacturing Coordinator:
Laura Burns

Product Marketing Manager:
Jason Sakos

Associate Product Manager:
Tim Gleeson

Editorial Assistant:
Nick Lombardi

Cover Design:
Julie Malone

Text Designer:
GEX Publishing Services

Compositor:
GEX Publishing Services

TABLE OF
Contents

CHAPTER FIVE
WAN Concepts

CHAPTER SIX
Router and IOS Basics

Introduction

The proliferation of networks in the workplace and the popularity of the Internet has contributed to an increasing need for networking professionals with both LAN and WAN configuration skills. Employers are looking for qualified individuals to fill the demand for these networking jobs, and certification is a great way to prove you have what it takes. The primary objective of this book is to help you prepare for and pass the Cisco Certified Network Associate Exam (CCNA), the foundation certification upon which other Cisco certifications are built. The undisputed worldwide leader in networking equipment, Cisco manufactures routers, switches, access servers, and network management software designed to interconnect LANs and WANs around the globe.

INTENDED AUDIENCE

The *CCNA Guide to Cisco Networking, Second Edition* provides a comprehensive guide for anyone wishing to obtain a solid background in basic Cisco networking concepts, and is an ideal tool to use to prepare for CCNA certification. This book guides you through the basics of networking, configuring, and troubleshooting Cisco routers and switches. To best understand the material in this book, you should have a background in basic computer concepts and have worked with PC hardware. This book is intended for use in a classroom or an instructor-led training environment with access to Cisco routers and switches. When you finish the book, you should understand and be able to perform all objectives covered on CCNA Exam #640-607.

CHAPTER DESCRIPTIONS

Chapter 1, "Introducing Networks," introduces the OSI Reference Model and identifies why the industry uses this layered approach to networking. The five steps of data encapsulation, the function of a MAC address, and the difference between connection-oriented and connectionless network service are explored.

In **Chapter 2**, "Network Devices," you learn all about the different devices used on a network and the advantages and disadvantages of using particular devices. The devices include hubs and repeaters, bridges and switches, brouters and routers, and gateways. Devices are discussed in the context of network segmentation, because it is important to understand which devices segment the network and which do not.

In **Chapter 3**, "TCP/IP and IP Addressing," you learn about TCP/IP—the language of the Internet. TCP/IP is a suite of many protocols including ICMP, UDP, TCP, ARP, and RARP. IP addressing and subnetting is also covered in this chapter. Finally, the benefits of using ping and trace to troubleshoot IP is discussed.

In **Chapter 4**, "Network Topology and Design," you review physical and logical LAN topologies as well as cabling standards. Various network management tools are also reviewed.

In **Chapter 5**, "WAN Concepts," you are introduced to the various WAN physical standards and data link protocols operating on WAN links today. Discussion includes an introduction to various WAN technologies and protocols including ATM, T1, ISDN, X.25, Frame Relay, PPP, HDLC, and SDLC.

In **Chapter 6**, "Router and IOS Basics," you learn about the components of the router and the basic configuration commands. This includes various configuration modes and prompts, passwords, context-sensitive help, and enhanced editing features. It also includes instructions on how to configure the HyperTerminal program in Windows to access the router and how to configure the router using the System Configuration Dialog. An introduction to the Cisco 1900 series switch user interface is also incorporated.

Chapter 7, "Router Startup and Configuration," explains the boot process in a Cisco router and how to manipulate that process. CDP, Cisco's proprietary protocol, which is enabled by default on all Cisco routers and switches, is introduced. In addition, configuration of IP on the router and the 1900 series switch is discussed. Finally, troubleshooting connection problems using show commands, ping, trace, and telnet are included.

In **Chapter 8**, "Routing Protocols," you learn to differentiate between routable, nonroutable, and routing protocols. Routing protocols are categorized as either Exterior Gateway Protocols or Interior Gateway Protocols. The focus of this chapter is Interior Gateway Protocols and the two categories therein, which include distance-vector and link-state. The count-to-infinity problem with distance-vector routing protocols is discussed, as are the different ways to combat this problem. Finally, you will learn how to configure the two most popular distance-vector routing protocols, RIP and Cisco's proprietary IGRP.

Chapter 9, "IPX/SPX," delves into Novell's proprietary protocol suite. Topics include the description of the IPX/SPX protocol stack and how its protocols map to the OSI model. The parts of an IPX/SPX network address are identified. The Data Link layer frame formats supported by NetWare and the Cisco IOS are described, as well as the function of Service Advertisement Protocol (SAP) advertisements and the processes Cisco routers use when dealing with SAP advertisements. Finally, you will learn how to configure and monitor IPX/SPX on a Cisco router.

Chapter 10, "Access Lists," covers the dual purpose of access lists, which are flow control and security. You will learn the syntax of the five types of lists found on the CCNA exam. These include standard IP and IPX lists, extended IP and IPX lists, and SAP filters. You will learn the usage and rules of access lists and how to configure and apply them. Finally, you will learn how to monitor your lists on the router.

In **Chapter 11**, "PPP/ISDN," you learn about PPP encapsulation and how to configure PPP and its options on a Cisco router. You will also learn about PPP multilink and how to enable it. You will explain how to implement ISDN BRI and dial-on-demand routing on Cisco routers and learn how to configure an ISDN BRI connection.

In **Chapter 12**, "Frame Relay," you learn about Frame Relay standards and equipment and about the role of virtual circuits and performance parameters in Frame Relay. Finally, you will learn about the various Frame Relay topologies and how to configure and monitor Frame Relay on Cisco routers.

In **Chapter 13**, "Switching and VLANs," you learn about the features and benefits of Fast Ethernet, as well as the guidelines and distance limitations of Fast Ethernet. In addition, you will learn about defining full- and half-duplex Ethernet operation. You will learn to distinguish between cut-through and store-and-forward LAN switching, and to define the operation of the Spanning Tree Protocol and its benefits. You will also learn about the benefits of virtual LANs. Finally, you will learn about the configuration basics for the Cisco 1900 series switch.

Appendix A, "CCNA Certification Objectives," lists each CCNA certification objective, along with the chapter and section where information about the objective is covered.

Appendix B, "Additional Resources," provides additional sources for information on subjects covered in this course.

Appendix C, "A Networking Professional's Toolkit," provides pictures of networking tools, along with their proper names and uses.

Appendix D, "Command Summary," provides a list of the commands presented in this course. You should review these commands before you attempt the CCNA certification examination.

FEATURES

To aid you in fully understanding Cisco networking concepts, this book includes many features designed to enhance your learning experience:

- **Chapter Objectives**—Each chapter begins with a detailed list of the concepts to be mastered. This list gives you a quick reference to the chapter's contents and is a useful study aid.

- **Chapter Summary**—Each chapter's text is followed by a bulleted summary of the concepts introduced in that chapter. These summaries provide a helpful way to recap and revisit the ideas covered in each chapter.

- **Key Terms**—All of the terms within the chapter that were introduced with boldfaced text are gathered together in the Key Terms list at the end of the chapter. This provides you with a method of checking your understanding of all the terms introduced.

- **Review Questions**—The end-of-chapter assessment begins with a set of review questions that reinforce the ideas introduced in each chapter. Answering these questions will ensure that you have mastered the important concepts. The review questions can also be used to help prepare for the CCNA exam.

- **Case Projects**—Located at the end of each chapter are several case projects. In these case examples, you implement the skills and knowledge gained in the chapter through real design and implementation scenarios.

TEXT AND GRAPHIC CONVENTIONS

Additional information and exercises have been added to this book to help you better understand what's being discussed in the chapter. Icons throughout the text alert you to these additional materials. The icons used in this book are described below.

 Tips offer extra information on resources, how to attack problems, and time-saving shortcuts.

 Notes present additional helpful material related to the subject being discussed.

 The Caution icon identifies important information about potential mistakes or hazards.

 Case project are more involved, scenario-based assignments. In these extensive case project examples, you are asked to independently apply what you have learned in the chapter.

INSTRUCTOR'S MATERIALS

The following supplemental materials are available when this book is used in a classroom setting. All of the supplements available with this book are provided to the instructor on a single CD-ROM.

Electronic Instructor's Manual. The Instructor's Manual that accompanies this textbook includes:

- Additional instructional material to assist in class preparation, including suggestions for classroom activities, discussion topics, and additional projects.

- Solutions to all end-of-chapter materials, including the review questions and case projects.

- An electronic CCNA certification game.

ExamView®. This textbook is accompanied by ExamView, a powerful testing software package that allows instructors to create and administer printed, computer (LAN-based), and Internet exams. ExamView includes hundreds of questions that correspond to the topics covered in this text, enabling students to generate detailed study guides that include page references for further review. The computer-based and Internet testing components allow students to take exams at their computers and also save the instructor time by grading each exam automatically.

PowerPoint presentations. This book comes with Microsoft PowerPoint slides for each chapter. These are included as a teaching aid for classroom presentation, to make available to students on the network for chapter review, or to be printed for classroom distribution. Instructors, please feel at liberty to add your own slides for additional topics you introduce to the class.

Figure files. All of the figures and tables in the book are reproduced in bitmap format on the Instructor's Resource CD. Similar to the PowerPoint presentations, these are included as a teaching aid for classroom presentation, to make available to students for review, or to be printed for classroom distribution.

CoursePrep Test Prep Software

Exam preparation software from MeasureUp is included on the CD-ROM at the back of this book. This CoursePrep software provides 50 sample exam questions that mirror the look and feel of the CCNA #640-607 exam. For more information about MeasureUp test prep products, or to order the complete version of this software, visit their Web site at *www.measureup.com*.

Lab Manual

The Lab Manual for CCNA Guide to Cisco Networking, Second Edition was written to accompany this book. The Lab Manual provides hands-on instruction on topics that correspond to the objectives on Cisco's CCNA Exam #640-607, and skills that every networking professional should possess. To order a copy, consult your sales representative, or visit our Web site at *www.course.com*.

ACKNOWLEDGMENTS

Many talented people have participated in the creation of this book. The Development team would like to thank the Production Editor, Brooke Albright, for her resourcefulness and flexibility, and the Technical Editor, John Bosco, for his dedication and for squeezing this book into his busy schedule. We would also like to thank the reviewers for their quick and thoughtful feedback: Lionell Craddock, Bluefield State College; Russ Davis, Pittsburg Technical Institute; Tony Vargas, El Paso Community College; and Dietrich Quiring, Provo College.

Kurt Hudson

This project has quite seriously been a team effort. Steve Elliot rounded us up for the task. Amy Lyon and Dave George really made this project happen (start to finish). Kelly Cannon took an early lead in getting this book ready to go and remained a binding force throughout. Cannonball (Cannon) and KFC (Caudle) made this book great. I would like to thank our technical and production editors John Bosco and Brooke Albright for doing a very thorough job. They both caught many items that were above and beyond. Pre-copies of chapters go out to reviewers and their feedback is most helpful in making this publication better—I thank them for their efforts. Thanks to Rob Pinion for allowing me to take pictures of his routing and switching setups. Thanks to Neal Allen, Nichelle Williams, and Fluke Networks for their help. I would also like to thank my colleague Terry Bright for taking on additional tasks, which freed me up to work on this project. Lastly and most importantly, I cannot be more grateful for the amazing patience and support of my true love and wife Laura; she was my fiancée when this project began.

Kelly Caudle

First, I would like to thank the Lord for the opportunity to work on this book. I also thank Course Technology for the chance to work on this project. Additionally, I wish to thank Dave George and Amy Lyon for their help and support. Furthermore, I want to thank Kurt Hudson and Kelly Cannon for all their hard work during this project; it was a pleasure to work with such good co-authors. Last, but definitely not least, I want to thank my wife Susan for all her love and support.

Kelly Cannon

I would like to thank Course Technology for the opportunity to be involved in the world of academic publishing. I would also like to thank Kurt Hudson and Kelly Caudle for giving me the chance to work with them. In addition, I am grateful to Dave George and Amy Lyon for all of their hard work on this project. Foremost and finally I would like to thank my wonderful family, Jim, Veronica, and Adrienne.

1

INTRODUCING NETWORKS

After reading this chapter and completing the exercises, you will be able to:

♦ Identify and describe the functions of each of the seven layers of the OSI reference model

♦ Identify the reasons why the networking industry uses a layered model

♦ Define and explain the conversion steps of data encapsulation

♦ Define and describe the function of a MAC address

♦ Describe connection-oriented network service and connectionless network service, and identify the key differences between them

This chapter introduces the fundamentals and evolution of computer networking. You will learn about the reasons for networking, some networking terminology, and a bit about the different types of networks. Specifically, you will learn about networking standards and types of networking equipment. As the course progresses, the concepts presented in this chapter will be periodically revisited and expanded upon.

INTRODUCTION TO NETWORKING

A computer network, or simply a **network**, is a term that describes the connection of two or more computers by some type of medium. For example, a computer connected to the Internet over the public telephone system is part of a network. Two computers connected by a wire cable also form a network. In addition to wire cables, you can use **fiber-optic cable**, **infrared**, and radio equipment to create and maintain a connection between two or more systems, thereby forming a network.

Origin of Networking

Industry experts find it difficult to place the actual origin of networking because many devices have been networked throughout history. For example, in the 1930s, electrical engineers used a device called the Network Analyzer for simulating electrical power grids. The earliest mainframe computers also were placed in networks, in that cables connected them in order to share computing power. Today, networks include a wide variety of computers and peripheral components.

Systems that are part of a network do not have to be identical. As a matter of fact, the largest computer network in the world, the Internet, connects a wide variety of computer systems. Mainframes, IBM and IBM-compatible personal computers (PCs), and Macintosh, UNIX, and NetWare systems are all part of the Internet. Televisions, vending machines, and light switches are also part of computer networks today because creative electrical engineers have developed methods to add network interfaces to these devices.

Why Do We Use Networks?

Some people might use the words "efficiency" or "necessity" in answering the preceding question. Realistically, the question could be answered in one word: convenience. As people have grown more dependent on technology, their need for networked devices has increased.

People expect interoperability from electronic devices. For instance, every person who has a videocassette recorder (VCR) expects it to work with the television set. When connected, the two devices are essentially networked to provide the user with the ability to watch television, play movies, and record television programs. Many people integrate their televisions and VCRs with their home stereos in order to form a larger networked system. In many ways, a computer network is no more complex than a home entertainment system.

Networked computers can share data and peripherals. Without a network, people have to find other methods for transferring data between computers. These other methods include copying the data to a floppy disk or another type of storage media, and physically moving that data to another system—a method called "sneakernet," since shoes provide the transport medium between computers.

Computer networks allow for the transfer of files, data, and even shared applications without copying anything to floppy disk. In addition, networks allow computers to share items such as printers, scanners, fax machines, processors, disk drives, and other resources.

Networking Terminology

New terminology for networking and networking components emerges almost daily. Therefore, the creation of a complete and up-to-date list of networking terminology would be impossible. In this section, you will learn the most widely used networking terminology.

Connection Media

All networks use connection **media**. Wire cabling, such as twisted pair or coaxial, forms the connection in most networks. Some networks employ fiber-optic cable. It is more expensive than wire cabling, but less susceptible to **electromagnetic interference (EMI)**, which is frequently caused by nearby motors or fluorescent lighting. Still other networks use **wireless** transmission media, such as infrared or radio signals. With wireless communication, a connection is made between the devices sending and receiving the signals, with air, rather than cable, used to host the communication.

Client/Server Networks

Client/server networks have computers that are **servers** and computers that act as **clients** to those servers. In a client/server network, the servers host the resources for the clients to utilize, while a client is the computer that requests resources from the server. The term client sometimes also refers to a user. For example, a server might have a printer, or resource, attached to it for clients to use. You may see a variety of servers on a network:

- Print server: Hosts the connection to a printer so that clients can send print jobs to the printer
- File server: Maintains storage space for data that is shared with clients
- Database server: Hosts a database that clients can use to read/write and share information in an organized system with other clients
- Remote access server (RAS): Allows clients to dial-in, usually over the public telephone system, to establish connections and to access network resources from a remote location
- Web server: Provides content on the Internet for clients to connect to when "browsing" the Internet

Peer-to-Peer

When every computer on a network acts as both a client and a server, the network is a peer-to-peer network. In a **peer-to-peer network**, all computers can share resources, such as files, printers, and applications, with other computers. Peer-to-peer networks are also known as "workgroups" because all computers are on the same level and can share resources with other computers.

LAN, WAN, MAN, SAN

Depending on the size of the network, you can use different terms to describe it. For example, a **local area network (LAN)** is contained within a company or department and located in a single geographic area, usually a building or part of a building. A **wide area network (WAN)** spans multiple geographic areas and is usually connected by common telecommunication carriers. A **metropolitan area network (MAN)** is the intermediate stage between a LAN and a WAN. (The term, which is used infrequently, attempts to describe a network that is within the boundaries of a city, campus, or town, but that is larger than a LAN.) A **storage area network (SAN)** is a relatively new term that describes a series of storage devices, such as tapes, hard drives, and CDs, that are networked together to provide very fast data storage for a network or subnetwork. The devices are physically separate from the servers. This makes the network more scalable and flexible, because any server can exchange data with any storage device and additional storage devices can be added more quickly and simply.

Network Operating System

A **network operating system (NOS)** allows communication over a network. In the early days of PC computing, most PCs could not communicate on a network with other computers. This gave rise to two distinct terms: the stand-alone operating system (OS), which could not communicate on a network, and the networking OS, which could communicate on a network.

 Network administrators sometimes call the device or computer at which a user works an **end system**.

NIC

A **network interface card (NIC)** is a device that allows a computer or other device to connect to a network. This device is also known as an adapter, network card, or network interface. The NIC is a physical component that connects to the internal hardware of the computer system. The NIC allows a physical connection to the network media.

Networking Hardware

Networking hardware is a generic term that describes all the physical components of a network, such as the NIC, cable, and any related connectors. Any device or physical component that is used to connect computers in a network is considered to be network hardware.

Networking Software

The software programs used to run a network are known as networking software. These programs include the NOS and all client/server networking software programs, such as shared applications like e-mail and database applications.

UNDERSTANDING THE OSI MODEL

As computer networks became popular in the early 1980s, many different networking implementations were created. In the following years, compatibility and communication problems among these different network implementations became pervasive. The wide variety of hardware and software made communication between heterogeneous systems nearly impossible.

In 1984, the **International Organization for Standardization (ISO)** presented the **Open Systems Interconnection (OSI)** model. In developing the OSI model, ISO examined existing protocols, such as Transmission Control Protocol/Internet Protocol (TCP/IP), Systems Network Architecture (SNA) from IBM, and DECNET (Digital Equipment Corporation's proprietary networking model). Based on their examination of existing protocols, the ISO recommended a seven-layer network model called the OSI model.

Most networking vendors agreed to support the OSI model in one form or another. The model allows vendors to implement networks that permit communication among the wide variety of network implementations. The OSI model is not an absolute standard for computer networks; it is used as a reference model for how networks should be built. Because it is a reference model, it makes an ideal tool for learning how networks function.

Reasons for Layering

As previously mentioned, the OSI model has seven layers. A layered networking model is advantageous because it:

- Simplifies the networking model by dividing it into less complex components, which makes it easier to comprehend and use

- Enables programmers to specialize in a particular level or layer of the networking model

- Provides design modularity, which allows upgrades to a specific layer to remain separate from the other layers

- Encourages interoperability by promoting balance between different networking models

- Allows for standardized interfaces to be produced by networking vendors

Figure 1-1 shows the layers of the OSI model: **Physical layer**, **Data Link layer**, **Network layer**, **Transport layer**, **Session layer**, **Presentation layer**, and **Application layer**. The number beside each layer represents the number associated with that particular layer. For instance, the Network layer is commonly referred to as layer 3.

Figure 1-1   OSI reference model

As a group, these layers form the OSI protocol stack. A **protocol** is a defined method for communicating between systems. Computers must use a common protocol in order to communicate properly. Many different protocols are available for use on networks today; two examples are TCP/IP and IPX/SPX. You can think of a protocol as a common language that is used between two computers. Just as humans must be able to speak a common language in order to communicate, computers must use a common protocol.

If you need an easy way to remember the seven layers, from layer seven to layer one, use the following saying: All People Seem To Need Data Processing (Application, Presentation, Session, Transport, Network, Data Link, Physical). To remember layer one to layer seven, use Please Do Not Throw Sausage Pizza Away (Physical, Data Link, Network, Transport, Session, Presentation, Application).

Peer OSI Communication

The seven layers of the OSI reference model communicate with one another via **peer communication**. In other words, each layer will only talk to its peer on the opposite side of the communications process. As a result, each layer is unaware of the activities of all other layers of the model. Figure 1-2 shows peer communication, where the layers on the source node only talk with the opposite and equivalent layers on the destination node.

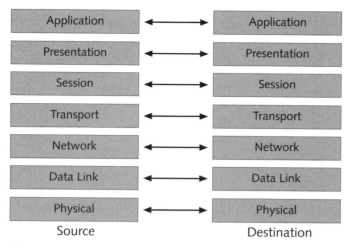

Figure 1-2   Peer communication

Each layer will only communicate with its opposite equivalent. Peer communication allows error checking to occur on two separate layers simultaneously. Even if the Transport layer is already providing reliable transmission of data, the Data Link layer is unaware of what goes on above it and will provide Data Link error control in the form of the **cyclical redundancy check (CRC)**.

Each layer does provide services to the layer above it and receives services from the layer below it, but the layers do not acknowledge these services in any way. Instead, each layer concentrates just on its function in the overall communications process. As a result, each layer of the OSI model takes information from the layer above, encapsulates that information into specific formats, and passes that information to the layer below.

Layer Functions

As previously stated, each layer in the OSI model performs a specific function in the transmission process. Although most modern networks do not implement the OSI model exactly as it is defined, the model remains an excellent reference and learning tool. In light of that, the functions of each layer of the OSI model are defined in the following sections.

Although the OSI model specifies seven layers to the communication process, most real-world implementations of protocol stacks do not use seven distinct layers. For example, TCP/IP uses a four-layer approach, while IPX/SPX loosely maps to the OSI model. Still, as mentioned earlier, the model is useful to help conceptualize the network communication process.

Physical (Layer 1)

Layer 1 in the OSI model is the Physical layer. It has the following responsibilities:

- Definition of the physical characteristics of the network hardware, including cable and connectors
- Representation of binary digits as voltages (encoding)
- Transmission of signals on the wire

The Physical layer defines the mechanical, electrical, and procedural events that occur during the physical transmission of electronic signals on the wire. In essence, the Physical layer's job is to transmit the actual signals on the network. This layer defines the physical characteristics of the transmission media (cable, air, glass, etc.), the network card, and other physical items, such as connectors and wall jacks.

As an example of a Physical layer definition, consider the Electronic Industries Association/Telecommunications Industry Association (EIA/TIA) 568B specification. The 568B specification defines a wiring system for data-grade cable, as shown in Figure 1-3.

Figure 1-3   568B twisted pair wiring scheme

Because a computer stores information in binary form (as a one or a zero digit), the Physical layer must convert that information into a signal for physical transmission. The network card at the Physical layer converts the data into electrical, radio, or light signals and transmits the signal on the network media. At a set measurement interval, the receiving NIC detects the presence of a signal as a binary one and its absence as a binary zero. Signals are sent by the source and received by the destination at a common interval so that the code (signal on/signal off) is interpreted correctly at the destination.

Logically, the physical devices must follow some type of standard when encoding and decoding these binary digits into and from electrical signals. The most common standard used in LANs is the Manchester Encoding method. This encoding method defines specific measurement intervals that are to be used when interpreting signals as binary digits.

Connectors, cables, and devices such as **repeaters** and hubs are all items that you can associate with the Physical layer. In the process of choosing cable, networking administrators often consider the following criteria:

- Expense
- Physical location
- Distance
- Security requirements
- Transmission speed required

Network devices and networking media will be discussed in greater detail later in this course.

Data Link (Layer 2)

The layer just above the Physical layer on the OSI protocol stack is the Data Link layer. This layer has several responsibilities:

- NIC software functions, including the identification of the source and destination nodes via their physical addresses (Media Access Control addresses)
- Definition of how data is packaged for transport as frames
- Error detection
- Flow control of information sent across the link

In the Data Link layer, the information to be transmitted receives its final formatting. The data packet is prepared for transmission, and a CRC is added to the packet, or unit of data. The CRC is information that is used to determine whether a packet was corrupted during transmission. Once assembled, the data packet is placed in a frame.

The Data Link layer has two sublayers that further articulate its functions: the **Logical Link Control (LLC) layer** and the **Media Access Control (MAC) layer**. The **Institute of Electrical and Electronics Engineers (IEEE)** created these sublayers to identify and isolate the separate responsibilities required at this level of the protocol stack. The LLC layer defines how data is packaged for the network. The LLC function is significant because it allows data frames to be packaged differently for different types of networks. Essentially, the LLC is the portion of the Data Link layer that provides the linking function between the Physical layer and the higher layers. Figure 1-4 shows the OSI layers, including the two sublayers.

Figure 1-4   Data Link layer subdivision

The MAC layer defines the media access method and provides a unique identifier for the network card. The unique identifier, called a MAC address, is a 48-bit address represented as a 12-digit **hexadecimal** number given to each network card during production, as shown in Figure 1-5. Every network interface card on your network must have a unique MAC address. This **physical address** provides a way to distinguish one computer from another on the network.

Figure 1-5   MAC address

When network-card manufacturers produce network cards, they burn the MAC address into the circuitry of the NIC. IEEE assigns the first six hexadecimal digits of a MAC address to NIC manufacturers. Thus each manufacturer has its own six-digit identifier, sometimes called the Organizational Unit Identifier (OUI) or block ID. The last set of six hexadecimal digits is assigned by the vendor itself and is sometimes called the serial number or the device ID. Together, the twelve digits in a MAC address must form a unique number. Note that since the MAC address is added during the manufacturing process, it is a permanent marking. The only way to change your computer's MAC address is to replace the network card.

Because a computer uses a MAC address to identify itself on the network, the MAC address is an integral component when computers open communication pathways to transmit data on the network. On an **Ethernet** or **CSMA/CD** network, when one computer (the source) wants to communicate with another (the destination), the source computer sends the data packet out on the wire. The data packet is then routed to the appropriate portion or segment of the entire network. On that segment, every network interface receives and evaluates the message. When a NIC finds a match between its MAC address and the one listed in the data packet, the packet is copied and passed up the protocol stack. Even when one NIC finds a match, the data packet is still moved along the network until each NIC on the segment has evaluated the packet. When computers send out broadcast messages (messages intended for every machine on a given segment), every computer will accept the packet and pass it up the protocol stack.

Many LANs and WANs contain several segments. Dividing a network into segments enhances performance. If you didn't divide a network, every NIC on that network would take the time to receive and evaluate every message, which is costly. When networks are segmented, regular broadcasts and packets meant for the local segment are not passed to other segments. Because segmentation reduces the amount of packets that each NIC must check and evaluate, it increases network performance.

Network (Layer 3)

Layer 3 in the OSI model is the Network layer. This layer has the following functions:

- Error handling
- Software addressing for data packets
- Best path selection

The Network layer routes data and handles communication errors. (The error-handling feature of the Network layer is rarely used in LAN implementations because LANs are largely error-free.) The Network layer contains software-addressing information for data packets, which makes network segmentation and routing possible.

The protocols at the Network layer allow computers to route packets to remote networks. The addressing mechanism at the Network layer allows data packets to move between segmented networks. Routers operate at the Network layer to move packets back and forth between segments, pushing them to the correct segment of the network. The Network layer contains a **logical address** for the computer. The type of logical address depends on the type of Network layer protocol used. For example, if the network uses the Internet

Protocol (IP), an example of a logical address could be the following IP address: 192.168.1.1. Like the MAC address, the logical address must be unique for the computer on the network. Unlike the MAC address, however, the logical address usually can be assigned and modified by the person in charge of the network.

The Network layer and IP addresses are discussed in greater detail as this course progresses.

Transport (Layer 4)

The Transport layer provides point-to-point data transportation. The responsibilities of the Transport layer include the following:

- End-to-end error-free transmission and delivery
- Data segmentation into maximum transmission unit (MTU) size
- Messaging service for the Session layer

Protocols that reside at the Transport layer can be connection-oriented or connection-less. **Connection-oriented** protocols require an acknowledgment (ACK) of the receipt of data packets. If an ACK is not returned for a given packet in a given time, the connection-oriented protocol will re-transmit the packet. Conversely, **connectionless** protocols do not require an ACK for received packets.

Connectionless services are often deemed unreliable because they do not ensure that the data was received properly. A packet sent by a connectionless transport is also called a **datagram**. A letter sent through the post office is similar to a datagram. A person who sends regular mail through the post office does not receive an acknowledgment from the post office when the letter is delivered. If the person wants an acknowledgment, he or she has to confirm with the letter recipient. Connection-oriented services are termed reliable because they ensure the receipt of packets. Using the post office analogy again, assume that a letter was sent through the post office with a return receipt requested. This type of delivery could be considered reliable, because the sender receives notification when the letter is successfully delivered. The connection-oriented services of the Transport layer help create a "session" between two computers. Computers that share large amounts of data often establish sessions. This is especially true when computers are linked for application-sharing purposes.

The Transport layer protocols can often be adjusted to alter the packet size for the given network. This type of control allows for optimization of the packet, based on the type of data transfers that are being conducted. Generally, the size of the packet should be correlated to the size of the data transfer. For instance, if a system typically transfers large files over the network, you should use larger packet sizes.

Session (Layer 5)

The Session layer enables two applications on the network to have an ongoing conversation or dialog. This is especially useful when applications are shared across the network or when computers are joined for game playing. Examples of Session layer protocols include **SQL**, **RPC**, and **X-Windows**.

The Session layer provides the following services:

- Control for data exchange (full or half duplex)
- Data synchronization definition
- Failure recovery
- Communication setup and teardown

The Session layer tells the receiving computer where a transmission begins and ends. When a large amount of data must be passed between one computer and another, the data most likely is broken into several pieces. The Session layer ensures clear identification of the beginning and the end of such a data transfer.

The Session layer allows the transfer of a large set of data across the network. For example, if you want to save a file to a network file server, your computer will attempt to open a session with the network server. Once the session is established, your computer will break the data into tiny packets and send the packets across the network until all the packets have been received by the server and written to the file server's disk drive. The Session layer also provides the ability to interrupt and recover the session if there is a need to wait for other data transmissions that are occurring on the local segment. If the line fails momentarily, the Session layer will also attempt to recover the session.

Presentation (Layer 6)

The Presentation layer prepares the data from the Application layer for transmission over the network. It also reformats data received from the lower layers in the protocol stack for the Application layer. Presentation layer components include extensions and coding schemes such as **BMP**, **WAV**, **EBCDIC**, and **ASCII**.

The Presentation layer has these responsibilities:

- Data translation
- Data formatting
- Data syntax restructuring
- Data encryption
- Data compression

The Presentation layer receives data from the Application layer. Because the data can come in several different formats, the Presentation layer must translate the data into a format that all computers on the network can interpret. In some cases, the Presentation layer must restructure the data in order to be sent across the network.

This layer also provides the encryption services when data encryption is used in network communications. For outbound communications, the Presentation layer will encrypt data prior to transmission. For inbound data, the Presentation layer decrypts the data before passing it up to the Application layer. The Presentation layer may also compress outbound data or decompress inbound data. Data compression reduces the size of the data that is sent across the network and, in many cases, improves network performance.

After the Presentation layer reformats, compresses, and/or encrypts data, no further restructuring of the data takes place. The lower layers add headers and trailers, but they do not reconfigure the data.

Application (Layer 7)

Layer 7 is the Application layer. It has the following responsibilities:

- Initiating the request for network services
- Providing services to applications

The Application layer is at the very top of the OSI protocol stack. This layer is concerned with user interaction with the computer and the network. In this layer, the user's actions may result in network access and the beginning of communications. The Application layer contains many protocols and utilities, which provide services to the network applications the user is using. Note that application programs like Microsoft Word, Eudora Mail, Netscape, etc. are not in the Application layer. Application programs, as well as the users of those programs, are outside the model, above the Application layer. For example, a user may use the Outlook e-mail program. That program is not in the Application layer, but the e-mail protocol SMTP (Simple Mail Transfer Protocol) that supports programs such as Outlook is in the layer. Data from the Application layer is passed directly to the Presentation layer.

Data Encapsulation

Data is sent from one computer to another in a data **packet**. The packet contains data from the sending application and additional information added by the protocol stack. Prior to transmission across the network, the data is organized into a data **frame** at layer 2.

Each layer in the protocol stack adds a **protocol data unit (PDU)** to the data as it is passed down the layers. A PDU, which is also known as a header or a trailer, is specific information that is sent from one layer on the source computer to the same layer on the destination computer. This type of communication is called peer communication. As the layers pass the data through the stack, the addition of a header and/or trailer is called **encapsulation**. When data is passed down the protocol stack, the header or trailer of the next-lower layer encapsulates it. It is helpful to think of encapsulation as "wrapping."

The data packet is passed over the network from the source computer to the destination computer. It is assembled as it travels down the protocol stack of the source computer and disassembled as it travels up the protocol stack of the destination computer, as shown in Figure 1-6.

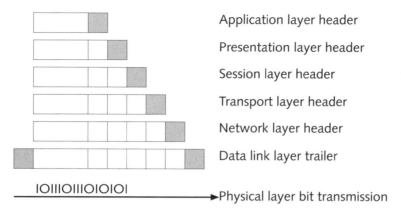

Application layer header

Presentation layer header

Session layer header

Transport layer header

Network layer header

Data link layer trailer

IOIIIOIIIOIOIOI → Physical layer bit transmission

Figure 1-6   Encapsulation

As the destination computer unpacks the data packet, the data is checked. Once the data packet is completely disassembled, the original information that was transmitted is delivered to the receiving application. Table 1-1 lists and describes the steps of data encapsulation.

Table 1-1   Five steps of data encapsulation

Step Number	Event	Description
1	Data Conversion	When the application generates a message to be sent out on the network, the data is converted into a standard data format. This occurs at OSI layers 5, 6, and 7, which are also known as the "upper layers"
2	Segmentation header added	The Transport layer segments the data into maximum transmission units (MTUs) to ensure that hosts on both ends can communicate.
3	Packet creation with network header	Data is placed into a data packet or datagram, and a network header with logical addressing information is added. This occurs at layer 3, the Network layer.
4	Frame header and trailer for network link	The data frame is prepared for the type of network protocol that is in use. A frame header and trailer are added at the Data Link layer.
5	Bit transmission	The frame is sent across the wire as bits at the Physical layer; ones and zeros are encoded and transmitted along the physical network as pulses.

CHAPTER SUMMARY

❑ Two or more computers connected by media form a network. Computers can use a network to share resources such as printers, disk space, and applications.

❑ Before computers were networked, file transfers were usually conducted by users physically walking copies of data (on floppy disk or other magnetic media) to another computer, a system called "sneakernet."

❑ The earliest networks had no standardization, so interoperability between the various proprietary network implementations was rare. The ISO developed the OSI model in the mid-1980s to standardize networking models.

❑ Data transmission can be connection-oriented or connectionless. Connection-oriented transmission requires that packets be acknowledged as received. Connectionless transmission does not require acknowledgments.

❑ The OSI networking model has seven layers, which simplify the networking model by dividing it into less complex components. This layering allows engineers to specialize in specific layers, and the modularity allows them to upgrade components at one layer without affecting other layers. The layered model also encourages interoperability between the various networking vendors by providing them with a standard architecture.

❑ The Physical layer, the first and lowest layer of the OSI model, handles the physical transmission of data across the network.

❑ The Data Link layer, the second layer of the OSI model, interacts with the networking hardware by controlling the link and supporting communications with the network interface; this layer also interacts with the MAC address.

❑ The Network layer, the third layer of the OSI model, supports addressing and routing of data packets.

❑ The Transport layer, the fourth layer, segments and optimizes data that is to be sent out on the network.

❑ The Session layer, the fifth layer, establishes and maintains connections between computers during data transfers.

❑ The Presentation layer, the sixth layer, handles data translation, encryption, and formatting for transmission on the network or for interpretation by the Application layer.

❑ The Application layer, the seventh and highest layer, handles the interface between the network and the user.

❑ When the network user sends data to the network, it goes through a five-step data encapsulation process. This process takes place as the data packet travels down the OSI protocol stack.

KEY TERMS

1

American Standard Code for Information Interchange (ASCII) — A standardized method for formatting binary information and text for communications and printer control. The acronym ASCII is pronounced "ask-ee."

Application layer — The seventh layer of the OSI model, which is responsible for requesting network services and for providing services to applications.

BMP — A Windows Bitmap (BMP) file, a graphical image type used with Microsoft Windows applications.

Carrier Sense Multiple Access with Collision Detection (CSMA/CD) — The network access method used by Ethernet networks.

client — A computer that operates on a network and that requests and uses the services of other computers on the network, but that does not necessarily provide any services to other computers.

client/server — A type of networking in which a few dedicated computers, called servers, share files, printers, disk drives, and other resources with a group of client computers.

connection-oriented — Network communications that require acknowledgment. On the OSI reference model, the decision to use connection-oriented communications is made at the Transport layer.

connectionless — Network communications that do not require acknowledgment. On the OSI reference model, the decision to use connectionless communications is made at the Transport layer.

cyclical redundancy check (CRC) — The process that ensures that data was not corrupted during transmission. This is accomplished by comparing CRC calculations before and after transmission.

Data Link layer — The second layer of the OSI protocol stack, which defines the rules for sending and receiving information across the network media. It encodes and frames data for transmission and provides error detection and control. This layer has two parts: LLC and MAC.

datagram — A message or packet that is sent across a network and that does not require acknowledgment by the destination station.

electromagnetic interference (EMI) — Electronic noise that disrupts signals on cables. This noise is frequently caused by motors and generators, but can also be caused by sunspots and other natural EMI-producing phenomenon.

encapsulation — A process that occurs during transmission through the protocol stack in which data from the higher layers is wrapped in a protocol header and/or trailer.

end system — The location and/or set of controls that the user can manipulate to interact with a computer or a network.

Ethernet — A standard networking architecture that defines the physical layout, lengths, and types of media that can be used. There are many variations of Ethernet but most use the CSMA/CD network access method.

Extended Binary Coded Decimal Interchange Code (EBCDIC) — A standardized formatting method for both binary and text files for communications and printer control. IBM developed EBCDIC. The acronym EBCDIC is pronounced "eb-see-dick."

fiber-optic cable — A type of cable that conducts light signals through glass or plastic to generate network signals. Fiber-optic cable allows for transmission rates of 100 megabits per second or greater. It is impervious to electromagnetic interference because it sends light signals rather than electric signals along the cable.

frame — A segment of data. The words "frame" and "data packet" are often used interchangeably, although technically a frame is found at layer 2 of the OSI model and a packet is found at layer 3.

hexadecimal — A numbering method that relies on a base of 16. Hexadecimal digits can be 0, 1, 2, 3, 4, 5, 6, 7, 8, 9, A, B, C, D, E, or F.

infrared — Invisible light at the upper end of the electromagnetic spectrum. It is used in most hand-held remote control devices for televisions, stereos, and videocassette players. It is also used in some types of computer networking, especially for data transfers between laptop and desktop systems.

Institute of Electrical and Electronics Engineers (IEEE) — A technical professional society that fosters national and international standards. Their web site is *http://www.ieee.org*.

International Organization for Standardization (ISO) — A multi-industry association that attempts to standardize and define items that increase communication and compatibility in many different industries.

local area network (LAN) — A group of computers and other devices typically connected by a cable. Is normally located in a single geographic region such as a building or floor in a building.

logical address — A network address that can be assigned and modified by the person in charge of the network. This type of address appears at the Network layer of the OSI model.

Logical Link Control (LLC) layer — A sublayer of the Data Link layer that forms the connection between the other software in the protocol stack and the networking hardware (such as the NIC and the cables).

media — The cable, glass, or telephone lines that host the signal from one computer to another on a network.

Media Access Control (MAC) layer — A sublayer of the Data Link layer that defines the hardware address of the physical network interface. In addition, it discards corrupted packets and identifies which packets were directed to the local system.

metropolitan area network (MAN) — An intermediate specification that defines networks confined to a fairly restricted geographic area, such as a campus, town, or city. These private networks span multiple geographically separate locations that are near to one another.

network — Two or more computers connected by some type of media.

network interface card (NIC) — A hardware device that transmits and receives electronic signals on a network.

Network layer — The third layer of the OSI conceptual networking model, which allows communications to be routed on a network. It provides a logical address for computers on a network.

network operating system (NOS) — Operating software that has networking components built into its structure.

Open Systems Interconnection (OSI) — A seven-layer reference model created by the International Organization for Standardization (ISO) to define and separate networking hardware and software into distinct layers and functions. This model makes it easy for developers and manufacturers to ensure that their networking implementations are compatible with other implementations in the industry.

packet — A group of data that is transmitted across a network.

peer-to-peer network — A type of network in which the clients can also function as servers.

peer communication — The method of communication among the levels of the OSI model in which each protocol in the OSI protocol stack encodes its own protocol data unit into the network hierarchy, so that it can communicate with the equivalent layer on the destination computer.

physical address — Also called the MAC address. It is burned into the network interface card (NIC) during the manufacturing process.

Physical layer — The first layer of the OSI conceptual networking model, which defines the physical media and electronic transmission methods used in networking.

Presentation layer — The sixth layer of the OSI network model, responsible for data formatting and encryption.

protocol — A definition of rules for communication between two or more computers. Computers must have a common protocol (or a translator) in order to communicate.

protocol data unit (PDU) — Information added to a data packet by the layers of the protocol stack. It can be header or trailer information that is attached to the data packet prior to transmission.

Remote Procedure Call (RPC) — A method used to establish communications between computer systems at the Session layer.

repeater — A device that repeats or boosts a network signal along network wire. It reduces signal degradation and increases the maximum usable length of network cable.

server — A computer that shares resources with other devices on a network.

Session layer — The fifth layer of the OSI model, which controls the connection between two computers sharing data. It maintains, defines, and recovers connections that are established between two computers.

storage area network (SAN) — A subsystem of networked storage devices physically separate from the servers.

Structured Query Language (SQL) — A computer language used to query, manipulate, and communicate with databases.

Transport layer — The fourth layer of the OSI reference model, which segments and reassembles data frames. It also provides for connection-oriented and connectionless communications.

WAV — A Windows Audio (WAV) file, an audio file format used with Microsoft Windows applications.

wide area network (WAN) — A network that spans two or more geographically diverse locations and typically uses public telecommunications carriers in order to connect its individual segments.

wireless — Communications that are not conducted over physical wires or cables. These communications can include infrared, radio, and other types of transmissions that are sent through the air between two or more locations.

X-Windows — A standard graphical user interface (GUI) used on UNIX systems.

REVIEW QUESTIONS

1. Which of the following best describes the Presentation layer?

   a. Establishes, maintains, and manages sessions between applications

   b. Translates, encrypts, or prepares data from the Application layer for network transmission

   c. Handles routing information for data packets

   d. Provides the electrical and mechanical transmission of data

   e. Handles link control and uses the MAC address on the network interface card (NIC)

2. Which of the following best describes the Network layer?

   a. Handles routing information for data packets

   b. Provides the electrical and mechanical transmission of data

   c. Handles link control and uses the MAC address on the network interface card (NIC)

   d. Establishes, maintains, and manages sessions between applications

   e. Translates, encrypts, or prepares data from the Application layer for network transmission

3. Which of the following best describes the Session layer?

   a. Translates, encrypts, or prepares data from the Application layer for network transmission

   b. Handles routing information for data packets

   c. Provides the electrical and mechanical transmission of data

1

    d. Handles link control and uses the MAC address on the network interface card (NIC)

    e. Establishes, maintains, and manages sessions between applications

4. Which of the following best describes the Transport layer?

    a. Provides the electrical and mechanical transmission of data

    b. Handles link control and uses the MAC address on the network interface card (NIC)

    c. Establishes, maintains, and manages sessions between applications

    d. Segments and reassembles data and provides either connection-oriented or connectionless communications

    e. Translates, encrypts, or prepares data from the Application layer for network transmission

5. Which of the following best describes the Data Link layer?

    a. Provides the electrical and mechanical transmission of data

    b. Handles link control and uses the MAC address on the network interface card (NIC)

    c. Establishes, maintains, and manages sessions between applications

    d. Translates, encrypts, or prepares data from the Application layer for network transmission

    e. Handles routing information for data packets

6. Which of the following best describes the Physical layer?

    a. Establishes, maintains, and manages sessions between applications

    b. Translates, encrypts, or prepares data from the Application layer for network transmission

    c. Provides the electrical and mechanical transmission of data

    d. Handles link control and uses the MAC address on the network interface card (NIC)

    e. Provides network services to the user

7. Which of the following best describes the Application layer?

    a. Establishes, maintains, and manages sessions between applications

    b. Translates, encrypts, or prepares data for network transmission

    c. Provides network services to the user

    d. Handles routing information for data packets

    e. Provides the electrical and mechanical transmission of data

8. Which of the following accurately describe the Media Access Control (MAC) address? (Choose all that apply.)

   a. It is a physical number set during the manufacturing process.

   b. This address is a layer in a network segment.

   c. MAC addresses contain 12 hexadecimal numbers.

   d. Computers use this address to uniquely identify themselves on the network.

   e. An IP address is one example of this type of address.

9. Which of the following accurately describe the network address? (Choose all that apply.)

   a. It is a physical number set during the manufacturing process.

   b. This address is used when routing communications between different network segments.

   c. The Data Link layer uses this address.

   d. This address is set at layer 3 of the OSI model.

   e. An example of this type of address is an IP address.

10. Connection-oriented services are also known as _____ services.

    a. reliable

    b. unreliable

    c. datagram

11. Connectionless services are also called _____ services.

    a. reliable

    b. acknowledgment

    c. unreliable

12. Which of the following services receive an acknowledgment from the destination? (Choose all that apply.)

    a. Datagram

    b. Reliable

    c. Connection-oriented

    d. Connectionless

    e. Unreliable

13. Place the following steps of data encapsulation in their correct descending order:

    a. Frame headers and trailers added

    b. Segment header added

    c. Bit transmission

    d. Packet creation and network header

    e. Data conversion

14. Which of the following correctly defines a WAN?

    a. A network contained within a single geographic location and usually connected by a privately maintained media

    b. A network spread over multiple geographic areas and usually connected by publicly and privately maintained media

    c. A network spread over a single metropolitan area

15. Which of the following best describes a LAN?

    a. A network that is contained in a single geographic area such as a building or floor in a building

    b. A countywide network that spans multiple geographic locations

    c. A large network that is connected by both publicly and privately maintained cabling spread over multiple geographic regions

16. Which of the following reasons for providing a layered OSI architecture are correct? (Choose all that apply.)

    a. To provide design modularity, which allows upgrades to a specific layer to remain separate from the other layers

    b. To simplify the networking model by dividing the networking model into 14 layers and 12 sublayers

    c. To discourage interoperability between disparate networking models

    d. To enable programmers to specialize in a particular layer

    e. To allow for standardized interfaces from networking vendors

17. On a network, computers must use a common _____ in order for communication to occur.

    a. protocol

    b. operating system

    c. manufacturer

    d. hardware platform

18. Before networks, what did people use to transfer files?

    a. Sneakernet

    b. Protocols

    c. Interface cards

    d. Ethernet

19. A protocol is to a computer as a(n) _____ is to a person.

    a. identity

    b. personality

    c. language

    d. personal philosophy

20. Which of the following are network hardware? (Choose all that apply.)

    a. NIC

    b. NOS

    c. LLC

    d. Network media

    e. Connectors

21. Which of the following are network software? (Choose all that apply.)

    a. Components that map to the Application layer of the OSI model

    b. NIC

    c. NOS

    d. Media connectors

22. All networking vendors follow the OSI model and design seven-layer architectures.

    a. True

    b. False

23. Communications on a network originate at the _____.

    a. destination

    b. breaker

    c. peak

    d. source

24. Transmitted signals are bound for a(n) _____ computer.

    a. destination

    b. breaker

    c. peak

    d. source

25. Information transmitted on a network is called a(n) _____.

    a. package

    b. expresser

    c. data destination

    d. data packet

    e. E-pack

26. Which of the following are layers of the OSI model? (Choose all that apply.)

    a. OSI

    b. Physical

    c. IEEE

    d. Data Link

27. Which layer of the OSI model is responsible for media access and packaging data into frames?

   a. Network layer

   b. Physical layer

   c. Data Link layer

   d. Transport layer

28. At which layer of the OSI model will encryption and compression occur?

   a. Presentation layer

   b. Session layer

   c. Application layer

   d. Network layer

29. Which of the following lists the layers of the OSI model from layer 7 to layer 1?

   a. Application, Session, Transport, Network, Presentation, Data Link, Physical

   b. Physical, Data Link, Network, Transport, Session, Presentation, Application

   c. Application, Presentation, Session, Transport, Network, Data Link, Physical

   d. Presentation, Application, Session, Network, Transport, Data Link, Physical

30. The _____ layer is responsible for finding the best path to route packets within an internetwork.

   a. Transport

   b. Network

   c. Session

   d. Data Link

CASE PROJECTS

Case Projects

1. Jennifer, Moe, and Lisa recently passed the Network+ certification exam and have been hired to perform network support at your company. Moe has been complaining that memorizing the layers of the OSI model was difficult and a waste of time. He understands why protocol developers need to know about it, but thinks that network administrators and support people only need to know which protocols are operating on the network in question. Explain to Moe the reasons for using the OSI model. How could detailed knowledge of the model be valuable in Moe's network-support position?

2. Lisa overhears your conversation with Moe and asks your opinion about data encapsulation. She is confused about the layers in which encapsulation occurs. Explain the five steps of data encapsulation to her.

3. Jennifer is unsure in which layer the MAC addresses function. Because the MAC is on the NIC and is associated with the physical media, she asks why this address is associated with the Data Link layer. Explain to Jennifer the functions of the Data Link layer and the sublayers within this layer. Where exactly does the MAC address fit in?

4. Give Jennifer, Moe, and Lisa a helpful way to remember the layers of the OSI model. Identify three words to associate with each layer.

5. This afternoon, you will be explaining the OSI model to senior management. Design a flow chart showing how the OSI model facilitates the transferring of data from a source to a destination node.

2

NETWORK DEVICES

After reading this chapter and completing the exercises, you will be able to:

- ♦ Explain the uses, advantages, and disadvantages of repeaters
- ♦ Explain the uses, advantages, and disadvantages of hubs
- ♦ Define network segmentation
- ♦ Explain network segmentation using bridges
- ♦ Explain network segmentation using switches
- ♦ Explain network segmentation using routers
- ♦ Explain network segmentation using brouters and gateways

Many devices help control and extend the usable size of a growing network. These devices have a wide variety of functions and are added to networks to allow a greater number of computers to exist on the network; to extend the usable distance of the network; to segment, or localize, traffic on the network; to subdivide the network so problems are easier to isolate; and to join existing networks together. In this chapter, you will learn about the different devices that can be used to accomplish the preceding objectives. These devices include repeaters, hubs, bridges, switches, routers, brouters, and gateways.

REPEATERS

The number of **nodes** on a network and the length of cable used influence the quality of communication on the network. As data leaves the source or transmitting station, the NIC converts the data to electrical impulses, if copper wire is used, or to light signals, if a fiber-optic cable is used. As the signal travels the length of the cable, the distance that it must traverse weakens it. The nodes that copy and pass the signal on also degrade it. This degradation of signal clarity is called **attenuation**.

Repeaters work against attenuation by repeating signals that they receive on a network, typically cleaning and boosting the digital transmission in the process. For example, a digital signal communicates one of two different states (one or zero) in its communication stream. On a network connected by wire media, the presence of voltage creates a one, and the absence of voltage creates a zero. However, as attenuation occurs, the digital signal may become increasingly difficult to decipher. If left uncorrected, attenuation could make the signal unreadable. A repeater takes the attenuated signal, cleans it up, and then sends the clear and crisp digital stream to the rest of the network, as shown in Figure 2-1.

Figure 2-1   Repeater

Note that on **analog** networks, devices that boost the signal are called **amplifiers**. These devices do not have the same signal regeneration capabilities as repeaters because they must maintain the shape of the received signal. Therefore, noise tends to be amplified with the signal.

Because repeaters work with the actual physical signal, and do not attempt to interpret the data being transmitted, they are Physical layer (layer 1) devices on the OSI model. This means that most repeaters cannot tell the difference between a good signal and a corrupt signal. Thus, they normally repeat everything.

Some repeaters can be used to connect two physically different types of cabling. For example, a repeater might connect a twisted-pair cable to a coaxial cable. However, repeaters cannot reformat, resize, or otherwise manipulate the data packet. In other words, when a network uses different physical media but the same data type and packet structure, a repeater can be used as a connection device.

HUBS

A **hub** is a generic connection device used to tie several networking cables together to create a link between different stations on a network. Hubs that are plugged into electric power are called **active hubs**. They usually amplify or repeat signals that pass through them. Because they have multiple inbound and outbound connections, these hubs are also known as multiport repeaters. A hub that merely connects different cables on a network and provides no signal regeneration is called a **passive hub** and is not a repeater.

 "Hub" is a generic term applied to many different network-connection devices. A hub can accomplish two different tasks: if it only connects cables together, it is a passive hub; if it actually boosts the network signal, it is an active hub. If a hub in some way **segments** or subdivides the traffic on a network, it is an intelligent, or switching, hub. For the purposes of the CCNA exam, the term hub, by itself, is a device that does not segment the network.

Often, a hub forms a central point on a network where the cables come together. A star topology often has a hub at its center. **Topology** usually refers to the physical layout of network cable and devices. When all stations are connected to a central hub, the topology is known as a star because of its appearance. Figure 2-2 shows a star topology with a hub in the center.

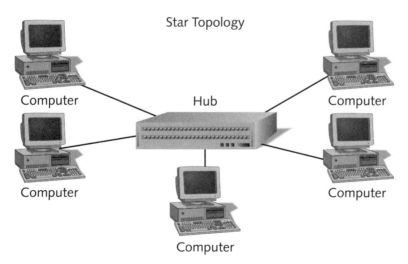

Figure 2-2   Star topology

ADVANTAGES AND DISADVANTAGES OF REPEATERS AND HUBS

Because repeaters simply repeat, amplify, and clean up a signal, network administrators mainly use them to increase the usable distance of a network. Repeaters have little impact on network speed because they do not do any packet processing.

Familiarize yourself with the following advantages of using repeaters on your network:

- Repeaters can extend a network's total distance.

- Repeaters do not seriously impact network performance.

- Certain repeaters can connect networks using different physical media.

Although repeaters provide many advantages, they do have disadvantages. The following list describes the disadvantages of using repeaters on the network:

- Repeaters cannot connect different network architectures, such as **Token Ring** and Ethernet.

- Repeaters do not reduce network traffic.

- Repeaters do not segment the network.

Repeaters do not reformat data packets, so they cannot connect networks that require different types of packet structures. Also, they do not reduce network traffic because they repeat everything they receive. Because they repeat everything without discrimination, the number of repeaters must be limited on your network. Too many repeaters on a network could throw off network communication timings by repeating packets after they normally would have been dropped. Such a circumstance would create noise on the wire and increase the likelihood of packet collisions, which would reduce network performance.

Repeaters also do not segment a network. That is, they do not create logical or physical divisions of the network. On an Ethernet network, packets that are broadcast on a given segment may collide. This happens when two or more stations transmit at the same time. Because repeaters do not segment a network, devices that are separated only by a repeater are susceptible to data packet collision, since they are part of the same **collision domain**.

NETWORK SEGMENTATION

Network **segmentation** is an essential concept you must understand in order to complete the CCNA exam successfully and understand the contents of this book. In particular, you must understand network segmentation using bridges, switches, and routers.

Ethernet networks, which are characterized by the IEEE 802.3 standard, define the use of a **Carrier Sense Multiple Access with Collision Detection (CSMA/CD)** access method. CSMA/CD specifies that each node (before placing packets onto the networking media) must first listen to the network media to determine if the media is currently free of packets. If so, the node can place packets on the media. Obviously, it is possible for two nodes to listen, find a wire empty, and send packets at the same exact time. The end result is a collision in which both packets are destroyed. The CSMA/CD access method specifies that nodes involved in a collision on the network perform a **backoff algorithm**, which causes them to wait a random amount of time, called a **backoff period**, before making an attempt to retransmit data. The randomness of the period greatly reduces the likelihood of a second collision.

Problems occur when network administrators place too many nodes on the same network segment. As the number of nodes increases, the amount of traffic on a segment increases, as does the chance that two nodes will transmit data at exactly the same time. This causes the number of collisions to increase. The result is a large amount of network bandwidth being used to retransmit packets that have been destroyed by collisions. Segmentation is the answer to this problem.

Segmentation is the breaking down of a single heavily populated network segment into smaller segments, or collision domains, populated by fewer nodes. Figure 2-3 shows an example of network segmentation.

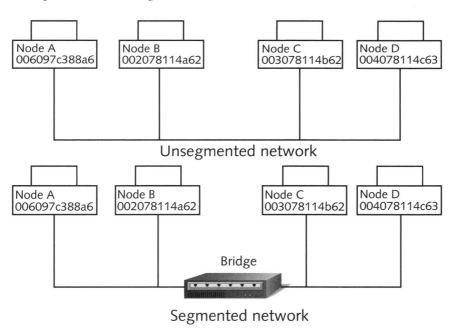

Figure 2-3   Network segmentation

In Figure 2-3, the upper graphic depicts a network consisting of four nodes sharing a single segment—in other words, a single collision domain. In this unsegmented network, all computers would be affected by the traffic of other nodes. The lower graphic shows a bridge separating the four computers into two collision domains. This segmentation reduces the number of computers that must contend for use of the network. For example, on a 10 Mbps network, each collision domain shares its own 10 Mbps. In the upper graphic, four computers would share this 10 Mbps. In the lower graphic, only two computers would share the bandwidth. As a result, network collisions and retransmissions are reduced. A bridge is one networking device that can be used to segment networks.

BRIDGES

Bridges operate at the Data Link layer of the OSI model. A bridge filters traffic between network segments by examining the destination MAC address. Based on this destination MAC address, the bridge either forwards or discards the frame. If the destination MAC address is located on a segment other than the originating segment, the bridge forwards it. If the frame was meant for the local segment, the bridge discards the frame. In this way, the bridge reduces network traffic by keeping local traffic on the local segment. However, when a client sends a **broadcast** frame to the entire network, the bridge will always forward the frame. In addition, if a bridge has no destination MAC address in its table, it will send the frame out to all interfaces except the one it came in on.

The bridge functions like a repeater in that it listens to incoming frames and repeats them on other segments. The only real difference is that it actually reads the MAC address and chooses whether to repeat or discard a frame.

Consider the network shown in Figure 2-4. The bridge divides the network into two segments (Segment A and Segment B). Communications between computers on Segment A do not pass through to Segment B, and vice versa. However, communications between computers on Segment A and Segment B will be repeated through the bridge to the other segment. For example, when Computer 1 sends a message to Computer 4, the bridge discards the frame, and only Computers 2, 3, and 4 receive it. Computer 4 will accept the frame, while Computers 2 and 3 will discard it after determining that it was not destined for their MAC address. However, when Computer 2 sends a frame to Computer 5, all computers on Segment A and Segment B will examine the frame. Only Computer 5 will accept the frame, and the rest will discard it after determining that the MAC address on the frame does not match theirs.

Bridges can use two different methods to determine which segment includes a specific MAC address. One method is transparent bridging, and the other is source-route bridging.

Transparent Bridges

Transparent bridges are also called learning bridges because they build a table of MAC addresses as they receive frames. This means that they "learn" which addresses are on which segments. When a bridge first receives power, its bridging table is empty. Over time, though, it learns which segments have which MAC addresses as frames are forwarded. The bridge uses the source MAC addresses to determine which addresses are on which segments. By determining a frame's origin, the bridge knows where to send frames in the future. Ethernet networks mainly use transparent bridges. Token Ring networks usually employ source-routing bridges.

2

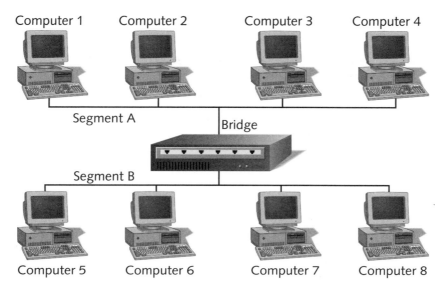

Figure 2-4   Bridge

Source-Routing Bridges

In Token Ring networks, source-routing bridges rely on the source of the frame transmission to provide the routing information. The source computer determines the best path by sending out explorer frames. When the destination computer receives the explorer frames, it determines the best routes and sends that information back to the source. Then, the source includes the routing information returned by its explorer frames in the frame sent across the network. The bridge uses this information to build its table.

Translation Bridges

Although bridges tend to connect similar networks, translation bridges can connect networks with different architectures, such as Ethernet and Token Ring. These bridges appear as transparent bridges to an Ethernet host and as source-routing bridges to a Token Ring host.

Advantages and Disadvantages of Bridges

Bridges do more than repeaters because they evaluate frames; however, their additional capabilities bring both advantages and disadvantages. The advantages of using a bridge include the following:

- Bridges can extend a network by acting as a repeater.
- Bridges can reduce network traffic on a segment by subdividing network communications.

- Bridges increase the available bandwidth to individual nodes because fewer nodes share a collision domain.

- Bridges reduce the likelihood of network collisions.

- Some bridges connect networks using different media types and architectures.

Because bridges regenerate the network signal when they pass it from segment to segment, they can extend the cable's usable distance. Bridges selectively forward frames, which effectively reduces the number of messages circulating around the network. Because this also reduces the number of frames and broadcasting stations, the likelihood that two stations will broadcast at the same time on the same segment and cause a collision is reduced. Bridges also connect different media types, and some can connect different architectures. Bridges, however, do have some disadvantages:

- Because bridges do more than repeaters by viewing MAC addresses, the extra processing makes them slower than repeaters.

- Bridges forward broadcast frames indiscriminately, so they do not filter broadcast traffic.

- Bridges are more expensive than repeaters.

The fact that bridges forward broadcast traffic can be a major disadvantage on a network during a **broadcast storm**, which happens when two or more stations engage in the transmission of excessive broadcast traffic. For example, Microsoft operating systems use broadcasts to determine which computer will be in charge of creating a browse list (i.e., a map of network resources). In the early Microsoft networks, broadcast storms occurred when two or more machines would not relinquish the browse list responsibility to a higher-ranked machine. Such an error condition can cease network communications altogether. Because bridges simply forward broadcast traffic, they do nothing to reduce the storm.

SWITCHES

Like bridges, switches operate at the Data Link layer of the OSI model. **Switches** increase network performance by reducing the number of packets transmitted to the rest of the network. In an Ethernet network, computers are usually connected directly to a switch. Unlike bridges, a switch opens a **virtual circuit** between the source and the destination. This prevents communications between just two computers from being broadcast to every computer on the network or segment. This is called **microsegmentation** because the segment, or collision domain, is effectively just the sending and receiving nodes.

 Sometimes switches are called "switching hubs."

When two machines have a virtual circuit, they do not have to share the wire with any other computers. Thus, if the total network transfer capacity is 10 Mbps, the two communicating machines get the full **bandwidth**, which is, in this case, 10 Mbps. Multiple virtual circuits can be in use at the same time, each with its own 10 Mbps. This is called "switched bandwidth." Conversely, a hub will divide the 10 Mbps among each communicating node connected to its ports. This is called "shared bandwidth." When machines must share a wire and compete for available bandwidth with other machines, they experience **contention**. A switch reduces contention by subdividing a network into virtual circuits.

Switches filter based on MAC addresses and build tables in memory just like bridges, but the switching table will have a mapping of switch port number to MAC address instead of bridge segment number to MAC address. Switches can have an unlimited number of ports, which can be connected directly to workstations. Usually bridges have fewer than 10 ports, and so those ports are connected to hubs rather than directly to workstations. Bridges are software-based devices while switches are hardware-based.

The advantages of switches include the following:

- Switches increase available network bandwidth.

- With switches, there is reduced workload on individual computers.

- Switches increase network performance.

- There are fewer frame collisions because switches create collision domains for each connection (a process called microsegmentation).

- Switches have an unlimited number of ports and connect directly to workstations.

Even though the benefits of switching are great, switching has its disadvantages. Here are a few to consider:

- Switches are significantly more expensive than bridges.

- Network connectivity problems can be difficult to trace through a switch.

- Broadcast traffic may be troublesome.

Switches usually cost more than bridges, but they do a lot more. Unfortunately, because switches are constantly creating and dropping virtual circuits, network problems may be difficult to trace. Broadcast traffic is also a problem for switches, because the hardware address indicates that all computers should receive a packet. The switch can either block or send these broadcasts. When a switch blocks the broadcasts, network performance improves, but applications that rely on broadcasts to keep track of resources are not able to communicate using broadcasts. However, if the switch sends the broadcasts, they will be transmitted to every machine on the network by the switch. In that case, virtual circuits provide no benefit. Of course, other types of network communications will still benefit from switches' involvement. A switch is the device of choice for improving network performance, and many companies are replacing hubs and bridges with switches. Switching, and the Cisco 1900 series switch in particular, are covered in greater detail in Chapter 13.

This section discusses Ethernet switches (primarily used in LANs), but several implementations of switching for WAN configurations also exist. Public telecommunications carriers such as AT&T, Sprint, and MCI provide most of these switching services. These services include packet switching, switched-56, AT&T Switched Digital Services, and MCI Communications Virtual Private Data Services.

ROUTERS

As networks grow more complex, network administrators may need to utilize routers on their networks. **Routers** provide filtering and network traffic control on LANs and WANs. These devices can connect multiple segments and multiple networks. Networks connected by multiple routers are called **internetworks** because they create a larger network of interconnected, smaller networks.

Routers operate at the Network layer of the OSI model. Routers are similar to switches and bridges in that they segment a network and filter traffic. However, instead of evaluating the physical address of a packet (as do switches and bridges), routers use the logical address. Like bridges and switches, routers use a table to determine how to forward packets. You will learn more about these routing tables in Chapter 3.

When a router is introduced into a network, it creates more networks. This is because every interface on a router represents a different network. Routers create collision domains and they also create **broadcast domains** because a router will not pass broadcast traffic. A broadcast domain is a group of network devices that will receive LAN broadcast traffic from each other.

Physical versus Logical Addresses

The NIC manufacturer burns the physical address or MAC address into the network card during the manufacturing process. The MAC address, which is found at the Data Link layer of the OSI model, is used by bridges and switches to make forwarding decisions within a network or **subnetwork**. On the other hand, the type of Network and Transport protocols used by the devices on a network dictate the format of the logical address. For example, the TCP/IP and IPX/SPX protocol suites span the Network layer and Transport layer of the OSI reference model. Both of these protocols are routable, which means that they can be used for communication between networks or subnetworks that are divided by a router or routers.

When TCP/IP is used on an internetwork, the logical address is known as an **IP address**. Routers utilize the IP address to route packets to the correct network segment. Software, not hardware, implements IP addresses. This means that routers use the logical Network layer software address to route packets to the appropriate network segment. Figure 2-5 illustrates a router connecting four different network segments. Notice that each **port** (connection) on the router has its own unique IP address.

Figure 2-5   Router

Advantages and Disadvantages of Routers

Although routers offer several advantages for the network, they have some inherent disadvantages. First, let us take a look at the advantages:

- Routers can connect different network architectures, such as Ethernet and Token Ring.

- Routers can choose the best path across the network using dynamic routing techniques. These techniques are described in Chapter 8.

- Routers create collision domains by segmenting the network.

- Routers reduce network traffic because they do not retransmit network broadcast traffic; in other words, they create broadcast domains.

The disadvantages of using routers on the network include the following:

- Routers work only with routable network protocols; not all protocols are routable.

- Routers are more expensive than bridges or repeaters.

- Dynamic router communications (inter-router communication) cause additional network overhead, which results in less bandwidth for user data.

- Routers are slower than bridges or switches because they must analyze a data transmission from the Physical through the Network layer, whereas bridges and switches only read two layers of information: the Data Link and Physical.

BROUTERS

Several types of hybrid devices exist in the networking world. One such device is the **brouter**. A brouter functions as both a bridge for nonroutable protocols and a router for routable protocols.

A brouter provides the best attributes of both a bridge and a router. The brouter acts as a bridge when it receives a packet that contains a nonroutable protocol, such as NetBEUI. To accomplish its bridging task, the brouter uses the MAC address. In contrast, the brouter acts as a router when it receives a packet that contains a routable protocol, such as TCP/IP or IPX/SPX. To accomplish its routing task, the brouter uses network address information. Routers operate at the Network layer of the OSI model; bridges operate at the Data Link layer. Because the brouter performs a dual role, it operates at both the Data Link and Network layers.

GATEWAYS

A **gateway** is usually a combination of hardware and software. Its purpose is to translate between different protocol suites. The packets must be rebuilt not just at the lower levels for conversion between, for example, Ethernet and Token Ring, but at the very upper levels so that the actual data content can be converted into a format the destination can process. Because gateways must rebuild the packets at the upper layers of the OSI model, gateways have the most negative effect on network performance. That is to say, they create the most **latency** of all the devices discussed in this chapter. One example of a common gateway would be Services for Macintosh. This is software installed on a Windows NT or 2000 server so that Macintosh computers, which use the AppleTalk protocol, can communicate with the server, which is most likely using the TCP/IP protocol.

CHAPTER SUMMARY

- ❏ Network administrators use devices to control and extend the usable size of a network. These devices include repeaters, hubs, bridges, switches, routers, brouters, and gateways.

- ❏ Repeaters work against attenuation by cleaning and repeating signals that they receive on a network. Repeaters work at the Physical layer of the OSI model. They cannot connect different network architectures. Repeaters do not reduce network traffic or segment the network.

- ❏ A hub ties several networking cables together to create a link between different stations on a network. An active hub has its own electrical power and acts as a repeater, whereas a passive hub provides no signal regeneration. Hubs operate at the Physical layer of the OSI model and do not segment the network.

- ❏ Network segmentation is the process of isolating hosts onto smaller segments to reduce the possibility of collisions. Bridges and switches are two devices commonly used to segment networks.

- ❏ Bridges provide network segmentation by examining the MAC address that is sent in the data frame. Bridges can use transparent bridging or source-route bridging to determine which segment includes a specific physical address. Bridges operate at the Data Link layer of the OSI model.

❏ Switches increase network performance by reducing the number of frames transmitted to the rest of a network. They do this by opening a virtual circuit between the source and the destination. Switches operate at the Data Link layer of the OSI model.

❏ Routers operate at the Network layer of the OSI model and provide filtering and network-traffic control on LANs and WANs. They can connect multiple segments and networks. On a TCP/IP network, routers use IP addresses to route packets to the correct network segment. Routers use information from routing tables to move packets from one network to another.

❏ A brouter is a hybrid device that functions both as a bridge for nonroutable protocols and as a router for routable protocols. Brouters operate at both the Data Link and Network layers.

❏ Gateways are usually a combination of hardware and software and are used to translate between different protocols. They usually operate at layer 4 and above in the OSI model.

KEY TERMS

active hub — A device that connects multiple nodes and/or networks, is connected to external power, and repeats and regenerates signals on a network.

amplifier — A device used to boost analog signals on a broadband network.

analog — A method of signal transmission on broadband networks.

attenuation — The natural degradation of a transmitted signal over distance.

backoff algorithm — A mathematical calculation performed by computers after a collision occurs on a CSMA/CD network, which forces machines to wait a random amount of time before resending the destroyed packet. A backoff algorithm is run by computers to set the length of time for the backoff period.

backoff period — A random time interval used after a collision has been detected on an Ethernet network. Use of a backoff period minimizes the likelihood of another collision.

bandwidth — The available capacity of the network. The greater the network bandwidth, the greater the speed in data transfer.

bridge — A device that operates at the Data Link layer, used to filter traffic between network segments by evaluating the MAC address of packets that are sent to it.

broadcast — A packet meant for the entire network.

broadcast domain — A group of network devices that will receive LAN broadcast traffic from each other.

broadcast storm — Excessive broadcast messages to every host on the network, launched by multiple computers; usually triggered by some error condition on the network.

brouter — A device that functions as a bridge for nonroutable protocols and a router for routable protocols. The brouter operates at both the Data Link and Network layers.

Carrier Sense Multiple Access with Collision Detection (CSMA/CD) — An access method specified by the IEEE Ethernet 802.3 standard. In this method, a node will listen to see if the line is clear and then, if the line is clear, send data. Two nodes may still send at the same time and cause a collision, in which case the two nodes will then perform the backoff algorithm.

collision domain — In Ethernet networking, a single segment on a network. Any station on the same physical segment or separated by a repeater is in the same collision domain. Bridges, routers, and switches (depending on how they are configured) can separate collision domains.

contention — The condition that occurs when computers on a network must share the available capacity of the network wire with other computers.

gateway — A combination of hardware and software that translates between different protocols on a network.

hub — An active or passive device that connects network segments. Passive hubs are connection points; active hubs repeat and regenerate signals.

internetwork — A large network comprised of smaller interconnected networks.

IP address — A 32-bit binary address used on TCP/IP networks; consists of a host portion and a network portion.

latency — A delay on a network caused by a variety of factors, including the addition of devices.

microsegmentation — The type of segmentation that occurs through the use of virtual circuits between switches and nodes. Each connection enjoys the total bandwidth. Bandwidth is not shared as it is through hubs.

node — A connection point or junction on the network. A node can be a terminal or computer connected to the network.

passive hub — A device that connects network segments, but does not perform signal regeneration.

port — A connection point, usually for network cable, on a device such as a hub, bridge, switch, or router.

repeater — A device that repeats and cleans signals on the network, and extends the usable distance of the network.

router — A device that connects multiple segments, subdivides a network, filters broadcast traffic, and maintains a routing table. A router uses the logical address to move data packets from point to point.

segment (noun) — A section of a network that has been subdivided by routers, switches, or bridges.

segment (verb) — To subdivide a network with a networking device, such as a bridge, switch, or router.

segmentation — The process of breaking a network into smaller broadcast or collision domains.

subnetwork — A portion of the network created by manipulating a network address and breaking it down into smaller parts.

switch — A device used between nodes on a network or between networks to create virtual circuits between two points. A switch increases bandwidth by isolating traffic between two points.

Token Ring — A networking method developed by IBM that organizes the network into a physical or logical ring. The token is a logical device and, because stations may only broadcast on the network when they have the token, traffic does not collide.

topology — The physical layout of network components. The topology can take the form of a ring, star, or bus.

virtual circuit — A private connection between two points created by a switch that allows the two points to use the entire available bandwidth between those two points without contention.

REVIEW QUESTIONS

1. Routers operate at which layer of the OSI model?

   a. Data Link

   b. Presentation

   c. Session

   d. Network

2. Bridges operate at which layer of the OSI model?

   a. Network

   b. Data Link

   c. Session

   d. Transport

3. Bridges provide which of the following benefits? (Choose all that apply.)

   a. Reduced network traffic

   b. Reduced broadcast traffic

   c. Minimized collisions

   d. Faster response time than repeaters

4. Which of the following is an appropriate description of a broadcast storm?

    a. Noise on the network

    b. A large amount of traffic that passes directly through routers

    c. An electrical condition caused by the sun

    d. An error condition in which many broadcasts are sent simultaneously across the entire network

5. Which of the following best describes a network segment?

    a. A section of the network that has been separated from other segments by a router, bridge, or switch

    b. A piece of broken twisted-pair cable

    c. A piece of broken coaxial cable

    d. A portion of the network that has been isolated with a repeater

6. A router that has eight ports will require how many IP addresses?

    a. Four

    b. Six

    c. Eight

    d. Nine

    e. Ten

7. If a bridge receives a frame that has a destination MAC address located on the same segment from which it came, what will happen to the frame at the bridge?

    a. It will be forwarded.

    b. It will be dropped.

    c. The source signal will be repeated on all segments.

    d. The destination address will be repeated on all segments.

8. Which of the following is not true about bridges?

    a. Bridges do not forward broadcast traffic.

    b. Bridges segment the network.

    c. Bridges reduce the likelihood of a collision.

    d. Bridges operate at the Data Link layer.

9. Which of the following is not true about routers?

    a. Routers operate at the Network layer.

    b. Routers segment the network.

    c. Routers reduce broadcast traffic.

    d. Routers are faster than repeaters.

2

10. Which of the following is not true about switches?

    a. Switches operate at the Data Link layer.

    b. Switches create virtual network segments.

    c. Switches do not segment the network.

    d. Switches create private connections between two points.

11. Which type of addresses do routers use?

    a. Logical

    b. Physical

    c. MAC

    d. Data Link

12. A _____ can reduce broadcast traffic.

    a. bridge

    b. router

    c. repeater

    d. connector

13. Which of the following is the correct name for a device that operates at both the Data Link and Network layers of the OSI reference model?

    a. router

    b. bridge

    c. switch

    d. brouter

    e. hub

14. When two stations broadcast at the same time on a single segment of an Ethernet network, what happens?

    a. contention

    b. crash

    c. collision

    d. interruption

15. Which type of addresses do bridges use?

    a. Logical

    b. Physical

    c. IP

    d. TCP

16. When must you change the IP address of a given host on a network segmented with routers?

    a. When that computer is moved to a different segment on the network

    b. When the network card is replaced

    c. When the router is replaced

    d. When a bridge is replaced

17. Which of the following OSI layers contains media access control information?

    a. Physical

    b. Data Link

    c. Transport

    d. Presentation

    e. Session

    f. Network

18. A switch divides network communications at which layer of the OSI model?

    a. Presentation

    b. Network

    c. Transport

    d. Data Link

19. Which of the following devices translates between different protocols?

    a. bridge

    b. switch

    c. router

    d. gateway

20. Rank the following devices from lowest to highest latency.

    a. hub

    b. switch

    c. gateway

    d. router

21. Typically, which is the best device for increasing performance on your LAN?

    a. hub

    b. bridge

    c. switch

    d. router

2

22. What kind of bridges do Ethernet networks use?

 a. Translation

 b. Source-routing

 c. Transparent

 d. Brooklyn

23. What kind of bridges will connect an Ethernet network to a Token Ring network?

 a. Translation

 b. Source-routing

 c. Transparent

 e. Brooklyn

24. Why don't repeaters and hubs segment the network?

 a. They only work at the physical layer where there is nothing to filter.

 b. They are not considered devices.

 c. They operate at the network layer where segmentation can't occur.

 d. They do segment the network.

25. Another name for IP address is _____ address and another name for a MAC address is _____ address.

 a. Ethernet, logical

 b. Physical, Ethernet

 c. Logical, physical

 d. NIC, software

CASE PROJECTS

1. Winslow Networks wants to increase the performance of Sampson's network. As senior network administrator for Winslow, you assign Lisa to the job. That afternoon, while preparing to work on a lab assignment from her Cisco CCNA class, Lisa mentions that she would use a router to increase the performance of Sampson's network because routers are better than bridges. Explain to Lisa when and where a router would be the best choice. Under what circumstances would a router not be the best choice?

2. Another Winslow technician, Jennifer, overhears the discussion as she sits down to examine the lab materials spread out on Lisa's desk. Jennifer thinks Winslow should use a bridge to solve the problem. She reminds you that Sampson has a relatively small network and that a router would be more equipment than necessary. The Sampson network is running nonroutable protocols. What do you tell Jennifer?

3. Moe works at Winslow also. As a graduate of the Cisco CCNA course, he thinks that a brouter would be the best choice. He has read that a brouter performs as both a router and a bridge, but he isn't sure how this works. Explain to Moe how a brouter works. Is a brouter the best choice for Sampson? Are other devices worth consideration?

4. Moe and Lisa want you to settle an argument. Moe says a repeater is not the same as a hub. Lisa says it is. Moe argues that if you say a hub is a repeater, you might as well say that a bridge is a repeater too. Give Moe and Lisa your opinion and defend it.

5. Your colleague is preparing a presentation for new clients. She asks you to prepare a short part of that report, in which you describe the differences between segmentation with repeaters, routers, and bridges. Prepare this short report.

3

TCP/IP AND IP ADDRESSING

After reading this chapter and completing the exercises, you will be able to:

♦ Discuss the origins of TCP/IP

♦ Understand the different classes of IP addresses

♦ Configure and verify IP addresses

♦ Subdivide an IP network

♦ Identify and discuss the different layer functions of TCP/IP

♦ Describe the functions performed by protocols in the TCP/IP protocol suite, including ICMP, UDP, TCP, ARP, and RARP

♦ Use ping and trace and describe their functions

The acronym TCP/IP stands for Transmission Control Protocol/Internet Protocol, but this acronym has evolved to represent more than just these two protocols; TCP/IP is now a protocol suite that contains a variable number of protocols, depending on the specific manufacturer and network. In this chapter, you will learn about the most common and important protocols associated with TCP/IP networks.

Origins of TCP/IP

The invention and evolution of the **Transmission Control Protocol/Internet Protocol (TCP/IP)** protocol suite resulted from a coordinated effort by the United States Department of Defense (DOD). In the late 1960s, the DOD had a research branch named the **Advanced Research Projects Agency (ARPA)**. ARPA was charged with creating a wide area network (WAN) capable of surviving a nuclear attack. One of the results of the initial research was the TCP/IP protocol suite.

After completing the initial research and development, ARPA chose four university sites to help formulate the initial network: the University of California at Santa Barbara (UCSB), the University of California at Los Angeles (UCLA), the Stanford Research Institute (SRI), and the University of Utah. Initially, these sites were connected with 50 Kbps leased lines, which formed the **Advanced Research Projects Agency Network**. The name was later shortened to **ARPANET**.

 ARPA is now known as the Defense Advanced Research Projects Agency, although the agency's Web site is under *http://www.arpa.mil*.

Although the initial research was conducted for military purposes, academic researchers found the network to be a great way to communicate with one another. Because the U.S. government never classified or restricted the technology used to create the network, researchers at other organizations used the information gained from the project to create their own TCP/IP networks. This furthered the development of the protocol stack as various groups developed more protocols for the TCP/IP suite.

To further increase the popularity of TCP/IP, the DOD funded two projects. The first was the adaptation of TCP/IP to work with the UNIX operating system. The second was the inclusion of the TCP/IP protocol with Berkeley UNIX (Berkeley Software Distribution UNIX [BSD UNIX]). At the time, 90% of the university science departments in the United States used BSD UNIX, so TCP/IP quickly increased in popularity and use.

Eventually, this network interconnected so many different organizations and sites that it became known as the Internet. Because taxpayer money funded the project and the government did not classify it, it was considered to be in the public domain. This opened the Internet to everyone, organizations and individuals alike.

Overview of the TCP/IP Protocol Suite

The TCP/IP protocol suite is a network model with four layers: **Application**, **Transport**, **Internetwork**, and **Network Interface**. A series of documents called **Requests for Comments (RFCs)** define, describe, and standardize the implementation and configuration of the TCP/IP protocol suite. The **Internet Network Information Center (InterNIC)** is responsible for maintaining these standards.

Figure 3-1 compares the TCP/IP protocol suite to the OSI reference model. Notice that the Application layer and the Network Interface layer of the TCP/IP model support multiple functions that require five different layers in the OSI model.

Figure 3-1   Protocol architecture comparison

- Application layer: The Application layer in the TCP/IP model maps to the OSI Application, Presentation, and Session layers. This layer defines the functionality of the upper layers, including support for data formatting, conversion, and encryption. Also, the layer provides an application interface while providing session-establishment and control services.

- Transport layer: The Transport layer in both models determines the connectionless or connection-oriented services. Two main protocols—TCP and **UDP (User Datagram Protocol)**—operate at this layer.

- Internetwork layer: The Internetwork layer in the TCP/IP model is a direct equivalent to the Network layer in the OSI reference model. Logical addressing information, such as the IP address, occurs here.

- Network Interface layer: The Network Interface layer of the TCP/IP model maps to both the Data Link and Physical layers of the OSI reference model. Network functions at this level include hardware addressing, media access control, physical topology, and electrical and mechanical specifications.

Application Layer

The TCP/IP Application layer includes protocols for e-mail, remote logins, file transfers, Web browsing, network management, and name management. Specific protocols that exist at the TCP/IP Application layer include the following:

- FTP: The **File Transfer Protocol (FTP)** sends data over a reliable connection. This protocol can be used to send, delete, and move files to and from an FTP server and client.

- TFTP: The **Trivial File Transfer Protocol (TFTP)** sends data using an unreliable connection. This protocol functions similarly to FTP, but is faster and less reliable. A file transferred with TFTP is more likely to be corrupted than if it were transferred with FTP.

- NFS: The **Network File System (NFS)** is a distributed file system developed by Sun Microsystems that allows data to be shared across a network, regardless of the type of computer, operating system, network architecture, or protocol. This standard UNIX file system allows remote files to be manipulated as if they resided on the local computer.

- SMTP: The **Simple Mail Transfer Protocol (SMTP)** is the messaging or e-mail transfer protocol. This connection-oriented protocol allows mail to be transferred on TCP/IP networks and the Internet between e-mail servers.

- Telnet: A telnet client can use this **terminal emulation protocol (telnet)** to log onto a remote machine or telnet server. The telnet user can then run programs on the remote computer, using the remote computer's processor. Telnet is usually the first utility used when troubleshooting routers.

- rlogin: The **remote login application (rlogin)** allows you to gain access to TCP/IP hosts that support rlogin. This command-line utility allows you to navigate and manipulate a remote computer's directory structure.

- SNMP: You can install the **Simple Network Management Protocol (SNMP)** on TCP/IP hosts, including routers and other devices that support TCP/IP. SNMP is a connectionless protocol that permits remote tracking and management of TCP/IP hosts. For example, SNMP clients can report information such as hard drive space, network statistics, and various performance data. The SNMP manager can remotely monitor and control the SNMP clients.

- DNS: The **Domain Name System (DNS)** service provides TCP/IP host name to IP address resolution. For example, when you type *www.cisco.com* into a Web browser and do so while connected to the Internet, the name must be resolved to an IP address before the communication can traverse the Internet. DNS servers on the Internet provide this name resolution so that you can establish a connection to the Cisco Web server.

- HTTP: The World Wide Web uses the **Hypertext Transfer Protocol (HTTP)**. This connection-oriented protocol allows you to connect your computer to other computers on the Internet and view Web page content.

Transport Layer

3

The TCP/IP Transport layer performs several functions, the most notable being end-to-end packet delivery, reliability, and flow control. Two protocols, TCP and UDP, reside in the Transport layer of the TCP/IP model. TCP provides reliable, connection-oriented communications between two hosts. UDP provides connectionless datagram services between two hosts. Of the two protocols, TCP requires more network overhead because data is acknowledged as it is received. UDP is faster, but less reliable, because the recipient does not acknowledge data as it is received. Applications and utilities are written (programmed) to use either UDP or TCP. With UDP, communication reliability is left to the Application layer.

Ports

Both TCP and UDP use port numbers for communications between hosts. Port numbers are similar to phone numbers in that Transport layer services can be "called" by their port number. For example, if you want to order a pizza delivery, you can look up the number of a pizza place and dial the correct digits on your phone to request delivery. A similar event happens when a computer wants service from the TCP/IP Transport layer. When a computer wants to transfer a file over FTP, it uses TCP port 21 to establish and control the connection and TCP port 20 to transfer the data. TCP ports 20 and 21 are called **Well Known Port numbers** because applications expect to find FTP services on TCP port 21 and to transfer their data on TCP port 20.

IANA has a database of Well Known Port numbers located at *http://www.iana.org/assignments/port-numbers*.

You should be familiar with the following Well Known TCP and UDP port numbers from RFC 1700:

- TCP port 20 — FTP data transfer
- TCP port 21 — FTP control port
- TCP port 23 — Telnet
- TCP port 25 — SMTP
- TCP & UDP port 53 — DNS (also known as name or domain server)

- TCP port 80 — HTTP Web services
- TCP & UDP port 123 — Network Time Protocol (NTP)
- TCP port 110 — **Post Office Protocol version 3 (POP3)**
- TCP port 119 — Network News Transport Protocol (NNTP)
- UDP port 69 — TFTP
- UDP port 161 — SNMP

Each IP transport protocol has its own port numbers. This means that TCP has 65,535 ports available and UDP has another 65,535 ports available. Sometimes a service will exist on the same port number on both protocols. For example, DNS can use TCP port 53 or UDP port 53. Even if a Well Known Port number exists for a certain service, you do not have to use it for that service. For example, if you wanted to hide a Web server on the Internet, you might set its HTTP service port number to TCP 1055 (a randomly chosen number). Then, your Web clients would have to know the port number in order to contact your Web services. The port numbers are divided into three ranges: Well Known Ports, Registered Ports, and Dynamic/Private Ports.

- Well Known Ports are those from 0 through 1,023.
- Registered Ports are those from 1,024 through 49,151.
- Dynamic/Private Ports are those from 49,152 through 65,535.

To understand the use of ports in network communications, consider the diagram shown in Figure 3-2. The FTP client calls the FTP server on TCP port 21 to establish communication. Then the FTP server responds to the client. The client computer dynamically configures the client software to use a port above TCP 1023; in the figure, that TCP port is 1029. Then, the FTP data transfer port is established. Again, the client calls the server on the Well Known Port of TCP 20. After the necessary acknowledgments, the client computer sets the FTP client software to use a port above TCP 1023 (port 1030 in the figure) to conduct the actual data transfer.

TCP Three-way Handshake

To establish a reliable connection between two points, TCP uses a **three-way handshake**. To do this, TCP transmits three packets before the actual data transfer occurs between two hosts. In order to transfer data reliably, the hosts must synchronize their communications to ensure that no packets are missed during communication.

Figure 3-2   TCP port usage in FTP communications

As an analogy for the three-way handshake process, consider the following example: Assume that two pilots want to communicate with one another during a mission. The first pilot uses the call sign "Maverick" and the other pilot uses the call sign "Iceman." A call from Maverick to Iceman might be similar to the following:

Maverick: "Iceman, this is Maverick; do you copy?"

Iceman: "This is Iceman; I copy you, Maverick."

Maverick: "Roger, Iceman."

After this initial interaction, Maverick would begin sending information to Iceman. The major difference between the human interactions in the example above and how computers communicate via TCP is that the computers will use data packets with sequence numbers. Each host computer must acknowledge the sequence number of the sender and include its own sequence number in the following packet. This allows the computers to keep track of each packet and to ensure that none are lost during transmission. If a given packet does not arrive within a given time interval, the source computer will retransmit it. If the destination computer receives packets out of order, it can use the sequence numbers to reassemble those packets into the correct order.

Before investigating the three-way handshake process further, look at Figure 3-3, which illustrates a conceptual drawing of the TCP packet header structure. In the following text, you will be concerned with the sequence number field and the acknowledgment number field.

Source Port (16 bits)	Destination Port (16 bits)
Sequence Number (32 bits)	
Acknowledgment Number (32 bits)	
Offset, Reserved Bits, Flags (16 bits)	Receive Window Size (16 bits)
Checksum (16 bits)	Urgent Pointer (16 bits)
Options and Padding (32 bits)	
Data (variable length) Information for the next higher layer (Application layer)	

Figure 3-3   TCP packet header

 TCP is defined in RFC 793 *(ftp://ftp.isi.edu/in-notes/rfc793.txt)*. The RFC describes all of the data fields in the TCP packet structure, as well as the other TCP concepts discussed in this chapter.

Before two computers can communicate over TCP, they must synchronize their **initial sequence numbers (ISN)**. These sequence numbers ensure that the communications are assembled in the proper order and that no missing packets exist. The synchronization process occurs when each host sends its own ISN and receives a confirmation and an ISN from the other host. When a synchronization request is sent, it is abbreviated SYN. When an acknowledgment is sent, the abbreviation is ACK. This process has four steps:

1. Host A sends a SYN packet to Host B, which indicates a sequence number represented here as ISN_A. The ACK field contains a zero in this first packet.

2. Host B composes an ACK packet for Host A, which acknowledges A's sequence number by adding one to the number of the sequence number that Host A submitted (ISN_A+1). This is called an **expectational acknowledgment**.

3. Host B adds its SYN data for Host A, which indicates its sequence number ISN_B, and sends that information to Host A in the ACK packet composed in Step 2.

4. Host A submits an ACK packet to Host B. The packet includes a sequence number of ISN_A+1 (expected by Host B) and an acknowledgment number of ISN_B+1, which indicates that Host A received the last packet and now expects a sequence of ISN_B+1 from Host B.

Even with four steps, only three packets need to be exchanged because the SYN packet from Host B also serves as the acknowledgment to the SYN packet from Host A. This process is called the TCP three-way handshake because only three packets travel the network to negotiate and synchronize the TCP connection, as shown in Figure 3-4.

Figure 3-4   TCP three-way handshake

Notice in Figure 3-4 that the ACK number in the TCP packet from Host B is one number higher than the SYN number sent by Host A. This process shows that Host B expects to see SEQ number 201 next (ISN_A+1). The process is considered expectational (and not necessarily sequential because packets can get out of sequence). This allows hosts to detect and recover from failures or problems with TCP communications. RFC 793 states: "The principal reason for the three-way handshake is to prevent old duplicate connection initiations from causing confusion." A number of possible error conditions are described in the RFC. One example of how TCP recovers from old duplicate connections is illustrated in Figure 3-5.

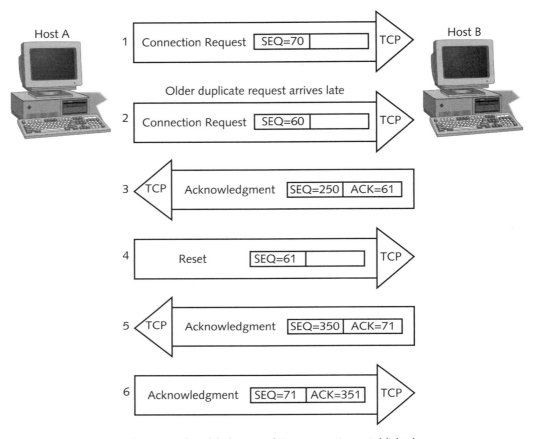

Three-way handshake complete: connection established

Figure 3-5 TCP connection recovery

In the example, the packets are numbered to help you follow what is happening. Packet 1 is a connection request that arrives before a previous connection request (shown as packet 2). Host B acknowledges the connection request with the lower sequence number first (packet 3). Host A realizes that Host B is acknowledging an old connection request and sends a reset packet (packet 4). A **reset packet (RST)** indicates that a TCP connection is to be terminated without further interaction. Host B then acknowledges the newer connection request from Host A with packet 5 (ACK=71, which is one higher than the SEQ in packet 1). Host A then completes the three-way handshake with Host B by sending data packet 6 with SEQ=71 and ACK=351 (which is one higher than packet 5). In this example, TCP packets 1, 5, and 6 complete the three-way handshake.

3

TCP Sliding Windows

Once the three-way handshake is complete and data transfer begins, TCP **sliding windows** control the flow and efficiency of communication. The size of the TCP sliding window determines the number of acknowledgments sent for a given data transfer because it constrains the amount of data that will be received before an acknowledgment is sent to the transmitting host. Essentially, once the window fills with data, the destination host sends an acknowledgment for all the packets received in that window. Then, the window slides over in order to accept new packets. It is important to note that it is the sender that controls the sliding window's size.

Networks that perform large data transfers should use large window sizes. During a connection for a large data transfer on a network with few collisions, a large TCP sliding window would work well. Large window sizes can cause problems, however, on a network with lots of traffic or on one that does small data transfers. The large window may force the sending host to wait for an acknowledgment. If the sending host waits too long, it will retransmit data. Then, that sending host may receive an acknowledgment of both the original and the retransmitted data.

A small TCP window size produces frequent acknowledgments. Networks that transfer small amounts of data should use small window sizes; however, if the receiving computer is forced to acknowledge every data packet because of a small TCP sliding window, the increase in network traffic and the additional load placed on the hosts would be inefficient. Fortunately, TCP window sizes can adjust dynamically during the life of a connection, so that the window can be expanded or contracted as needed to make the communications more efficient.

TCP sliding windows is one of three methods used to control the flow of packets on a network. The other two are **buffering** and **congestion avoidance**. Buffering is a capability that most network devices have and use to keep up when packets are flowing in too quickly for them to keep process. The **buffer** is a portion of memory where the device stores incoming packets until they can be processed. Congestion avoidance is a communication method for network devices to reduce the flow of packets from their source. Devices implement congestion avoidance by sending a "slow down the transmission rate" request to the device that is sending packets too rapidly. The ICMP Source Quench (covered in the next section) is a type of congestion avoidance.

Internetwork Layer

The Internetwork layer in the TCP/IP model handles software, or logical, addressing. Four main protocols function at this layer:

- IP: The **Internet Protocol (IP)** provides a connectionless delivery service. The IP moves packets around the network, including through routers. IP is covered in greater detail later in the chapter.

- ICMP: The **Internet Control Message Protocol (ICMP)** controls and manages IP communications. This protocol, defined in RFC 792 (*ftp://ftp.isi.edu/in-notes/rfc792.txt*), provides message control and error-reporting services between two TCP/IP hosts or between a host server and a gateway to the Internet. ICMP uses eight different message types to manage eleven different aspects of IP communications. The eight types of ICMP messages are **destination unreachable**, **time exceeded**, **parameter problem**, **source quench**, **redirect**, **echo request/reply**, **timestamp request/reply**, and **information request/reply**.

- ARP: The **Address Resolution Protocol (ARP)** resolves IP addresses to MAC addresses for source hosts that know the IP address of the destination host but not the MAC address. The source host issues an ARP broadcast requesting the MAC address for the corresponding IP address. Every station on the local subnet receives the ARP broadcast, but only the destination host responds.

- RARP: The **Reverse Address Resolution Protocol (RARP)** provides IP address to MAC address resolution in a manner similar to that of ARP, but does so under different circumstances. In the case of a **diskless workstation**, a source host will know its MAC address (because it is burned into the NIC) but not its IP address, because the IP address is implemented in software and a diskless workstation cannot store information locally. This host will get its IP address by issuing a RARP request to a RARP server.

ARP

The Internet Protocol (IP), Address Resolution Protocol (ARP), and Reverse Address Resolution Protocol (RARP) are all routed protocols associated with TCP/IP. A **routed protocol** is one that contains enough information in its header that it can be routed on a network. Protocols at the Internetwork layer of the TCP/IP stack are routed. The Address Resolution Protocol (ARP) maps IP addresses to MAC addresses. In essence, the source of the network packet sends the information to the destination. Unique MAC addresses reference the end-points in the exchange.

Many network devices maintain tables of the MAC and IP addresses of other devices on the network. These tables are called **ARP tables** and are maintained in volatile Random Access Memory (RAM). Many devices allow the network administrators to modify the ARP table (also known as ARP cache), but this is not a typical activity. Normally, devices automatically obtain and update their own ARP tables.

When a computer transmits a packet to a destination on the local network, it checks its ARP cache for an IP to MAC address mapping for the destination node. If the computer finds an appropriate IP to MAC address mapping, the source computer uses the IP and MAC addresses to encapsulate the data that it is ready to transmit. The source computer then sends the packet directly to the destination computer.

```
MS-DOS Prompt                                    _ □ ×
  10 x 18 ▼   □ □ □ ⊠ □ □ A

C:\>arp -a

Interface: 208.128.20.163 on Interface 0x1000002
  Internet Address      Physical Address     Type
  204.70.128.1          20-53-52-43-00-00    dynamic
  204.181.89.153        20-53-52-43-00-00    dynamic
  204.181.89.154        20-53-52-43-00-01    static

C:\>
```

Figure 3-6 IP host's ARP table

Figure 3-6 illustrates the ARP cache of a Windows 98 TCP/IP host attached to the Internet. Notice that the IP address is listed first, the MAC address next, followed by information about whether the entry is static or dynamic. Most entries are dynamic, which means that the system performed IP to MAC resolution as needed. Static entries, which are rarely used, provide semi-permanent IP to MAC address mappings that an administrator entered manually. An administrator makes these manual mappings to reduce ARP traffic on the network only when he or she knows that a specific hardware address and IP address combination will remain constant.

ARP Request

If a source computer cannot locate an IP to MAC address mapping in its ARP table, it must obtain the correct mapping, because both an IP and MAC address for the source and destination are required to send data. To do this, the device initiates an **ARP request** to gain the destination's MAC address.

 This section focuses on obtaining the MAC address for a specific IP address and assumes that the device already knows the destination's IP address. If the source computer has only the destination computer's host name, the source must first obtain the IP address, which is beyond the scope of the address resolution discussed here.

A source computer broadcasts an ARP request to all hosts on the local segment. Each device determines whether the packet is destined for its IP address. The one device that discovers that the ARP request broadcast packet is destined for its IP address responds to the ARP request.

 Because it is a broadcast mechanism, ARP is only used on the local segment of a network. Routers will not pass ARP broadcasts. If the destination host is not on the same network segment as the source host, the source will send the packet to the **default gateway** (router) and will not ARP.

ARP Request Frame

The ARP frame has a logical configuration. As you have learned, the lower layers in the protocol configuration encapsulate data frames. With ARP, the computer is seeking an IP to MAC address resolution, so the ARP frame includes both the MAC and IP addresses. The frame header includes the MAC header and the IP header, followed by the ARP message. The MAC header contains the destination and source MAC address, and the IP header contains the destination and source IP addresses. Figure 3-7 represents the ARP request frame configuration.

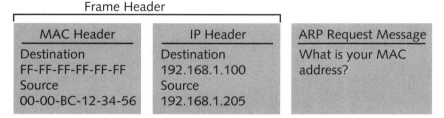

	Frame Header	
MAC Header	**IP Header**	**ARP Request Message**
Destination FF-FF-FF-FF-FF-FF Source 00-00-BC-12-34-56	Destination 192.168.1.100 Source 192.168.1.205	What is your MAC address?

Figure 3-7   ARP request packet

The packets shown in the figure are simplified to illustrate a specific point. Real packets have 28 octets (28 sets of eight binary digits), which identify hardware types, protocol types, and message lengths. Because these components are not significant to the current discussion, they are not shown in the figure. RFC 826 (*ftp://ftp.isi.edu/in-notes/rfc826.txt*) contains a detailed discussion of ARP.

Since the source host does not know the MAC address of the destination, the ARP request frame is a broadcast to all MAC addresses (FF-FF-FF-FF-FF-FF) and all devices on the local segment will investigate the frame to determine whether their IP addresses match that of the destination. The device that discovers its own IP address in the IP header reads the rest of the packet and returns an **ARP reply**. The rest of the devices on the segment discard the packet.

The ARP reply supplies the MAC address of the destination host in a unicast packet. When the computer that sent the ARP request receives the ARP reply from the host, it has the information necessary to properly address the data it wants to send to the destination computer. The source computer extracts the MAC address from the ARP reply and updates its ARP table. Then, the source computer creates and properly addresses its data packet and sends it with the MAC address of the destination computer.

Devices on the network that receive and eventually discard an ARP request use the source information to update their own ARP tables. Recipients enter the source computer's MAC address from the ARP request packet into their local ARP tables.

ARP Cache Life

Because the source checks its local ARP cache prior to sending packets on the local network, the ARP cache must contain current information. If the ARP cache contains stale information, data packets could be routed to the wrong host. Because the ARP table directs data packets to a specific network card based on the mapping, it is important that the mappings are correct. Host IP addresses can change, so old ARP table mappings can cause misrouted packets. To ensure that old ARP table entries do not become a serious problem, network devices place a **time-to-live (TTL)** on ARP entries. For example, Microsoft operating systems use a two- to ten-minute TTL for their ARP cache, and initial mappings through ARP have a two-minute TTL. Any entry that is used twice within those first two minutes is automatically given a life of 10 minutes. After the 10 minutes, the ARP entry is removed from the ARP table.

By using TTLs, an operating system ensures that an ARP cache is never outdated for more than 10 minutes. The process of removing ARP entries from an ARP table is known as aging out the ARP table. In addition to aging out, devices on a network also replace ARP entries whenever new information is received. For example, if a computer receives a packet from a host that contains an IP and MAC address that is different from what it has listed in the ARP table, the computer updates its ARP table.

Even though the ARP tables are revised frequently, and their entries have short lives, they reduce network traffic. Without an ARP table, a device would have to perform an ARP for each packet, which could significantly increase network traffic on the local segment. As discussed earlier, increased traffic usually results in increased collisions and network delays.

RARP

The Reverse Address Resolution Protocol (RARP) is similar to ARP in that computers use it to bind MAC addresses to IP addresses. However, RARP is used primarily by diskless workstations, which have MAC addresses burned into their network cards but no IP addresses. Because these workstations have no disks, they have no hard drives to hold IP configuration information. Therefore, they must obtain their IP configuration information each time they boot on the network.

To do this, a client's IP configuration must be stored on a RARP server. The RARP server maintains a table of IP to MAC address mappings for RARP clients. During the boot process, RARP clients call the RARP server to obtain their IP configuration information.

RARP Request Frame

As mentioned earlier, a RARP packet has the same structure as an ARP packet. However, it contains different pieces of information. Figure 3-8 illustrates a RARP request frame.

Notice that the IP header does not have a specific destination or source IP address in the RARP frame. The source does not know which device is the RARP server, so it must broadcast to all devices on the segment.

RARP

Figure 3-8   RARP request frame

RARP Client

Once a RARP client receives a RARP reply, it configures its IP networking components. The client copies its IP address configuration information into its local RAM. After the client receives the configuration settings, it can use the MAC and IP address to send packets on the network to other clients.

When the diskless workstation reboots or is shut down, the respective IP configuration information is lost. Consequently, each time the diskless workstation boots, it must obtain its IP configuration settings from a RARP server.

ARP and RARP Compared

The RARP process and the ARP process are both concerned with IP to MAC address mapping. In addition, they use the same packet format and utilize broadcast addresses to accomplish their tasks. Although they share similarities, they have certain differences as well:

- ARP is concerned with obtaining the MAC address of other clients by using an IP address, but RARP obtains the IP address of the local host by using the local host's MAC address. Computers broadcast ARP packets on the local network by using the broadcast MAC address, but RARP uses the broadcast IP address (255.255.255.255) as well as the broadcast MAC address.

- The local host maintains the ARP table. A RARP server maintains the RARP table.

■ The local host uses an ARP reply to update its ARP table and to send packets to the destination. The RARP reply is used to configure the IP protocol on the local host.

Routers and ARP

As you have learned, routers segment networks. Segmenting a network reduces network traffic because routers do not forward broadcast traffic from one segment (**subnet**) to another by default. (Although you can configure most routers to forward broadcasts, such an action would increase network traffic unnecessarily.)

Because hosts rely on ARP requests to determine MAC addresses, and ARP requests use broadcasts, hosts must create broadcast traffic in order to determine the MAC address of other hosts. However, routers filter broadcast traffic, which means that ARP requests can go no further than the local segment (subnet). What happens when the source computer needs to send a message to a host on a remote segment? In such a case, the source must forward the packet to the router. This section explains how routers use their routing tables and ARP to correctly route packets across a network.

ARP Tables

Like other network devices, routers maintain ARP tables to assist in transmitting packets from one network to another. If the destination IP address of a packet is on a segment to which a router is attached, the router will forward the packet directly to the destination. To do this, the router must obtain the MAC address for that destination. If the router has the MAC to IP mapping in its ARP table, the router can forward the packet directly. However, if the router does not have that mapping in its ARP table, the router must issue an ARP request.

A router uses ARP just as other hosts use ARP. However, the router is bound to have a larger ARP table because it typically deals with more hosts. It connects to multiple networks; a typical TCP/IP host only connects to and receives ARP mappings for its local segment. Of course, the actual number of ARP table entries depends on the amount of traffic sent between and within the various segments. Routers have multiple network interfaces and therefore also include the port numbers of their NICs in the ARP table. Thus, routers can make routing decisions for incoming packets quickly by forwarding the packets to the appropriate interface.

The Ping Utility

Network administrators and support personnel commonly use the **Packet Internet Groper (ping)** utility to verify connectivity between two points. The ping utility uses ICMP echo request/reply messages to verify connectivity at the Internetwork Layer of the TCP/IP model, which is one reason that ICMP echo request/reply messages are the most commonly used ICMP message. When you issue the ping command, the source node sends out ICMP echo request packets to the specified destination node. The destination node, if it is up and running correctly, replies with ICMP echo reply packets. A simple ping request can be issued by typing the ping [ip #] command. Figure 3-9 shows the output of the ping command.

```
RouterB>ping 172.22.5.1
Type escape sequence to abort.
Sending 5, 100-byte ICMP Echoes to 172.22.5.1, timeout is 2 seconds:
!!!!!

Success rate is 100 percent (5/5), round-trip min/avg/max = 68/70/76 ms
RouterB>
```

Five exclamation points represent five successful ping replies

Figure 3-9   ping example

The reply of five exclamation points means that all five echo request packets were responded to with echo reply packets. The following table shows a list of possible replies:

Table 3-1   Ping Responses

Ping Response	Result
!	Echo request successfully replied to with Echo reply
.	Time-out (no response from destination)
U	Destination unreachable
?	Unknown packet type
&	Time-to-live exceeded
C	Packet experienced congestion

Cisco routers include two ping commands: standard ping and extended ping. Figure 3-10 shows the proper syntax for the extended ping command. The extended ping allows you to specify more echo request packets and larger packets. You can also use this command to ping IPX nodes with the IPX protocol. Overall, the standard and extended ping commands give you an excellent tool for determining the status of remote hosts on your network.

You must type the enable command and enter privileged mode before the extended ping command is available

Ping without a following IP address will invoke the extended ping command

```
RouterB>en
Password:
RouterB#ping
Protocol [ip]: ip
Target IP address: 172.22.5.1
Repeat count [5]: 25
Datagram size [100]: 100
Timeout in seconds [2]:
Extended commands [n]:
Sweep range of sizes [n]:
Type escape sequence to abort.
Sending 25, 100-byte ICMP Echoes to 172.22.5.1, timeout is 2 seconds:
!!!!!!!!!!!!!!!!!!!!!!!!!
Success rate is 100 percent (25/25), round-trip min/avg/max = 68/93/120 ms
RouterB#
```

You can specify the exact number and size of packets you wish to use for the ping command

Figure 3-10   Extended ping commands

3

The Trace Utility

The **trace** utility also uses ICMP echo request/reply messages. Trace shows the exact path a packet takes from the source to the destination. This is accomplished through the use of the TTL counter. The packet is sent out first with a time-to-live of one. Once it finds the first hop (router) on the path to the destination, the packet is returned with a **destination unreachable** message. The TTL is incremented to two and the packet is resent. This process continues until the packet reaches the destination or times out. The net effect is that you see the hops (transitions from one device to another) that a packet takes as it travels the network. Figure 3-11 shows a trace to a router port with IP address 172.22.5.1. You can use the trace utility to determine where communications are breaking down along a particular path.

```
RouterB>trace ip 172.22.5.1
Type escape sequence to abort.
Tracing the route to 172.22.5.1
  1 172.22.3.1 20 msec 20 msec 20 msec
  2 172.22.4.2 36 msec 40 msec *
RouterB>
```

The trace command shows you the exact route packets take to reach a destination. You can use this information to pinpoint where network problems are occurring.

Figure 3-11   Trace command example

Be aware that some routers can be configured to discard ICMP echo requests and therefore become invisible to the trace command. This feature is often used as a security measure because some network administrators do not want all of their network devices and IP addresses exposed to people who decide to run a trace. Several different malicious network attacks have also been created using ICMP messages; one in particular is called an **ICMP flood**. An ICMP flood is caused by a malicious user or program that sends a large quantity of ICMP echo requests (pings) to a target device in an attempt to crash or greatly reduce the performance of the target device. This is another reason network administrators may choose to turn off ICMP support on key devices, such as routers.

Using ping and trace on a PC workstation is slightly different than on a Cisco router.

Network Interface Layer

The TCP/IP Network Interface layer plays the same role as the Data Link and Physical layers of the OSI model. The MAC address, network card drivers, and specific interfaces for the network card function at this level of the TCP/IP protocol stack. No specific IP functions exist at this layer because the layer's focus is on communication with the network card and other networking hardware such as cable, hubs, and repeaters.

IP Addressing

An IP address has 32 bits divided into four octets (four sets of eight binary digits). To make the address easier to read, people use decimal numbers to represent the binary digits. For example, the IP address 192.168.1.1 is 11000000.10101000.00000001.00000001 when written in binary. Notice that 32 binary digits create the address. The lowest number of any octet is 00000000, or zero, and the highest number of any octet is 11111111, or 255. When binary IP addresses are written in decimal format, it is often called dotted decimal notation.

To understand how eight binary ones are equal to the decimal 255, you must look at the places for each of the binary values. Table 3-2 illustrates the places of the binary digits 128, 64, 32, 16, 8, 4, 2, and 1. Notice that the number 192 is created when the first two binary digits are ones and the following six digits are zeros. To determine the decimal equivalent, you add the binary places that are identified by ones. In the second row of Table 3-2, the 128 and 64 places have ones, which creates the decimal number 192 (i.e., 128 + 64 = 192).

Table 3-2   Binary to decimal conversion

	128	64	32	16	8	4	2	1
192	1	1	0	0	0	0	0	0
168	1	0	1	0	1	0	0	0
1	0	0	0	0	0	0	0	1
255	1	1	1	1	1	1	1	1
0	0	0	0	0	0	0	0	0

MAC to IP Address Translation

The MAC address identifies a specific computer on a network, so each MAC address is unique. TCP/IP networks can use MAC addresses in communication. However, network devices could not efficiently route traffic on a large internetwork or on the Internet with MAC addresses; MAC addresses are not grouped logically, they cannot be modified, and they don't give information about physical or logical network configuration. Therefore, another addressing scheme called **IP addressing** was devised for use on large networks. Unlike MAC addresses, IP addresses have a hierarchical structure and do provide logical groupings. The structure of the IP address makes packet routing possible on large networks.

You can compare driver's license numbers to MAC addresses. The driver's license allows you to drive a car, and it uniquely identifies you as a vehicle operator. However, when people want to talk with you, they don't call your driver's license number. Instead, they call your phone number. Phone numbers identify your location with an area code and other digits specific to you. Similarly, IP addresses identify the specific network on which you reside and your computer on that network. For example, if your IP address is 192.168.1.3, your computer is host 3 on network 192.168.1.0.

Because the IP address identifies both a network and a host, you can route communications through large networks, including the Internet. Routers can send communications in a more efficient manner by using the hierarchical IP address. If the Internet used MAC addresses, huge tables would have to be maintained containing not only the MAC addresses of each and every computer, but also each device along the path to that computer. Clearly, that would be unmanageable, especially given that network cards can malfunction. Every time someone replaced a network card, the giant MAC table would have to be updated!

IP Classes

The **Internet Assigned Numbers Authority (IANA)** devised the hierarchical IP addressing structure, and the **American Registry of Internet Numbers (ARIN)** assigns IP addresses to public, private, and government organizations. Five different groups of IP addresses (labeled Class A through E) exist on the Internet. The first three classes, Classes A, B, and C, are assigned to governments, companies, schools, and public entities for use on the Internet. The other two classes (D and E) are reserved for **multicasting** and experimentation. Therefore, you will mainly be concerned with managing Class A, B, and C addresses.

Class A

ARIN reserves Class A IP addresses for governments throughout the world. Class A addresses, when written in binary format, will always begin with a zero. You can tell what class an Internet address belongs to by looking at its first octet. For example, Class A addresses in decimal notation will have 1 to 126 as their first octet. Figure 3-12 displays the binary digits associated with these decimal numbers.

Binary Place Values

128	64	32	16	8	4	2	1		Decimal Equivalent	Description
0	0	0	0	0	0	0	0	=	0	Subnet identifier
0	0	0	0	0	0	0	1	=	1	Bottom of Class A range
0	1	1	1	1	1	1	0	=	126	Top of Class A range
0	1	1	1	1	1	1	1	=	127	Loopback address

Figure 3-12   Class A addresses

Notice that all zeros identify the subnet, which is not a usable IP address. The first Class A address that can be assigned is 1.0.0.0 (decimal) or 00000001.00000000.00000000.00000000 (binary). The last Class A address that can be assigned is 126.0.0.0 in decimal notation, which is 01111110.00000000.00000000.00000000 in binary format.

It seems that 127.0.0.1 (decimal) is the highest assignable Class A address, but that particular address range is reserved as the **loopback** address. The loopback address is widely known as 127.0.0.1, but all addresses with 127 as their first octet are part of the loopback range. You can use the loopback address range for diagnostics, such as ping. If you ping 127.0.0.1

or any other IP address on the 127.0.0.0 network, your internal IP configuration should respond. This response verifies a properly installed TCP/IP protocol suite. Because the entire 127 Class A address is reserved for diagnostics, the highest Class A that can be assigned is 126. (It is important to note that a successful loopback test does not mean the device can communicate with other devices. You can get a successful loopback response from a computer with no network cable attached to the NIC card.)

Notice that you cannot create a decimal number higher than 127 with eight binary digits if the first digit must be zero. The IANA specified that the first binary digit in a class A address would be zero to separate it from the other four categories (B, C, D, and E).

For Class A addresses, the ARIN only assigns the first octet. However, the same is not true for Class B and Class C addresses. Class B addresses are assigned with the first two octets set. Class C addresses are assigned with the first three octets set. This means that there is a difference between the number of hosts that you can assign based on the type of address you are assigned:

- Class A: Each Class A address supports 16,777,214 hosts.
- Class B: Each Class B address supports 65,534 hosts.
- Class C: Each Class C address supports 254 hosts.

Why is there such a difference in the number of hosts supported? When you are assigned a Class A network, you can use the last three octets for your network hosts. When you use a Class B network, only the last two octets can be used. A Class C address only has a single octet for you to modify.

Class B

Class B IP addresses are assigned to large- and medium-sized companies. The IANA specifies that Class B addresses will lead with 10 when written in binary format. This means that the range in decimal notation for the first octet of Class B addresses is 128 through 191. Figure 3-13 illustrates the binary to decimal calculations that specify this range.

Binary Place Values   Decimal   Description
                                   Equivalent

128	64	32	16	8	4	2	1			
1	0	0	0	0	0	0	0	=	128	First Class B address
1	0	1	1	1	1	1	1	=	191	Last Class B address

Figure 3-13   Class B addresses

With the first two binary digits of the first octet in the Class B category defined, the address range is limited. When the last six configurable bits of the first octet are set to zero, the lowest configurable number is obtained (128). When those same six digits are set to one, the highest configurable number is set (191).

Class C

Class C IP addresses are assigned to groups that do not meet the qualifications to obtain Class A or B addresses. The IANA specified that the first three binary digits of a Class C address must be 110, which means that Class C addresses can range from 192 through 223 in decimal notation. Figure 3-14 illustrates the binary to decimal equivalents for the Class C addresses.

Binary Place Values   Decimal   Description
                                             Equivalent

128	64	32	16	8	4	2	1
1	1	0	0	0	0	0	0	= 192	First Class C address
1	1	0	1	1	1	1	1	= 223	Last Class C address

Figure 3-14   Class C addresses

In Class C addresses, the last five digits are configurable. The graphic shows that when the last five digits are set to all zeros, the decimal equivalent is 192. When those same five digits are set to binary ones, the decimal equivalent is 223.

Class D

Class D addresses (also known as **multicast addresses**) are reserved for multicasting. Multicasting is the sending of a stream of data (usually audio and video) to multiple computers simultaneously. Compared to broadcasting, this saves bandwidth. Many routers forward multicasts, and computers configured to receive the multicast information accept the packets and can receive the data stream. Because Class D addresses must have 1110 as their first four binary digits, the range for Class D starts with decimal 224 and ends at 239 in the first octet. Figure 3-15 illustrates the binary and decimal range for Class D addresses.

Binary Place Values   Decimal   Description
                                             Equivalent

128	64	32	16	8	4	2	1
1	1	1	0	0	0	0	0	= 224	First Class D address
1	1	1	0	1	1	1	1	= 239	Last Class D address

Figure 3-15   Class D addresses

Class E

The IANA reserves Class E addresses for research, testing, and experimentation. The Class E range starts where Class D leaves off. Notice that Figure 3-16 illustrates the first address in the "experimental" range as 240. No top range is listed because Class E is the final range defined. Therefore, Class E is everything above and including 240 (decimal) as the first octet.

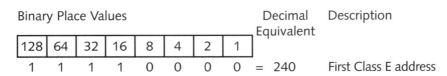

Figure 3-16   Class E addresses

Private IP Ranges

Many companies today utilize private IP addresses for their internal networks. This prevents the organizations from having to obtain official IP addresses from the InterNIC or their ISP every time they add a host to the network. Class A, B, and C private address ranges have been defined by RFC1918 (*ftp://ftp.isi.edu/in-notes/rfc1918.txt*). Table 3-3 illustrates the private IP address ranges that network administrators can use. If these private ranges are used for an internal network, they will not be routable on the Internet. This is fine for most organizations because they have one or more gateway devices (such as routers, firewalls, or proxy servers) that provide connectivity to the Internet. These gateway devices have network interface connections to both the internal network and the Internet and route packets between them (thereby providing Internet connectivity to internal clients). The company will simply have to obtain one or more official IP addresses if the organization chooses to provide services (like an organizational Web site) to people using the Internet.

Table 3-3   The private IP ranges

Class	Private Address Range
A	10.x.x.x
B	172.16.x.x – 172.31.x.x
C	192.168.x.x

Subnet Addressing

As previously mentioned, IP addresses identify both the network and the host. However, the division between the two is not specific to a certain number of octets. In an earlier example, the IP address 192.168.1.3 was used to illustrate that 192.168.1.0 was the network and 3 was the host identifier on that network. This suggests that the first three octets comprise the network identifier and the last octet is the host identifier, but that is not always true. In fact, the network portion can be as small as the first octet or as large as 30 of the 32 binary digits of the IP address.

How do you determine how many digits are used for the network identifier? You must look at the **subnet mask**, which is a required component for all IP hosts. On every TCP/IP network, hosts must have both an IP address and a subnet mask. The subnet mask indicates how much of the IP address represents the network or subnetwork. Standard (default) subnet masks are as follows:

- Class A subnet mask is 255.0.0.0 or
  11111111.00000000.00000000.00000000

- Class B subnet mask is 255.255.0.0 or
  11111111.11111111.00000000.00000000

- Class C subnet mask is 255.255.255.0 or
  11111111.11111111.11111111.00000000

Notice that Class A addresses come from the InterNIC with the first octet masked; Class B addresses have the first two octets masked; Class C addresses have the first three octets masked. This is directly correlated to the number of octets that are defined by the InterNIC.

The mask is essentially a continuous string of binary one digits. TCP/IP hosts use the combination of the IP address and the subnet mask to determine if other addresses are local or remote. The binary AND operation is used to perform the calculation. The binary AND operation is simple—each of the 32 binary digits in the IP address is compared with the corresponding digit on the subnet mask to arrive at the ANDing result. One and one results in one, and all other combinations result in zero. When devices AND the IP address with the corresponding subnet mask, the network (or subnetwork) number is the result. Computers and routers use the AND computation to determine the subnet identifier for each IP address. If the subnet identifier for the local IP address is the same as that of the IP address to which it wants to communicate, then the packet is sent on the local subnet (ARP is used, as necessary, to locate the destination MAC address on the local subnet). However, if the subnet identifiers are different, then the packet is sent to the default gateway (usually the local router) to be routed to the remote subnet. Figure 3-17 illustrates ANDing.

Source IP:	64.168.1.1	01000000.10101000.00000001.00000001
Subnet mask:	255.255.255.0	11111111.11111111.11111111.00000000
ANDing result:	64.168.1.0	01000000.10101000.00000001.00000000
Destination IP :	64.168.5.7	01000000.10101000.00000101.00000111
Subnet mask:	255.255.255.0	11111111.11111111.11111111.00000000
ANDing result:	64.168.5.0	01000000.10101000.00000101.00000000

When the mask 255.255.255.0 is used the hosts are remote.

Source IP:	64.168.1.1	01000000.10101000.00000001.00000001
Subnet mask:	255.255.0.0	11111111.11111111.00000000.00000000
ANDing result:	64.168.0.0	01000000.10101000.00000000.00000000
Destination IP:	64.168.5.7	01000000.10101000.00000101.00000111
Subnet mask:	255.255.0.0	11111111.11111111.00000000.00000000
ANDing result:	64.168.0.0	01000000.10101000.00000000.00000000

When the mask 255.255.0.0 is used the hosts are local.

Figure 3-17   ANDing operations

In the figure, the first comparison uses the subnet mask 255.255.255.0, which defines the first three octets as the network identifier. A quick look will tell you that these hosts are on two different subnets. Notice that the first three octets from the ANDing result of the source host are 64.168.1, while those of the destination host are 64.168.5. This means that the source is on network 64.168.1.0 and the destination is on subnet 64.168.5.0. The source host will have to send communications for 64.168.5.7 through its default gateway.

Now, consider the calculations shown on the bottom half of Figure 3-17. The subnet mask has been changed to 255.255.0.0. Given this configuration, the two hosts are on the same subnet because the network identifier in this case is 64.168.0.0 for both. This means that the source host would use ARP, if necessary, to determine the MAC address of host 64.168.5.7 and then transmit its data to that MAC address. Notice that in both of these examples, the default mask is not used. The 64 in the first octet identifies this as a Class A address, which would have a default subnet mask of 255.0.0.0. This means the network administrator has manipulated the mask to get more network numbers. This is called **subnetting** and is discussed later in this chapter.

Subnet Address

If you look at the preceding network and host number divisions, you will notice that the network is identified by the first, or first few, octets. Notice that after the masked portion of the subnet mask, the network identifier changes to zero(s). For example, the network identifier of a host that has IP address 192.168.23.45 with subnet mask 255.255.255.0 is 192.168.23.0.

One of the IP networking rules stipulates that a TCP/IP host must have a nonzero host identifier. From this information, you can determine that on a subnet using mask 255.255.255.0, the IP address 222.12.150.4 is a valid host IP address. However, the address 222.12.150.0 is not a host address, but a network identifier. In other words, you could not assign 222.12.150.0 to a computer.

Do not expect all subnetwork identifiers to end in a decimal zero. It is true that subnetworks are identified by all the binary digits in the host portion being zero, but that does not mean that the entire last octet will be zero. For example, 199.192.65.32 could be a subnetwork identifier using subnet mask 255.255.255.224. In this case, the host identifier will be the last five binary digits of the last octet. Because 32 is 00100000 in binary, the final five digits are all zero, which indicates the subnetwork. This concept is described in greater detail as the chapter progresses.

Broadcast Address

IP addressing has another rule that you must commit to memory. On any subnet, when the entire host portion of an IP address is all binary ones, it is a broadcast to all of the computers on that segment. For example, on subnet 192.168.1.0, the IP address 192.168.1.255 is a broadcast. This also can apply to larger subnetworks such as 190.55.0.0; the IP address 190.55.255.255 is a broadcast on that network.

Converting these addresses into binary digits can quickly show if an IP address is a broadcast. If all the binary digits in the host identifier are ones, the address is a broadcast. Figure 3-18 illustrates a broadcast address for a subnet.

```
Subnet ID:      199.192.65.0      11000111.11000000.01000001.00000000
Subnet Mask:    255.255.255.0     11111111.11111111.11111111.00000000
Broadcast:      199.192.65.255    11000111.11000000.01000001.11111111
```

Figure 3-18   Broadcast addresses

By looking at Figure 3-18, you can quickly determine the broadcast address (199.192.65.255) because the decimal 255 represents eight binary ones. The binary calculation is not necessary if you know that all bits in the octet that represents the host portion are ones. However, the determination is not so easy when an octet is partially masked, as shown in Figure 3-19.

```
Subnet ID:      199.192.65.32     11000111.11000000.01000001.00100000
Subnet Mask:    255.255.255.224   11111111.11111111.11111111.11100000
Broadcast:      199.192.65.63     11000111.11000000.01000001.00111111
```

Figure 3-19   Broadcasts on partially masked octets

In Figure 3-19, you can see that subnetwork identifiers don't always end in a zero decimal value. In this case, the last octet has been partially masked (three binary places), leaving the last five binary digits of the last octet to represent the host identifier. In decimal format, it may be difficult to determine that 199.192.65.63 is a broadcast address for the subnet 199.192.65.32, but in binary format, it is much easier. You can see quickly that the last five binary digits are all ones, which indicates a broadcast on the local subnet.

Notice how important the subnet mask is in determining the logical subdivision of the network. For example, if the subnet mask in Figure 3-19 were 255.255.255.0 instead of 255.255.255.224, the broadcast address would not be 199.192.65.63. Instead, 199.192.65.255 would be the correct broadcast address.

SUBDIVIDING IP CLASSES

By now, you know that ARIN assigns Class A, B, and C addresses. You have also seen how these address groups can be further subdivided into subnetworks. Organizations that are not connected to the Internet can define their own subnets however they desire. In this section, we will look closer at how networks can be logically segmented using IP subnets.

When a private organization decides to subnet its network identifier, the outside world does not see a difference in the organization; only the internal structure of the organization's network changes. An organization may decide to subnet for various reasons:

- To match the physical layout of the organization: A group may want to configure the network to mirror the organizational structure. For example, if the company occupies a six-story building with 30 hosts per floor, the network administrator may create six different subnets, one for each floor.

- To match the administrative structure of the organization: Some organizations may choose to divide their network by administrative structure. For example, the administrator might subdivide the network by department. Each department could have its own subnetwork.

- To plan for future growth: If a network administrator foresees and plans for organizational growth, he or she may decide to subnet the network based on that expectation.

- To reduce network traffic: This is one of the most common reasons to divide an IP network into smaller subnetworks. Because routers are required for each network division, the number of routers on the network must increase when subnetting occurs. Typically, routers do not forward broadcast traffic, which means that there will be less broadcast traffic on the network. Routers, as their name implies, also route packets along a path instead of broadcasting them to all hosts on a segment. Overall, this equates to a more efficient use of the network and a corresponding reduction in network traffic.

As an example, assume that a private organization had the Class B address 190.45.0.0; the network manager of this organization might decide to subnet the Class B address in order to mirror the internal administrative structure of the organization. This decision would not affect the external network (Internet); it would only influence the structure of the network inside the private organization. The organization's internal routers would be responsible for handling inbound communications for that Class B address.

You can divide the 190.45.0.0 address by adding 255 to the third octet of the subnet mask. By default, the subnet mask for a Class B address is 255.255.0.0, but the network administrator might decide to use 255.255.255.0. Figure 3-20 illustrates what the subnetting does to the Class B address.

Figure 3-20 Dividing a Class B network

The example address in the figure shows how the different octets can be broken out. Notice that the third octet now defines the subnet. By masking the third octet, the administrator can create 254 different subnetworks, each of which can contain 254 hosts.

Subnet Masking

3

When network administrators create subnets, they borrow bits from the original host field to make a set of subnetworks. The number of borrowed bits determines how many subnetworks and hosts will be available. Whenever you subnet a network address, you lose some of the host addresses that you could have had without the subnetting. For instance, in the example from the previous section, the network administrator divided the Class B address 190.45.0.0 by masking the third octet. You know from the previous section that Class B addresses support 65,534 hosts. However, when the third octet is masked, there is only room for 254 subnetworks, each containing 254 hosts. This means that the number of addresses is reduced to 64,516 (254 x 254). Table 3-4 illustrates the types of subnet masks that can be used and how these masks affect the number of hosts available per subnet.

Table 3-4   Class B subnet masks

Subnet mask	Subnets on network	Hosts per subnet
255.255.192.0	2	16,382
255.255.224.0	6	8,190
255.255.240.0	14	4,094
255.255.248.0	30	2,046
255.255.252.0	62	1,022
255.255.254.0	126	510
255.255.255.0	254	254
255.255.255.128	510	126
255.255.255.192	1,022	62
255.255.255.224	2,046	30
255.255.255.240	4,094	14
255.255.255.248	8,190	6
255.255.255.252	16,382	2

When the host portion of an IP address is all binary zeros, that address is the subnetwork identifier. When the host portion of an IP address is all binary ones, that address is a broadcast address.

The network administrator can use up to 14 bits to subnet a Class B address. Two bits must be left for host numbers.

Class C addresses also can be subdivided, but not as many options or available masks exist because only the last octet can be manipulated with this class. Table 3-5 illustrates the five available subnet masking options for Class C addresses.

Table 3-5   Class C subnet masks

Subnet mask	Subnets on network	Hosts per subnet
255.255.255.192	2	62
255.255.255.224	6	30
255.255.255.240	14	14
255.255.255.248	30	6
255.255.255.252	62	2

 The network administrator can use up to six bits of the last octet to subnet the Class C address. Two bits must be left for host numbers.

Each example in Table 3-5 follows a pattern in the last octet. If you refer to Table 3-4, you will see the same numbers in the last masking octet in those examples. This pattern exists because subnet masks must have continuous binary one digits from the left side. Figure 3-21 illustrates the possible binary combinations that can be used as subnet masks.

Figure 3-21   Subnet mask values

The subnet masks have a clear binary pattern. They must have a continuous string of ones from the left side of the octet. Such a table would be easy to recreate, if you remember the binary places at the top. Then, you need only to add up the binary places to get their decimal equivalents. For example, the mask 11000000 can be calculated by adding binary places 128 and 64 (128 + 64 = 192).

Learning to Subnet

The best way to learn to subnet a network is to use a Class C address. A Class C address only allows the administrator to subnet the last octet. Also, as Table 3-5 shows, you can use only five different numeric masks on the last octet of a Class C address.

Suppose you had a network with five different segments and somewhere between 15 and 20 TCP/IP hosts on each network segment. You just received your Class C address from ARIN (199.1.10.0). Refer to Table 3-5 to decide which subnet mask you will use. Notice that only one subnet mask can handle your network configuration: 255.255.255.224. This subnet mask will allow you to create six subnetworks and to place up to 30 hosts per network. The other subnet masks will give you either too few subnetworks or too few hosts.

Deciding on the subnet mask is fairly straightforward. You just select the mask that meets your needs. Your next task is to assign the addresses to your network. You must find the IP address of each subnet identifier and a valid range of IP addresses for each subnet. A quick way to determine the subnet identifiers (IP addresses) is to write the last masking octet as a binary number. Then, you can determine the binary place of the last masking digit, as shown in Figure 3-22.

Class C Address: 199.1.10.0
Standard Mask: 255.255.255.0
Selected Mask: 255.255.255.224

	128	64	32	16	8	4	2	1
224	1	1	1	0	0	0	0	0

Figure 3-22   Subnet masking example

Notice that the last masking digit in this example occupies the binary place of 32. To calculate the subnets, begin with the major network number and increment by 32. Stop counting when you reach the value of the mask (224):

- 0 (binary 00000000) — unusable
- 32 (binary 00100000)
- 64 (binary 01000000)
- 96 (binary 01100000)
- 128 (binary 10000000)
- 160 (binary 10100000)
- 192 (binary 11000000)
- 224 (binary 11100000) — unusable

Now, you have determined the different subnet identifiers. You cannot use the first subnet because the resulting IP address would be the same as the major network number (the network number with no subnetting). It is also known as "subnet zero." You also cannot use 224 because it is the mask, so you have six numbers left. These six numbers will be the last octets of the IP addresses identifying your six subnets. You can quickly determine that they are subnet identifiers because the host portions (last five binary digits in this case) are all zero.

 RFC 1878 (*ftp://ftp.isi.edu/in-notes/rfc1878.txt*) discusses the inclusion and exclusion of all zero and one subnets. Subnet zero can be used in special circumstances, which are beyond the scope of the CCNA exam.

Next, you must determine the valid ranges for your hosts on each subnet. These are IP addresses that can be configured on the computers on your network. For this operation, you need only take the ranges between each subnet identifier. In doing this, you must remember to remove the broadcast address for each subnet from the list of valid ranges. Each subnet has a broadcast address, and it is the last number before the start of each new subnet, because the last number is equivalent to placing all binary ones in the host portion of the IP address. Table 3-6 illustrates the subnet identifier, valid host range, and broadcast address for each subnet.

Table 3-6   Class C address 199.1.10.0 masking 255.255.255.224

Subnet identifier	Valid host range	Broadcast address for subnet
199.1.10.32	199.1.10.33 – 199.1.10.62	199.1.10.63
199.1.10.64	199.1.10.65 – 199.1.10.94	199.1.10.95
199.1.10.96	199.1.10.97 – 199.1.10.126	199.1.10.127
199.1.10.128	199.1.10.129 – 199.1.10.158	199.1.10.159
199.1.10.160	199.1.10.161 – 199.1.10.190	199.1.10.191
199.1.10.192	199.1.10.193 – 199.1.10.222	199.1.10.223

As first described in Table 3-5 and shown in Table 3-6, there are six available networks with 30 available hosts per network. One address on each subnet is the subnetwork identifier, and one is the broadcast address for that subnet. You also lose the addresses below the first network identifier (199.1.10.32, in this case) and the addresses that are greater or equal to the last masking octet (224 in this example).

Notice that the masking digits in the last octet cover the first three binary digits, as shown in Figure 3-23. Each valid subnet in the list has a different combination of the first three binary digits. However, all zeros or all ones in the first three places (the network identifier) are not allowed. If three zeros lead the octet, the address is equivalent to the assigned IP network address (199.1.10.0). If three ones lead the octet, the address is equivalent to a broadcast for the entire Class C address.

Automated subnet calculators on the Internet are quite useful for determining the number of subnets versus the number of hosts. One example is the IP Subnet Calculator from WildPackets (*http://www.wildpackets.com*).

		Binary				Binary
Decimal	32	001 00000	Decimal	128	100 00000
Mask	224	111 00000	Mask	224	111 00000
Decimal	64	010 00000	Decimal	160	101 00000
Mask	224	111 00000	Mask	224	111 00000
Decimal	96	011 00000	Decimal	192	110 00000
Mask	224	111 00000	Mask	224	111 00000

Figure 3-23   A binary look at the mask

Subnetting Formulas

If you take an exam on IP subnetting, you probably will not be permitted to use a subnet calculator. Although you can write the numbers out in binary format and create tables to determine the subnet identifiers and ranges, you also can use formulas to solve these problems. Consider memorizing the following two formulas:

- $2^y - 2 = $ # of usable subnets (where y is the number of bits borrowed)
- $2^x - 2 = $ # of usable hosts per subnet (where x is the number of bits remaining in the host field after borrowing)

To demonstrate how these formulas can be used, assume that you have the subnet mask 255.255.255.240 on your Class C network address of 199.4.10.0. To determine the number of subnets, you would figure out how many masked bits (borrowed bits) exist in the final octet, as shown in Figure 3-24.

```
C Address        199.4.10.0       11000111.00000100.00001010.00000000
Standard Mask    255.255.255.0    11111111.11111111.11111111.00000000
Mask             255.255.255.240  11111111.11111111.11111111.11110000

y = 4 (borrowed bits)
x = 4 (bits left in host field after borrowing)

Formulas:
2^y - 2 = # of usable subnets
2^x - 2 = # of usable hosts per subnet
2^4 - 2 = 14 usable subnets
2^4 - 2 = 14 usable hosts per subnet
```

Figure 3-24   Sample calculation using formulas

Figure 3-25 illustrates the subnets created when the Class C address 199.4.10.0 is used with the subnet mask 255.255.255.240. Notice that the last octet of the subnet increments by the decimal value of the right-most significant binary digit in the mask, which in this case is 16. The zero subnet range is invalid because when any of those IP addresses are ANDed with the subnet mask 255.255.255.240, they are identical to the network identifier (subnet zero). The 15th subnet range is invalid because when any of those IP addresses are ANDed with the subnet mask 255.255.255.240, they are identical to the broadcast range for the Class C IP address.

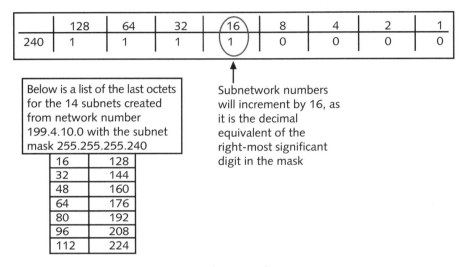

Figure 3-25   255.255.255.240 subnet mask

 Refer back to Figure 3-17 for an illustration of ANDing.

Besides the dotted decimal notation and the binary notation for IP addressing, there is another method for showing an IP address and its subnet mask—CIDR.

CIDR

The **Classless Inter–Domain Routing (CIDR)** notation method specifies the number of masked bits in an IP address/subnet mask combination. Standard notation for showing a subnet mask is, for example, 255.255.255.240; with CIDR, you need only list the number of masked digits. You can see that 28 masked bits and four unmasked bits exist in the mask 255.255.255.240 (11111111.11111111.11111111.11110000). Thus, the network identifier is 28 bits long and the host identifier is four bits long. The CIDR notation for the address 192.168.4.30 with this mask would be 192.168.4.30/28. You designate a mask by putting a forward slash after the IP address, followed by the number of bits in the network portion of the IP address. CIDR notation is based on assigning IP addresses on other than octet boundaries. This has helped slow the exhaustion of Class B addresses. CIDR is now used by all backbone routers and most ISPs. However, knowledge of the original class system is essential in order to understand subnetting and CIDR. (Other than the notation method described above, CIDR is beyond the scope of the CCNA exam. However, it is covered in detail in a CCNP Routing course.)

To figure out the subnet of the address 192.168.4.30/28, you must determine the binary value of the lowest masking bit. Then, you can use that number (16) to determine the last octet of your subnets (see Figure 3-25). The first valid range of host identifiers is on subnet 192.168.4.16 and includes the host addresses 192.168.4.17 through 192.168.4.30; this means that 192.168.4.30/28 is a host on subnet 192.168.4.16.

 Do not forget that the last address before the next subnet is a broadcast. In our example, the address 192.168.4.31/28 would be a broadcast for subnet 192.168.4.16. This is not a valid host identifier because the number 31 (binary 00011111) requires that the host portion (last four digits) be all ones.

Broadcast Types

There are two different types of broadcasts: flooded and directed. **Flooded broadcasts** are broadcasts for any subnet and use the IP address 255.255.255.255. A router does not propagate flooded broadcasts because they are considered local. When a host sends a packet to the IP address 255.255.255.255, the packet remains on the local subnet.

On the other hand, **directed broadcasts** are for a specific subnet. Routers forward directed broadcasts. For example, a packet sent to the Class B address 129.30.255.255 would be a broadcast for network 129.30.0.0. The router would forward that packet to the identified network.

UNDERSTANDING PACKET TRANSMISSION

As packets travel a given network segment, each host on the segment evaluates the packet to determine whether the destination MAC address listed in the packet matches its own or is a broadcast to all hosts. The host makes a copy of the packet and sends the original packet along the network path. If the copy of the packet is for the local host's MAC address, a broadcast, or a multicast for which the local host is configured to receive, the packet continues up the protocol stack. If the packet is not for the local host, the copy is discarded.

MAC address checking occurs at the Network Interface layer of the TCP/IP model, or the Data Link layer (layer 2) of the OSI model. In the TCP/IP networking model, if the data is destined for the local host's MAC address or is a broadcast, the Network Interface layer information is removed. Next, the protocol stack passes the packet to the Internetwork layer. There, the destination IP address contained in the packet is compared to the local host's IP address. If the IP address listed in the data packet matches the local host address, or is a broadcast, the protocol stack strips off the Internetwork layer information and moves the packet up the protocol stack again.

As you learned previously, the Internetwork layer of the TCP/IP protocol stack is equivalent to the Network layer of the OSI model. The Network Interface layer and the Internetwork layer of the TCP/IP protocol stack ensure that data gets from one host to another on a TCP/IP network. The MAC address, at the Network Interface layer, uniquely identifies a specific device on any network. The IP address, at the Internetwork layer, identifies a specific host on a specific network. For a packet to be routed on a TCP/IP internetwork, both an IP address and MAC address are required for both the source and destination hosts.

Routers on the Network

Routers connect two or more network segments. In doing so, a router must have a separate identity for each network it is connecting. A router requires an IP address for every network segment to which it is connected and a separate network interface or port for each network segment. For example, if a router connects four different network segments, it must have four different IP addresses and four different network interfaces. Figure 3-26 illustrates the configuration of a router that connects four segments.

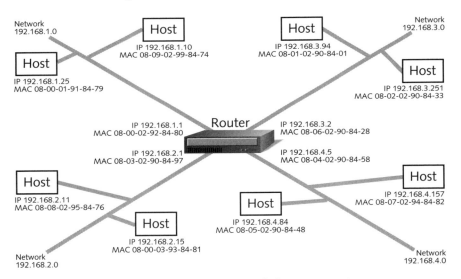

Figure 3-26   Configuration of a router with four segments

Notice that the router has an IP and MAC address for each of its ports that are valid for each of the network segments to which it is connected. Figure 3-26 also illustrates hosts configured on each network segment. Each device on the network has a unique IP address and MAC address.

Serial interfaces—in other words, those attached to WAN links—typically do not have their own MAC addresses. The serial interfaces use MAC addresses assigned to LAN interfaces on the router.

When computers need to send packets to destinations not on their segment, they send the packets to the router (default gateway) instead. The router connected to the segment on which the packet originated recognizes that the destination host is on a different subnet. The router must determine which subnet should receive the packet. The router first removes the Network Interface information (OSI Data Link layer header), which contains the router's MAC address, since it was addressed to the router. (The sending computer obtained the router's MAC address either from looking in its ARP cache or by sending an ARP request if the address was not in its table.) Then, the router analyzes the Internetwork layer information—specifically, the destination IP address. The destination IP address will be the IP address of the final destination, not the IP address of the router. In fact, the source and destination IP addresses do not change throughout the journey of a packet from source to destination. Only the MAC address changes. The router references its **routing table** to determine which of its interfaces is connected to the destination network. Then the router rebuilds the Network Interface layer information with the appropriate format for the destination network and sends the packet out through the correct interface.

Network to Network

Routers maintain routing tables, which they use to route packets from one network to another. When a network uses TCP/IP, each port on a router requires an IP address, which allows the router to correctly forward the packet to the appropriate network segment. For example, consider the router connections shown in Figure 3-27. Assume the router port 192.168.1.1 connects to network segment 192.168.1.0. If a packet comes in for a host computer that connects to 192.168.1.0, the router knows to forward this packet to the 192.168.1.1 port because that port attaches to the correct network. The router's routing table tells it that packets destined for 192.168.1.0 should be sent to the interface with IP address 192.168.1.1.

Figure 3-27 Router

On a TCP/IP network, the logical addresses on a certain segment must be matched. For example, if the network segment is 192.168.1.0, all the hosts on that segment must have addresses that start with 192.168.1. They also will have unique identifiers for the last octet. This means that if you move a computer from one segment to another, the IP address will have to be changed to make it a member of the new segment.

You only need to ensure that the logical address, such as the IP address, matches the network because MAC addresses are a permanent part of the NIC and do not change when the computer is moved to a new network.

Dynamic or Static Tables

Routing tables match network addresses with the addresses of the routers that handle those networks. The tables can be built statically or dynamically. A static routing table requires manual configuration by the network administrator. Each route must be entered by hand, and the router always uses the same route to send packets to a specific network address, even if that route is not the most efficient.

Dynamic updates are provided through **routing protocols**. Routing protocols allow the routers to be updated automatically. Routers automatically build dynamic routing tables; a router capable of dynamic routing can choose from among the various routes on a network without input from the administrator. The router communicates with other dynamic routers to determine the most efficient route from one point to another on the network. The routers can also track multiple paths to the same location so that alternate routes are available. Dynamic routers can use different methods to determine the best path across a network. One method is the distance-vector algorithm, which considers the number of hops between two points. A hop is a transition from one network segment to another. Each router along a network path is considered one hop. The packet takes the path with the smallest number of hops. A second method used in dynamic routing is the **link-state** algorithm. Using the link-state algorithm, the router takes into consideration network traffic, connection speed, and other assigned costs.

Transmitting Packets to Remote Segments

When TCP/IP hosts transmit a packet to a remote segment, they cannot use ARP to obtain the correct MAC address because the router would filter the ARP request broadcast. In such a case, the TCP/IP host must use the services of the router. When TCP/IP hosts transmit packets to remote segments, they contact their default gateway, which is the network interface to which the client sends traffic that is destined for remote segments. The default gateway is usually a router connecting that local segment to other networks on the LAN or WAN. The TCP/IP host sends the data packet with the destination MAC address of the router. However, since the ultimate destination for the packet is a client on a remote network, the IP address listed as the destination is that of the remote host. When the router receives the packet, it pulls off the Network Interface information and analyzes the packet at the Internetwork layer.

The router checks its routing tables against the destination IP address to locate the appropriate network interface through which to forward the packet. If the router is directly connected to the network for which the packet is destined, it will readdress the packet at the Network Interface layer (OSI layer 2) with the MAC address of the destination host. It will get this MAC address from its ARP cache. If the information is not in its ARP table, the router will send an ARP request on the destination's segment and attempt to obtain the MAC address. If the router is not directly connected to the network in question, the router will send the packet to the next router in the path on the way to the destination. In this case, the destination IP address will stay the same but the destination MAC address will be that of the next router. The packet will be transferred around the internetwork until the destination is found or the TTL (hop count) reaches its maximum. Routers automatically discard packets that meet the packet's maximum hop count. This prevents packets from endlessly looping around the network or Internet. The process of moving a packet from one router to another in hopes of locating the correct IP address to MAC address mapping is known as indirect routing.

Routing Packets

This section discusses the journey of a packet across a network, from Host A to Host B, as shown in Figure 3-28.

Figure 3-28   Routing a packet

Table 3-7 lists the IP address, network interface, and network identifier for each device. The assumed subnet mask for this network is 255.255.255.0.

Host A

Host A composes its data at the Application layer and then encapsulates that data in the appropriate Transport layer protocol. The data is then passed to the Internetwork layer. At the Internetwork layer of the TCP/IP protocol stack, the IP address (192.168.4.22) for the destination host (Host B) is added. Because Host A is communicating with a remote host, it uses the MAC address of its default gateway (Router 1; 192.168.1.1) when encapsulating the data at the Network Interface layer.

Table 3-7   Information surrounding the journey of a packet

Device IP	Address	Interface	Network
Host A	192.168.1.14		192.168.1.0
Router 1	192.168.1.1	Ethernet 0	192.168.1.0
Router 1	192.168.2.1	Ethernet 1	192.168.2.0
Router 2	192.168.2.2	Ethernet 0	192.168.2.0
Router 2	192.168.3.1	Ethernet 1	192.168.3.0
Router 3	192.168.3.2	Ethernet 0	192.168.3.0
Router 3	192.168.4.1	Ethernet 1	192.168.4.0
Host B	192.168.4.22		192.168.4.1

Once Host A has properly composed, formatted, and addressed the packet, it transmits the packet on the network. The other hosts on the network (Q and X) receive and discard the packet because the MAC address does not match theirs. Router 1 accepts the packet because the MAC address does match.

Router 1

Router 1 picks up the packet. After the router strips the Network Interface layer information off the packet, the router determines that the packet is destined for IP address 192.168.4.22. Given the subnet mask, the router determines that the network identifier is 192.168.4.0. Router 1 then consults its routing table to determine to which router port the packet should be sent. Table 3-8 contains essential information from the routing table of Router 1. To make the example simple, the routing table shown here has only two pieces of information, the network and interface addresses. In reality, routing tables contain several additional items, including subnet masks (or netmasks), default gateways, and cost metrics.

Table 3-8   Router 1 routing table

Network	Interface
192.168.1.0	192.168.1.1
192.168.2.0	192.168.2.1
192.168.3.0	192.168.2.2
192.168.4.0	192.168.2.2

When Router 1 consults its routing table, it sees that packets destined for network 192.168.4.0 must be sent to 192.168.2.2, which is the interface on the next hop in the path, Router 2.

Router 1 repackages the Network Interface part of the data packet and transmits the packet out interface 192.168.2.1 using the MAC address of Router 2. The destination IP address, 192.168.4.22, remains unchanged.

Router 2

Router 2 picks up the packet destined for its MAC address and strips off the Network Interface information. Router 2 analyzes the IP Header destination address and identifies that it is destined for network 192.168.4.0. Next, Router 2 checks its routing table, as shown in Table 3-9.

Table 3-9 Router 2 routing table

Network	Interface
192.168.1.0	192.168.2.1
192.168.2.0	192.168.2.2
192.168.3.0	192.168.3.1
192.168.4.0	192.168.3.2

According to its routing table, Router 2 must send the packet destined for network 192.168.4.0 to the next router interface, which is 192.168.3.2 on Router 3. Therefore, Router 2 repackages the Network Interface layer of the packet, adding the MAC address for Router 3 to the packet. The destination IP address remains 192.168.4.22, and the data packet is sent to Router 3.

Router 3

Router 3 receives the data packet destined for its MAC address and strips off the Network Interface layer information to reveal the IP address. Router 3 determines that the traffic is destined for network 192.168.4.0 and checks its routing table, as shown in Table 3-10.

Table 3-10 Router 3 routing table

Network	Interface
192.168.1.0	192.168.3.1
192.168.2.0	192.168.3.1
192.168.3.0	192.168.3.2
192.168.4.0	192.168.4.1

The routing table shows that one of Router 3's interfaces is directly connected to network 192.168.4.0. Because of this, Router 3 must then determine which host on the network has the IP address 192.168.4.22. Router 3 checks its ARP table to get a MAC address mapping for the client. If no mapping exists, Router 3 issues an ARP request on network 192.168.4.0 to get a mapping. Once the router has the correct MAC to IP mapping, it repackages the Network Interface layer using the MAC address of the destination. After the packet is properly addressed, Router 3 transmits it to Host B through interface 192.168.4.1.

Host B

Both Host B and Host T receive the traffic forwarded by the router. However, Host T discards the packet because it is not addressed to its MAC address. Host B accepts the packet at the Network Interface layer and continues to process the data frame. At the Internetwork layer, Host B confirms that the packet is intended for its IP address. Then, it passes the data packet up the protocol stack for further processing.

CHAPTER SUMMARY

◻ TCP/IP is more than just the Transmission Control Protocol/Internet Protocol; it is an entire suite of protocols that provides data transportation, management, and diagnostic capabilities for networks that use it.

◻ TCP/IP was started by the Defense Advanced Research Projects Agency (DARPA). That group was charged with developing a national communication system that could survive a nuclear war. Later, their network, ARPANET, was turned over to the public, especially universities. From there, the Internet grew into what it is today, a large worldwide commerce and communications network.

◻ TCP/IP maps to a four-layer network model: Application, Transport, Internetwork, and Network Interface. These layers map to equivalent functions in the OSI reference model.

◻ The Application layer in the TCP/IP model covers the Application, Presentation, and Session layers of the OSI reference model. The TCP/IP Transport layer maps directly to the OSI Transport layer. The Internetwork layer of the TCP/IP model maps directly to the Network layer of the OSI model. Finally, the Network Interface layer of the TCP/IP model is equivalent to the Data Link and Physical layers of the OSI model.

◻ The TCP and UDP protocols reside at the Transport layer of the TCP/IP networking model. UDP is an unreliable and connectionless communications protocol that does not guarantee packet delivery. TCP is a reliable and connection-oriented protocol that guarantees packet delivery. TCP uses a three-way handshake in order to establish a communications link between two points. TCP also uses a sliding window to control the flow of packets and the number of acknowledgments between the two hosts.

◻ Both TCP and UDP use port numbers from 1 to 65,535 to establish their communications between two points. Ports with numbers 1023 and under are Well Known Port numbers, as defined in RFC 1700. These ports describe common Internet services that hosts can use to contact public servers for specific types of services, such as Web, FTP, and Telnet.

◻ The Internet Protocol (IP) resides at the Internetwork Layer. It provides the logical address that can be passed through a router. The IP address allows networks to be divided into subnetworks.

❐ You can use the ping utility with IP and ICMP to diagnose and troubleshoot network connections. Also, you can use the trace utility with IP to determine all the hops that a packet makes along its path to a remote TCP/IP host.

❐ Address Resolution Protocol (ARP) and Reverse ARP (RARP) reside in the Internetwork layer. These protocols allow the TCP/IP host to map the IP address to a MAC address.

❐ The MAC address is the final leg of communication between hosts. Packets are transmitted via the MAC address to the destination host once the packets arrive at the destination network or subnetwork.

❐ The Internet Assigned Numbers Authority (IANA), the Internet Network Information Center (InterNIC), and the American Registry of Internet Numbers (ARIN) work together to subdivide and issue addresses for Internet clients. Three classes of addresses (A, B, and C) are available to organizations. Class A addresses are for governments worldwide. Class B addresses are assigned to medium to large companies and universities. Class C addresses are assigned to organizations and individuals who require an IP address but who do not meet the criteria to have a Class A or B address.

❐ Two other address categories, Class D and Class E, exist. Class D addresses are used for multicasting information. Multicasting allows anyone with the correct setup to broadcast a simultaneous transmission to multiple computers. Class E addresses are used for experimentation and research.

❐ You can subdivide addresses assigned by the InterNIC. This process is called subnetting. The subnet mask divides the network portion of the IP address from the host portion of the address. The network or subnetwork IP address must always have zeros for the host identifier portion. IP addresses that identify TCP/IP hosts must be nonzero in the host portion. When the host portion of an IP address is all binary ones, the address is a broadcast address.

❐ Routing tables can be created manually and dynamically. Network administrators manually create static routing tables. A manual table requires more administrative overhead but gives the administrator greater control over the routing process. Dynamic updates are provided through routing protocols. The routing protocols allow the routers to be updated automatically.

KEY TERMS

Advanced Research Projects Agency (ARPA) — The government organization operating in the Department of Defense (DOD) that was responsible for the creation and proliferation of the Internet and the TCP/IP protocol suite.

Address Resolution Protocol (ARP) — A protocol that works at the Internetwork layer of the TCP/IP networking model; resolves a known IP address to an unknown MAC address, which is the final leg of communication between the source and destination.

Advanced Research Projects Agency Network (ARPANET) — The original name of the Internet.

American Registry of Internet Numbers (ARIN) — The independent organization in charge of the allocation of IP addresses.

Application layer — The TCP/IP layer that corresponds to the Application, Presentation, and Session layers of the OSI model.

ARP reply — A reply sent by the device that discovers its own IP address in the IP header of the ARP request frame and includes the requested MAC address.

ARP request — A process used to obtain the correct mapping when a source computer cannot locate a MAC address for a known IP address in its ARP table.

ARP table — A table used by a network device that contains MAC to IP address mappings.

buffer — A portion of memory used to store information that is being sent or created too fast for a system to process.

buffering — A way in which devices on a network are able to handle packet flows that exceed their processing capabilities. Packets are stored in a buffer until the system can process them.

Classless Inter-Domain Routing (CIDR) — The notation method that specifies the subnet mask following an IP address as the number of masked bits. For example, the IP address 192.168.1.1 with subnet mask 255.255.240.0 could be represented by 192.168.1.1/20 because the subnet mask 255.255.240.0 represents the masking of 20 bits.

congestion avoidance — A method by which a system on the network can reduce the flow of packets on a network by sending a message request to the sender to reduce the rate at which they are being transmitted.

default gateway — The address that a host or IP device sends a packet to when it does not have a record of where to send the packet. TCP/IP clients send packets to the default gateway when the destination host is not on their subnet. The default gateway is usually an interface on a router.

destination unreachable — An ICMP message sent back to the source host when a gateway cannot deliver an IP datagram.

directed broadcasts — Broadcasts sent to specific segments. For example, a broadcast on segment 192.168.1.0 would be 192.168.1.255.

diskless workstation — Workstations configured to download their operating systems from a central server. These workstations typically do not have a hard drive.

Domain Name System (DNS) — A hierarchical naming service that is used on the Internet and IP networks to provide host name to IP address resolution.

echo request/reply — The most commonly used ICMP message. ICMP echo request/reply messages are used to check the availability of a remote host, the devices along a network path (intermediate gateways), and to verify the installation of the TCP/IP protocol on the local source host.

expectational acknowledgment — A TCP acknowledgment process in which the acknowledgment number refers to the sequence number expected next. If the expected sequence is not received within an expected time interval, a retransmission is requested.

File Transfer Protocol (FTP) — A part of the TCP/IP protocol suite that provides reliable file transfers across the Internet or other TCP/IP networks. FTP uses TCP to transfer files.

flooded broadcasts — A broadcast for any subnet that uses the IP address 255.255.255.255. Routers do not pass flooded broadcasts.

Hypertext Transfer Protocol (HTTP) — A protocol used for communications on the World Wide Web. Web servers are HTTP servers.

ICMP flood — A large quantity of ICMP echo requests sent to a target device by a malicious person or program in an attempt to crash or greatly reduce the performance of the target device.

information request/reply — ICMP messages that are typically used to determine the subnet mask used by the destination. This message allows a host to determine the number of the network it is on.

initial sequence number (ISN) — Sequence numbers that allow communicating hosts to synchronize their communications in a TCP three-way handshake. When the communication is initiated, two hosts communicating over TCP will synchronize their initial sequence numbers.

Internet Assigned Numbers Authority (IANA) — The regulatory agency responsible for subdividing and administering the address hierarchy used on the Internet.

Internet Control Message Protocol (ICMP) — A protocol in the TCP/IP protocol suite at the Internetwork layer. ICMP messages control and manage IP protocol communications.

Internet Network Information Center (InterNIC) — The main regulatory agency of the Internet. It is responsible for administrative tasks involving the Internet and individuals and/or public or private organizations.

Internet Protocol (IP) — The Network layer (Internetwork layer) protocol that is responsible for addressing, which allows IP to be routed.

Internetwork layer — The layer of TCP/IP that is equivalent to the Network layer of the OSI model.

IP addressing — The act of assigning (unique) IP addresses to devices on the network.

link-state — A routing protocol that uses cost when calculating the best path between two points. It considers items such as network traffic, router congestion, bandwidth, reliability, and other factors that could affect network performance.

loopback — The TCP/IP Class A address 127.x.x.x that is reserved for diagnostic purposes. This address allows you to check if TCP/IP has been properly installed on the system. (Specifically, the IP address 127.0.0.1 is the address usually given as the loopback.)

multicast address — A special subdivision of IP categories reserved for data streaming. Multicast addresses are used to send information to groups of computers. The range for multicasting addresses is 224.0.0.0 to 239.255.255.255.

multicasting — The sending of a stream of data to multiple computers simultaneously.

Network File System (NFS) — A file system associated with the UNIX operating system that allows for network communications between hosts.

Network Interface layer — In TCP/IP, the layer that is equivalent to the Physical and Data Link layers of the OSI model.

Packet Internet Groper (ping) — A troubleshooting utility that verifies that a remote host is currently running and accessible.

parameter problem — An ICMP message sent whenever incorrect datagram header information is received. The message identifies the octet in the datagram that caused the problem.

Post Office Protocol version 3 (POP3) — A protocol used by client machines, which allows users to check their e-mail boxes on an e-mail server.

redirect — An ICMP message sent to source hosts requesting that they change routes since the one they chose was not optimal. This packet is used to update a source host's internal routing table.

remote login application (rlogin) — A utility that allows remote computers to connect to other computers or devices.

reset packet (RST) — A packet indicating that the receiver should delete the TCP connection without further interaction.

Requests for Comments (RFC) — A group of Internet-related documents maintained by the InterNIC that specify Internet protocols and standards.

Reverse Address Resolution Protocol (RARP) — A protocol used to resolve the client's unknown IP address to the client's MAC address for the final leg of communication between an IP source and destination. RARP clients broadcast a request for their IP address. A RARP server has a table of IP to MAC mappings and responds to the client with a RARP reply.

routed protocol — A protocol that contains enough OSI Network layer information that its packets can be routed from a source to a remote destination on an internetwork.

routing protocols — Used to dynamically create routing tables so that routed protocols can route the data.

routing table — A table used by a router to determine which of its interfaces is connected to the destination network.

Simple Mail Transfer Protocol (SMTP) — The main protocol that transfers electronic mail on the Internet between e-mail servers.

Simple Network Management Protocol (SNMP) — A protocol that provides network administrators the ability to centrally control and monitor the network.

sliding windows — A feature of TCP used to control the flow of communications between two hosts. The size of the TCP sliding window regulates how often acknowledgments will be sent to the transmitting host from the receiving host.

source quench — An ICMP message request to reduce the rate at which the sender is transmitting packets to the destination. This message is used for flow control, when packets arrive too fast (the receiving host runs out of buffer space for the message), or if the system is near capacity (network is congested).

subnet — A portion of a network that has been separated out from the main network by using a different subnet mask.

subnet mask — A required component for all IP hosts used in combination with an IP address to determine to which subnet the local host belongs. The local host uses this information to determine if the destination is local or remote to the source. Based on this information, the source will either broadcast information on the local network or send its packet to the default gateway for delivery to a remote network.

subnetting — The act of subdividing a network logically with subnet masks.

TCP/IP — *See* **TCP** and **IP**.

terminal emulation protocol (telnet) — A connection-oriented, Application layer utility that allows TCP/IP clients to login to a remote system and operate on that system as if the connection between the two were local.

three-way handshake — The method used by TCP to negotiate a reliable connection between two hosts on a network. This process involves the exchange of three data packets before the communication process begins.

time exceeded — An ICMP message sent whenever a packet's time-to-live (hop count) reaches zero and the datagram is dropped.

time-to-live (TTL) — The number of hops (routers) that a packet can make before it is discarded. The router discards a packet when its TTL is zero, which prevents a packet from looping endlessly around the network. Routers normally decrement the packet TTL by one before passing the packet to the next router.

timestamp request/reply — ICMP messages that are used to synchronize clocks by requesting the destination machine's current time of day value, which is given in milliseconds since midnight Universal Time.

trace — A utility that uses ICMP messages to determine the path between a source and destination host. Trace can discover all of the hops (routers) along the path between two points.

Transmission Control Protocol (TCP) — The protocol that guarantees the delivery of a packet by sending an acknowledgment for each window of data received. This protocol operates at the Transport layer and sends its data encapsulated in the IP protocol. TCP communications are also known as connection-oriented because TCP negotiates a communication path between hosts on the network.

Transport layer — The TCP/IP layer that maps directly to the OSI model Transport layer.

Trivial File Transfer Protocol (TFTP) — A file transfer utility used on the Internet. TFTP uses UDP to transfer files and is therefore less reliable than FTP, which uses TCP in transferring files.

3

User Datagram Protocol (UDP) — The protocol that operates at the Transport Layer and transports data unreliably over IP. This is sometimes known as connectionless communication because the messages are sent without expectation of acknowledgment. There is no connection negotiation process as in TCP. The packets that are sent by UDP are also known as datagrams. Since UDP does not negotiate a connection, it is faster than TCP.

Well Known Port numbers — TCP and UDP ports from 0 through 1023 on which client applications expect to find common Internet services.

REVIEW QUESTIONS

1. Which of the following is a reliable communications protocol?

   a. UDP

   b. TCP

   c. IP

   d. ICMP

2. Which of the following is used by the TFTP protocol?

   a. UDP

   b. TCP

   c. ICMP

   d. Telnet

3. Which of the following is a layer in the TCP/IP protocol stack? (Choose all that apply.)

   a. Application

   b. Presentation

   c. Physical

   d. Data Link

   e. Internetwork

4. Which of the following is a TCP/IP Application layer protocol? (Choose all that apply.)

   a. DNS

   b. FTP

   c. UDP

   d. IP

   e. ICMP

5. Which of the following is a TCP/IP Internetwork layer protocol? (Choose all that apply.)

   a. ICMP

   b. FTP

   c. DNS

   d. ARP

   e. IP

6. Which of the following is a TCP/IP Transport layer protocol? (Choose all that apply.)

   a. ARP

   b. RARP

   c. IP

   d. UDP

   e. TCP

7. If your Class C address has a three-bit subnet mask, which of the following would be a subnetwork identifier?

   a. 203.16.34.33

   b. 203.16.34.135

   c. 203.16.34.32

   d. 203.16.34.240

8. Which of the following would be a broadcast address for a Class C network?

   a. 190.15.23.255

   b. 190.42.25.255

   c. 221.21.23.255

   d. 129.21.15.255

9. Which of the following Class C IP addresses is a broadcast (assuming the subnet mask is 255.255.255.224)?

   a. 219.129.32.5

   b. 219.129.32.63

   c. 219.129.32.97

   d. 219.129.32.161

10. For a Class B broadcast, which octets will be completely binary ones?

   a. 2nd

   b. 2nd and 3rd

   c. 1st and 2nd

   d. 3rd and 4th

11. Which of the following is a Class A broadcast?

    a. 11.255.255.255

    b. 127.75.255.255

    c. 193.255.255.255

    d. 14.25.255.255

12. What is the purpose of the reserved numbers in a Class D address?

    a. Unicast

    b. Experimental

    c. Broadcast

    d. Multicast

13. What is the purpose of the reserved numbers in a Class E address?

    a. Unicast

    b. Broadcast

    c. Multicast

    d. Experimental

14. In a Class C address, which octets identify the network?

    a. All of them

    b. The first octet only

    c. The first and second octet

    d. The last octet

    e. The first three octets

15. Class B addresses allow you to configure how many octets on your network for host IP addresses?

    a. One

    b. Two

    c. Three

    d. Four

16. Which of the following are valid network identifiers for Class A addresses?

    a. 1-127

    b. 1-126

    c. 192-223

    d. 224-240

    e. 128-191

3

17. What would the value of the first octet of the subnet mask be if the CIDR notation for an address is 192.168.1.16/27?

    a. 224

    b. 254

    c. 255

    d. 265

18. What would the value of the last octet of the subnet mask be if the CIDR notation for an address is 192.168.1.16/28?

    a. 192

    b. 224

    c. 240

    d. 248

    e. 252

19. Assuming that the address 165.24.3.6 uses the correct default mask, what is the host identifier?

    a. 165.24

    b. 24.3.6

    c. 3

    d. 3.6

20. How many bits (maximum) can be used from the last octet of a Class C address to subnet your network?

    a. 2

    b. 4

    c. 6

    d. 8

21. Which of the following address classes allows you to use up to 14 bits to create a subnet mask?

    a. Class A

    b. Class B

    c. Class C

    d. None of the above

22. A subnet mask of 255.255.252.0 on a Class B network indicates that
    _____ bits have been borrowed from the host portion to subnet the
    network.
    a. 2
    b. 4
    c. 6
    d. 8
    e. 10

23. Given the following CIDR address and mask, which of the following is a broadcast
    on its subnetwork 162.17.12.125/24?
    a. 162.17.15.255
    b. 162.17.12.255
    c. 162.17.255.255
    d. 255.255.255.255
    e. None of the above

24. Given the address 190.14.20.255/20, which of the following statements is true?
    a. This is a broadcast address.
    b. This is a network address.
    c. This is a host address.
    d. This address is on network 190.14.20.0.
    e. This address is on network 190.14.16.0.

25. Given the address 190.14.20.0/22, which of the following statements is true?
    a. This is a broadcast address.
    b. This is a network address.
    c. This is a host address.
    d. This address is on network 190.14.20.0.
    e. This address is on network 190.14.16.0.

26. The TCP acknowledgement process is _____.
    a. expectational
    b. sequential
    c. exceptional
    d. sesquicentennial

27. Which of the following are NOT ICMP message types?

   a. echo & destination unreachable

   b. source quench & redirect

   c. relay and reroute

   d. parameter problem & information

   e. timestamp & time exceeded

3

CASE PROJECTS

1. Moe is having a difficult time with IP subnetting. He knows the basics but has some specific questions. He wants to know why certain numbers are unavailable for use. For example, he was told that he cannot use 10 or 127 or any numbers over 223 in the first octet. Why are these numbers off limits? Explain your answer to Moe.

2. Moe wants to understand the concept of sliding windows. Explain to Moe the purpose of sliding windows. When should networks use large sliding windows? When should they use smaller sliding windows? What could happen if small data transfers occur in a large sliding window?

3. Moe and Jennifer want you to explain step by step what occurs when a host wants to send a message. Discuss where ARP fits in and how exactly ARP facilitates the communications.

4. Lisa does not understand the purpose of the RARP protocol or the RARP server. Explain to her how RARP works and why a computer might have a MAC address but no IP address.

4

NETWORK TOPOLOGY AND DESIGN

After reading this chapter and completing the exercises, you will be able to:

♦ Discuss the different physical topologies

♦ Determine which types of network media to use given a set of requirements

♦ Understand horizontal cabling standards and wiring closets

♦ Consider performance requirements and improvements for given situations

♦ Install a telecommunications connector

♦ Wire a patch panel

♦ Test network cable

♦ Describe various network architecture models

♦ Discuss LAN design

♦ Describe the function that network management tools perform on a network

In this chapter, you will learn about the different physical topologies and types of cabling available for networks. In addition, this chapter explains standards and suggests ways to correctly and effectively design and implement the physical media and devices of a network. You will learn about wiring closets and performance considerations, how to wire a wall jack, and how to test cable for proper operation. You will also be introduced to the most common network architectures and their specifications. Finally, you will learn about the hierarchical network design models and network management tools.

PHYSICAL TOPOLOGIES

A network's physical topology consists of the physical layout of the networking components. The three most common topologies are the bus, star, and ring. This section examines these network topologies and discusses the advantages and disadvantages of each.

Bus

A **bus** topology connects all stations in a linear fashion, which accounts for the name "linear bus." The wire on a bus network has two distinct end points, which are capped by terminators. Terminators absorb electronic signals so that they are not reflected on the network. Figure 4-1 illustrates this concept.

Figure 4-1   Bus topology

On a bus topology, all stations receive the signals transmitted by other stations. Network signals travel in both directions down the bus network, and each station checks the data frame as it passes by. If the receiving station identifies its own MAC address in the destination address of the data frame, it will accept the data. Otherwise, the frame is discarded, but the signal continues along the bus. Although the stations are all on one cable segment, the bus continues to work when stations are off line because the media does not actually pass through the individual stations.

The bus topology has several advantages:

- It is inexpensive.
- It is easy to design and implement because the stations are simply daisy-chained together.

The bus topology has disadvantages as well:

- It is difficult to troubleshoot. If a cable break occurs at any location on the bus, the entire bus fails and it can be difficult to locate the point of failure.
- It requires termination. If the last computers on the chain are not terminated correctly, stations cannot transmit.

Star

The **star** network configuration is the most popular physical topology. As Figure 4-2 shows, in a star configuration all computers or stations are wired directly to a central location, which is usually a **concentrator** (a.k.a. hub) or a **Multistation Access Unit (MAU)**. A data signal from any station goes directly to this central device, which transmits the signal according to the established **network access method** for the type of network.

Figure 4-2   Star topology

The star topology has several advantages:

- A break in one cable does not affect all other stations as it does in bus technologies because there is only one station per segment, making the star generally more reliable.

- In a star, problems are easier to locate because symptoms often point to one station.

- The star is the second-easiest topology to design and install, after the bus.

- The star does not require manual termination. Instead, the media is terminated in the station at the **transceiver** on the network interface card (NIC) and in the hub or MAU.

The star topology has disadvantages as well:

- Hubs, which are required for a star topology, are more expensive than bus connectors.

- A failure at the hub can affect the entire configuration and all connected stations.

- Star topologies use more cable than bus topologies because separate wires run to each individual station.

Repeaters can extend the maximum usable distance of the bus or star topology. Typically, active hubs function as repeaters in a star configuration.

 The bus and star topologies can be combined to form a **star/bus** or **bus/star** physical topology. Hubs that have connectors for coaxial cable as well as for twisted-pair wiring are used to form these types of networks. When different physical topologies are applied to a network, the result is often called a **mixed media** network.

Ring

Physical rings are most often seen in **Fiber Distributed Data Interface (FDDI)** networks. FDDI is a WAN technology and is discussed later in this chapter. Stations on a **ring** are wired to one another in a circle around the entire network.

A ring topology resembles a bus topology except that it has no termination points. Data is passed around the ring and, unlike a bus network, stations in a ring regenerate the signal before passing it along. This makes the ring topology active, as opposed to the passive bus topology.

The ring topology has these advantages:

- It prevents network collisions because of the **media access method** or architecture required.

- Each station functions as a repeater, so the topology does not require additional network hardware, such as hubs.

However, as with any topology, disadvantages exist:

- As in a bus network, a failure at one point can bring down the network.

- Because all stations are wired together, to add a station the network must be shut down temporarily.

- Maintenance on a ring is more difficult than on a star topology because an adjustment or reconfiguration affects the entire ring.

Influence of the 5-4-3 Rule on Topologies

The Institute of Electrical and Electronics Engineers (IEEE) identifies a maximum number of repeaters, segments, and populated segments that can be used on any given 10-Mbps Ethernet network using repeaters and/or hubs. These maximums are known collectively as the **5-4-3 rule** because no more than five segments of cable and four repeaters can exist between any two stations on the network, and only three of the five segments can be populated with computers, bridges, or routers. The other two segments can only interconnect the repeaters and/or hubs. Typically, the 5-4-3 rule is represented graphically as shown in Figure 4-3.

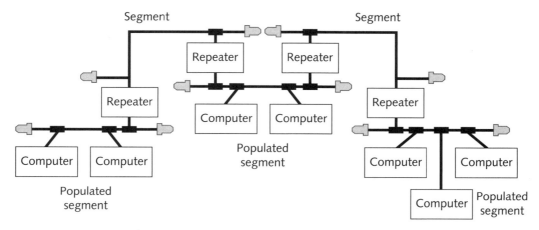

Figure 4-3   5-4-3 rule

The drawing illustrates a linear bus network. This network has five interconnected segments and four repeaters, and only three of the five segments are populated. It is easy to verify that this network complies with the 5-4-3 rule.

When networks employ different types of media, it can be difficult to verify compliance with the 5-4-3 rule. For example, bus networks (using coaxial cable) are easily identifiable as segments because they have one wire with many stations. However, when bus networks are combined with star networks (using twisted-pair cable), each cable running from the hub is a segment.

Evaluate the network configuration shown in Figure 4-4 for 5-4-3 rule violations. While doing so, remember that the hubs in this illustration function as multiport repeaters and that the terms station, host, terminal, server, and computer are used interchangeably to reflect industry use.

In the figure, one violation of the 5-4-3 rule exists: the separation between Station 3 and Server 1 and Host 2 because six segments and five repeaters exist between these stations. Either the hub and segment of Station 3 must be moved, or the hub and segments of Server 1 and Host 2 must be moved.

Figure 4-4 Mixed topologies

MEDIA

Modern networks can use several types of network media. Most networks use some type of cable for the connection medium; however, air is also considered a medium when used in wireless networks. Wireless technologies, such as infrared and satellite communications, will become increasingly important in the future. This section covers twisted-pair, coaxial, and fiber-optic cabling.

Twisted-Pair Cabling

Most networks are connected with twisted-pair cabling. The cable that runs from your telephone to the wall is probably twisted-pair. Different types and categories of twisted-pair cable exist, but they all have some things in common:

- The wires are copper.
- The wires come in pairs.
- The pairs of wires are twisted around each other.
- The pairs of wires are usually enclosed in a cable sheath individually and as a group of wires.

The twisting of network wires inside the cable sheath reduces **crosstalk**—the bleeding of a signal from one network wire to another, which can corrupt signals and cause network errors. Transmitting cables have a naturally created magnetic field around them. When two networking wires are twisted around one another (inside the same cable sheath), their electronically created magnetic fields cancel each other out. This **cancellation** insulates the signal from the effects of signal bleeding. The twisting of the wires not only protects the signal inside from internal crosstalk, but also guards against other external forms of signal interference (bleeding of energy or signals from other wires or appliances that may be near the twisted wires).

Unshielded Twisted-Pair (UTP)

Unshielded twisted-pair (UTP) cabling is used for a variety of electronic communications. UTP cable supports data transmissions of 4, 10, 16, 100, and (theoretically) 1000 Mbps. The maximum segment length for UTP is 100 meters. Although additional categories of UTP are being developed and are expected to reach speeds greater than 100 Mbps, currently there are five accepted categories of UTP that you should know about. Table 4-1 shows these five different categories of UTP wiring.

Table 4-1 Categories of UTP

Type	Description
CAT 1	Voice-grade communications only; CAT 1 twisted-pair does not support data transmission.
CAT 2	Data-grade 4 Mbps; CAT 2 is an older, rarely used specification of UTP.
CAT 3	Data-grade 10 Mbps; CAT 3 cable meets the minimum transmission rate for 10BaseT networking.
CAT 4	Data-grade 16 Mbps; CAT 4 is an intermediate UTP specification that has largely been replaced by CAT 5 cable.
CAT 5	Data-grade 100 Mbps; CAT 5 is the most widely implemented cabling in networks today. Some recent network specifications outline using CAT 5 cable for up to 1000 Mbps transmission rates.

Most building codes require that **plenum**-grade cable be used when installing networking cable in ceilings or walls. The jackets of certain types of network cable give off a toxic gas when burned, which is unacceptable for most fire codes. Plenum-grade cable does not give off a toxic gas when burned and is often required by fire codes.

The advantages of UTP cable include:

- It is a thin, flexible cable that is easy to string between walls.
- Most modern buildings come with **CAT 5** UTP already wired into the wall outlets or at least run between the floors.

- Because UTP is small, it does not quickly fill up wiring ducts.

- UTP costs less per foot than any other type of LAN cable.

Using UTP also has disadvantages:

- It is more susceptible to interference than most other types of cabling. The pair twisting does help, but it does not make the cable impervious to electrical noise.

- Its unrepeated length limit is 100 meters.

RJ-45 Connectors

Twisted-pair wiring is fitted with a plastic connector and inserted into a transceiver on a NIC at the computer end and a hub, switch, or wall connector at the other end. These connectors are known as **Registered Jacks (RJ)**. Typically, RJ-45 connectors connect UTP networks. The RJ-45 connectors resemble the typical RJ-11 connectors that connect your phone to the wall. The difference between the RJ-45 connectors and the RJ-11 connectors is that the former has eight wire traces (four-pair) and the latter has only four (two-pair). These extra wire traces result in the RJ-45 connector being larger than the RJ-11 connector.

 Some RJ-11 connectors are used with three-pair (six-wire) UTP.

Shielded Twisted-Pair (STP)

Shielded twisted-pair (STP) cabling is often seen in Token Ring networks and is similar to UTP in that the wire pairs are twisted around each other inside the cable. However, STP also has metal shielding around the cable to further protect it from external interference and crosstalk. Some types of STP have additional shielding around each individual pair as well as the bundle of pairs. Of course, shielding the individual wire pairs increases the overall diameter and weight of the cable. The maximum segment length of STP cable is 100 meters. The maximum bandwidth of STP is 155 Mbps.

The advantage of STP over UTP is that it has greater protection from interference and crosstalk due to the shielding.

The disadvantages to STP include the following:

- STP has a higher cost per foot.

- The STP shield must be grounded at one end; if grounded improperly, it can cause serious interference.

- STP is heavier and less flexible, and is more difficult to install.

- Because of its thickness, STP may not fit down narrow cable ducts.

Coaxial Cabling

Coaxial cable consists of either a solid inner core (often made of copper) or a wire strand **conductor** that is surrounded by insulation. Just outside of the insulation is a shield, which is a foil or copper braid that protects the inner conductor. A protective jacket (external coating) surrounds the outside of the cable.

Coaxial cable supports data transmission rates of 10 Mbps. The two most commonly used types of coaxial cable are **thicknet** and **thinnet**. Thicknet is simply a thicker form of coaxial cable than thinnet. Thicknet segments can be up to 500 meters long, whereas thinnet segments are limited to 185 meters. Figure 4-5 shows coaxial cable.

Figure 4-5   Coaxial cable

The advantages of using coaxial cabling on a LAN include the following:

- The segment lengths are longer than UTP or STP.
- Coaxial cable has greater interference immunity than UTP.
- Hubs between stations are not required.

Coaxial cable has disadvantages as well:

- It is not as easy to install as UTP because it is not as flexible or thin.
- It is more expensive than UTP.
- It supports a maximum bandwidth of only 10 Mbps.
- It requires more room in wiring ducts than UTP.
- It is relatively difficult to troubleshoot thinnet and thicknet networks.

Table 4-2 lists several types of coaxial cable you might encounter.

Table 4-2 Coaxial cable types

Cable type	Description
RG-8	50-ohm thicknet (10Base5) cabling
RG-58	50-ohm thinnet (10Base2) cabling RG-58/U — solid copper core RG-58 A/U — wire strand center conductor RG-58 C/U — military specification for thinnet
RG-59	75-ohm broadband cable (cable TV)
RG-62	93-ohm ARCNet

 Thinnet is sometimes referred to as **cheapernet**.

Thinnet and Thicknet Connectors

The most common connectors for **RG–58** cabling on thinnet networks are **barrel connectors**, **T-connectors**, and **terminators**. These connectors are known as **BNC** connectors. Terminators are placed on the T-connectors that are on the computers at the end of a thinnet segment. These devices absorb signals as they reach the end of the wire. This absorption keeps the signals from reflecting (signal bounce) and preventing other stations from transmitting. Barrel connectors are used to connect two cable segments, and T-connectors are used to connect two cable segments to a NIC. Figure 4-6 shows these connectors.

T-Connector

Barrel Connector

Terminator

Figure 4-6   Thinnet connectors

Although a thicknet network also uses coaxial cabling, the connectors can be different. Thicknet cable can be attached directly to computers using larger BNC-style connectors that are similar to thinnet connectors, but thicknet is extremely difficult to manipulate and usually is connected indirectly.

In this indirect method, a small device called a vampire tap pierces the thicknet cable to make a connection with the copper core. The tap is then attached to a transceiver external to the NIC. A drop cable, no more than 50 feet long, connects the transceiver to an **attachment unit interface (AUI)** port on the NIC. Unlike a BNC attachment or an RJ-45 attachment, the AUI attachment on the NIC is not a transceiver. The AUI interface is typically 15-pin and female.

 Thicknet is rarely seen on modern LANs. The most common utilization of thicknet today is as backbone cable running in elevator shafts and other areas where electrical interference is an issue. This is because of thicknet's good interference immunity.

Fiber-Optic Cable

Fiber-optic cable carries light pulses rather than electrical signals along its fibers. This cable is made of glass or plastic fibers, rather than copper wire like most other network cabling. The core of the cable is usually pure glass. Surrounding the glass is a layer of cladding made of glass or plastic, which traps the light in the core. The cladding is usually wrapped with an insulating layer. This is then surrounded with Kevlar fibers, which is the strong substance used in bulletproof vests. Finally, a protective outer sheath made of either PVC or Teflon (plenum grade) is added.

The light pulses carrying the signals in fiber-optic cable originate from a light-emitting diode (LED) (multimode cable) or laser (single-mode cable). Multimode cable can support transmissions up to 100 Mbps, over segments up to 2 km (1.2 miles). Single-mode cable can transmit up to 2 Gbps with segments that span up to 62 miles. Fiber-optic cable is the media of choice for connections between LANs, between buildings, across MANs (metropolitan area networks), and where there is excessive interference or security issues.

Fiber-optic cabling has several advantages:

- It can transmit over long distances, farther than any other network media.
- It is not susceptible to electromagnetic interference or crosstalk.
- It supports extremely high transmission rates.
- The cable has a small diameter and can be used in narrow wiring ducts.
- It is not susceptible to eavesdropping.

There are disadvantages to fiber-optic cable as well:

- It is more expensive than other types of networking media.

- It is more difficult and expensive to install than other types of network media. The ends of each cable must be polished perfectly flat and scratch-free before they are inserted into the connection devices.

- Because it is fragile, fiber-optic cable must be installed carefully and protected after installation.

Signal Degradation

Most media is susceptible to signal degradation. The sources of the degradation can be internal or external. When signals degrade over distance, attenuation results. Three internal factors can cause attenuation:

- **Resistance**: Opposition to the flow of electrons in a wire

- **Inductive reactance**: Opposition to the changes of electrical current in a wire

- **Capacitive reactance**: Opposition to voltage changes in a wire

When these internal opposition forces are combined and measured, the measure is called **impedance**. Each type of cabling has its own impedance rating, which is part of its specification. If all cabling on a network does not have the same impedance, the network can suffer from transmission errors or a reduction in the total usable segment length. For example, a 50-ohm coaxial cable should not be wired directly to a 93-ohm cable.

Internal signal degradations are naturally occurring and dictate the limitations on network cable lengths. In addition to the internal opposition of a wire to a signal, external forces can act on network signals. These external forces come in two main categories:

- **Electromagnetic interference (EMI)**

- **Radio frequency interference (RFI)**

Both types of interference can degrade and corrupt network signals as they travel through a wire. Electrical lighting (particularly fluorescent lighting), generators, elevators, machinery, and other electromagnetic equipment can be sources of EMI. Crosstalk is a form of EMI. Radio-transmitting devices cause RFI.

To reduce EMI/RFI on network cabling, you can do the following:

- Keep network media away from sources of EMI, such as lights, generators, and high-voltage electrical wiring.

- Ensure that network media is installed properly. Crosstalk is often the result of shoddy installation techniques.

- Use shielded cabling, which is more resistant to external interference. Token Ring STP even has shielding around each individual wire pair to protect from internal crosstalk.

- Use repeaters, which amplify and clean up networking signals. Of course, a repeater next to a noise source repeats the noise (if it appears to be valid data), which could cause more problems on the network. Repeaters are best used in the battle against attenuation.

- Ensure that you install high-quality cabling.

HORIZONTAL CABLING STANDARDS

Horizontal cabling is the twisted-pair or fiber-optic network media that connects workstations and **wiring closets**. The **Electronic Industries Alliance and Telecommunications Industry Association (EIA/TIA)** defines a set of specifications, **EIA/TIA-568**, which cover the outlets near the workstation, mechanical terminations in the wiring closets, and all the cable that runs along the horizontal pathway between the wiring closet and the workstation. The standards also specify the names given to cabling and devices on the network, as shown in Figure 4-7.

Figure 4-7   Horizontal cabling

The figure shows the following items:

- Workstation area cable: Connects the workstation to the wall outlet

- Telecommunications connector: Found at the wall outlet

- Horizontal cable: Runs between the wiring closet and the wall outlet

- Horizontal cross-connect patch cord: Connects devices in the wiring closet

Although EIA/TIA-568 specifies twisted-pair or fiber-optic cabling for horizontal cabling, the standard still recognizes 50-ohm coaxial cabling. However, this cable type is not recommended and will likely be removed from the standard at the next revision.

EIA/TIA-568B specifies that the maximum distance for a UTP horizontal cable run is 90 meters (295 feet). In addition, the **patch cords** (a.k.a. **patch cables**) located at any horizontal cross-connection cannot exceed six meters (20 feet), and those used to connect workstations in the work area can be a maximum of three meters (9.8 feet). Therefore, the total length of any unrepeated segment should not exceed the 100-meter limitation for UTP.

In addition to UTP, the following cable types may be used for horizontal pathways:

- Shielded twisted-pair (STP): Two pairs of 150-ohm cabling
- Fiber-optic cabling: A two-fiber 62.5/125-micron multimode cable

WIRING CLOSETS

Wiring closets serve as the center of a star topology. They contain the wiring and wiring equipment for connecting network devices, such as routers, bridges, switches, **patch panels**, and hubs. Since wiring closets are so significant to the physical cabling scheme of the network, their configuration and layout has been standardized by the Electronic Industries Alliance (EIA) and the Telecommunications Industry Association (TIA).

EIA/TIA-568 and **EIA/TIA-569** standards apply to the physical layout of media and wiring closets, with the latter stating that there must be a minimum of one wiring closet per floor. Further, when a given floor area **(catchment area)** exceeds 1000 square meters, or the horizontal cabling is in excess of 90 meters, additional wiring closets are required. In configurations in which more than one wiring closet is needed, a single wiring closet is designated the **main distribution facility (MDF)**. The MDF is the central junction point for the wiring of a star topology. The additional closets are called **intermediate distribution facilities (IDFs)**. The IDFs are dependent on the single MDF. IDFs are required when:

- The catchment area of the MDF is not large enough to capture all nodes.
- The LAN is in a multistory facility.
- The LAN encompasses multiple buildings.

If you are working with multistory buildings, you should place the MDF as close to the middle as feasible. For example, if there are three floors, place the MDF on the second floor, if possible.

Proximity to the POP

You should ensure that your main wiring closet is close to the **point of presence (POP)** to the Internet. Broadly defined, a POP is where two communications systems meet. In this context, the POP is the location where the telecommunications for a given building are located. It is where a LAN connects to the Internet via the telecommunications company's dial-up or leased lines. Placing the MDF near the POP facilitates your network's connection to the Internet. If you plan to have multiple wiring closets in support of a larger network, then your MDF should be located in the POP room if possible. Figure 4-8 illustrates the relationship of the MDF, IDF, and POP for a typical LAN that spans multiple buildings.

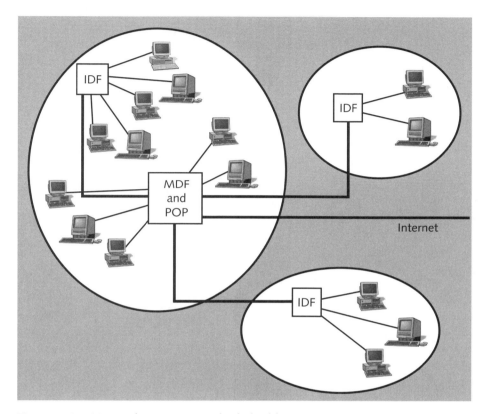

Figure 4-8   Network spanning multiple buildings

In the case of a multistory building, the POP will usually be on the ground floor, and the MDF should be on the middle floor. In this case, you cannot place the MDF and the POP in close proximity to each other

Figure 4-9 illustrates the relationship of the MDF, IDF, and POP for a typical multistory LAN.

Figure 4-9   Network spanning multiple floors

Backbone

When two or more wiring closets are implemented on a network, they must be connected to each other via **backbone** cable. Backbone cable connects wiring closets to each other in an extended star topology. Backbone cabling also connects wiring closets to the POP and wiring closets between buildings. It does not connect workstations, and is therefore sometimes called **vertical cabling** to distinguish it from horizontal cabling, which does connect hubs to workstations. EIA/TIA-568 specifies four different options for backbone cabling:

- 100-ohm UTP
- 150-ohm STP
- 62.5/125-micron optical fiber (most popular for new installations)
- Single-mode optical fiber

Since the vertical cabling carries the data traffic between the wiring closets, it is best for it to be the fastest link on a network. For this reason, network administrators using 10 Mbps networks often choose to make their vertical (backbone) cabling 100 Mbps. This allows them to increase performance and often increase the usable length of their vertical cabling. The length of the vertical cable depends on the type of cable that is used. As discussed previously, the maximum unrepeated distance for UTP is 100 meters. The maximum vertical cable distance for multimode and single-mode fiber is 2000 and 3000 meters respectively.

PERFORMANCE CONSIDERATIONS

When designing a network, you must keep in mind the network performance needs of the customer. Sometimes these are somewhat difficult to predict, especially if there isn't an existing network in place. However, it is still important to consider a customer's performance needs and, where possible, optimize the performance of the network. Items that you should consider when reviewing the performance needs of your customer include:

- Connection speeds
- Utilization and broadcast traffic
- Collisions and contention
- Resource placement

In the following sections, each of the above-listed items is discussed. You will learn a technique for analyzing the bandwidth requirements of an organization. In addition, you will review several of the factors that influence the way in which a network performs.

Connection Speeds

The complexity of the data being transferred affects bandwidth. For example, it takes more bandwidth to download a graphic in one second than it takes to download a text file in the same amount of time. Although your network may have a theoretical bandwidth of 10 Mbps, what you experience in terms of network capacity at any given time may be far less than 10 Mbps. The real capacity of a network is sometimes referred to as **throughput**. Factors that affect throughput include the type of network devices being used on the network, the number of nodes, power issues, **network architecture**, and other variables. The bandwidth calculations most commonly required involve determining either the time to download a file under best conditions or the actual rate of a file transfer.

Utilization

Network utilization is an important factor that influences the performance of a network. The higher the utilization, the greater the impact on performance. The typical rule of thumb for an Ethernet network is that more than 40% utilization for a sustained period should be investigated. Many factors influence the overall utilization of a network. However, when investigating causes (or potential causes) of high utilization, be sure to consider the following items:

- Video or audio streaming/teleconferencing
- Client/server applications
- Host/terminal applications
- Routing protocols
- Routine maintenance tasks (file backup and database copying)
- Broadcast traffic
- Ethernet collisions

You must be aware of the type of information that will be passed on the network. In most cases, it is best to find a network similar to the one you are designing, so that you can estimate the performance requirements. If this is not possible, you should attempt to get calculations from application vendors and equipment manufacturers concerning performance. You want to ensure that the average and peak requirements of applications do not exceed your available bandwidth. In the next section, you will learn a way to estimate bandwidth and throughput.

The most common solution for reducing network utilization is to segment a network with a connectivity device such as a bridge, switch, or router. Other solutions may include the following:

- Reducing the number of services provided on the segment
- Reducing the number of protocols in use on the segment
- Disabling bandwidth-intensive applications or protocols, such as those that support audio or video streaming
- Relocating the systems consuming the most bandwidth on the segment

Calculating Bandwidth and Throughput

As you consider the bandwidth that is required by an organization, you should attempt to discover the types of bandwidth-intensive communications that will be conducted on its network. You can then use that information to calculate the bandwidth requirements. For example, assume that you know that a 300 MB file must be transferred across a WAN link that runs at 56 Kbps every night. You want to estimate the time that it will take that file to transfer and see if the performance is acceptable to your client. The time that it takes a file to transfer from one location to another is called **transmission time**. You can calculate the transmission time by dividing the file size by the bandwidth, as shown in the following formula:

Transmission Time = File Size/Bandwidth   (T = Fs/Bw)

As an example of the use of this formula, consider the different units of measure for the file size 300 megabytes and the transmission speed 56 kilobits per second. The first task is to obtain a common unit of measurement, which in this case is bits. 300 megabytes equals 300,000,000 bytes, which must then be multiplied by eight to convert to bits (eight bits in a byte). That is 2,400,000,000 bits that must be transferred over the link. Since a kilobit is 1000 bits, 56 Kbps means that the transfer rate is actually 56,000 bits per second. Now, plug those numbers into the formula and you will see how long it takes to transfer the file:

2,400,000,000/56,000 = 42,857 seconds

Convert the number of seconds into hours and minutes to make it more recognizable: 42,857 seconds is 11 hours, 54 minutes, and 17 seconds. Assuming that the client wants to complete the file download in eight hours, this performance would be unacceptable, and a faster link would have to be considered.

If you have an existing connection, you can time a file transfer and determine your actual throughput for the link. Throughput is a more realistic measure of transmission time because it is based on the observed transfer rate. Throughput equals the size of the file divided by the actual download time. Consider this formula:

Throughput = File Size/Download Time   (Tp = Fs/Dt)

If you send actual data across your network connection, you can time the transfer and calculate the throughput. For example, assume that you transfer four gigabytes of data across your network connection and it takes six minutes. First, you convert the numbers to a common format. (Four gigabytes is four billion bytes, which is 32 billion bits. Six minutes is 360 seconds.)

Then, plug the numbers into the formula:

32,000,000,000/360 = 88,888,889 bits per second

To make the throughput figure more recognizable, convert it into megabits per second by dividing by one million. When you do this, you discover the throughput is roughly 89 Mbps.

You may find a throughput of 89 Mbps on a network that has a 100-Mbps connection and wonder why you didn't get the full 100 Mbps of bandwidth. This is because bandwidth and actual throughput aren't equal. Throughput is affected by variables other than the connection speed, including other traffic on the wire, the latency of connectivity devices, and the capabilities of the source and destination to receive packets. If you were calculating the speed of the file transfer based on your 100-Mbps connection speed, you would expect the 4-GB transfer to complete in about 5 minutes and 33.3 seconds, as shown in the following:

32,000,000,000 bits/100,000,000 bits per second = 320 seconds

 Keep in mind that you may need to factor in additional bandwidth to account for the variables affecting actual throughput.

By performing these calculations, you can ensure that your proposed network design and equipment will be able to meet the needs of your client.

Collisions and Contention

All stations on an Ethernet segment must share the available connection with each other. This means that the stations contend with one another for the opportunity to transmit on the wire. Two stations cannot transmit at the same time, or a collision will occur. Collisions cause delays because, for a short period, all transmissions cease on the wire, and the stations that caused the collision must reset and wait to transmit again.

When you are considering upgrading an existing network, you can check the rate of collisions on the network using a **protocol analyzer** or other network performance-monitoring tool. Although collisions are expected to occur on Ethernet networks, a high rate of collisions can cause serious performance problems. As a rule of thumb, collision rates of 5% or more should be investigated. If no errors, such as faulty adapters, are detected when you investigate the collision rate, the collisions may be caused by too many stations trying to contend for the same bandwidth on the segment. In such a case, one course of action may be to segment the network with a bridge, router, or switch.

Resource Placement

One important item that can improve the performance of a network is the proper placement of resources. When possible, network users should be on the same network segment as the resources they need to access. When resources that are frequently accessed by users are not placed on the same segment as the user, increased traffic across the network results. For example, consider the placement of the accounting database in Figure 4-10.

Assume that the most frequent users of the accounting database are in the Accounting Department. Since the file server is located in a segment that is mostly used by the Marketing Department, traffic between the marketing and accounting segments is higher than necessary. If the Accounting Department is using the accounting database server more than the Marketing Department, then the database server should be part of the Accounting Department's segment.

Deciding where to place resources on a network is a very important part of configuring the most efficient communication paths. Of course, the need for security and centralized control may sometimes outweigh the need for increased performance.

Figure 4-10 Resource placement

INSTALLING TELECOMMUNICATIONS CONNECTORS

Once you have run the horizontal cable from the closets to the various locations to be networked, you must attach it to the telecommunications connectors. If you have decided to use surface mounting, then the connection can be made quickly outside the wall by simply wiring the cable to the box and jack. However, if you have selected a flush mounting, you must fish the cable from the interior of the wall and run it outside the hole you previously cut for the connection box or bracket.

If you are using a box connector, cut or snap out a portion of the back of the box and bring the wire through it. Then, insert the box into the hole in the wall. You can secure the box by turning the screws in the corners, which extends tabs behind the wall to secure the box. If a bracket is used, then push out the side flanges to attach it to the hole.

As previously discussed, the type of wall jack that is specified in the 568B standard for connecting Category 5 UTP is RJ-45. The RJ-45 connector, as shown in Figure 4-11, is similar in design to a standard (RJ-11) telephone jack, but it is larger and has more pins (eight, instead of two to six).

The side of the RJ-45 jack that faces out from the wall has a female plug where the male connector of the workstation area cable connects. The portion of the plug inside the wall must be wired. In order to connect the wire from the wall to the RJ-45 jack, you must strip back the cable's jacket to expose the eight individual wires, as shown in Figure 4-12.

Figure 4-11   RJ-45 connector

Figure 4-12   UTP wires

Be sure to strip back only about one to two inches of the jacket. If you strip too much of the jacket, the connection may be degraded. Be careful not to untwist the wire too much; the EIA/TIA-568 standard allows for CAT-5 untwisting of up to a half-inch.

The individual wires should be placed according to their corresponding color-coded pins into the back of the RJ-45 jack. If the back of the jack does not have color-coded pins, you should place the wires in the **568A** or 568B order. Note that a mixture of 568A and 568B should not be used. Figure 4-13 shows the 568B wiring scheme.

4

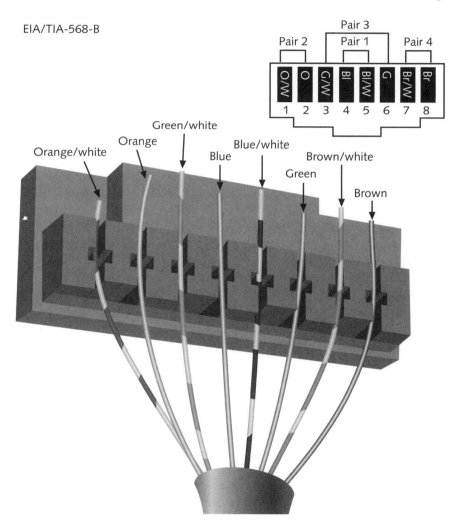

Figure 4-13   Jack wiring

Once the wire is inserted into the pins on the back of the plug, use a **punch tool** to punch down the wire into the back of the plug. Do this carefully; skewed wires can negatively affect the transmission rate. The punch tool should simultaneously complete the connection and remove the excess wire. If any excess wire remains, be sure to remove it. If the wires do not make a good connection, the network performance may degrade or transmission may even stop altogether. Be sure that there are no wire shorts (one wire touching another) at the connector. Try to keep the wire jacket within ⅛ inch from the connector (the shorter the distance of the exposed wire, the better).

Once all of the wires have been properly punched into the connector, place the clips on the jack. Ensure that they are tight so that they will properly protect the wiring. Place any excess cable inside the wall (flush mounting) or inside the connector box (surface mounting). Next, snap or screw the faceplate into the box or bracket that you installed earlier.

PATCH PANEL

The patch panel is a device with rows of pins and ports that connects the horizontal cabling to the patch cables inside the wiring closets. The side with the ports is considered the front of the patch panel. The side with the pins is considered the back side. Patch panels are located at the center of a star or extended star topology and serve as a switchboard interconnecting the devices on a network. Figure 4-14 shows the pins side of a patch panel.

Figure 4-14   Patch panel pins

Figure 4-15 shows the ports side of a patch panel.

The horizontal cables coming in from other parts of the network are punched into the exposed groups of pins on the patch panel. Each group of pins represents a connection for one cable and directly corresponds to a port on the opposite side of the patch panel.

The pins are color-coded to facilitate wiring. The process for punching these wires into the panel is similar to that of wiring an RJ-45 telecommunications connector:

Step 1   Strip back 1½ to 2 inches of UTP cable.

Step 2   Untwist the individual wires no more than ½ inch for Category 5 UTP.

Step 3   Match the wires with the corresponding colors on the patch panel pins.

Step 4   Punch down the cables with the appropriate punch tool—Krone or 110.

Ports on front of patch panel

Figure 4-15   Patch panel ports

The punch tool should simultaneously connect and cut the cable. The specific type of tool that you use depends on the type of patch panel in use. Figure 4-16 shows a 110 punch tool. Be sure to check the documentation or with the manufacturer to determine which type of tool is appropriate.

Figure 4-16   110 Punch tool

With any punch tool, you must hold it with the cutting edge away from the connectors you are punching down or the wires will not be cut when they are punched down.

On the opposite side of the patch panel, patch cables are used to connect the patch panel ports to other devices inside the wiring closet, such as hubs, routers, and switches. The patch panel ports accept RJ-45 connectors, so no punching down of cable is necessary for this side. However, the patch cable itself must be fitted with RJ-45 connectors on both ends so that it can connect from the port on the patch panel to the intended network device (i.e., hub, switch, or router).

TESTING CABLE

Once cabling is installed, be sure to test it. There are several types of tests you can run on your network cable to ensure that it will perform optimally. All cable testing devices can be used to check basic connectivity. More advanced cable testers can be used to check cable performance characteristics in addition to connectivity. In this section, you will learn about the common cable connectivity tests and performance measures.

Cable Testers

There are many different cable testers available with a wide variety of features. Cable testers with limited features can be as inexpensive as $50 to $100. More advanced models can be priced above $5000. Important measurements that cable testers can make are:

- Wire map
- Attenuation
- Noise
- Near end crosstalk (NEXT) (Only the very high-end cable testers have this capability.)
- Distance measure

EIA/TIA and IEEE specify standards for these measurements, which gives a reference point for acceptable measurements. To ensure that the network is performing optimally, take periodic measurements and compare them with EIA/TIA and IEEE specifications. In the following sections, the preceding measurements are explained, and tips for correcting and minimizing cable problems are presented.

Wire Map

A **wire map** is an important measurement that a cable tester makes to check the wiring sequence. Regardless of which wiring method you use, EIA/TIA-568A or EIA/TIA-568B, wire pairings will always be the same, as follows: 1+2, 3+6, 4+5, and 7+8. An incorrectly wired cable can prevent or degrade signal transmission. The test shows whether the installer properly or improperly connected the wires to the jack or plug. Table 4-3 illustrates and defines the various cabling problems that a wire map can detect.

Table 4-3 Wire map error detection

Condition	Visual	Description
Crossed wires		A wire from pair 1 and 2 is crossed with a wire in the 3 and 6 pair.
Reversed pairs		The wires 1 and 2 are crossed.
Crossed pairs		Pair 1 and 2 is crossed with pair 3 and 6.
Short		Wires 1 and 3 are shorted.
Open		Wire 2 is open and does not complete the circuit.

Crossed wires, reversed pairs, and crossed pairs all indicate incorrect wire placement at the jack, connector, or patch panel. Figure 4-17 illustrates the condition known as crossed pairs.

Figure 4-17   Crossed pairs

Shorts are caused when two wires make contact with each other at some point, which usually means that the cable was bent or creased more than 90 degrees. A short can also occur if cable is pierced, any open wire is broken at some point inside the wire, or a wire is not properly connected.

There is another condition—a split pair—that only very high-end cable testers can detect. A simple wire map cannot detect a split pair because there are no incomplete circuits, as shown in Figure 4-18.

Figure 4-18   Split pairs

A split pair usually results from poor wiring at the jack and the patch panel. The sequence must be incorrectly wired in both places in order for the pair to be split. This problem can result in crosstalk because the actual twisted wires are carrying two different signals. Normally, one pair is used to send and the other to receive, but in this configuration, the wire pair is twisted incorrectly, which increases the likelihood of crosstalk during signal transmission. Although wire maps cannot detect this problem, a NEXT test or visual inspection can detect a split pair.

Attenuation

Attenuation is the loss of signal power over the distance of a cable. To measure attenuation on a cable, the cable tester must be assisted by a second test unit called a **signal injector**. The signal injector sends electric pulses down the wire from one end, and the cable tester picks them up at the other end. In this way, the loss in pulse strength is measured and the level of attenuation can be calculated.

Often, the cable tester is preprogrammed with the level of attenuation allowed according to the EIA/TIA-568A specification; otherwise, you must check the specification to see what an acceptable attenuation is at various frequencies. The pulse from the signal injector for Category 5 cable should be set at 100 MHz to test the cable fully. The lower the attenuation, the better: for example, attenuation of 10 decibels is better than 20 decibels.

Noise

Noise consists of unwanted electrical signals that alter the shape of the transmitted signals on a network. Noise on a cable can be produced by many different sources, such as other wire pairs, fluorescent lights, radios, electronic devices, heaters, and air-conditioning units. When the wiring in a wall is too long, it can act as an antenna for noise by picking up EMI and RFI from other devices and sending the noise along with the electrical signals that it is meant to transmit between devices on the network.

Alternating current (AC) signal noises are called **oscillations** and can alter the digital signal that computers receive on the wire. Network signals are typically digital transmissions, which means they have two states—on and off. Network devices interpret the on state as a digital "one" and the off state as a digital "zero." The network card samples the wire continuously as it receives transmissions bit by bit. If oscillations mask the transmission, the network card may incorrectly interpret the data or discard the data frames as corrupt.

Improper grounding can also cause noise. The motherboard and other internal integrated **circuits** of a computer use the chassis as their ground (zero reference). However, the chassis is also the ground for the incoming power. If there is a wiring error, it could not only electrify the chassis but cause internal component errors as well. Faulty AC wiring can also cause problems with transmissions because the **signal reference ground** is the computer chassis and grounding plate. If the ground is wired incorrectly, the reference voltage may be something other than zero. When the computer attempts to interpret a signal from the wire with a skewed signal reference ground, the data could be misinterpreted.

 Keep only one **transformer** on a LAN to reduce problems caused by faulty wiring, overloaded circuits, different grounds, and long AC wiring runs acting as antennas.

Cable testers can listen for noise on a wire. To perform a test for cable noise, the horizontal cable should be unplugged from the network jacks and patch panel. The cable tester then listens for noise on the cable. If noise is found on the cable, the path of the wire should be traced to determine if there is any possible noise source in the area. Unplug devices where possible to see if the noise disappears. You can eliminate oscillations by rewiring electrical connections.

NEXT

Near end crosstalk (NEXT) is a measure of interference from other wire pairs. A signal may bleed from one set of wires to another, causing crosstalk. The NEXT measure seeks to determine how much signal bleed is occurring. The cable tester measures NEXT by placing a series of different frequency signals on the wire (usually up to 100 MHz for Category 5 cable). A good cable tester displays the NEXT readings against the acceptable limits put forth in the EIA/TIA standard. For example, Figure 4-19 illustrates a cable tester displaying NEXT results against the standard.

The test for NEXT should be done at both ends of a cable. This is because the crosstalk can be affected by attenuation. Typically, a cable tester measuring NEXT sends a signal out on a pair of wires. The NEXT measurement represents the effect of the test signal on another pair of wires. Higher NEXT values correspond to less crosstalk and better network performance. If the signal experiences significant attenuation, the crosstalk may be seen as insignificant. Therefore, both ends of the cable should be tested for NEXT. Causes of NEXT include:

- Split pairs
- Too much wire untwisted at the patch panel, jack, or connectors
- Bends, kinks, or stretches in the cabling

Figure 4-19   NEXT test on a cable analyzer

To minimize NEXT, be sure to handle cable carefully. Never apply more than 25 pounds of pressure when stringing or fishing cable. (Some vendors sell 10-pound-rated pulling string that will break before too much tension is placed on the wire.) Be sure not to step on, cut, crush, or twist the wire during installation. Finally, ensure that jacks and patch panels are wired correctly to avoid split pairs.

Visually check the horizontal cables if NEXT is detected; look for untwisted wires, stretched areas, or kinks in the cable.

Distance Measure

EIA/TIA-568A specifies maximum cable lengths for network media. Cables that are too long can cause delays in transmission and network errors. Cable testers use time-domain reflectometry to find the distance of a cable. Time-domain reflectometry is similar to radar in that a signal is sent, it bounces off an object, and it is reflected back to the emitting device. The time it takes for the signal to travel between the two points indicates the distance to the object.

A cable tester that uses time-domain reflectometry is called a **time-domain reflectometer (TDR)**. TDR measurements can detect the overall length of a cable or the distance to a cable break or opening. This is because the signal is reflected anytime that the wiring is open.

Good TDRs can even show various levels of signal change along the way. These measurements can tell the efficiency of the wiring at a connector or patch panel. If the measurement is made through a wall jack or patch panel, tiny spikes may appear at the connector showing the signal transition. A large spike could indicate a wiring problem or faulty connection. The accuracy of the measurement is fairly high, usually within two feet or less.

Baseline

After a network is up and running, it is important to take a baseline measurement to tell you how well the network is performing at a given moment. The baseline measurements can then be compared with future measurements. Baseline measurements can include the following:

- Error rates
- Collision rates
- Network utilization

When the network is in full operation, you can determine the utilization, number of collisions, and network errors. This helps you determine how efficiently the network is running. Then, periodically, you can take measurements of the network to see how it compares to the baseline. If the network seems generally slow, you can check the statistics at that moment against the baseline.

When you compare the two measurements, you may see immediately why the network seems to be running slowly. If the network utilization is above 40% (for Ethernet), then you might consider segmenting the network. You also may find a higher number of network errors, which could indicate a bad network card tying up the bandwidth.

NETWORK ARCHITECTURE

The term network architecture refers to a network's physical and **logical topology**. This includes its physical structure or layout, the media used, the network access method, and the standards and protocols employed. The network access method, which is the same thing as logical topology, defines how the signal gains access to and travels on a wire. Logical topologies operate at the Data Link layer of the OSI model. The most common network architectures include Ethernet, Token Ring, FDDI, and AppleTalk.

Network architectures are defined primarily at the Physical and Data Link layers of the OSI model. The 802 standard defines these architectures.

IEEE 802

IEEE 802 covers issues concerning all types of networks—local area (LAN), metropolitan (MAN), wide area (WAN), and wireless. As originally written, IEEE 802 only addressed issues related to the first two layers of the OSI networking model—Physical and

Data Link. Thus, by necessity, the standard is constantly evolving as committees research, discuss, and propose additions, revisions, and other modifications.

Several different specifications in the 802 standard are particularly interesting in basic networking architectures. This section covers the following specifications:

- 802.2 — Logical Link Control
- 802.3 — CSMA/CD
- 802.5 — Token Ring
- 802.11 — Wireless technologies

Logical Link Control (IEEE 802.2)

To better define and modularize the technologies used to transmit data on a network, the IEEE subdivided the Data Link layer of the OSI networking model. In the IEEE **802.2** specification, the Data Link layer is divided into the **Media Access Control (MAC) sublayer** and the **Logical Link Control (LLC) sublayer**, as shown in Figure 4-20.

Figure 4-20   802.2 specification

The LLC sublayer is closer to the software components of the protocol stack because it controls data link communication and defines **Service Access Points (SAP)**, which are used to transfer information from the Logical Link Control layer to higher layers of the protocol stack.

The MAC sublayer is closer to the underlying hardware architecture because it is in direct contact with the network interface card (NIC). This sublayer is responsible for error-free data transmission and for providing electronic access to one or more NICs at the Physical layer. The MAC sublayer contains the hardware address for the NICs.

CSMA/CD (802.3)

IEEE **802.3** defines the **access method** used by most Ethernet networks (Ethernet being the most common LAN technology today). The network access method used by Ethernet was developed in the 1960s at the University of Hawaii. Xerox Corporation eventually adopted the access method in the 1970s. Xerox, Digital Equipment Corporation, and Intel furthered the development of Ethernet. The IEEE adopted the 802.3 standard in the early 1980s. Different types of Ethernet networks exist within the generic 802.3 specifications. These specifications call for different transmission rates, cable types, and minimum and maximum cable lengths.

Ethernet uses the Carrier Sense Multiple Access with Collision Detection (CSMA/CD) network access method. In fact, the 802.3 standard is typically referred to as CSMA/CD. To understand where the name originated, consider that on an Ethernet network, before transmitting, any device must listen to the wire for a carrier signal, which is present only when another station is transmitting. Listening to the wire is called carrier sense (CS). If no signal is detected, devices can send data. All devices have equal access to the wire, which is what the multiple access (MA) portion of CSMA/CD describes.

The last part of the name, CD, stands for collision detection, which means that the devices can detect collisions in the event that two individual transmissions collide on the network. Collisions occur when two hosts transmit data on the network at the same time. The area in which the collision originates and affects other stations is referred to as the collision domain. Because a collision of frames makes them unintelligible to the hosts on the network, such a situation is undesirable.

Although stations are required to listen to the wire before sending a transmission, two stations could listen to the wire simultaneously and not sense a carrier signal. In such a case, both stations might transmit their data at the same time. Shortly after the simultaneous transmissions, a collision would occur. Ethernet NICs can detect collisions on the wire. This ability further explains the collision detection (CD) piece of the CSMA/CD network access method.

Once the sending devices detect a collision, they transmit a 32-bit **jam signal** that tells all other devices except the collision parties that they are not to transmit for a brief period (9.6 microseconds or slightly longer). After the transmittal of the jam signal, the two stations that experienced the collision use an algorithm to enter a backoff period, which causes them not to transmit for a random interval. The backoff period ensures that those two stations do not immediately cause another collision.

The CSMA/CD access method uses a logical bus topology. This means that the signal will go out from the sending station in all directions to every host on the segment. The physical topology (or layout) may be a bus or a star. The five most well-known Ethernet specifications are 10BaseT, 10Base2, 10Base5, 100BaseT, and Gigabit Ethernet.

The most popular Ethernet specification is **10BaseT** and describes an Ethernet network connected by twisted-pair cable that can support transmissions of 10 megabits per second (Mbps) using **baseband** (digital) signals. The physical topology resembles a star, as each host is connected to a central device (in this case, a hub). Because each segment terminates in the workstation and the hub, there is only one host per segment. This is known as a star-bus topology. The minimum segment length is 2 meters, and the maximum length of any segment is 100 meters.

Another Ethernet specification, **10Base2**, describes a coaxial cable network that has a 10-Mbps baseband transmission rate over a maximum segment length of 185 meters. This specification is also known as **thin Ethernet**, or thinnet, because of the type of cabling used. Each end of a thinnet network must be terminated. This is because (unlike the 10BaseT specification) the wire does not terminate in the workstation and a hub. The physical topology of a thinnet network is a bus. Computers are daisy-chained together by segments of coaxial cable. There is a maximum of 30 hosts per segment.

A third Ethernet specification, **10Base5**, is a coaxial cable specification that indicates a 10-Mbps baseband transmission using a physical bus topology. 10Base5 networks allow segment runs of 500 meters. This specification is also known as Standard Ethernet, **thick Ethernet**, or thicknet, because of the type of cabling used. The longer allowable segment length is related to less attenuation on the wire because of the wider cable diameter. The maximum number of hosts on a thicknet segment is 100, and the computers on each end must be terminated.

A fourth specification, **Fast Ethernet**, is also known as **100BaseT** because it provides a 100-Mbps baseband transfer rate over twisted-pair wire. Fast Ethernet uses the same network access method (CSMA/CD) and the same topology as 10BaseT, which is star-bus, but provides 10 times the data-transmission rate. Of course, different NICs and network devices are required to obtain the higher rate.

When converting to 100BaseT, existing 10BaseT network wiring can be used and the entire network does not have to be converted to 100BaseT, because the access method still employs CSMA/CD and other specifications are compatible with 10BaseT. Newer NICs support both 10- and 100-Mbps transmission rates.

The fifth specification, **Gigabit Ethernet**, is a more recent addition to the IEEE 802.3 specifications. It supports 1 Gbps baseband transmission. This new type of Ethernet is used primarily as a backbone to connect networks over fiber-optic cable. The standard employs the CSMA/CD access method and is backward compatible with 100BaseT and 10BaseT technologies.

Token Ring (802.5)

IBM developed Token Ring technology, and the IEEE updates the standard to keep current with changes by IBM. In the **802.5** specification, Token Ring networks use token-passing to keep track of which node is communicating. Although the specification does not mandate the physical topology of Token Ring, almost all Token Ring networks are connected in a physical star. The device at the center of the star is a MAU instead of a hub or switch. Token Ring networks typically use twisted-pair cable, and the transmission rates can be either 4 or 16 Mbps.

In the physical star configuration, the logical ring is implemented in the MAU. The token is passed from host to host through the MAU. So, although the physical layout of a Token Ring network is a star just as in the 10BaseT networks, the signal is traveling in a ring—thus, the term **star-ring**. Recall that in the 10BaseT star-bus network, the signal is sent through the hub to all hosts. This would be a logical bus instead of a logical ring. MAUs can be connected to other MAUs on the network. Up to 33 MAUs can be connected on a Token Ring network.

In the **token-passing** access method, a single token is passed from station to station. From the perspective of any given station, the token is received from the **nearest active upstream neighbor (NAUN)** and passed to the **nearest active downstream neighbor (NADN)**. The token is, in fact, a small data frame. Stations may transmit on the network only when they have received the token. Each station requires the token in order to transmit. Thus, no two stations transmit at the same time, which prevents collisions. Because the token is passed from one station to another, a break in the cable or a loss of a host can interrupt the flow of the token.

As stations are powered on in a Token Ring network, the first station turned on becomes the **active monitor**. It ensures that the network continues to function by periodically sending a packet around the ring to ensure ring integrity. Any Token Ring NIC can detect a failure on the ring. If a NIC does detect a failure, it starts **beaconing**. Beaconing means that the NIC sends frames to all other NICs on the wire. The frame includes the address of the NIC originating the frame and its NAUN. The NAUN should recognize its own address in the beacon frame and remove itself from the network to run self-diagnostics. If the diagnostics pass, the NIC will reinsert itself on the wire; otherwise, it will remain disconnected from the ring. Once the failure point is detected, the ring is automatically reconfigured around the failed NIC. Token Ring technology provides for traffic prioritization, is more reliable than Ethernet technologies, and works in industrial environments where interference from EMI sources makes many Ethernet installations untenable.

Wireless Technologies (802.11)

Wireless LANs connect users over the air using electromagnetic waves, and are usually used where there are limitations to installing cable. The IEEE **802.11** standard for wireless LANs specifies parameters at both the Physical and Data Link layers of the OSI model. At the Physical layer, infrared or spread spectrum technologies are supported.

Infrared (IR) transmission requires line-of-sight between the transmitter and receiver. If you use a remote control to change the channels on your TV, you are most likely using an IR transmitter. Infrared transmissions cannot go through walls and can be degraded by sunlight, but they are relatively secure because they are highly directional (point-to-point).

Spread spectrum, which is a form of radio frequency (RF) transmission, involves the deliberate spreading of the transmitted signal over many different frequencies, or over a wide bandwidth, and does not require line-of-sight. This technology requires greater bandwidth than standard RF transmission. There are two flavors of spread spectrum transmission: frequency-hopping spread spectrum (FHSS) and direct-sequence spread spectrum (DSSS). In FHSS, a relatively high-power signal is continually switched between different frequencies. With DSSS, the transmission is spread across a wide signal bandwidth at low power levels. FHSS and DSSS provide some degree of security from unauthorized interception.

At the Data Link layer, 802.11 specifies **Carrier Sense Multiple Access/Collision Avoidance (CSMA/CA)** as the network access method. This is similar to CSMA/CD where the node first listens to see if the channel is clear. However, in the case of CSMA/CA, if the channel is not clear, the node chooses a random backoff time to determine how long to wait until it can transmit. When it is time to transmit, the node first sends out a ready-to-send (RTS) packet. If the destination node gets the RTS, it sends a clear-to-send (CTS) packet, and subsequently, the data is sent. The 802.11 standard is still being reviewed and reworked. Wireless LAN implementations are expected to increase exponentially as the technology develops and improves.

FDDI

The Fiber Distributed Data Interface (FDDI) standard is the responsibility of the **American National Standards Institute (ANSI)**. The standard describes a network that can span up to 100 kilometers (62 miles) over single-mode fiber-optic cabling. The transmission rate on a FDDI network is 100 Mbps, and FDDI allows up to 500 devices per network. The FDDI access method is based on the Token Ring (802.5) specification but does not have the same limitations. FDDI is a physical and logical ring.

The FDDI network has two rings, the primary ring and the secondary ring. Data travels on the primary ring. The secondary ring is used as a backup, in case the primary ring fails. However, if the secondary ring is not used for backup, it can increase the effective transmission rate to 200 Mbps. Although regular Token Ring networks are limited to one token on the ring at a time, FDDI networks can circulate more than one token. Thus, data can be transmitted more quickly on the network.

LAN DESIGN MODELS

You can choose many different network design models to implement on your network. However, there are two basic design strategies that are typically followed: **mesh design** and **hierarchical design**. Mesh designs are less structured than hierarchical designs. In a mesh design, there is typically no clear definition of where certain network functions are performed. Routers in a mesh design act as peer devices and perform essentially the same functions. As shown in Figure 4-21, the mesh is a flat structure in which expansion of the network is done laterally.

Figure 4-21   Mesh network design

Hierarchical designs, on the other hand, are more structured and defined. These types of designs separate different equipment and network media by their connectivity functions. Compared to a mesh design, a hierarchical design:

- Is easier to manage: Mesh designs are not as organized as hierarchical networks, so they can be considerably more difficult to manage.

- Is easier to troubleshoot: The defined structure of the hierarchical design makes it easier to identify, locate, and isolate network problems.

- Has improved scalability: A well-defined hierarchical design can be modified and redefined to support a larger organization more easily than a mesh design. The more organized the network, the easier it is to expand. Furthermore, the structure allows for additional users, equipment, and media to be added without extensive investigations into the distance between nodes and the number of nodes per segment.

- Allows easier analysis: Measurements of performance are easier to obtain when a network has a defined structure. The measurements are also easily applied to future expansion plans for the network.

In the following sections you will learn more about three hierarchical network models: the three-layer network model, the two-layer network model, and the one-layer network model.

Three-Layer Network Model

The **three-layer network model** is the most complex of the three models. It consists of a **core layer**, a **distribution layer**, and an **access layer**. The following list describes each in turn:

- Core layer: Provides WAN connectivity between sites located in different geographic areas

- Distribution layer: Used to interconnect buildings with separate LANs on a campus network

- Access layer: Identifies a LAN or a group of LANs that provides users with access to network services

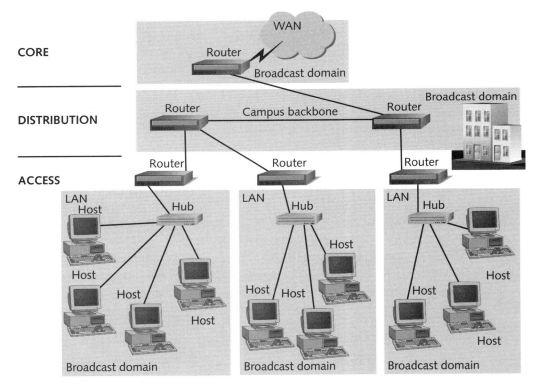

Figure 4-22   Three-layer network model

Figure 4-22 illustrates how each layer would be categorized in a large network environment. As you can see, the core layer connects networks in different cities, the distribution layer connects several LANs within the same part of the city, and the access layer is where each group of users gains access to the greater network.

Each layer is separated into its own broadcast domain because the layers are separated by routers. Notice that within the access layer, there are several broadcast domains, each providing users with access to the network. Therefore, the separation between the layers in the three-layer network model is mostly due to function. However, there is also a separation of broadcast domains between the layers because of the connectivity equipment used to create the configuration.

Core Layer

The core layer provides WAN connections between the various locations of the network. Since the core layer mostly consists of point-to-point WAN connections, hosts are not typically part of this layer. Organizations usually lease the connections used for the core layer from a telecommunications company. Organizations use the core layer to provide a fast connection path between remote sites. Therefore, efficient use of the available bandwidth is a concern for those negotiating, designing, and administering the core layer connections. Often, network administrators establish multiple connections at the core layer to ensure that connectivity is maintained between each remote site and the main site.

Distribution Layer

The distribution layer consists of all the equipment necessary to make the connection between different LANs in a single geographic area or campus. This includes the backbone connection and all the routers used to form the connections to each LAN. At this level of the network, network administrators usually implement **policy-based connectivity**. This means that the network administrator determines the type of traffic (such as Web or FTP) to allow on the backbone and the type of traffic that the router will filter. The network administrator can use routers to filter the traffic from the incoming WAN connection and between the various LAN connections. This allows the network administrator to control users' access to services and broadcast traffic between LANs.

The administrator of the distribution layer can also control the LAN interconnections by establishing path metrics between the LANs. This allows the network administrator to predict and control the path a network packet should traverse between two points. By doing this, the network administrator may reserve certain network communication paths for certain types of traffic. For example, the network administrator could choose a specific path on the network to filter all traffic except that which is related to e-mail communications. Since e-mail is transferred over TCP port 25, the administrator could configure the router to allow only TCP port 25 traffic. This would mean that no matter how congested the rest of the network became, e-mail communications would have a dedicated path across the wire.

The best practice is not to place any end stations at the distribution layer, because those stations will have access to traffic traversing the LANs. Sitting a user at an end station at the distribution layer would essentially allow that user access to all traffic flowing between the LANs, which could become a security threat. Placing a server at the distribution layer would mean that traffic would be originating and terminating at the distribution layer, which compromises the separation of the layers. Controlling traffic and troubleshooting would be more complex because the traffic filters, which apply to servers at the access layer, could not apply to a server placed at the distribution layer. For example, if you place a Web server at the distribution layer, users will only have access to it if you allow Web traffic through the routers that separate the distribution and access layers. This means that you can no longer filter Web traffic between the LANs.

Access Layer

In the three-layer model, the end systems should be located in the access layer. The access layer provides a logical grouping of users by function. This results in a logical segmentation of the network. This segmentation is typically based on boundaries defined by the organization. For example, the Marketing, Accounting, and Human Resources Departments in a company are typically segmented from one another. These departments may share some common information, but for the most part, their daily functions are separate. While each would be part of the access layer, connectivity devices such as bridges, switches, or routers would typically separate their domains. The main goal at this layer is to isolate the traffic between the individual workgroups, segments, or LANs.

The three-layer network model works well for large network environments. However, network administrators find that the two-layer or one-layer model works best for smaller network environments. These two models are discussed in the following sections.

Two-Layer Network Model

The difference between the **two-layer network model** and the three-layer network model is that the distribution layer or campus backbone is not defined or implemented in the former. Network administrators use WAN connections to interconnect separate LANs, as shown in Figure 4-23.

Notice that each broadcast domain is still separated by access-layer routers, yet the domains may be further subdivided by switching equipment. The structure is still in place so that the network administrator can add a distribution layer and implement a three-layer model at a later date.

One-Layer Network Model

Smaller networks can employ a one-layer network model design strategy. The one-layer network model has less need for routing and access-layer separation than the two-layer or three-layer models. Typically, the **one-layer network model** includes a LAN with a few remote sites. In the one-layer network model, servers may be distributed across the LAN or placed in one central location. Figure 4-24 illustrates a one-layer network configuration.

4

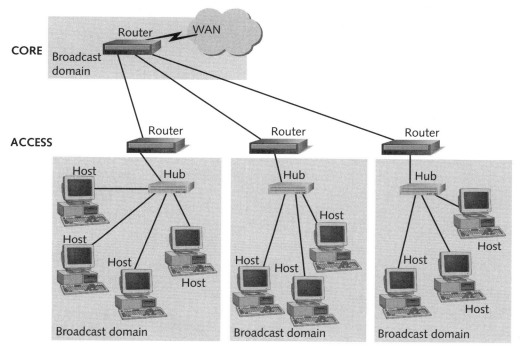

Figure 4-23   Two-layer network model

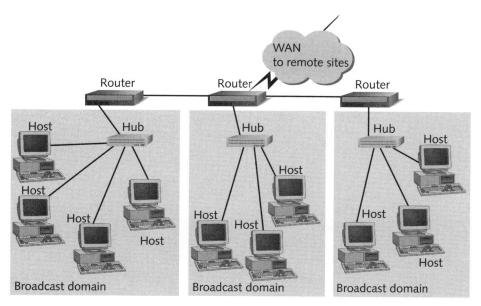

Figure 4-24   One-layer network model

Most of the traffic in the one-layer network will be concentrated on the LAN. The WAN should only have a light traffic load, because the remote sites will not be generating much traffic. The network users gain access to the rest of the network via routers that may connect other segments of the LAN or parts of the WAN. Network administrators can change the one-layer design model into a two- or three-layer structure as the network grows.

As you can see by reviewing the illustrations of the one-layer, two-layer, and three-layer network models, the main difference between these hierarchical models is the number of routers deployed in each configuration. In the three-layer model, there are three levels of routers: one at the core layer for the WAN, one at the distribution layer for the campus backbone, and one at each site in the access layer. In the two-layer network, two levels of routers divide the structure. The one-layer model only has one layer of routers, all of which operate at a peer level.

The main difference between the one-layer design model and the mesh design is the definition of structure. With a mesh network, the chances of having to restructure the entire network configuration as the network increases in size are greater.

NETWORK-MANAGEMENT TOOLS

Network-management tools allow you to perform management functions, such as monitoring network traffic levels, finding bottlenecks, and monitoring software usage. The most common tools are cable testers, **network monitors**, and **network analyzers**. Because you have previously learned about cable testers, this section discusses only network monitors and analyzers.

The differences between a network monitor and a network analyzer can be small. Usually a network monitor is implemented in software while a network analyzer is implemented in hardware. In fact, in many situations, the term analyzer is more of a marketing slogan than a distinction of service. In reality, however, the network analyzer (or protocol analyzer) provides a more sophisticated level of service than a monitor.

To illustrate the differences between network monitors and network analyzers, Table 4-4 compares some of the features of the Microsoft Network Monitor and the Fluke LANMeter, which is a network analyzer.

Table 4-4 Monitor and analyzer

Feature	Microsoft Network Monitor	Fluke LANMeter
Collects network statistics	Yes	Yes
Stores and opens network packets	Yes	No
Uses Simple Network Management Protocol (SNMP) to query devices	No	Yes

Table 4-4 Monitor and analyzer (continued)

Feature	Microsoft Network Monitor	Fluke LANMeter
Analyzes network statistics	No	Yes
Troubleshoots network devices	No	Yes
Provides diagnostic tools	Yes	Yes
Generates traffic for the analysis	No	Yes
Analyzes types of devices on network	No	Yes
Analyzes types of collisions	No	Yes
Analyzes types of errors	No	Yes
Ranks top broadcasting hosts	No	Yes

In addition to the tools presented in the table, other sophisticated network–management tools can be used for daily network-management and control functions. These management tools typically have three components:

- **Agent**: The agent is the client software part of the management tool. It collects information for use by the management system. The agent resides on each network device.

- **Manager**: The manager is a centralized software component that manages the network. The management software stores the information in a standardized database.

- **Administration system**: The administration system is the centralized management component that collects and analyzes the information from the managers. Most administration systems provide information, alerts, and automatic modifications. Often, the administration system is coupled with the management application.

There are two main management protocols used with network management systems: SNMP and CMIP. The following sections discuss these protocols and their basic operations.

SNMP

The Simple Network Management Protocol (SNMP) is a TCP/IP standard protocol included in all major TCP/IP protocol suites. SNMP is a connectionless protocol that operates at layer 7 of the OSI model and port number 161. The U.S. Department of Defense and TCP/IP developers released SNMP in 1988; today, it is the most widely implemented network-management tool.

SNMP allows SNMP agents (client devices on a network that use SNMP agent software) to collect information and statistics for SNMP management software. An SNMP manager can then query a device to obtain the information that the agent has trapped, as shown in Figure 4-25.

Figure 4-25   SNMP in action

A **Management Information Base (MIB)** is a database that maintains the statistics and information that the SNMP reports and uses. Typically stored measurement items include disk space available, network packets transmitted/received, network errors, and system-utilization statistics. Because a network administrator can edit the MIB and insert additional measurement items, any number of statistics can be tracked. The only requirement is that the MIB on both the SNMP management software and the SNMP agent software be configured to track and retrieve the new measurement items.

Network administrators commonly use SNMP to manage hubs and routers. Management tasks include:

- Network traffic monitoring
- Automatic disconnection of problem nodes
- Connection or disconnection of nodes based on time and/or date
- Port isolation for testing purposes
- Remote management capabilities

SNMP managers can also provide network topology maps, historical management information, alerts, and traffic monitoring throughout a network. Examples of SNMP management systems include OpenView, by Hewlett-Packard; NetView, by Tivoli Systems and IBM; and SunNet Manager, from Sun Microsystems.

Although SNMP is an extremely popular management tool, it is not the only one available. Another well-known management protocol is CMIP.

CMIP

The **Common Management Information Protocol (CMIP)** is similar to SNMP in that it uses the MIB to monitor the network. Although this protocol has not been as widely implemented as SNMP, it is more efficient because the clients report the information to the management device. This means less network traffic because the management device doesn't have to call for the information, as is the case with SNMP.

In summary, in SNMP, continuous calls must be exchanged to keep the management device updated, even if those calls only determine if a component has reached a certain threshold. In CMIP, the client makes one call to notify the management tool when a particular threshold is reached. A threshold is set manually to alert the administrator when a certain criterion is met, such as 80% capacity on a hard drive.

CHAPTER SUMMARY

- There are three basic physical LAN topologies: bus, star, and ring.

- These topologies, or layouts, typically involve cable, such as UTP, STP, coaxial, or fiber. The network architecture used on a LAN defines the physical topology, the media used, and the network access method. The most popular architectures are 10BaseT and Token Ring.

- The IEEE has defined many standards that have influenced the way networks are designed and implemented. It has also defined different network access methods, which include CSMA/CD, token-passing, and CSMA/CA.

- One of the largest contributions from the IEEE is the 802 standard, which has subsets that define Ethernet (802.3), Token Ring (802.5), and wireless (802.11) network architectures.

- The 802.2 standard from the IEEE subdivided the OSI Data Link layer into two parts to make functional distinctions between the Media Access Control (MAC) sublayer and the Logical Link Control (LLC) sublayer.

- Ethernet is also known by its access method, CSMA/CD (Carrier Sense Multiple Access with Collision Detection).

- Token Ring uses an entirely different access method that is governed by token-passing. The token, a small data frame, is passed from station to station around the ring, and a station can transmit only when it has the token.

❏ FDDI uses token-passing like Token Ring networks, but it is not subject to the same limitations.

❏ CSMA/CA is a network access method specified by the wireless LAN standard—802.11. This standard supports spread spectrum and infrared technologies for use on wireless LANs. CSMA/CA nodes listen before sending but determine when to send based on a random backoff factor. Before transmitting, CSMA/CA nodes send a notification that they are going to transmit.

❏ Installing media on a network is a multifaceted project. The layout of the network should be determined and documented. The number of wiring closets necessary, as well as their locations, must be determined. Standards for wiring closets, cable runs, distances, and cable must be considered when the routes are established.

❏ Obstructions and EMI/RFI must be overcome. After you install cable, you should test it for wiring, performance, and configuration problems. Cable testers can be used to determine if cables are wired correctly, if they meet length standards, and if they have attenuation or noise problems.

❏ When implementing a network, you can choose one of three hierarchical network models: one-layer, two-layer, or three-layer.

❏ The one-layer network model is the least complex, and is a flat structure where all components function at essentially the same level. The two-layer model separates the WAN from the rest of the internal network, which is usually done by adding routers with packet filters. In the three-layer model, the internal LANs are further divided by backbone cabling, which has additional routers with packet filters. In this model, the WAN connection is called the core layer, the backbone cabling and routers form the distribution layer, and the individual LANs function at the access layer.

❏ Network administrators use network monitors and network analyzers to manage a network on a daily basis. These tools can also be used to troubleshoot abnormal situations.

❏ The main difference between a network monitor and network analyzer is the level of service provided. The network analyzer typically offers more advanced features, such as SNMP querying, remote administration, and even automatic problem correction.

KEY TERMS

100BaseT — An Ethernet standard that provides a 100-Mbps baseband transfer rate over twisted-pair cabling. Also called Fast Ethernet.

10Base2 — An Ethernet standard that specifies a 10-Mbps baseband transmission over thin Ethernet (RG-58); the maximum transmission distance of any single segment is 185 meters.

10Base5 — An Ethernet standard that indicates a 10-Mbps baseband transmission over a maximum segment length of 500 meters; the type of cable used in this standard is called thick Ethernet or thicknet and uses RG-8 coaxial cable.

10BaseT — An Ethernet standard that specifies a 10-Mbps baseband transmission over twisted-pair cabling; the maximum segment length is 100 meters.

5–4–3 rule — The rule that stipulates that between stations on a LAN, there can be no more than five network segments connected, the maximum number of repeaters between the segments is four, and the maximum number of segments with stations on them is three.

802.2 — A standard of the IEEE that specifies the subdivision of the Logical Link Control sublayer from the Media Access Control (MAC) sublayer. These sublayers are part of the OSI Data Link layer.

802.3 — The IEEE standard that defines CSMA/CD or Ethernet networking.

802.5 — The IEEE standard that defines Token Ring networking.

802.11 — The IEEE standard that defines wireless LANs.

access layer — The layer in the three-layer network model that provides users access to the network. This is the layer in which end systems are connected to the network.

access method — The rules that determine which station can send data and how collisions are managed. The two most popular access methods are CSMA/CD and token-passing. Access method is also known as logical topology.

active monitor — The computer in a Token Ring network that is powered on first and that manages the beaconing process.

administration system — The centralized management component that collects and analyzes the information from the managers in a network-management system, such as SNMP or CMIP.

agent — The client software part of the management tool in a network-management system, such as SNMP or CMIP; responsible for collecting the information that is used by the management system; resides on each network device.

alternating current (AC) — Type of current that is delivered to homes and office buildings. It changes polarity cyclically as it is manufactured by power plants.

American National Standards Institute (ANSI) — The organization that guides the process of standardization by ensuring that consensus, openness, and due process are maintained during the development process. ANSI is responsible for the FDDI standard.

attachment unit interface (AUI) port — A 15-pin physical connector interface between a computer's network interface card (NIC) and an Ethernet network that uses 10Base5 (thicknet) coaxial cable. On 10Base5 Ethernet, the NIC uses the AUI to connect to a transceiver cable that in turn taps into the main cable.

backbone — Cabling used to connect wiring hubs in an extended star topology; typically, 62.5/125-micron multimode cable is used for this connection. However, 100-ohm UTP, 150-ohm STP, and single-mode fiber can also be used to connect wiring closets to wiring closets, wiring closets to the POP, and wiring closets between buildings; sometimes called vertical cable.

barrel connector — Used in coaxial networks; connects one coaxial cable segment to another, effectively forming a single cable.

4

baseband — A digital signal used in network transmissions where a single carrier frequency is used to transmit the signal.

beaconing — A fault-detection method implemented in Token Ring networks where stations broadcast packets to other stations on the ring in an attempt to find a break in the wire or a faulty interface.

BNC — A hardware connector for coaxial cable that has a cylindrical shell with two small knobs that allow it to be locked into place when twisted. Depending on the source, the letters BNC are said to stand for Bayonet Navy Connector, British Naval Connector, Bayonet Neill Concelman, or Bayonet Nut Connection. See also barrel connector.

bus — In the physical sense, a network topology where computers are daisy-chained together on the same coaxial cable segment; in the logical sense, refers to the CSMA/CD access method that sends data frames to all other stations simultaneously.

bus/star — A physical bus and physical star can be combined to form a star/bus or bus/star physical topology; hubs that have connectors for coaxial cable as well as twisted-pair wiring are used to form these types of networks. When different topologies are applied to a network, it is often called a mixed-media network.

cancellation — The desirable situation in which magnetic fields generated by two different wires carrying electronic signals cancel out each other; cancellation provides limited protection from crosstalk and external interference.

capacitive reactance — A naturally occurring opposition to voltage changes in a wire used for electronic signal transmission.

Carrier Sense Multiple Access/Collision Avoidance (CSMA/CA) — The network access method used by wireless LANs as outlined in IEEE 802.11. Nodes must first listen to a channel before transmitting. If the channel is busy, nodes configure a random backoff time to wait before transmitting.

CAT 1 — Category 1 unshielded twisted-pair (Cat 1 UTP) is a voice-grade only communication medium that should not be used as network media.

CAT 2 — Category 2 unshielded twisted-pair (Cat 2 UTP) is a voice- or data-grade medium that is rarely used in modern networks but that does have the rating to transmit up to 4 Mbps.

CAT 3 — Category 3 unshielded twisted-pair (Cat 3 UTP) is a voice- or data-grade medium that can transmit at 10 Mbps and that supports 10BaseT networking.

CAT 4 — Category 4 unshielded twisted-pair (Cat 4 UTP) supports voice or data and is capable of a 16-Mbps transmission rate.

CAT 5 — Category 5 unshielded twisted-pair (Cat 5 UTP) is the most popular installation medium today; this media type supports 100-Mbps transmission rates, but new standards attempt to achieve 1000 Mbps over CAT 5 cabling.

catchment area — The area serviced; for example, the area serviced by a wiring closet is the catchment area of that wiring closet.

cheapernet — A reference to RG-58 thin Ethernet cable.

circuit — Path in which electrical current can flow.

Common Management Information Protocol (CMIP) — A standard developed by the International Organization for Standardization (ISO) to provide a method for monitoring and managing network resources.

concentrator — A term used to describe a hub.

conductor — Material with low resistance to electron flow.

core layer — The layer that provides fast WAN connectivity for large network designs using the three-layer network model.

crosstalk — Signal bleed from one cable to another; this type of error usually occurs in poorly wired media.

distribution layer — Provides the backbone for a network; this layer is used in the three-layer network model to allow for access and protocol control and to increase security on the network.

EIA/TIA — *See* **Electronic Industries Alliance** and **Telecommunications Industry Association**.

EIA/TIA-568 — Defines and describes operational parameters for various grades of unshielded twisted-pair cabling.

EIA/TIA-568A — A wiring method used to indicate which colors are assigned to which pin for UTP cable.

EIA/TIA-568B — A wiring method used to indicate which colors are assigned to which pin for UTP cable.

EIA/TIA-569 — Describes various network media configurations, such as those for horizontal pathways, entrance facilities, wiring closets, equipment rooms, and workstations.

Electronic Industries Alliance (EIA) — The organization that provides standards that define how cabling should be configured on a network; often, these standards are done as a joint operation with the TIA.

Fast Ethernet — *See* 100BaseT.

Fiber Distributed Data Interface (FDDI) — Describes the general specifications for the use, installation, configuration, and limitations of fiber-optic networking; pronounced "fiddy;" this standard is the responsibility of ANSI.

Gigabit Ethernet — New 802.3 standard that allows 1-Gbps transmission, usually across fiber-optic cable.

hierarchical design — In network design methodology, a network that is structured in a layered hierarchical fashion, such as the one-layer, two-layer, and three-layer network models; the opposite would be a mesh design.

horizontal cabling — Media that connects workstations and wiring closets.

IEEE 802 — Standard that focuses on the Physical and Data Link layers of the OSI model; developed in February 1980.

impedance — Measure of the total opposition to electron flow, changes in current, and changes in voltage in cable; causes attenuation.

inductive reactance — Opposition to the changes of electrical current in a wire.

4

infrared — One of the wireless technologies defined in IEEE 802.11. This technology requires line-of-sight between the transmitter and receiver. It is low power but cannot be intercepted.

intermediate distribution facility (IDF) — Dependent upon the MDF in a star topology; another wiring closet used to support devices on a network.

jam signal — A 32-bit message to all computers on an Ethernet network that tells all stations not to transmit.

Logical Link Control (LLC) sublayer — A networking sublayer defined by the IEEE to further modularize the software functions versus the hardware functions (defined by the MAC sublayer) of the OSI Data Link layer.

logical topology — Describes the way a signal travels in a network, which is a function of the access method; the logical topology is usually a bus or a ring.

main distribution facility (MDF) — The central wiring closet in an extended star topology; typically, an MDF houses the POP, patch panel, and network-interconnection devices (bridges, routers, switches, repeaters, and concentrators).

Management Information Base (MIB) — A central repository of network statistics used by SNMP and CMIP; allows management protocols to maintain network statistics; can be modified to control workstations and other network devices.

manager — A centralized software component that is used to manage the network in a network management system, such as SNMP or CMIP.

Media Access Control (MAC) sublayer — A networking sublayer defined by the IEEE to further modularize the hardware functions versus the software functions (defined by the LLC sublayer) of the OSI Data Link layer.

media access method — *See* **access method**.

mesh design — In network design methodology, a network that has no organized structure; the opposite would be a hierarchical design.

mixed media — When different physical topologies are applied to a network, it is often called a mixed media network; for example, the bus and star topologies can be combined to form a star/bus or bus/star physical topology.

Multistation Access Unit (MAU) — The central device in a Token Ring architecture; forces the signal to be transmitted in a logical ring topology.

near end crosstalk (NEXT) — A measure of crosstalk performed at the location nearest the cable tester; the cable tester injects a signal of varying frequencies on a wire and measures signal bleed between other pairs of wires.

nearest active downstream neighbor (NADN) — The station on a Token Ring network that, during normal operations, receives the token from its nearest active upstream neighbor (NAUN).

nearest active upstream neighbor (NAUN) — The station on a Token Ring network that, during normal operations, passes the token to its NADN.

network access method — *See* **access method**.

network analyzer — A device that can collect and analyze information obtained by monitoring network traffic; may be able to query and manage network devices; also called protocol analyzer.

network architecture — A network's physical and logical topology, including its physical structure or layout, the media used, the network access method, and the standards and protocols employed.

network monitor — A program that collects information by monitoring network traffic; typically, does not have the advanced features of analysis and device management common to network analyzers.

4

one-layer network model — Includes WAN connectivity equipment and organizes a network so that it can be easily adapted to the two- and three-layer design models in the future.

oscillations — Undesirable, irregular signals (noise) riding on top of the desired signal.

patch cable — *See* **patch cord**.

patch cord — Cables used to terminate communication circuits in a wiring closet or between a workstation and a telecommunications outlet. See also cross-connect jumpers.

patch panel — A device that includes ports and pin locations used to connect devices in a wiring closet to devices on the network; acts as a switchboard for the network.

physical ring — *See* **ring**.

plenum — A space or enclosure in which air or gas is at a higher pressure than that of the outside atmosphere; a rating for network cable that specifies that the cable does not give off a toxic gas when burned.

point of presence (POP) — The point of interconnection between the telephone company and the building, floor, or company.

policy-based connectivity — A method that the network administrator uses to control access. The network administrator creates policies, such as "no video streaming is allowed at site 1," then implements them on the network, using equipment such as routers and switches.

protocol analyzer — *See* **network analyzer**.

punch tool — Used to punch down cable at the patch panel or RJ-45 wall jack; completes the connection while simultaneously removing excess wire.

radio frequency interference (RFI) — Electronic signal interference caused by radio transmissions.

Registered Jack (RJ) — A type of telecommunications connector that is used for twisted-pair cabling.

resistance — Opposition to the flow of electrons in a wire.

RG-58 — A type of thin coaxial cable that meets the 10Base2 Ethernet specification.

RG-8 — A type of thick coaxial cable that meets the 10Base5 Ethernet specification.

ring — A physical topology in which computers or other devices are connected in a circle or ring.

Service Access Point (SAP) — A protocol located in the Logical Link Control layer; defines how data can be passed up to higher layers.

shielded twisted-pair (STP) — Describes a type of cabling in which pairs of wires are twisted around one another inside a wire bundle; the wire bundle is then shielded by a foil coating, which protects it from external interference.

signal injector — Puts traffic on a wire so that a cable tester can measure attenuation and crosstalk.

signal reference ground — Zero-volt reference point on a computer cabinet or chassis; incoming signals are measured against this ground to determine if they are a "one" or a "zero."

spread spectrum — One of the wireless technologies defined in IEEE 802.11. This technology involves radio frequency transmission with the deliberate spreading of the signal over different frequencies.

star — Most popular physical topology in which computers are connected to a central device, usually a hub or a MAU.

star-bus — A network architecture that utilizes a physical star topology with a logical bus topology.

star-ring — A network architecture that utilizes a physical star topology with a logical ring topology.

T-connector — Used with coaxial cabling to connect a workstation NIC to a coaxial network.

Telecommunications Industry Association (TIA) — Provides standards that define how cabling should be configured on a network; often, these standards are done as a joint operation with the EIA.

terminator — A device used at the end of a coaxial segment to absorb a signal and prevent it from reflecting back along the wire.

thick Ethernet — *See* **thicknet**.

thicknet — An Ethernet networking standard that employs RG-8 coaxial cabling; a thicknet network can have segments of up to 500 meters and provides a 10-Mbps baseband transmission rate.

thin Ethernet — *See* **thinnet**.

thinnet — An Ethernet networking standard that employs RG-58 coaxial cabling; the specification includes a 10-Mbps baseband transmission rate and up to 185-meter segments.

three-layer network model — Divides a network into three connectivity layers: core, distribution, and access.

throughput — The observed transfer rate of a network; transfer rate is affected by device latency, network traffic, and capacity of source and destination to send and receive traffic.

time-domain reflectometer (TDR) — Cable tester that can detect the overall length of a cable or the distance to a cable break or opening by measuring the distance to where the signal is reflected anytime the wiring is open.

token-passing — A network access method that employs the use of a data token to enable a computer to transmit information.

transceiver — A device that converts a data signal into an electronic signal for transmission; designed to attach to a specific type of wiring or network media; transceivers for thinnet and UTP are on the NIC; transceivers for thicknet are usually attached to a vampire tap on the cable itself.

transformer — Device that steps voltage up or down where the hot lead originates and the neutral wire is grounded.

transmission time — Time that it takes a file to transfer from one location to another.

two-layer network model — Divides a network into two connectivity layers: core and access.

unshielded twisted-pair (UTP) — A type of cabling in which pairs of wires are twisted around one another inside a wire bundle.

vertical cabling — *See* backbone.

wire map — A function that displays the connections of UTP wiring from point to point; used to see if the connectors were properly wired.

wiring closet — A central junction point, usually located in a separate room, used for interconnecting various network devices.

REVIEW QUESTIONS

1. Which of the following UTP cable types are not rated for at least 10-Mbps transmissions? (Choose all that apply.)

   a. Category 1

   b. Category 2

   c. Category 3

   d. Category 4

   e. Category 5

2. Which of the following are true statements about Ethernet? (Choose all that apply.)

   a. Stations must have a token before they can transmit.

   b. Stations can transmit at anytime.

   c. Stations can detect collisions.

   d. Stations beacon during error conditions.

3. Which of the following devices extends the network at the Physical layer while serving as a central connection point?

   a. Active hub

   b. Router

   c. Gateway

   d. Passive hub

4. Which of the following are benefits to installing fiber-optic cable? (Choose all that apply.)

   a. Impervious to EMI

   b. Small diameter

   c. Easy to install

   d. Low cost

5. Which of the following is the correct specification for wireless technologies?

   a. 802.3

   b. 802.4

   c. 802.5

   d. 802.11

6. Which of the following is an advantage to using the bus topology?

   a. Centralized connection point

   b. Low implementation cost

   c. Ease of troubleshooting

   d. Fault tolerance

7. Which of the following specifications defines Token Ring?

   a. 568B

   b. 802.2

   c. 802.5

   d. 802.3

8. Which of the following can cause the complete failure of a star network?

   a. Failure of one station

   b. Break in a cable

   c. Failure of the hub

   d. Bad port on the hub

9. What does an active hub do that a passive hub does not?

   a. Connect media

   b. Route traffic

   c. Segment a network

   d. Repeat network signals

10. Which of the following is desirable as it relates to network media?

    a. High-voltage lines in close proximity

    b. Attenuation

    c. Cancellation

    d. Crosstalk

11. Which type of cable is usually required by fire codes?

    a. Voice-grade

    b. Plenum-grade

    c. CAT 1

    d. CAT 5

12. Which of the following is the most expensive type of cabling?

    a. Thinnet

    b. Coaxial

    c. Twisted-pair

    d. Fiber-optic

13. Which type of connector is used with twisted-pair cabling?

    a. BNC

    b. Barrel

    c. T-connectors

    d. RJ-45

14. Which of the following cables have shielding that protects them from EMI? (Choose all that apply.)

    a. Fiber-optic

    b. RG-58

    c. STP

    d. UTP

15. Which media should be installed if there is significant concern for the security of the data carried within?

    a. Thicknet

    b. Thinnet

    c. Fiber

    d. UTP

    e. STP

16. Which wireless technology requires line-of-sight between the transmitter and the receiver?

    a. Spread spectrum

    b. Direct sequencing

    c. Frequency-hopping

    d. Infrared

17. Which of the following describes a loss of signal strength over the length of a wire?

    a. Crosstalk

    b. Split pair

    c. Attenuation

    d. EMI

18. Which of the following are true of star topology cables? (Choose all that apply.)

    a. Patch cables connect the telecommunications outlet to the patch panel.

    b. The horizontal cable is terminated at the patch panel.

    c. The horizontal cable is terminated at the RJ-45 jack.

    d. The horizontal cable runs between hubs.

19. What is the main purpose of monitoring a network when there are no known problems on the network?

    a. Helps to pinpoint the location of a network bottleneck

    b. Allows you to establish a baseline for normal operations

    c. Increases network security

    d. Makes people more cautious

20. Which of the following devices can actually increase network traffic but do nothing to decrease it?

    a. Bridge

    b. Router

    c. Repeater

    d. Switch

21. At which layer of the three-layer network model should users connect to the network?

    a. Core

    b. Central

    c. Access

    d. Distribution

    e. Campus

22. Which of the following is also known as vertical cabling?

    a. Horizontal

    b. Parallel

    c. Backbone

    d. Serial

23. What is another name for the MDF and IDF?

    a. Backbone

    b. Vertical cabling

    c. Wiring closets

    d. Bandwidth

24. In a three–layer network model, each layer is part of a separate _____.

    a. LAN

    b. WAN

    c. organization

    d. broadcast domain

    e. area of responsibility

25. The cable that connects a workstation to a wall outlet is called _____.

    a. telecommunications connector

    b. vertical cable

    c. horizontal cable

    d. patch cable

26. In an organization in which multiple wiring closets are required, the central junction point for the wiring of the star topology will be located in the _____.

    a. MDF

    b. IDF

    c. workstation area

    d. catchment area

27. When the distance between wiring closets exceeds 500 meters, which of the following cable types could be used to traverse the distance without the use of intermediate wiring closets or connectivity devices?

    a. UTP

    b. STP

    c. Copper

    d. Fiber-optic cabling

28. When possible, the POP should be located near the _____.
    a. IDF
    b. workstation area
    c. MDF
    d. bathroom
29. The usable distance of the UTP cable between the MDF and IDF is
    _____.
    a. 90 meters
    b. 200 meters
    c. 150 meters
    d. 100 meters
30. If single-mode fiber-optic cable is used between the MDF and IDF, what is the maximum usable distance?
    a. 100 meters
    b. 1000 yards
    c. 3000 meters
    d. 2000 meters

CASE PROJECTS

1. Your company is sending you and your team to the Americanus Corporation to set up a 100BaseT network. Jennifer wants to know why 100BaseT and other star configurations are referred to as "star-bus" networks. Explain to her where "bus" comes from and how the CSMA/CD access method works to manage collisions.

2. Moe mentions that the token-passing access method can also look like a star. This topology is known as a "star-ring." Moe wants to know how "star-ring" networks differ from "star-bus" networks and how collisions are managed in the "star-ring" configuration.

3. Lisa has learned that determining the networking media is the most important network design decision. She wants to know which factors led to the decision of the Americanus Corporation to choose Category 5 UTP cable and the 100BaseT architecture. Discuss the advantages of using Category 5 UTP cable and the 100BaseT architecture.

4. You have just learned that the Americanus Corporation may decide to connect its new 100BaseT LAN to another LAN in a different building several miles away. What cable type can be used for this connection? Can you think of any other alternatives?

5. Jennifer has been asked to do a presentation for a Winslow Network client. The focus of the presentation is the different media included in the EIA/TIA-568 standards for backbone cabling. Tell her what cables to include, the distance limitations, and when and where to use these different cable types.

5

WAN CONCEPTS

After reading this chapter and completing the exercises, you will be able to:

♦ Describe WAN standards

♦ Explain the WAN connection methods

♦ Discuss WAN data link protocols

♦ Understand the WAN Physical layer

♦ Recognize the various WAN physical topologies

♦ Understand the purpose and operation of network address translation

---

The information in previous chapters was oriented toward local area networks (LANs). This chapter focuses on wide area networks (WANs) and the standards and devices specific to WAN communications. Throughout the chapter, the differences between LANs and WANs are highlighted.

WAN STANDARDIZATION

Wide area networks (WANs) differ from local area networks (LANs) in several ways. First, WANs connect geographically separate LANs. Second, WANs historically used low-speed connections over serial interfaces. This has changed in recent years as new WAN technologies have reached speeds in the gigabit per second range. Third, WAN standards differ from LAN standards at the Physical and Data Link layers of the OSI reference model. Fourth, WANs often carry more than just data. Other traffic types seen on WAN links include audio, video, and voice.

Several organizations contributed to the standardization of WAN technologies. These organizations created standards that applied to both the Physical and Data Link layers of WAN implementations:

- International Organization for Standardization (ISO)
- American National Standards Institute (ANSI)
- Electronic Industries Alliance (EIA)
- **Internet Engineering Task Force (IETF)**
- International Telecommunication Union-Telecommunication Standardization Sector (ITU-T)

 ITU-T was formerly the Consultative Committee for International Telegraph and Telephone (CCITT).

These organizations concentrated on standardizing the equipment and Data Link layer protocols used to transfer data over WAN connections. The standards applied to WANs are based on the type of facilities in which the WAN is expected to operate.

WAN Connection Methods

You can configure WAN connections in different ways. As the following section discusses, the type of connection partially determines the appropriate data link protocol for the connection. Networking standards recognize three different connection methods for WANs.

The first method is the dedicated point-to-point connection. Dedicated lines are also known as leased lines. The connection is made between two points and used only to transfer data between those two points. One office LAN connecting to another office LAN in a geographically separate location is an example of a dedicated point-to-point connection, as shown in Figure 5-1.

The second type of connection is a variation of the dedicated point-to-point connection. The only difference is that more than one dedicated point-to-point connection exists. This type of connection is called a multipoint facility connection, which is based on dedicated facilities, as shown in Figure 5-2.

Figure 5-1   Dedicated point-to-point facilities

Figure 5-2   Multipoint facility based on dedicated facilities

Dedicated lines provide service 24 hours a day, seven days a week. They can typically carry data, voice, and video. These different traffic streams are **multiplexed** onto a single physical line using **Time Division Multiplexing (TDM)**. Multiplexing refers to the combining of different traffic streams onto a single physical medium. Since this kind of service is expensive, it should be used when bandwidth is used in a constant and steady pattern, because you pay for the service even when no traffic is being transmitted. The most common dedicated service is a T1 line. T1s provide point-to-point connectivity at 1.544 Mbps.

The third connection type uses a switched WAN connection between facilities. This means that the communication path between the points is not necessarily the same each time. This type of connection is called a multiaccess switched service because none of the lines is dedicated. Instead, the service switches the lines as necessary, as shown in Figure 5-3.

Figure 5-3   Multiaccess switched services

The cloud that appears in Figure 5-3 represents a switched network, as it is labeled in the figure. The cloud illustrates that the network uses switched or unknown paths between connection points. This cloud also could represent the Internet because specific paths across the Internet are not defined.

The standards organizations also defined several types of data link protocols to be used with the WAN connections listed previously. These protocols are discussed next.

WAN Data Link Protocols

The data link protocols available for WAN communications define how networks will carry the data frames on a given data link. The data link protocols used for WANs come in three categories:

- Interface to IBM enterprise data centers: Synchronous Data Link Control (SDLC)

- WAN connections using peer devices: High-level Data Link Control (HDLC) and Point-to-Point Protocol (PPP)

- Switched or relayed services: X.25/Link Access Procedure Balanced (LAPB), Frame Relay, Integrated Services Digital Network (ISDN)/Link Access Procedure D-channel (LAPD), and Asynchronous Transfer Mode (ATM)

Some of these protocols provide functionality as high as in the Network layer of the OSI reference model, and all of these protocols transfer data over a WAN data link.

SDLC

IBM developed the **Synchronous Data Link Control (SDLC)** protocol in the 1970s to allow IBM host systems to communicate over WAN connections. IBM systems can use the SDLC protocol for point-to-point or point-to-multipoint connections between remote devices and a central mainframe computer. In SDLC, the network has one primary station and one or more secondary stations. SDLC networks always make connections between the primary station and one of the SDLC secondary stations because secondary stations cannot communicate with each other directly.

Cisco routers can interface with the IBM mainframe systems and pass native SDLC traffic via point-to-point serial links; also, other protocol traffic can be multiplexed with SDLC over those links. In addition, Cisco routers can encapsulate SDLC data frames into IP datagrams so that SDLC communications can traverse non-SDLC networks.

Communications over SDLC are **synchronous**, which means that the clock or timing mechanism between the source and destination must be synchronized. The synchronization is maintained by a bit pattern encoded into the **bit stream**. **Asynchronous**, the opposite of synchronous, means that timing devices are not required for transmission. In asynchronous communication, the bit stream is interpreted by start and stop bits. The destination uses the start and stop bits to ascertain where the transmission begins and ends. Because synchronous communication does not require start and stop bits, it is more efficient than asynchronous communication.

Other WAN protocols have been derived from the SDLC protocol. For example, the ISO developed High-level Data Link Control (HDLC) from SDLC. HDLC is the default protocol on WAN links.

HDLC

The **High-level Data Link Control (HDLC)** protocol is a superset of the SDLC protocol. Another name for HDLC is **Advanced Data Communication Control Procedures (ADCCP)**, which came from the American National Standards Institute (ANSI). However, the most widely accepted name for this protocol remains HDLC.

Devices can use HDLC for both point-to-point and multipoint connections. The protocol also supports **full-duplex** communication, which means that information can be transmitted and received simultaneously. HDLC also permits both synchronous and asynchronous communications. In **half-duplex** communication, devices can send data in both directions, but not simultaneously. With **simplex** transmissions, devices can send data in one direction only.

HDLC does not support multiple protocols (by default) because its packet structure does not have a field for indicating higher-layer protocols. However, Cisco's proprietary HDLC frame has a field that allows for the specification of a protocol type. The **Point-to-Point Protocol (PPP)** further extends the typical HDLC data frame by providing a protocol field.

Figure 5-4 illustrates the frame formats of HDLC, Cisco modified HDLC, and PPP.

Figure 5-4   HDLC and PPP

The following list details the common fields between these frame formats:

- **Flag**: Placed at the beginning and ending of a frame to mark the start and finish of that frame.

- **Address**: Indicates the destination address.

- **Control**: The sequence number that ensures that the data is handled and reassembled in correct order.

- **Frame Check Sequence (FCS)**: A field that calculates a checksum for the frame, which is used for error checking.

In the HDLC frame, the data field contains the information that is to be passed to the Network layer. In a PPP frame, the area occupied by data in HDLC identifies the encapsulated protocol and holds the Link Control protocol (LCP).

LCP is similar to the Logical Link Control (LLC) in the IEEE 802.2 definition for LAN protocols. PPP uses LCP to establish, configure, maintain, and terminate point-to-point connections. The data for the Network layer is also located inside the LCP.

PPP

As mentioned earlier, PPP extends the functionality of the HDLC protocol by providing Network layer protocol encapsulation. WAN devices commonly use PPP over dial-up or leased lines to provide connections to IP networks. However, because PPP makes use of **Network Control Protocols (NCPs)**, WAN devices can use it to transfer IP, IPX, AppleTalk, and other Network layer protocols over PPP connections.

 The **Serial Line Internet Protocol (SLIP)** was the predecessor to PPP; it only supported IP connections. PPP replaced SLIP because PPP is more efficient and because it supports more protocols and interfaces.

PPP is an Internet standard protocol defined in RFCs 2153 and 1661. The Internet Engineering Task Force (IETF) defined PPP to provide router-to-router, host-to-router, and host-to-host connections. You can use PPP over several different physical interfaces, including:

- Asynchronous serial

- ISDN/Synchronous serial

- High-Speed Serial Interface (HSSI)

Asynchronous serial connections are used with analog modems, which connect directly to existing phone lines and outlets in residential areas throughout the United States. ISDN/**Synchronous serial** connections require special modem (**ISDN modem**) equipment to interface with the **Integrated Services Digital Network (ISDN)** provided by many public carriers. HSSI is a serial device that was developed by

Cisco and T3Plus Networking. It defines a serial connection that operates at speeds of up to 52 Mbps over distances of up to 15 meters (50 feet), and is typically used to connect a router to a T3 line.

PPP and HDLC are both methods for accessing the services of WAN providers by using protocols that connect peer devices. In this context, "peer" means devices on the same level. The final group of protocols to discuss are those that provide switched or relayed services, such as X.25, ISDN, Frame Relay, and ATM.

 PPP configuration details are discussed in Chapter 11 of this book.

X.25/LAPB

X.25 is a CCITT (ITU-T) specification that describes the connection of PCs and terminals through packet-switching networks. Packet switching is a technology whereby individual packets, each with source and destination addresses, are routed through the network based on the best path. The packets may not necessarily take the same route. They are put back in order, if necessary, at the destination.

X.25 is one of the most widely implemented techniques for international communications because almost every country with a telephone system has an X.25 addressable network. In the United States, AT&T, Sprint, CompuServe, the Regional Bell Operating Companies (RBOCs), and others provide X.25 services.

X.25 provides communication between two points over **virtual circuits**. A virtual circuit is a logical circuit and not a dedicated physical link. The virtual circuit is a point-to-point connection across the WAN. Because the communication can travel any path inside the WAN switched network, the WAN is often indicated by a cloud.

Originally, X.25 was created to function over existing and unreliable analog telecommunications lines, so error correction and flow were built into the protocol. Although this provides a reliable transmission, it also negatively affects the performance of the protocol. X.25 originally (in 1992) had a throughput of 56 Kbps, but the CCITT revised the standard and boosted the throughput to 2 Mbps. Even so, up to 70 percent of the throughput is used for error checking.

The X.25 specification is older than the OSI model, so its terminology does not directly translate. However, the X.25 standard defines three layers that are similar to the lower three layers of the OSI model.

- Physical layer: Defines the physical and electrical interface from the computer or terminal to the attachment of the X.25 packet-switching network. The Physical layer is also known by its interface, either X.21 or RS-232-C (described later in this chapter). This layer is equivalent to the OSI Physical layer.

- Link Access layer: Defines the data-transmission and framing sequence. The actual name of the protocol used with X.25 communications is **Link Access Procedure Balanced (LAPB)**. This protocol was derived from HDLC. This layer is similar to the OSI Data Link layer.

- Packet layer: Is the virtual-circuit transmission through packet-switched networks. This layer describes a point-to-point connection as opposed to a point-to-multipoint connection. This layer is roughly equivalent to the OSI Network layer.

Figure 5-5 compares these X.25 layers with the OSI model.

Figure 5-5   OSI and X.25 layer comparison

Although X.25 is similar to the Frame Relay protocol, Frame Relay provides speed advantages over X.25, as the following section describes.

Frame Relay

Frame Relay is a Data Link layer protocol that the telecommunications companies created to improve upon the X.25 standard. Frame Relay is also a service. This protocol/service operates between 56 Kbps and 45 Mbps over a WAN connection, and relies on higher-layer protocols to provide error checking and flow control. Like X.25, Frame Relay is a packet-switching technology. Unlike X.25, which was created in the 1970s, Frame Relay assumes a more reliable connection provided by modern fiber and digital networks. Frame Relay shares bandwidth with other Frame Relay subscribers. In this sense, Frame Relay is not a dedicated service. Because it is not dedicated, it is less expensive than a leased line.

Frame Relay uses high-quality digital connections and is the fastest WAN-only protocol described in this chapter.

Frame Relay defines the connection between the **customer premises equipment (CPE)**, usually a router, and the service provider's local access switching equipment, or Frame Relay switch. Frame Relay services are available in the United States from telecommunications carriers such as MCI, Sprint, AT&T, and the RBOCs. Because Frame Relay is a Layer 2 protocol, it can operate over virtually any Physical layer interface. However, it is most often implemented between a router and a Frame Relay switch. The Frame Relay service provider supplies the Frame Relay switches.

 CPE is defined as both customer-premises equipment and customer-provided equipment. Both definitions indicate equipment under the customer's control.

5

Two types of virtual circuits, **switched virtual circuits (SVC)** and **permanent virtual circuits (PVC)**, connect Frame Relay ports. SVCs are controlled by software and are active only while a connection to the WAN is active. The software dials the WAN as required, establishes an SVC, and terminates the SVC that has the connection to the WAN when the communication ends. More often, Frame Relay connections are configured with PVCs, which (as their name implies) remain connected to the WAN. The PVC is defined manually by the network administrator and exists until it is manually removed. Frame Relay uses **statistical multiplexing** to allocate bandwidth to the virtual circuits. Statistical multiplexing is a method for transmitting several types of data simultaneously across a single line in which bandwidth is dynamically allocated to the virtual circuits on a packet-by-packet basis.

The network administrator and the telco define the following information when setting up a Frame Relay connection between a router and a Frame Relay switch.

- **Access Rate**: The speed of the line that indicates transfer rate. Common U.S. access rates are 64 Kbps and 128 Kbps, which are provided by Integrated Service Digital Network (ISDN) connections, and 1.544 Mbps, which are provided by **T1** connections.

- **Committed Information Rate (CIR)**: The minimum average transfer rate of the Frame Relay circuit. This is usually lower than the access rate because the transfer rate may exceed the CIR during short bursts. This is the most important parameter.

- **Committed Burst Size (CBS)**: The maximum amount of data bits that the service provider agrees to transfer in a set period under normal conditions.

- **Excess Burst Size (EBS)**: The amount of excess traffic (over the CBS) that the network will attempt to transfer during a set period. The network can discard EBS data, if necessary.

- **Data Link Connection Identifier (DLCI)**: Pronounced *dell-see*, this is configured on the router and used to identify the PVCs and SVCs. In this way, DLCI identifies which path leads to a specific Network layer address (i.e., IP address). The DLCI is not a network-wide unique address, as is a MAC address; instead, the DLCI is only locally significant, meaning that it can, and usually does, change on each physical link.

- **Local Management Interface (LMI)**: A standard signaling mechanism between the CPE and the Frame Relay connection. The LMI can provide the network server with a local DLCI and give DLCI global (network wide) significance rather than merely local significance. In addition, it can provide keep-alive and status information to the end user (router) regarding the connections. The LMI also uses inverse ARP to automatically determine the protocol address of remote devices.

- **Discard-Eligible (DE)**: Certain frames can be configured at the router as discard-eligible; thus, during times of congestion, DE frames are discarded in order to provide a higher, more reliable, service to those frames that are not discard-eligible.

Frame Relay switches attempt to control congestion on the network. When congestion is recognized, the Frame Relay switch sends a **Forward Explicit Congestion Notification (FECN)** message to the destination. This message tells a router that congestion was experienced on the virtual circuit. In addition, the switch sends a **Backward Explicit Congestion Notification (BECN)** message to the transmitting or source router. In response to the BECN, the router should reduce the amount of traffic it is sending.

When the sum of the data arriving over all virtual circuits exceeds the access rate, the situation is called oversubscription. This can occur when the CIR is exceeded by burst traffic from the virtual circuits. Oversubscription results in dropped packets. In such a case, the dropped packets must be retransmitted.

Frame Relay configuration details are discussed in Chapter 12 of this book.

As mentioned, Frame Relay can be connected over ISDN connections. Although ISDN can host Frame Relay, it can be used for WAN connections without Frame Relay as well. The following section describes ISDN.

ISDN/LAPD

ISDN is a circuit switching technology. This means there is a dedicated circuit for the length of the transmission. All data takes the same path. Regular phone calls are circuit switched. Circuit switching is usually preferred for data that must be received in real-time, such as video streaming. Network devices can use ISDN over existing digital telephone lines to transmit both voice and data. **B-channels (bearer-channels)** transmit the data and **D-channels (data-channels)**, maintain ISDN connections. ISDN service is available from most communication providers in the United States, including Sprint, MCI, AT&T, and the RBOCs.

There are two basic service levels for ISDN connections: **Primary Rate Interface (PRI)** and **Basic Rate Interface (BRI)**. PRI provides a throughput of up to 1.544 Mbps over its 23 B-channels and single 64 Kbps D-channel, whereas BRI provides two B-channels at 64 Kbps each and one D-channel at 16 Kbps. This means that BRI provides a throughput of 128 Kbps because the 16 Kbps line is used to control the connection. The **Link Access Procedure D-channel (LAPD)** protocol specification developed by the CCITT (ITU-T) defines the method of using the D-channel to control communications. The CCITT derived this protocol from the HDLC protocol.

ISDN connections also can provide X.25 and Frame Relay connections. ISDN configuration is discussed in Chapter 11 of this book.

Another protocol used to connect LANs is considered both a WAN and a LAN protocol. This technology is called ATM.

ATM

Asynchronous Transfer Mode (ATM) is a communications protocol that is used within and between LAN connections. Telecommunications companies based the ATM on the foundations of Frame Relay, although ATM is circuit-oriented in the sense that ATM cells follow the same path for the duration of the connection. ATM provides high-speed data transmission rates for voice, data, video, audio, and imaging. Public carriers such as Sprint and AT&T offer ATM.

ATM requires devices capable of ATM communications. Cisco 4000, 7000, and 7500 router families support ATM communications. ATM communications can be conducted over T1, **fractional T1**, and **T3** lines. ATM can be used between LANs as a WAN connection, within LANs as a backbone, and/or wired directly to desktops using ATM NICs and hubs.

ATM is similar to Frame Relay and X.25 in that it runs over a switched service. Also, like Frame Relay, ATM does not provide the redundant error checking that X.25 utilizes. Unlike both Frame Relay and X.25, the ATM packets (called cells) have a fixed length (53 bytes). The fixed length of each cell allows ATM to efficiently plan and disperse packets quickly. (Variable-length packets can introduce traffic delays.) ATM switching is implemented in the hardware, making it much faster than the other switching techniques covered in this section. Currently, ATM can reach speeds of 10 Gbps.

Since ATM can be used both between LANs and inside LANs, it is not just a WAN protocol. The fastest WAN-only protocol presented in this chapter is Frame Relay.

WAN Physical Layer

Thus far, you have learned about Data Link layer components and standards that apply to WAN connections. However, WAN standards apply to both the Data Link and Physical layers of the OSI model. In this section, you learn more about the connections, equipment, and standards in the physical connections of the WAN.

As described, WAN connections usually require service from a telecommunications provider, such as AT&T, MCI, or Sprint, over their **Public Switched Telephone Network (PSTN)**. Connections to the PSTN involve several pieces of equipment both at the customer location and the phone-company locations.

WAN Connections

WANs provide connections between two LANs. The WAN moves data and packets between routers at each end of the LANs that are supported by the WAN connection. RBOCs, or other telecommunications providers such as AT&T, MCI, and Sprint, provide these WAN connections.

Figure 5-6 illustrates the equipment commonly used to create a connection between two LANs.

Figure 5-6　WAN connection devices

Typically, two devices reside at the customer location—the **channel service unit/data service unit (CSU/DSU)** and the router. The CSU/DSU provides the connection from the customer site to the telecommunications company network. The CSU/DSU is the provider's side of the WAN link. The router provides the connection between the LAN and the CSU/DSU. The router is the subscriber's side of the WAN link.

The CSU/DSU is the interface between the DTE and the DCE. In some cases, the CSU/DSU is built into the router.

As shown in the graphic, the router is also called **data terminal equipment (DTE)**. A DTE can also be a computer or some other type of terminal; in all cases, it is a device at the user end of the network. The CSU/DSU is also called **data circuit-terminating equipment (DCE)**. A DCE can be a modem or a **terminal adapter (TA)**. In all cases, the DCE is a physical connection at the end of the WAN connection.

The **demarc**, or **demarcation**, is the next link in the chain from the DCE to the WAN. The demarc is the point at which the telecommunications company facility (POP) connects to the DCE. The connection between the demarc and the telephone company (WAN service provider) office is called the **local loop** or last mile.

The **Central Office (CO) switch** is the telecommunications company location that is the point of entry into the **toll network**. The toll network consists of the PSTN, including all the switches and trunks that comprise it. The toll network is so named because the telecommunications company bills the client to use the network. Billing can either be a flat fee or a rate based on usage.

5

Most of the connections between two LANs over a PSTN are the responsibility of the telecommunications company. Typically, the network administrator is responsible for the WAN connection from the router (DTE) up to the CSU/DSU (DCE). These connections are defined in the Physical layer standards for WAN connections.

WAN Physical Standards

As you have learned, WAN standards describe communications at both the Physical layer and Data Link layer of the OSI model. The standards that focus on the Physical layer WAN connection center around the interface between the DTE and DCE—usually a serial interface.

The following is a list of the telecommunication standards that apply to the Physical layer WAN serial interface between the DTE and DCE devices:

- EIA/TIA-232: Also known as RS-232. Version numbers, such as RS-232-C and EIA/TIA-232-E, can follow both of these. This specification defines the interface for the connection between DTE and DCE data-communications devices. RS-232 can transfer data at up to 56 Kbps. RS-232 connections are made with 25-pin or 9-pin, D-shaped connectors. These connectors are known as DB-25 and DB-9 respectively. Most personal computers have an RS-232 interface.

- EIA/TIA-449: Also known as RS-449. This standard defines a faster serial interface version of RS-232. RS-449 can transfer data up to 2 Mbps. RS-449 connections are made by DB-37 connectors.

- EIA-530: The successor to RS-449. It is also known as the RS-530 specification. RS-530 defines the connection between DTEs and DCEs. Like EIA/TIA-449, this specification allows for up to 2 Mbps connection rates over the same DB-25 connectors that are used for RS-232 connections. However, RS-232 and RS-530 are not compatible standards.

- High-Speed Serial Interface (HSSI): Cisco and T3Plus Networking developed the HSSI standard. It operates at speeds of up to 52 Mbps over distances of up to 15 meters (50 feet). The cable is typically shielded twisted pair and the interface is a 50-pin connector.

- V.24: A list of definitions for interfaces between DTE and DCE to PSTNs.

- V.35: Used to define the trunk interface between a packet network and a network access device. The specification provides data-transfer rates up to 4 Mbps for DTE to DCE communication equipment that interfaces high-speed digital carriers.

- X.21: Defines the interface between the DTE and DCE for synchronous communication.

- G.703: The ITU-T recommended the G.703 standard to define European connections of 2.048 Mbps. It also includes specifications for the U.S. 1.544 Mbps transmission rates. This 1984 standard defines the physical and logical transfer of information over digital networks.

WAN TOPOLOGIES

You can use different topologies to create WAN connections. These topologies are the peer, the star, the partial mesh, and the full mesh (see Figure 5-7).

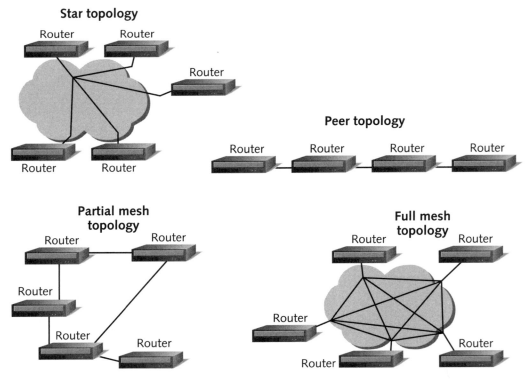

Figure 5-7   WAN topologies

The peer topology is like the bus LAN topology. Nodes are just strung along in a daisy-chained fashion. Very often, there will only be two routers connected. This is the simplest WAN topology. It is the least expensive and is easy to configure. The disadvantage to the peer WAN topology is that a failure between nodes will affect the WAN because there is no redundancy.

The star is the most popular WAN topology. This configuration is also called the hub-and-spoke topology because one router functions as a central point, or hub, in a simple hierarchical configuration. All other devices are connected to the central router as spokes would connect to a hub. Typically the network administrator will configure the central router with a single interface that makes a multipoint connection to all other routers.

The full mesh is the most expensive topology to implement because each router has a direct connection to every other router. However, this topology is the most fault-tolerant because there are always at least two routes to every router on the network. The more routers added to the full mesh, the more expensive the topology becomes, because multiple routes are required for each router.

The partial mesh is a compromise between the hierarchy of the star and the expense of the full mesh. A partial mesh is not as expensive as a full mesh because the principle of connecting every router to every other router is not required. Instead, connections are made according to need and traffic flow. If there is heavy traffic flow to one router, multiple circuits may be established between that router and the routers sending the most traffic to it. The partial mesh does not follow the hierarchical structure of the star, in that all routers do not have to be connected to a single central router.

NETWORK ADDRESS TRANSLATION

Network Address Translation (NAT) allows many home users, corporations, and organizations around the world to connect far more computers to the Internet than they would have otherwise been able to connect. NAT is defined in RFC 3022, which describes methods for connecting private (internal) IP addresses to the Internet. In Chapter 3 you learned that Private IP addresses could not be routed on the Internet, which is correct. However, NAT uses a one-to-one mapping or one-to-many mapping method to allow one or more private IP clients to gain access to the Internet using their own private IP address range.

Cisco developed NAT, and today the technology is used by routers, firewalls, and even individual computers with multiple network connections. There are two forms of NAT available:

- Static NAT
- Dynamic NAT

Static NAT

Static NAT is the simplest form of NAT in which a single private IP address is mapped to a single public IP address. For example, a router could be configured to translate all communications from the internal 192.168.0.1 address to the address 209.86.192.197. In this way, when the host 192.168.0.1 accesses the Internet, the router will translate its IP address as 209.86.192.197. The router will then translate communications between that host and any system on the Internet. Therefore, all Internet devices will be communicating with host 209.86.192.197, but the actual packets will be forwarded by the NAT router to host 192.168.0.1 on the local network.

In order for the NAT router to translate communications between the internal a external network, it must maintain a table in memory that maps internal IP addresses to addresses presented to the Internet (external addresses). With Static NAT, the mapping is one-to-one. For example, internal address 192.168.0.1 mapped to 209.86.192.197 and 192.168.0.2 mapped to 209.86.192.198, and so on.

The network configuration for NAT is quite simple in a small network because the NAT router will be the default gateway for all clients. In a larger network, the NAT router might be one of many routers on the network. Routers would have to be configured to use the NAT router for Internet communications.

When the local host 192.168.0.1 communicates with other hosts on the internal network (intranet), NAT will not be involved. For example, when host 192.168.0.1 sends packets to host 192.168.0.15, the packets will not go through the router. This is also true if the local host communicates with other hosts on different networks or subnetworks within the intranet. The router, even if enabled with NAT, will act as a router, sending packets to the appropriate internal network.

Dynamic NAT

Dynamic NAT means that the NAT router automatically maps a group of valid Internet IP addresses to a group of local IP addresses, as needed. This means that the network administrator really doesn't care which IP address the internal clients utilize, just that they are able to get an address. The network administrator also doesn't have to spend any time defining specific one-to-one mappings between the public and private IP addresses. Any private IP addressed host will be able to contact the NAT router (or server) and will automatically be translated to one of the available Internet IP addresses by the NAT router. The administrator need only define the internal and external IP ranges on the router.

Overloading

Overloading is a form of dynamic NAT that uses **port address translation (PAT)**. PAT allows multiple internal, unregistered IP addresses to use a single external registered address. In order to differentiate between the connections, PAT uses multiple public TCP and UDP ports to create unique sockets that map to internal IP addresses. The socket, as you learned earlier, is a combination of the IP address and port. For example, you may communicate with a Web server with IP address 209.120.178.205 over TCP port 80. The socket for that communication is 209.120.178.205:80 representing the IP address and port. When that Web server contacts your hosts, it will call your local IP address and the TCP socket you indicated in your three-way handshake, as you learned in Chapter 3. Now, assume that you have five clients on your LAN all communicating with different Web servers, but your NAT router only has one valid Internet IP address. How can the NAT router keep track of where the packets should be sent? The simple answer is by using PAT, which maps internal addresses and ports to the same external address but with different communication ports.

Consider the following example while referring to the sample NAT mapping table (Table 5-1). Assume an organization has five internal clients—Hosts A – E with IP address ranges 192.168.0.1 – 192.168.0.5. The organization also has a Web server at 192.168.0.100 hosting connections from Internet clients. The NAT server uses **port forwarding** to send connections from external clients to the Web server on the internal network. Hosts A, B, and C are communicating with a Web server that has the address 209.120.178.205 over port 80, which is socket 209.120.178.205:80. Host D is communicating with an FTP server with IP address 64.247.37.221 over TCP ports 21 and 20. Host E is connected to a Web server at 64.46.108.24. Each internal host had to supply one or more ports when it established communications. The organization only has one Internet IP available and that is 209.86.192.198.

Table 5-1 NAT mapping table

Host	Local Socket	Translated Socket	Remote Socket
A	192.168.0.1:1025	209.86.192.198:1025	209.120.178.205:80
B	192.168.0.2:1027	209.86.192.198:1026	209.120.178.205:80
C	192.168.0.3:1025	209.86.192.198:1027	209.120.178.205:80
D	192.168.0.4:1512	209.86.192.198:1049	64.247.37.221:21
D	192.168.0.4:1513	209.86.192.198:1050	64.247.37.221:20
E	192.168.0.5:1025	209.86.192.198:1029	64.46.108.24:80
Internal web server	192.168.0.100:80	209.86.192.198:80	72.13.15.24:1099

In Table 5-1, you can see how the NAT router would keep track of these individual connections uniquely. The local sockets will always be unique because the local hosts have unique IP addresses, even though they may end up using similar port numbers. Remote sockets called may be the same because multiple internal hosts can call the same external host. The only item that the NAT router has to make unique is the translated socket. The NAT router does this by not duplicating a port number for the unique IP addresses that it is configured to use. In the example above, the NAT router is configured to use a single IP address, making sure there is no port number duplication in the translated sockets. However, many NAT routers can be configured to utilize multiple public addresses and would therefore just have to ensure that the translated sockets were unique.

For example, if the NAT router had IP address 209.86.192.198 and 209.86.192.199 as public addresses, it could use dynamic port 1027 twice: once in socket 209.86.192.198:1027 and again in socket 209.86.192.199:1027.

Overlapping

Overlapping occurs in a situation where the internal network has been incorrectly configured for an IP range that actually exists on the Internet (registered to another entity). This problem usually only occurs when uninformed network engineers configure a network using arbitrary addresses. Sometimes the thought is that a connection to the Internet will never be required. In this case, the organization cannot connect directly to the Internet because it has an invalid IP range (registered to someone else). This overlapping problem can be solved using NAT because NAT hides the incorrectly configured internal IP scheme. The NAT router must be configured to translate the internal IP addresses to a valid external address or address range (actually available to the organization). This is really no different than previous forms of NAT except that the organization's internal IP address range really belongs to someone else (the "someone else" just doesn't know about it because those addresses are never exposed to the Internet – thanks to NAT). Most companies don't run into this problem because their network engineers and designers know to utilize one of the private IP address ranges (10.x.x.x, 172.16.x.x. – 172.31.x.x, and 192.168.x.x.) when configuring a private internal TCP/IP network.

CHAPTER SUMMARY

❑ WANs connect LANs in geographically separate areas.

❑ WAN connections typically function at the Physical and Data Link layers of the OSI reference model, and are made over serial connections.

❑ WAN connections are lower speed than LAN connections, and can be made as point-to-point, point-to-multipoint, and switched WAN connections.

❑ You can use several different data link protocols for WAN connections. The different types of WAN connections are: (1) interfaces to IBM mainframes provided by SDLC; (2) WAN connections using peer devices with HDLC and PPP; and (3) switched or relayed services including X.25, Frame Relay, ATM, and ISDN.

❑ X.25 is the oldest of the switched or relayed services and provides the least-efficient service because of its excessive error checking.

❑ Frame Relay is an enhancement over X.25 because it is faster and does not provide redundant error checking.

❑ ATM is similar to Frame Relay, except that it uses fixed-length cells instead of variable-length packets. In addition, the ATM protocol can be used on LANs as well as WANs.

❑ ISDN is a leased digital line that can support X.25 and Frame Relay connections, among others.

❑ ISDN comes in PRI and BRI levels. BRI only provides 128 Kbps throughput over two B-channels, and 16 Kbps over one D-channel that is used for controlling the connection. PRI provides 23 B channels of 64 Kbps each and one 64 Kbps D-channel for controlling the connection. This allows PRI to offer 1.544 Mbps throughput.

❑ The Physical layer WAN connections concern the interface between the DTE and DCE.

❑ The DTE is the endpoint of the user's network, which connects to the WAN interface. This is typically a router, computer, or terminal of some type. The WAN service provider usually provides the DCE, which is often a CSU/DSU, modem, or terminal adapter. The DCE is then connected to a demarc, which is a communications facility owned by the WAN service provider. The local loop is the connection (usually copper cable) that connects the demarcation to the WAN service provider's CO switch, which is actually part of the toll network or PSTN.

❑ The physical WAN topologies are: the peer, which is simply customer facilities connected in a daisy-chained fashion; the star, which involves connecting remote customer facilities to a central facility; the full mesh, which connects every location to every other location; and the partial mesh, which provides redundancy only where necessary.

❑ NAT is a technology that allows organizations to map valid external addresses to private or unregistered internal addresses. This allows organizations to maintain a separation between the Internet and the intranet (internal network) while still providing access to the Internet.

❑ Organizations can use NAT to allow many more people to access the Internet by sharing one or more valid public addresses.

KEY TERMS

Access Rate — The speed of the line that indicates transfer rate; common U.S. access rates are 64 Kbps and 128 Kbps, provided by Integrated Service Digital Network (ISDN) connections, and 1.544 Mbps, provided by T1 connections.

address — A field that indicates the destination address of the frame.

Advanced Data Communication Control Procedures (ADCCP) — The ANSI standard for HDLC.

asynchronous — Asynchronous communications rely on start and stop bits to define the end-points of a transmission; timing mechanisms are not needed to maintain clock synchronization between the source and destination.

asynchronous serial — Serial connections that are employed in most modems connected to residential phone lines.

Asynchronous Transfer Mode (ATM) — A networking implementation for both high-speed LAN and WAN connectivity.

Backward Explicit Congestion Notification (BECN) — When congestion is recognized, the Frame Relay switch sends a BECN message to the source router; should reduce the amount of traffic that is sent by the router.

Basic Rate Interface (BRI) — An ISDN service that provides two B-channels for data transfers up to 128 Kbps and one D-channel to control the communications.

B-channel (bearer channels) — An ISDN channel used to carry data; two or more B-channels, each supporting 64 Kbps, are provided with ISDN service.

bit stream — The stream of bits, or data, that flows between a source (transmitter) and a destination (receiver); can be communicated by synchronous or asynchronous methods.

Central Office (CO) switch — The telecommunications company location that is part of the PSTN or toll network; point of entry to the toll network from the demarc.

channel service unit/data service unit (CSU/DSU) — A telecommunications company device that provides connectivity between the WAN service provider network and the customer's LAN.

Committed Burst Size (CBS) — The maximum amount of data bits that the service provider agrees to transfer in a set period under normal conditions.

Committed Information Rate (CIR) — The minimum average transfer rate of the Frame Relay circuit; usually lower than the access rate because the transfer rate may exceed the CIR during short bursts.

control — A sequence number that ensures the data is handled and reassembled properly.

customer premises equipment (CPE) — Equipment under the customer's control; also known as customer-provided equipment, depending on the publication.

data circuit-terminating equipment (DCE) — Typically, the telecommunications-provided device on the customer side that allows the customer to connect to the WAN; often, a CSU/DSU, but can also be a modem or TA.

Data Link Connection Identifier (DLCI) — Pronounced *dell-see*, information in a Frame Relay connection that is configured on the router and used to identify which path leads to a specific Network Layer address (i.e., IP address). The DLCI is only locally significant, meaning that it can, and usually does, change on each Physical Link.

data terminal equipment (DTE) — A customer device that is used to connect to the telecommunications company equipment. This device is typically a router, but it can also be a computer or other type of terminal.

D-channel (data channel) — The control channel used in ISDN communications; can be 16 to 64 Kbps.

demarc — Location that is the responsibility of the telecommunications provider and that connects to the nearest telephone company office.

demarcation — *See* **demarc**.

Discard-Eligible (DE) — During times of congestion, DE frames are discarded in order to provide a higher, more reliable service to those frames that are not discard-eligible.

dynamic NAT — A type of network address translation in which the valid external IP addresses to be mapped to internal addresses are floating or not-fixed. The NAT router can then dynamically assign any of the available external addresses to any of the hosts on the internal network.

Excess Burst Size (EBS) — The amount of excess traffic (over the CBS) that the network will attempt to transfer during a set period; can be discarded by the network, if necessary.

flag — A field placed at the beginning and end of an HDLC and PPP frame to mark the beginning and end of the frame.

Forward Explicit Congestion Notification (FECN) — Message sent to the destination router on a frame relay circuit that tells the router that congestion was experienced on the virtual circuit.

fractional T1 — Instead of leasing a full T1 connection, customers may decide to lease the less-expensive fractional T1 connections. Connections range from one 64 Kbps channel up to the full T1 connection of 24 channels.

Frame Check Sequence (FCS) — A field in a frame that calculates a checksum for the frame, which is used for error checking.

Frame Relay — A Data Link layer protocol that relies on high-speed, reliable connections; can operate between 56 Kbps and 45 Mbps over a WAN connection.

full-duplex — A connection that allows communication in two directions simultaneously.

half-duplex — A connection that allows communication in two directions, but not simultaneously.

High-level Data Link Control (HDLC) — A superset of the SDLC protocol; a WAN protocol that can be used for both point-to-point and multi-point connections.

Integrated Services Digital Network (ISDN) — A service provided by most major telecommunication carriers, such as AT&T, Sprint, and the RBOCs; operates over existing phone lines and transfers both voice and data.

Internet Engineering Task Force (IETF) — Organization that defines Internet operating protocols; defines the serial line protocols PPP and SLIP.

ISDN modem — A modem used in ISDN communications that must be installed at ISDN subscriber locations.

Link Access Procedure Balanced (LAPB) — A derivative of the HDLC WAN protocol; adapted to provide WAN services over X.25 networks.

Link Access Procedure D-channel (LAPD) — A WAN protocol adapted from HDLC; used in communications over ISDN lines.

local loop — The connection between the demarcation and the telephone company (WAN service provider) office.

5

Local Management Interface (LMI) — A standard signaling mechanism between the CPE and the Frame Relay connection; can provide the network server with a local or global DLCI; can provide keep-alive and status information to the Frame Relay connection.

multiplexed — Combining different traffic streams onto a single physical medium. The traffic is separated (demultiplexed) at the receiving end.

Network Address Translation (NAT) — A method for using a router to separate an internal network from an external network (usually the Internet), which is defined in RFC 3022. Internal hosts with private or unregistered IP addresses can effectively utilize one or more public registered IP addresses to communicate with external systems.

Network Control Protocol (NCP) — A functional field that contains codes, which indicate the type of protocol that is encapsulated; allows PPP to encapsulate multiple protocols including IP, IPX, and AppleTalk.

Overlapping — A type of NAT used when an organization wants to connect to the Internet, but its internal addressing scheme is registered to another entity. Instead of renumbering the internal network, the organization uses NAT to translate its private addressing scheme to the addresses that it was assigned by the InterNIC or its ISP.

Overloading — A type of NAT that allows multiple internal hosts to utilize one or more external IP addresses. The NAT router uses a table to keep track of the IP addresses and ports of each host, dynamically mapping each internal socket to a valid external socket.

permanent virtual circuit (PVC) — A connection to the WAN that is established by the network administrator at the customer location; not expected to be terminated and therefore remains active.

Point-to-Point Protocol (PPP) — An Internet standard WAN protocol defined in RFCs 2153 and 1661; used to provide router-to-router, host-to-router, and host-to-host WAN connections.

port address translation (PAT) — A process used in overloading that allows multiple internal, unregistered IP addresses to use a single external registered address.

port forwarding — A method for sending packets from an external host system through a firewall or NAT router to an internal device. In this way, the internal device IP address is hidden from the external network and yet the internal device can still service requests from the external network.

Primary Rate Interface (PRI) — An ISDN service that provides 23 B-channels for data transfers up to 1.544 Mbps and one D-channel for controlling communications.

Public Switched Telephone Network (PSTN) — A telecommunications network that connects telephones around the country.

Serial Line Internet Protocol (SLIP) — A protocol that was originally used for IP connections over serial lines. It was replaced by the more efficient and versatile PPP.

simplex — A circuit that is unidirectional is called simplex because data can only be transmitted in one direction.

static NAT — A type of network address translation (NAT) that allows for a one-to-one mapping of internal to external addresses. One internal address is mapped to one specific external address.

statistical multiplexing — A method for transmitting several types of data simultaneously across a single line; bandwidth is dynamically allocated to the virtual circuits on a packet-by-packet basis

switched virtual circuit (SVC) — A temporary virtual circuit created when a network device calls the WAN to establish a connection; is terminated when the connection is terminated.

synchronous — Communications that rely on a clock. The clock of the source and destination must be synchronized so that the destination can pick up and interpret the transmitted frames correctly.

Synchronous Data Link Control (SDLC) — A protocol that was developed by IBM in the 1970s to allow IBM host systems to communicate over WAN connections; can be used for point-to-point or point-to-multipoint connections between remote devices and a central mainframe.

synchronous serial — The type of serial connection used with ISDN lines.

T1 — A leased line from a telecommunications carrier capable of carrying both voice and data with a 1.544 Mbps bandwidth.

T3 — A leased line from a telecommunications carrier that provides the bandwidth of 28 T1 connections, which equals 44.736 Mbps.

terminal adapter (TA) — An adapter that allows non-ISDN terminals to operate on ISDN lines.

Time Division Multiplexing (TDM) — A method for transmitting several types of data simultaneously across a single line; each path (circuit) has dedicated bandwidth allocated to that particular circuit for the duration of the call; less efficient than statistical division multiplexing.

toll network — A section of a WAN that is owned by a telecommunications provider; a monthly billed connection or a per-minute billed connection for the customer.

virtual circuit — Point-to-point connections through a switched network.

REVIEW QUESTIONS

1. Which of the following WAN services operates over existing telephone lines to provide voice and data communications?

   a. SDLC

   b. Frame Relay

   c. ISDN

   d. ATM

2. Which of the following is true about Frame Relay communication? (Choose all that apply.)

   a. Provides higher-speed communications over WAN links than X.25.

   b. Is slightly less efficient than X.25.

   c. Uses highly reliable digital facilities.

   d. Provides host-to-router and router-to-router communications.

3. Which of the following is the provider's end of the WAN link?

   a. DTE

   b. Computer

   c. DCE

   d. Dumb terminal

4. Which two devices would be considered part of the Physical layer for WAN equipment?

   a. Routers and hubs

   b. DTE and DCE

   c. Gateways and hubs

   d. Hubs and switches

5. Which of the following connection types can PPP support? (Choose all that apply.)

   a. Router-to-router

   b. Host-to-router

   c. Host-to-host

   d. Asynchronous

   e. Synchronous

6. Which of the following can HDLC support? (Choose all that apply.)

   a. Point-to-point

   b. Multipoint

   c. Synchronous

   d. Asynchronous

   e. Full-duplex

   f. Half-duplex

7. Which of the following is a data link protocol used for connecting LANs in geographically separate areas? (Choose all that apply.)

   a. TCP

   b. PPP

   c. OSPF

   d. Frame Relay

8. Which of the following data link protocols is most closely associated with the X.25 specification?

   a. LAPB

   b. LAPD

   c. PPP

   d. Frame Relay

9. Which of the following defines how frames are formatted and transmitted between systems on a single WAN link?

   a. Physical layer WAN standards

   b. Data Link layer WAN standards

   c. Network layer WAN standards

   d. Application layer WAN standards

10. In WAN communications, which of the following identifies the device that is located at the user's end of the WAN?

    a. DTE

    b. DCE

    c. CSU/DSU

    d. TA

11. A modem is an example of a DCE in a WAN connection. True or False?

12. Which of the following data link protocols is most closely associated with the ISDN specification?

    a. LAPB

    b. LAPD

    c. PPP

    d. Frame Relay

13. A computer is an example of a DTE in a WAN connection. True or False?

14. Which of the following can make use of ISDN lines? (Choose all that apply.)

    a. Frame Relay

    b. LAPD

    c. X.25

    d. SDLC

15. Which of the following WAN protocols was developed specifically to connect mainframe computers?

    a. PPP

    b. SDLC

    c. Frame Relay

    d. ISDN

16. WAN standards typically provide definitions for which two layers of the OSI model? (Choose all that apply.)

    a. Physical

    b. Data Link

    c. Application

    d. Presentation

    e. Transport

17. Which of the following defines communications that can flow in two directions, but not simultaneously?

    a. Full-duplex

    b. Simplex

    c. Half-duplex

    d. Quarter duplex

18. Which of the following communication methods rely on a timing device?

    a. Synchronous

    b. Asynchronous

    c. Full-duplex

    d. Half-duplex

19. Which of the following organizations was formerly known as CCITT?

    a. Internet Engineering Task Force

    b. International Organization for Standardization

    c. International Telecommunications Union

    d. Electronic Industries Alliance

20. Which of the following standards organizations has defined the RS-232, RS-449, and RS-530 standards?

    a. IETF

    b. ITU-T

    c. ISO

    d. EIA

21. What is utilized on routers to hide Intranet IP addresses from the Internet?

    a. PAP

    b. CHAP

    c. NAT

    d. FRAT

22. How does NAT deal with multiple internal IP addresses mapping to a single external address?

    a. PAP

    b. CHAP

    c. NAT

    d. PAT

23. How does overlapping occur?

    a. Network administrator doesn't plan for Internet connectivity.

    b. Network administrator uses registered IP addresses without getting permission.

    c. Both a and b

    d. None of the above

24. What is the purpose of multiplexing?

    a. to split up a signal into discrete chunks so it can be transported across the WAN

    b. to combine multiple signals onto a single medium

    c. to put packets back in order after they become disorganized during transport

    d. to acknowledge the receipt of packets

25. Which WAN technology can also be used on LANs?

    a. Frame Relay

    b. ISDN

    c. PPP

    d. ATM

CASE PROJECTS

1. It is obvious to Moe that WANs cover a larger area than LANs. He is not sure about the finer differences. Compare the characteristics of WANs and LANs for Moe.

2. The Americanus Corporation is ready to connect its network to the Internet. Jennifer helped set up this 100BaseT network and feels comfortable with the LAN devices. She has no idea how to interface with the Internet. Who usually provides Physical layer connectivity for WAN services? What WAN devices operate at the Physical layer? Who usually owns this equipment? What is the difference between a DTE, DCE, a CSU/DSU, and a terminal adapter?

3. Lisa thinks that the same protocols operating on LANs are also operating on WANs. Describe some of the WAN protocols operating at the Data Link layer to Lisa. What do these protocols describe?

4. Moe is curious. He dials into his Internet Service Provider (ISP) from home using regular phone lines. His friend has BRI service on an ISDN line. Explain to Moe the differences between these two methods of Internet access. Specifically, what kind of signal is being transmitted, what are the speed limitations, and what constitutes the DCE in each case? Would either of these connections be considered dedicated? What WAN protocols might be in play during a typical Internet session?

6

ROUTER AND IOS BASICS

After reading this chapter and completing the exercises, you will be able to:

♦ Describe the benefits of network segmentation with routers

♦ Understand the elements of the Cisco router user interface

♦ Configure the HyperTerminal program to interface with the Cisco router

♦ Describe the various router configuration modes

♦ Describe the various router passwords

♦ Understand the enhanced editing features of the Cisco IOS

♦ Understand the elements of the Cisco switch user interface

♦ Compare router components to typical PC components

This chapter revisits the benefits of routing. You will learn about the elements of the Cisco user interface, including the System Configuration Dialog, various configuration modes, and the many Cisco router passwords. You also will configure the Windows 98 program HyperTerminal for use with the router. In addition, the enhanced editing features of the Cisco IOS and router components will be explored.

BENEFITS OF ROUTING

As previous chapters explained, network administrators use routers in large networks to provide packet filtering, connections between local networks, traffic control, and wide area network (WAN) connections. Routers operate at the Network layer of the OSI reference model and because of Network layer addressing, routers can direct packets to both local and remote segments.

One of the main benefits of using a router is that it filters traffic. When a device sends a packet on the local segment, all other devices on that segment must receive or discard the packet. Bridges can segment the network at the Data Link layer, but broadcast traffic from one segment to another must still pass through the bridge because the bridge cannot distinguish addresses above layer 2. In a large network composed of one giant segment, this broadcast traffic could seriously affect performance. Routers solve the problem by filtering traffic and forwarding only packets that are addressed to hosts on other networks. In this way, routers reduce traffic by segmenting the network and filtering broadcasts. Said another way, routers create collision domains as well as broadcast domains.

When network administrators add routers to a network, they must configure those routers to operate within the network. To perform routine maintenance and troubleshooting, network operators and administrators must be able to check the status of the router and its components. This necessary interaction with the router requires an interface through which the routers can be configured.

CISCO ROUTER USER INTERFACE

Network administrators commonly configure and interact with a Cisco router via the **Cisco Internetwork Operating System (IOS)**. The Cisco IOS provides a command-line interface (CLI), which allows network operators to check the status of the router and network administrators to manage and configure the router. The software that interprets the commands is called the **command executive**, or **EXEC**.

A router can be accessed in several different ways. Each of these methods involves access through one of three lines. Network administrators typically access the router directly through the **console port** (also known as the **console**) located on the back of the router. The console port connects directly to a PC through an **RJ-45 to RJ-45 rollover cable** with an **RJ-45 to DB-9** or **RJ–45 to DB-25** connector included with the router. Whether you select the DB-9 or DB-25 connector will depend on the type of port on the back of the PC. The second line used to access the router is through the **auxiliary port (AUX)**, which is also on the back of the router. The auxiliary port allows a remote administrator to dial into the router through an external modem, which gets attached to the auxiliary port. The remote PC must also have a modem to use this method.

Figure 6-1 shows a laptop connected to a Cisco 2500 series router via the console port using the RJ-45 to RJ-45 rollover cable and RJ-45 to DB-9 connector. The DB-9 is attached to the COM1 port of the laptop in the picture.

Figure 6-1   Connecting a PC to the console

In addition to the AUX and the console ports, five **virtual terminals (VTY)** can be used to configure the router. Accessing the router through VTY lines is the same as telnetting to the router. The virtual terminals are numbered from zero to four. You can reference the virtual terminals by their abbreviation and numeric indicators: VTY 0, VTY 1, VTY 2, VTY 3, and VTY 4. Network administrators access the virtual terminals through a telnet session.

In addition to configuration through access via the AUX, console, or virtual terminals, the router can obtain configuration information from a **Trivial File Transfer Protocol (TFTP) server**. The router configuration information can be stored as a file on a TFTP server and can be downloaded to configure the router. (The process is described later in this chapter.) Also, network administrators can use network management software such as HP OpenView or CiscoWorks to manage Cisco routers. Figure 6-2 illustrates different methods for accessing a router for configuration purposes.

Figure 6-2 Methods for configuring a Cisco router

Connecting via Terminal Programs

When configuring the router through the console or AUX ports, you must first make the physical connection. Then, you can access the router through a terminal program. There are many different terminal programs that you can use, including HyperTerminal, MicroPhone Pro, ProComm Plus, Telix, Teraterm, and Terminal on Microsoft DOS and Windows systems; Kermit and Tip on Sun Workstations; Z-terminal on Apple Macintosh computers; and Minicom on Linux systems. For example, if the connection from the router to the PC attaches at the COM1 port on the PC, you would configure your terminal program to use COM1. You can use the following steps to configure HyperTerminal:

1. Open the HyperTerminal application. In Microsoft Windows 95 and Windows NT 4.0, it is under the Programs/Accessories group in the Start Menu. In Microsoft Windows 98 and Windows 2000, you should find HyperTerminal in the Programs/Accessories/Communications group in the Start Menu. If you cannot find HyperTerminal, you may have to install additional Accessories programs from the Add/Remove Programs icon in the Control Panel of your Microsoft Windows system. In Microsoft Windows XP, click **Start** and navigate to All Programs, Accessories, Communications, HyperTerminal.

2. Create a New Connection. If the New Connection Wizard does not come up automatically, click File, and then choose New Connection.

3. Enter a name for the connection. The name is for user reference only, so you can use whatever name you want that describes the connection. Click OK to continue.

4. You must then configure how you will connect to the router via the Connect To dialog box (you may be prompted to install a modem.) You will see a place to enter a phone number. If you are connecting to the router through the AUX port, you would provide the router phone number here. If connecting to the router through the console port, you should click on the "Connect using" dropdown list box and choose the COM Port to which the RJ-45 to DB-9 or DB-25 connector is attached. Click OK to continue.

5. Configure the following settings for the COM port: Bits per second, 9600; Data bits, 8; Stop bits, 1; Parity, None; Flow control, Hardware. Click OK to complete the configuration. Click File, Properties. Under Settings, make sure the keys are set to act as "Terminal" keys.

When the HyperTerminal configuration is complete, the program will attempt to connect to the router. At this point, you would turn on the router. On the screen, you should then see the router boot routine.

 If you see a series of miscellaneous characters after you turn on the router, you probably have incorrectly set the bits per second (a.k.a. baud rate). Choose the File/Properties menu and reconfigure your connection as described previously.

When the router boots, it should eventually show a prompt, such as **router>**, or you may be prompted to enter the **System Configuration Dialog** (also known as the Initial Configuration Dialog), which is an automated setup routine described below.

System Configuration Dialog

If the router hasn't been configured previously, or if the startup file has been erased, the Cisco IOS will prompt you to run the initial configuration dialog after the router boots. You can also access the system configuration dialog by typing the setup command at the privileged EXEC prompt. The System Configuration Dialog presents a series of prompts that guide you through the initial configuration for the router. Each question is followed by a default option in brackets. If you decide to accept the default option, you can press the Enter key. Beginning with version 12.0 of the IOS, there are two different levels of setup: basic management setup and extended setup. Basic management setup only configures enough connectivity for management of the system. Extended setup prompts you for configuration of all interfaces and provides enough configuration information to make the router operational.

The first item you are asked by the System Configuration Dialog is whether you would like to enter the initial configuration dialog. If you type "y", you will begin the router configuration process. The next question asked is "Would you like to enter basic management setup?" If you press "y" you will enter basic management setup. If you answer "n" you will enter extended setup mode. Figure 6-3 illustrates use of the setup command.

After the System Configuration Dialog program completes, the router will run through its typical startup process (this process is described in greater detail later in this chapter).

After this initialization process, you can begin to view and configure the router settings.

```
lab-a#setup


        --- System Configuration Dialog ---

Continue with configuration dialog? [yes/no]: y

At any point you may enter a question mark '?' for help.
Use ctrl-c to abort configuration dialog at any prompt.
Default settings are in square brackets '[]'.


Basic management setup configures only enough connectivity
for management of the system, extended setup will ask you
to configure each interface on the system.

Would you like to enter basic management setup? [yes/no]: y
Configuring global parameters:

  Enter host name [lab-a]:
```

Figure 6-3   Output from the setup command

User Interface

When the router completes its initialization process, you must press the Return or Enter key to reach the prompt. The initial prompt consists of two parts: the host name of the router followed by the greater than symbol (>). By default, the router's host name is router, so the default prompt is router>.

When the prompt displayed is the greater than symbol, the router is in **user EXEC mode** (or **user mode**). In this mode the network operator can check router status to see if the interfaces are operational, and review several of the router settings. From any prompt, you can see a list of possible commands at that prompt by typing a question mark (?), as shown in Figure 6-4. You do not need to press Enter after typing the question mark.

The question mark activates **context–sensitive Help** on the Cisco router. The term context-sensitive means that the router evaluates the command mode that you are in, and any command strings that you have entered on the line prior to the question mark, before providing the Help screen. For example, when you are in user mode and type the question mark, the help that follows will be commands available from user mode. However, if you type "ping ?", you will get a list of options that can be used with the ping command.

When the list of Help screen options does not fit on one screen, Help displays only the first screen of options. You can view additional commands line-by-line by pressing the Enter or Return key for each line. You can page through the list of commands by pressing the space bar. Pressing a letter on the keyboard will take you immediately back to the prompt.

```
RouterB(config)#? ◄
Configure commands:
aaa                          Authentication, Authorization and Accounting.
access-list                  Add an access list entry
alias                        Create command alias
arp                          Set a static ARP entry
async-bootp                  Modify system bootp parameters
banner                       Define a login banner
boot                         Modify system boot parameters
bridge                       Bridging Group.
buffers                      Adjust system buffer pool parameters
busy-message                 Display message when connection to host fails
cdp                          Global CDP configuration subcommands
chat-script                  Define a modem chat script
clock                        Configure time-of-day clock
config-register              Define the configuration register
default-value                Default character-bits values
dialer-list                  Create a dialer list entry
dnsix-dmdp                   Provide DMDP service for DNSIX
dnsix-nat                    Provide DNSIX service for audit trails
downward-compatible-config   Generate a configuration compatible with older
                             software
enable                       Modify enable password parameters
end                          Exit from configure mode
exit                         Exit from configure mode
frame-relay                  global frame relay configuration commands
help                         Description of the interactive help system
hostname                     Set system's network name
interface                    Select an interface to configure
ip                           Global IP configuration subcommands
ipx                          Novell/IPX global configuration commands
key                          Key management
line                         Configure a terminal line
logging                      Modify message logging facilities
login-string                 Define a host-specific login string
map-class                    Configure static map class
map-list                     Configure static map list
menu                         Define a user-interface menu
modemcap                     Modem Capabilities database
netbios                      NETBIOS access control filtering
no                           Negate a command or set its defaults
ntp                          Configure NTP
partition                    Partition device
priority-list                Build a priority list
privilege                    Command privilege parameters
prompt                       Set system's prompt
queue-list                   Build a custom queue list
resume-string                Define a host-specific resume string
rlogin                       Rlogin configuration commands
rmon                         Remote Monitoring
route-map                    Create route-map or enter route-map command mode
router                       Enable a routing process
scheduler                    Scheduler parameters
service                      Modify use of network based services
snmp-server                  Modify SNMP parameters
state-machine                Define a TCP dispatch state machine
tacacs-server                Modify TACACS query parameters
terminal-queue               Terminal queue commands
tftp-server                  Provide TFTP service for netload requests
username                     Establish User Name Authentication
x25                          X.25 Level 3
x29                          X29 commands

RouterB(config)#
```

Typing a ? invokes the help system of the IOS. In this case, all commands available in global configuration mode are displayed.

6

Figure 6-4   Output from the ? command

User mode does not allow you to configure the router. To do this, you must go into the **privileged EXEC mode**. To enter privileged EXEC, you can type the enable command at the user mode prompt. Next, you may be prompted for a password. If you have configured an enable password, you must enter it. As you type, the password will not be displayed on the terminal screen. If you have configured an enable secret password, then you will type the enable secret password. The different types of passwords are described in greater detail later in this chapter.

After you enter the enable password or the enable secret password, the greater than symbol (>) changes to a pound sign (#) to indicate that you are in privileged EXEC mode (**router#**). Most router configuration takes place in router modes beyond privileged EXEC mode; however, there are a few things that can be done at this prompt that can substantially effect router operations:

- Setup—the setup command will cause the router to enter the system configuration dialog, which allows the router to be completely reconfigured

- Copy—configurations can be copied from TFTP servers to the router and therefore change the router configuration

- Erase—configuration files as well as the entire IOS can be erased

Privileged EXEC mode is called **enable mode** because you must enter the enable command in order to access it.

Configuration Modes

There are several configuration modes that are accessible only through the privileged EXEC mode. This section discusses some of these basic **router configuration modes** and their respective options.

After you have placed the router into enable mode, you will be able to choose from various router configuration options. From the **enable mode prompt** (router#), you can view the router's configuration and access several other configuration modes. You access the basic configuration mode, called **global configuration mode**, by typing, "configure terminal" at the enable mode prompt.

From the global configuration mode, you can access several other configuration modes. For example, **interface configuration mode** allows you to configure the Ethernet and serial interfaces on your router. With **line configuration mode**, you can configure the virtual terminals, console, and AUX lines that let you access the router. Router configuration mode permits you to enable routing protocols such as RIP and IGRP. Table 6-1 lists these modes, the associated prompt, the method for entry and exit, and a brief description of what you can accomplish in each mode.

Table 6-1   Common configuration modes

Mode	Prompt	To enter	To exit	Used for
User EXEC	Router>	If there is a line password, enter it. Otherwise, press the Return or Enter key.	Logout or Exit	Shows the status of the router and allows network operators to manage connections
Privileged EXEC	Router#	Type enable at the prompt.	Disable Exit Logout	Copies, erases, sets up, and shows router settings
Global configuration	Router (config)#	Configure	Exit End	Allows you to configure various items, including clock, hostname, enable password, and enable secret password
Interface configuration	Router (config-if)#	Interface Ethernet0 or Interface Serial0	Exit End	Allows you to configure the settings, such as IP, for a specific interface
Line configuration	Router (config-line)#	Line console 0 or Line vty 0 4 or Line aux 0	Exit End	Configures lines, such as the console, virtual terminal, or auxiliary
Router configuration	Router (config-router)#	Router rip or Router igrp	Exit End	Adds or configures RIP, IGRP, or other routing protocols

Typing "exit" will take you back one level. For example, if your prompt shows "router(config-router)#" and you type "exit", your prompt will change to "router(config)#". Typing "end" or pressing the Ctrl+Z keys will take you all the way back to the enable prompt. For example, if you see "router(config-line)#" and you type "end", your prompt will revert to "router#", not "router(config)#". Note that if you are typing commands and you see the dollar sign "$", it means that the line is continued from a previous line.

All the commands shown in the table can be abbreviated. Usually, the abbreviation for a command is the fewest number of characters that can be used to uniquely identify the command. For example, to enter the enable mode, you can type "enable", or "en". (You also can type "enab" and "enabl".) On simulation questions on the CCNA exam, make sure to type the entire command, without abbreviations.

Often, you can discover abbreviated commands by simply trying them. If the command does not work, the router will tell you that the command is invalid. If you get part of the command correct, the router will show you the point at which you entered an incorrect character by pointing to the character with a caret symbol (^). For example, to show the current running configuration of the router, you can type "show running-config". However, if you accidentally type "show runing-config", the router will indicate that the command is incorrect by pointing to the first incorrect character. In Figure 6-5, the incorrect character is the letter "i".

```
router#show runing-config
                 ^
% Invalid input detected at '^' marker.

router#
```

Figure 6-5   Command error checking

 Using the shortcut for the show running-config command, which is "sh ru", reduces the chance of making a typo.

Once you have a basic understanding of the commands presented in Table 6-1, you are ready to start practicing basic router configuration tasks. One of the first areas that you might want to investigate is password configuration.

Plethora of Passwords

There are five passwords that can be set on a Cisco router. If you configure the router using the system configuration dialog (setup), you will be prompted for three of these five: the enable password, the enable secret password, and the **virtual terminal password**. You can add a **console password**, an **AUX line password**, and an individual password for each virtual terminal.

Table 6-2 lists and describes these router passwords.

Table 6-2   Router passwords

Enable	Used only when the enable secret password is not present. This password is not encrypted, but it does restrict access to enable mode if the enable secret password is removed.
Enable Secret	This is the primary password used to access enable mode because it supersedes the enable password. When the enable secret password is configured, only the enable secret password (not the enable password) allows you to access enable mode. This enable secret password is encrypted with the **MD5 algorithm**, which has no known method of reversal.

Table 6-2   Router passwords (continued)

Console	Protects the router from console access. When this password is set, someone attempting to access the router from the console connection will have to enter a password before he or she can enter any other commands. This password is not configured by default during setup.
AUX	The AUX line can also have a password configured. This password is requested whenever someone attempts to access the router by a modem through the AUX port.
Virtual Terminal	The router identifies each telnet session as a virtual terminal. You can configure a password for any number of virtual terminals or each one individually. Usually, a five-session limit is put on the router. If you type VTY 0 4 when configuring the password, you will be setting a single password for the five virtual terminals. To configure a password for a single virtual terminal, type VTY followed by the terminal number.

If you have an enable secret password set, you may see it as a string of miscellaneous characters when viewing your router configuration. Do not mistake those characters for the actual password; they are just a representation of an encrypted password.

 If you want to configure encryption for all of your router passwords, type "service password-encryption" at the global configuration prompt.

In the following sections, you will learn how to configure each of the passwords shown in Table 6-2.

Enable Password and Enable Secret Password Configuration

Both the **enable password** and **enable secret password** can be set from the global configuration mode (router(config)#) prompt. To add or change the enable password or enable secret password, simply type the name of the password you would like to configure and follow it with the password you would like to set.

Figure 6-6 illustrates the steps to configure the enable password and enable secret password from the terminal.

Figure 6-6   Setting enable password and enable secret password

Because it is encrypted, the enable secret password is more secure than the enable password. The enable password can be viewed from the configuration file, but the encrypted enable secret password cannot. To see the difference, type "show running-config" or "show run" at the enable mode prompt and read the configuration file as shown in Figure 6-7.

```
RouterB#show run
Building configuration...
Current configuration:
!
version 11.1
service udp-small-servers
service tcp-small-servers
!
hostname RouterB
!
enable secret 5 $1$RHhg$ngXce3OBeC7GprpPjtqsP1

enable password stuff

!
ipx routing 0060.474f.6506
!
interface Ethernet0
 ip address 172.22.2.1 255.255.255.0
 ipx access-group 800 out
 ipx network 300
!
interface Serial0
 no ip address
!
interface Serial1
 ip address 172.22.3.2 255.255.255.0
!
router rip
 network 172.22.0.0
!
no ip classless
access-list 800 deny 300 500
access-list 800 permit FFFFFFFF FFFFFFFF
!
!
!
!
line con 0
 password cisco
 login
line vty 0 4
 password password
 login
!
end

RouterB#
```

The enable secret password is stored in an encrypted form for increased security

The enable password is stored as plaintext and can pose a security risk

Figure 6-7   The enable password and enable secret password

If you want to remove the enable secret password, you can type "no enable secret" at the global configuration mode prompt. You can also type "no enable password" to remove the enable password. Of course, if you remove both the enable secret and enable password, the router can be configured by anyone who can log on.

To configure the console line, AUX line, and virtual terminal passwords, you must be in a line configuration mode, as the next section discusses.

Setting Line Passwords

Line passwords are the first line of defense against unauthorized intrusion into the router. You can set passwords for each line used to configure the router. As mentioned previously, these lines are the console line, the AUX line, and each of the five virtual terminal lines. By default, the virtual terminal passwords can be configured if you use the initial router setup process, but all virtual terminals are set for the same password.

One of the first passwords you might want to configure is the console line password. To configure a console password, you must enter line configuration mode. Figure 6-8 illustrates the process for configuring a console line password.

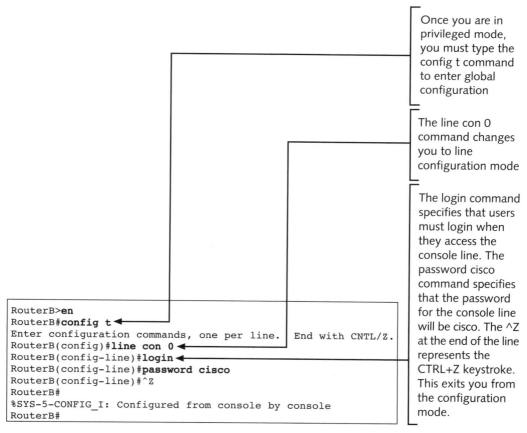

Once you are in privileged mode, you must type the config t command to enter global configuration

The line con 0 command changes you to line configuration mode

The login command specifies that users must login when they access the console line. The password cisco command specifies that the password for the console line will be cisco. The ^Z at the end of the line represents the CTRL+Z keystroke. This exits you from the configuration mode.

```
RouterB>en
RouterB#config t
Enter configuration commands, one per line. │ End with CNTL/Z.
RouterB(config)#line con 0
RouterB(config-line)#login
RouterB(config-line)#password cisco
RouterB(config-line)#^Z
RouterB#
%SYS-5-CONFIG_I: Configured from console by console
RouterB#
```

Figure 6-8   Applying a console password

After you have added the password to the console, you can check it by exiting global configuration mode and logging off the terminal. When you then attempt to log on to the terminal, you will be prompted for a password, as shown in Figure 6-9.

```
RouterB con0 is now available

Press RETURN to get started.
User Access Verification
Password:
```

You will see this prompt once the console session has been properly established. If the console password has been correctly set up, you will be prompted for the console password.

Figure 6-9   Console password example

You can also configure passwords on the virtual terminal lines (five virtual terminal lines exist on every router) in much the same way as on the console port. In fact, you must configure a vty password if you want to enable access via telnet. This is a safety precaution; without it, anyone with the IP address of the router will be able to access it. To configure the vty password, go into line configuration mode on the router for the vty lines and add the login and password commands. Figure 6-10 shows the process of applying a vty password.

If you just wanted to set an individual vty password for vty line 0, you would have typed "line vty 0" instead of "line vty 0 4" at the RouterB(config)# prompt shown in Figure 6-10. The same is true for any other vty port; they are individually numbered 0, 1, 2, 3, and 4 (five lines total).

Passwords can be placed on auxiliary ports in the same way they are placed on console or vty ports. Using all three of these passwords will at least slow down someone trying to enter your routers. If they happen to get through these passwords, the single most important password, the enable or enable secret password (depending on which one is in use) can stop them from actually modifying the router's configuration.

Enhanced Editing

By default, the router supports enhanced editing features that allow you to modify lengthy commands. The enhanced editing commands let you jump to the beginning or end of a command line. You also can jump ahead or behind, character by character, or word by word. Table 6-3 shows the shortcuts and the definitions. You must press the keyboard keys simultaneously in order to make these commands work. For example, the first key combination presented in the table is Ctrl+A, which means that you would press the Ctrl key and the A key simultaneously.

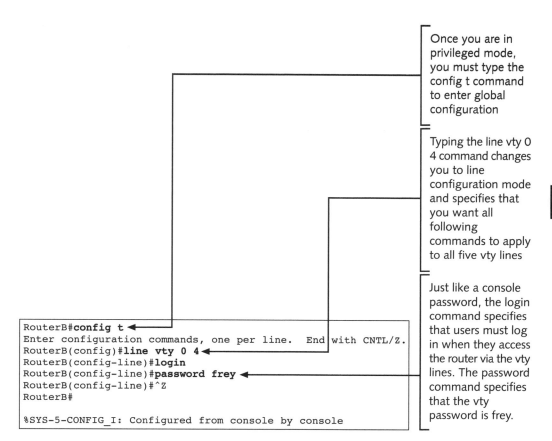

Once you are in privileged mode, you must type the config t command to enter global configuration

Typing the line vty 0 4 command changes you to line configuration mode and specifies that you want all following commands to apply to all five vty lines

6

Just like a console password, the login command specifies that users must log in when they access the router via the vty lines. The password command specifies that the vty password is frey.

```
RouterB#config t
Enter configuration commands, one per line.   End with CNTL/Z.
RouterB(config)#line vty 0 4
RouterB(config-line)#login
RouterB(config-line)#password frey
RouterB(config-line)#^Z
RouterB#

%SYS-5-CONFIG_I: Configured from console by console
```

Figure 6-10   Applying a vty password

Table 6-3   Editing commands

Key combination	Description
Ctrl+A	Moves the cursor to the beginning of the current line.
Ctrl+E	Moves the cursor to the end of the current line.
Ctrl+F	Moves the cursor one character to the right. You can also accomplish this by pressing the right arrow key.
Ctrl+B	Moves the cursor one character to the left. You can also accomplish this by pressing the left arrow key.
Esc+F	Moves the cursor one word forward.
Esc+B	Moves the cursor one word back.

You can turn off the enhanced editing features by typing "terminal no editing" at either the user EXEC or the privileged EXEC prompts. You can turn on terminal editing by typing "terminal editing".

When you type an incorrect command that the router cannot recognize, the bogus command might be mistaken for a host name. If this happens, the router will, by default, attempt to look up the host name and give you the corresponding IP address. If you would like to prevent the router from doing this, type "no ip domain-lookup" from the global configuration prompt. To cancel any command or process, press the Ctrl, Shift, and 6 keys simultaneously. You also may have to let go of those keys and then press the X key in order to initiate the escape sequence on some routers.

Command History

The command history allows you to retrieve previously typed commands. You can see up to 10 previously typed commands by typing "show history" from either the user EXEC or privileged EXEC mode. You can use the up arrow (or press Ctrl+P) to retrieve previous commands. The down arrow (or Ctrl+N) will retrieve recent commands, assuming that you are viewing previous commands. If you type part of a command, you can press the Tab key to complete the command.

To modify the number of commands stored by the router, you can use the terminal command. You can set the history buffer to zero so that it won't store commands, or you can set it to store up to 256 previous commands. For example, to decrease the number of commands stored from the default of 10 to three, you would type "terminal history size 3" at the enable prompt.

Configuring Router Identification

You can identify your router in several ways. The most obvious is the router host name. The default host name is simply "router", which is displayed at the beginning of every prompt. The command for configuring the host name for the router must be typed in global configuration mode. If you want to set the router host name, type "hostname" followed by the name that you would like to set. For example, to set the router's name to router57, type "hostname router57".

Another way to configure identification for the router is to configure a banner. A banner is a message that you can configure to display each time someone attempts to log in to the router. To configure the banner, you must be in global configuration mode (router(config#)); then type "banner motd", followed by a space and a delimiting character. Note that "motd" stands for "message of the day", and the delimiting character can be any keyboard letter or symbol.

When you type the delimiting character in a banner configuration, the router will interpret the character as the end of the banner; therefore, it is best to use a delimiting character that won't be typed in your banner message. A typical character used for delimiting the banner message is the pound symbol (#).

Figure 6-11 illustrates the configuration process for a banner page.

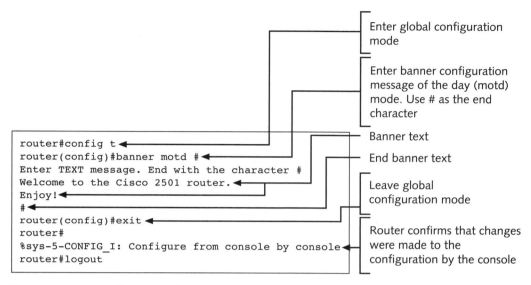

Figure 6-11 Configuring a banner message

Notice that once the delimiting character is typed, the router assumes that the banner message is complete. In order to see the banner message, log out and attempt to log on to the router. Figure 6-12 illustrates how the banner message in this section's example would look. To remove the banner, type "no banner motd" at the global configuration prompt.

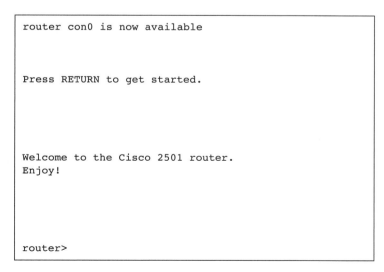

Figure 6-12 Banner message displayed

Another method of identifying router components is to configure an interface description. You can configure a description for each of the interfaces physically attached to your router by using the description command. The interface description helps you remember which network the interface services. For example, if you wanted to configure a description for the Ethernet0 interface to remind you that it is connected to the Department A LAN, you would type commands similar to those shown in Figure 6-13.

```
router#config t
router(config)#interface e0
router(config-if)#description Attached to Dept A LAN
```

Figure 6-13   Configuring an interface description

After you have configured the description for the interface, return to the basic privileged EXEC prompt (router#) and type "show interface" to check your work. The description for Ethernet0 should now have the text you typed.

Configuring the Time and Date

Another basic configuration task is to configure the router's time clock and time zone. Use the clock set command in enable mode to configure the time. You must be in global configuration mode to configure the time zone. The commands in Figure 6-14 show how to configure the time zone, the time, and the date.

```
router#config t
router(config)#clock timezone pacific -8
router(config)#exit
%SYS-5-CONFIG_I: Configured from console by console
router#clock set 02:46:10 29 August 2003
```

Figure 6-14   Configuring the time and date

When entering the time zone, you must include the name of the time zone and the offset from the **Universal Time Code (UTC)**. The UTC is based on the time in Greenwich, which is a city in the United Kingdom. All other time zones are either plus or minus a certain number of hours. For example, Eastern Standard Time is minus five, or five hours earlier than in Greenwich. After you have configured the time zone, you can configure the clock. If you do configure the time zone and clock in the opposite order, your clock will change after you configure the time zone. To confirm your settings, type "show clock" at the privileged EXEC prompt.

SWITCH USER INTERFACE

There are two types of operating systems in use on Cisco switches: IOS-based and set-based. An IOS-based system is one that you can configure from a command line interface. Switches that use IOS-based commands are Cisco Catalyst 1900, 2820, and 2900 switches. A set-based system is older and utilizes "set" commands at a command line interface. Cisco 1984G, 2926, 4000, 5000, and 6000 series switches employ the set-based configuration commands. In this book, the focus is on commands specific to the Catalyst 1900 IOS-based operating system because that is the switch model that appears on the CCNA exam. Basic Catalyst 1900 configuration is covered in this section. You'll receive additional configuration instructions for the Catalyst 1900 in future chapters as appropriate.

You can connect to a Cisco switch in the same way you connect to a Cisco router, as shown earlier in Figure 6-1. The Cisco switch has a console port to which you can connect your laptop or PC. Once you power-on the switch, a menu appears on your terminal program. The Catalyst 1900 menu includes the following options:

[M] Menus

[K] Command Line

[I] IP Configuration

You simply press the appropriate key (M, K, or I) on the keyboard to begin configuring the switch. In the sections to follow here and in other chapters, you'll learn the command line configuration methods for the Catalyst 1900. The command line interface is the focus because you can configure anything from that interface and that is the interface on which the CCNA exam focuses.

Modes and Passwords

You've already learned that enable mode is how you can actually make configuration changes on a Cisco router. The same is true for a Cisco switch with an IOS-based operating system. To enter enable mode, you can simply type enable at the command line prompt > and then press Enter. The prompt then changes to the pound # symbol and you are in enable mode (assuming a password hasn't been set yet). As a matter of fact, the next thing you should do is configure a password. To do so you must enter configuration mode by typing configure terminal (or an abbreviated version of the command such as config term or con t), which is the same command to enter global configuration mode on a router. Once there you can set the enable password, which is different from doing so on a Cisco router.

You can set the user mode password or enable mode password from the (config)# prompt. For example, if you type "enable password level ?", you will see that you can enter 1 through 15 to pick your password level. The level chosen dictates what commands can be used. Level 1 is for the user mode password and 15 for the enable mode password (each must be 4 to 8 characters). These passwords are all encrypted. Just like the router, you can also set an enable secret password, which usurps the enable password. The enable secret password also provides for levels 1 through 15. In addition, you can choose to use an encrypted or unencrypted secret password. To illustrate the configuration of passwords on a Catalyst 1900 switch, assume that you want a user level password to be *viewonly,* the enable password to be *ccnafix,* and an encrypted enable secret password to be *ccnasafe.*

(config)#**enable password level 1 viewonly**

(config)#**enable password level 15 ccnafix**

(config)#**enable secret ccnasafe**

There is no password recovery on the 1900 so if you forget your password you will have to call Cisco support!

Setting the Hostname

The actual task of setting the hostname on the Cisco Catalyst 1900 is identical to setting the hostname on a Cisco router. As with the router the hostname is only locally significant, so the function of the name is to identify the switch, not to provide any sort of Internet name resolution. The best idea is to set the name to identify the location of the switch. For example, if you worked for a company named HudLogic, Inc. and their switch was on the fourth floor of room 410, you might name the switch Rm410HL, which stands for Room 410 HudLogic. To configure this, you would type:

(config)#**hostname Rm410HL**

Rm410HL(config)#

Once the hostname is set, the prompt will change to reflect the name of the switch as shown above.

ROUTER COMPONENTS

A router is a computer and has many of the same hardware components that a typical PC does. This section discusses the hardware elements of the router, including:

- ROM
- Flash memory
- NVRAM
- RAM/DRAM
- Interfaces

ROM

Read-only memory (ROM) stores the bootstrap program, also called the ROM Monitor, that initializes the router's basic hardware components. ROM is not modified during normal operations, but it can be upgraded with special plug-in chips. The content of ROM is maintained even when the router is rebooted, which is similar to how ROM operates on a PC.

On the Cisco 2500, 4000, and 4500 routers, ROM contains a small version of the Cisco IOS as an emergency backup. Cisco 7000 and 7500 series routers have a full version of the Cisco IOS in ROM. You know that you are in **ROM monitor mode** when the prompt is just the greater than sign (>).

Flash memory

Flash memory is erasable, programmable, read only memory (EPROM). This means that flash memory is not typically modified during normal operations; however, it can be upgraded or erased when necessary. The content of flash memory is maintained even when the router is rebooted.

Flash memory contains the working copy of the current Cisco IOS and is the component that initializes the IOS for normal router operations. Flash memory on certain series of Cisco routers can store multiple versions of the IOS, which can make upgrading the IOS easier and safer. For example, if an upgrade to the IOS is implemented, but later found undesirable or difficult to use, the router can be configured to use the original copy of the IOS. The show version command displayed in Figure 6-15 provides a summary of IOS information.

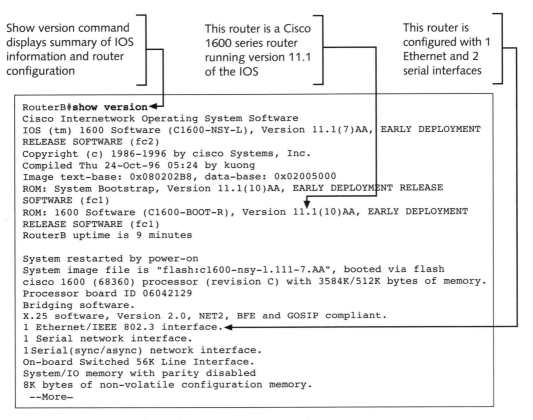

Show version command displays summary of IOS information and router configuration

This router is a Cisco 1600 series router running version 11.1 of the IOS

This router is configured with 1 Ethernet and 2 serial interfaces

```
RouterB#show version
Cisco Internetwork Operating System Software
IOS (tm) 1600 Software (C1600-NSY-L), Version 11.1(7)AA, EARLY DEPLOYMENT
RELEASE SOFTWARE (fc2)
Copyright (c) 1986-1996 by cisco Systems, Inc.
Compiled Thu 24-Oct-96 05:24 by kuong
Image text-base: 0x080202B8, data-base: 0x02005000
ROM: System Bootstrap, Version 11.1(10)AA, EARLY DEPLOYMENT RELEASE
SOFTWARE (fc1)
ROM: 1600 Software (C1600-BOOT-R), Version 11.1(10)AA, EARLY DEPLOYMENT
RELEASE SOFTWARE (fc1)
RouterB uptime is 9 minutes

System restarted by power-on
System image file is "flash:c1600-nsy-l.111-7.AA", booted via flash
cisco 1600 (68360) processor (revision C) with 3584K/512K bytes of memory.
Processor board ID 06042129
Bridging software.
X.25 software, Version 2.0, NET2, BFE and GOSIP compliant.
1 Ethernet/IEEE 802.3 interface.
1 Serial network interface.
1 Serial(sync/async) network interface.
On-board Switched 56K Line Interface.
System/IO memory with parity disabled
8K bytes of non-volatile configuration memory.
 --More-
```

Figure 6-15   Output from show version command

NVRAM

Nonvolatile random access memory (NVRAM) is a special type of RAM that is not cleared when the router is rebooted. The startup configuration file for the router is stored in NVRAM by default. When the router is first shipped, the configuration file is not present. This is the first file that the person who sets up the router creates.

NVRAM stores all the user-defined configuration information for the router, which can include the host name of the router, the protocol configurations, and the cache configurations.

The Cisco IOS uses the configuration file in NVRAM during the router boot process, which is explained in the next chapter. Whenever the configuration of the router is updated, the administrator copies the running configuration, which is the one that has just been updated, to the startup configuration. The startup configuration is maintained in NVRAM, whereas the running configuration is maintained in RAM/DRAM.

RAM/DRAM

Random access memory (RAM), also known as **dynamic random access memory (DRAM)**, is a **volatile** hardware component because its information is not maintained in the event of a router reboot. This is similar to how RAM operates in a PC. RAM/DRAM contains the working or running copy of the configuration file. During normal operations, changes to the router's running configuration take place in RAM/DRAM.

The IOS contains commands to view each of the router's components. To view the contents of RAM, you can issue one of several commands (because several components reside in RAM). One of the most common commands is the show running-config command. With this command, you can view the current configuration that is running in RAM, as illustrated in Figure 6-16. Two other common commands that can show the contents of RAM are the show memory and show buffers commands. Because they produce long, detailed output, their output has not been included in this text.

Another very useful command is the show startup-config command. With this command you can display the current startup configuration file on the router, which is stored in NVRAM. An administrator who wants to ensure changes are maintained, even if the system is rebooted, must copy the running configuration to the startup configuration. The command to do this is as follows:

Copy running-config startup-config

This command can be abbreviated as follows:

Cop ru st

These commands copy the configuration changes from RAM/DRAM to NVRAM. When the router is rebooted, the IOS will implement these changes through the startup-configuration file. If you want to combine your running configuration with the startup configuration stored in NVRAM, you can type "copy startup-config running-config" at the privileged EXEC mode prompt.

Interfaces

A router can ship with a variety of configurable interfaces. A common interface is Ethernet0, which is used to connect the router to an Ethernet LAN. Although this chapter focuses on the Ethernet, serial, console, and auxiliary interfaces, the router can have other types of interfaces, including:

- Token Ring
- Basic Rate Interface (BRI)
- Asynchronous Transfer Mode (ATM)
- Fiber Distributed Data Interface (FDDI)
- Channel Interface Processor (CIP) for System Network Architecture (SNA)
- High-Speed Serial Interface (HSSI)

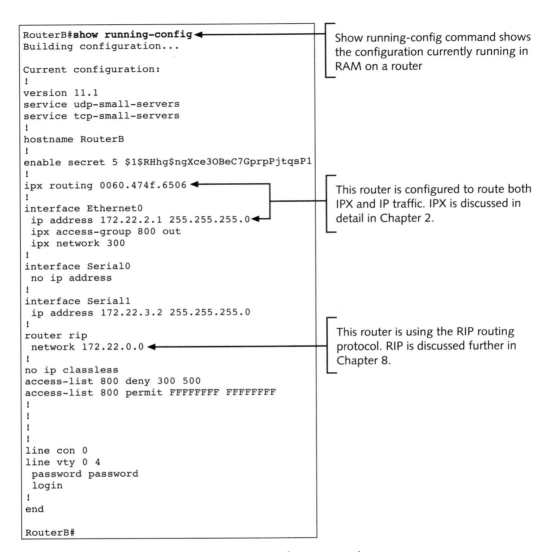

```
RouterB#show running-config                          Show running-config command shows
Building configuration...                            the configuration currently running in
                                                     RAM on a router
Current configuration:
!
version 11.1
service udp-small-servers
service tcp-small-servers
!
hostname RouterB
!
enable secret 5 $1$RHhg$ngXce3OBeC7GprpPjtqsP1
!
ipx routing 0060.474f.6506                           This router is configured to route both
!                                                    IPX and IP traffic. IPX is discussed in
interface Ethernet0                                  detail in Chapter 2.
 ip address 172.22.2.1 255.255.255.0
 ipx access-group 800 out
 ipx network 300
!
interface Serial0
 no ip address
!
interface Serial1
 ip address 172.22.3.2 255.255.255.0
!                                                    This router is using the RIP routing
router rip                                           protocol. RIP is discussed further in
 network 172.22.0.0                                  Chapter 8.
!
no ip classless
access-list 800 deny 300 500
access-list 800 permit FFFFFFFF FFFFFFFF
!
!
!
!
line con 0
line vty 0 4
 password password
 login
!
end

RouterB#
```

Figure 6-16   Output from show running-config command

You can view all of the configured interfaces for your router with the show interface command, as shown in Figure 6-17. Configuration options for the Ethernet and serial interfaces are covered in Chapter 7. The configuration options for the other interfaces are beyond the scope of this text.

```
RouterB#show interfaces

Ethernet0 is up, line protocol is up ◄
  Hardware is QUICC Ethernet, address is 0060.474f.6506 (bia 0060.474f.6506)
  Internet address is 172.22.2.1/24 ◄
  MTU 1500 bytes, BW 10000  Kbit, DLY 1000 usec, rely 255/255, load 1/255
  Encapsulation ARPA, loopback not set, keepalive set (10 sec)
  ARP type: ARPA, ARP Timeout 04:00:00
  Last input 00:00:10, output 00:00:00, output hang never
  Last clearing of "show interface" counters never
  Queueing strategy: fifo
  Output queue 0/40, 0 drops; input queue 0/75, 0 drops
  5 minute input rate 0 bits/sec, 0 packets/sec
  5 minute output rate 0 bits/sec, 0 packets/sec
     171 packets input, 25815 bytes, 0 no buffer
     Received 171 broadcasts, 0 runts, 0 giants
     0 input errors, 0 CRC, 0 frame, 0 overrun, 0 ignored, 0 abort
     0 input packets with dribble condition detected
     368 packets output, 37244 bytes, 0 underruns
     0 output errors, 0 collisions, 3 interface resets
     0 babbles, 0 late collision, 0 deferred
     0 lost carrier, 0 no carrier
     0 output buffer failures, 0 output buffers swapped out
Serial0 is down, line protocol is down ◄
  Hardware is QUICC Serial (with onboard CSU/DSU)
  MTU 1500 bytes, BW 1544 Kbit, DLY 20000 usec, rely 255/255, load 1/255
  Encapsulation HDLC, loopback not set, keepalive set (10 sec)
  Last input never, output never, output hang never
  Last clearing of "show interface" counters never
  Input queue: 0/75/0 (size/max/drops); Total output drops: 0
  Queueing strategy: weighted fair
  Output queue: 0/64/0 (size/threshold/drops)
  Conversations   0/0 (active/max active)
     Reserved Conversations 0/0 (allocated/max allocated)
  5 minute input rate 0 bits/sec, 0 packets/sec
  5 minute output rate 0 bits/sec, 0 packets/sec
     0 packets input, 0 bytes, 0 no buffer
     Received 0 broadcasts, 0 runts, 0 giants
     0 input errors, 0 CRC, 0 frame, 0 overrun, 0 ignored, 0 abort
     0 packets output, 0 bytes, 0 underruns
     0 output errors, 0 collisions, 84 interface resets
     0 output buffer failures, 0 output buffers swapped out
     0 carrier transitions
     DCD=down  DSR=down  DTR=up  RTS=up  CTS=down

Serial1 is up, line protocol is up
  Hardware is QUICC Serial
  Internet address is 172.22.3.2/24
  MTU 1500 bytes, BW 1544  Kbit, DLY 20000 usec, rely 255/255, load 1/255
  Encapsulation HDLC, loopback not set, keepalive set (10 sec)
  Last input 00:00:02, output 00:00:04, output hang never
  Last clearing of "show interface" counters never
  Input queue: 0/75/0 (size/max/drops); Total output drops: 0
  Queueing strategy: weighted fair
  Output queue: 0/64/0 (size/threshold/drops)
     Conversations   0/1 (active/max active)
     Reserved Conversations 0/0 (allocated/max allocated)
  5 minute input rate 0 bits/sec, 0 packets/sec
  5 minute output rate 0 bits/sec, 0 packets/sec
     355 packets input, 22240 bytes, 0 no buffer
     Received 354 broadcasts, 0 runts, 0 giants
     2 input errors, 0 CRC, 2 frame, 0 overrun, 0 ignored, 0 abort
     359 packets output, 22790 bytes, 0 underruns
     0 output errors, 0 collisions, 7 interface resets
     0 output buffer failures, 0 output buffers swapped out
     0 carrier transitions
     DCD=up  DSR=up  DTR=up  RTS=up  CTS=up
```

The show interfaces command lists a summary of the status of each interface. If the physical layer and Data Link layer protocols are up and running, the interface will be listed as Interface is up, line protocol up.

The configured network layer address is displayed with this command. A /24 after the IP address denotes a 24-bit subnet mask or a mask of 255.255.255.0.

This interface is listed as Serial0 is down, line protocol is down because neither a Physical layer or Data Link layer connection is active. In this case, a cable is not connected and a Data Link layer protocol has not been specified.

Figure 6-17   Output from show interfaces command

CHAPTER SUMMARY

❐ Cisco routers use the Cisco IOS to provide an interface for network operators and administrators.

❐ The first mode entered is user EXEC (router> prompt) and the next mode is privileged EXEC (router# prompt).

❐ In user EXEC, basic tasks such as checking the router status, checking connectivity, and viewing some configuration information can be accomplished.

❐ To actually configure the router, privileged EXEC mode must be accessed, as this mode leads to the two most common modes for router configuration: global configuration mode and interface configuration mode.

❐ The privileged EXEC mode is often called enable mode because it is entered using the enable command.

❐ The enable, enable secret, and vty passwords are set during initial configuration if the system configuration dialog is used, but they can be added and changed in global configuration mode (router(config)# prompt) also.

❐ When configured, the enable secret password supersedes the enable password. This is because the enable secret is an encrypted password that is not viewable in the configuration file, which means that it has less chance of being compromised. For this reason, it should be different from the enable password.

❐ The Cisco 1900 switch allows configuration from a command line just like a Cisco router. Hostnames and passwords, as well as other parameters, are configured on the Cisco 1900 switch in much the same way as they are configured on a router.

❐ The components of a router include ROM, flash memory, NVRAM, RAM/DRAM, and interfaces.

❐ ROM stores a limited version of the Cisco IOS and routines for checking the hardware during system boot. It is responsible for initializing the router.

❐ Flash memory stores the Cisco IOS that is loaded by default during system boot.

❐ NVRAM stores the startup copy of the router configuration file that is loaded by default during system boot.

❐ RAM/DRAM stores the working copy (running configuration) of the router configuration. This configuration is loaded into RAM from NVRAM by default during bootup. It is erased if the router is rebooted, unless it is saved to the startup configuration.

❐ Interfaces provide connectivity to various types of LANs and WANs.

KEY TERMS

auxiliary port (AUX) — A secondary port that allows connection to a modem that will be used for direct access to the router for configuration.

AUX line password — A password used to access the router through the AUX port.

AUX port — *See* **auxiliary port (AUX)**.

bootstrap — A small program used to load a much larger program. In the case of a router or switch, the bootstrap program loads the IOS.

Cisco Internetwork Operating System (IOS) — A router operating system that provides a command-line interface, which allows network operators to check the status of the router and allows network administrators to manage and configure the router.

command executive — The user interface that interprets commands and is provided by the Cisco IOS (a.k.a. the EXEC).

console — A physical connection on the back of the router to which you can connect a rollover cable to attach to a PC for router configuration (a.k.a. console port).

console password — The password that is used to access the router through the console port.

console port — *See* **console**.

context-sensitive Help — Help with the syntax of commands for the router that is based on the current router mode and prompt, as well as any part of a command that is typed.

dynamic random access memory (DRAM) — *See* **random access memory (RAM)**.

enable mode — Another name for the privileged EXEC mode. The enable or enable secret password must be entered in order to access this mode.

enable mode prompt — The prompt that indicates operation in privileged EXEC or enable mode. It has two elements: the host name of the router and the pound (#) symbol.

enable password — The password that protects enable mode in the event that the enable secret password has been removed.

enable secret password — An MD5 encrypted password that is not visible when viewing the system configuration; supersedes the enable password.

EXEC — *See* **command executive**.

flash memory — Erasable, programmable, read-only memory (EPROM). The content of flash memory is maintained when the router is rebooted. Flash memory contains the working copy of the Cisco IOS and it is the component that initializes the IOS for normal router operations.

global configuration mode — A router mode that allows manipulation of most of the router's generic settings. The prompt for global configuration mode is router(config)#.

interface configuration mode — A router mode that allows you to configure the Ethernet and serial interfaces. The prompt for this mode is router(config-if)#.

line configuration mode — A router mode that allows you to configure the virtual terminals, console, and AUX lines that let you access the router. The prompt for this mode is router(config-line)#.

MD5 algorithm — An algorithm used to encrypt an enable secret password. It has no known reversal.

nonvolatile random access memory (NVRAM) — A special type of RAM that is not cleared when the router is rebooted. NVRAM is where the startup configuration file for the router is stored.

privileged EXEC mode — A router mode used to configure the router.

random access memory (RAM) — Memory that stores the working copy of the router configuration. This configuration is erased if the router is rebooted, unless it is saved to the startup configuration.

read-only memory (ROM) — Memory that contains the necessary routines to boot the system and check its hardware. It also contains a limited version of the Cisco IOS for use only when the primary copies of the IOS in flash memory or on a TFTP server are accidentally lost.

RJ-45 to DB-9 — A connector that ships with the router to enable connection to a PC with a DB-9 COM port to the router console port.

RJ-45 to DB-25 — A connector that ships with the router to enable connection to a PC with a DB-25 COM port to the router console port.

RJ-45 to RJ-45 rollover cable — A cable that connects the console port on the back of the router to an RJ-45 to DB-9 or RJ-45 to DB-25 connector on the back of a PC. This cable ships with the router.

ROM monitor mode — A router mode that allows you to configure your router in the event that there is no valid IOS file in your flash memory.

router configuration mode — A router mode that allows you to enable routing protocols such as RIP and IGRP. The prompt for router configuration mode is router(config-router)#.

router# — *See* **enable mode prompt**.

router> — *See* **user EXEC mode**.

System Configuration Dialog — An automated setup routine that runs if you type "setup" from privileged EXEC mode or if the router is started/restarted without a configuration file.

Trivial File Transfer Protocol (TFTP) server — A computer that provides TFTP services and can be used to maintain the IOS and configuration file of a Cisco router.

Universal Time Code (UTC) — Based on the time in the city of Greenwich in the United Kingdom. All other time zones are either plus or minus hours of the clocks in Greenwich.

user EXEC mode — A router mode that allows a network operator to check router status, see if the interfaces are operational, and review several of the router settings.

user mode — *See* **user EXEC mode**.

virtual terminal password — A password that is used to access the router over a telnet connection.

virtual terminals (VTY) — Terminals provided with each Cisco router that can be used by telnet sessions to configure the router.

volatile — Contents of memory that are lost when the power is turned off. RAM is an example of volatile memory.

VTY — A Cisco IOS abbreviation for virtual terminal used in commands to reference virtual terminals.

6

REVIEW QUESTIONS

1. From which of the following prompts can you change the enable secret password?

   a. router(config)#

   b. router#

   c. router>

   d. router(config)>

2. If you type "show ?" at the router> prompt, what is the result of the command?

   a. You will see a list of usable show commands at the user mode prompt.

   b. You will see a list of connected users.

   c. You will see the current mode displayed.

   d. You will see the configuration register settings.

3. If you need to abort a command in the middle of execution, which key sequence will you press simultaneously?

   a. Ctrl+Esc

   b. Ctrl+X

   c. Ctrl+Shift+6

   d. Ctrl+Alt+Del

4. Which of the following commands will allow you to type a banner for your router?

   a. router(config-if)# banner message $

   b. router(config)# banner motd @

   c. router(config)# banner msg #

   d. router# banner config !

   e. router# banner motd #

5. By default, which of the router's components stores configuration files set up by the administrator?

   a. ROM

   b. Flash

   c. IOS

   d. NVRAM

6. If you are in global configuration mode, which router prompt will you see?

   a. global#

   b. router(config)#

   c. router(config-if)#

   d. router#

   e. router(config-gl)#

7. By default (during normal boot operations), where does the router look first for a working version of the Cisco IOS?

   a. NVRAM

   b. TFTP

   c. Flash

   d. ROM

8. What three commands can be used in privileged EXEC mode to alter the router configuration?

   a. setup, erase, and copy

   b. enable, setup, and tftp

   c. setup, show version, and show buffers

   d. erase, copy, and show run

9. The Cisco IOS image in ROM is always a full version of the IOS. True or False?

10. Which of the following are routing protocols? (Choose all that apply.)

   a. RIP

   b. IGRP

   c. IP route

   d. Cisco IOS

   e. TCP

11. From which of the following prompts can you modify the terminal vty password?

    a. router(config-line)#

    b. router#

    c. router>

    d. router(config)>

12. What does VTY 1 stand for?

    a. The first virtual Y connector

    b. Virtual terminal one

    c. Virtual test connection yes on 1

    d. v-modem terminal 1

13. How do network administrators usually access a VTY?

    a. ftp

    b. smtp

    c. telnet

    d. http

14. If, after connecting to the router via HyperTerminal, you see only illegible characters in the terminal window, what should you try?

    a. Adjust the baud rate.

    b. Change connectors.

    c. Use a telnet session.

    d. Turn on parity.

15. If you enter a VTY password during the automated setup routine, to which VTY will it apply? (Choose all that apply.)

    a. VTY 0

    b. VTY 1

    c. VTY 2

    d. VTY 3

    e. VTY 4

16. What are the two different levels of setup when using the System Configuration Dialog?

    a. initial and basic

    b. enable and enable secret

    c. basic and extended

    d. none of the above

6

17. What is the default number of significant bits in the subnet mask for the address 10.0.0.1?

18. From the router# prompt and the terminal, what must you type to enter global configuration mode?

    a. CON 0

    b. term gf

    c. conf t

    d. global conf

19. If you are at the router(config-if)# prompt and you press the Ctrl+Z keys simultaneously, which prompt will you see next?

    a. router>

    b. router#

    c. router(config)#

    d. Press Return to continue

20. Which of the following commands will allow you to enter privileged EXEC mode from the router> prompt? (Choose all that apply.)

    a. en

    b. ena

    c. enable

    d. enab

    e. enabl

21. What does the sh ru command show you?

    a. Remote users

    b. Running configuration

    c. Startup configuration

    d. Remote boot procedure

22. Which password can be used instead of the enable password?

    a. VTY 0

    b. console

    c. AUX

    d. enable secret

    e. login

23. Which password is encrypted by default?

    a. login

    b. MD5

    c. enable

    d. enable secret

    e. console

    f. VTY 0

24. If no hostname has been configured on a 1900 series switch, which of the following illustrates how the prompt will display in global configuration mode?

    a. router(config)#

    b. switch(config)#

    c. (config)#

    d. (switch)#

25. Which of the following best describes the operating system of the Cisco 1900 series switch?

    a. set-based

    b. IOS-based

    c. switch-based

    d. IP-based

CASE PROJECTS

1. Jennifer and Moe brought a client's router to the office to configure but they aren't sure how to make the physical connections. They want to use an older PC in Brad's office to configure the router. The COM2 port is available on this PC, and it has a DB-25 connector. How would you suggest the router be accessed? What hardware will you need? Where will you get this hardware?

2. You have helped Moe and Jennifer connect the router to the PC. Now, it is time to access the router and configure it. The old PC has the Windows 95 operating system on it. What program will you use to access the router? What are the important parameters to configure in this program, and what will the initial settings be?

3. Moe and Jennifer have accessed the router successfully. Explain to them which passwords the System Configuration Dialog will prompt them for during the initial configuration. Describe any particulars regarding those passwords. What other passwords are available to them? When and why might they want to implement these additional passwords?

4. Moe is a terrible typist. Lisa tells him to stop wasting time retyping router commands and use the command history and enhanced editing features of the Cisco IOS. When Moe asks her how to do this, she says that she read about it but doesn't remember exactly how these features work. Help Moe and Lisa by explaining to them the easy way to edit router commands. How do you retrieve previously typed commands? How do you move the cursor forward and back along the command line?

5. Lisa is planning to take a CCNA practice exam on the Internet. She is having a difficult time memorizing the components of the Cisco router. List the router components for her and give a brief description of the purpose of each component. How do similar components in a typical PC compare to the router components you have listed?

7

ROUTER STARTUP AND CONFIGURATION

After reading this chapter and completing the exercises, you will be able to:

♦ Understand router setup and startup

♦ Describe and use the Cisco Discovery Protocol

♦ Understand configuration management commands for Cisco routers and the 1900 series switch

♦ Configure IP on the Cisco router and the 1900 series switch

♦ Troubleshoot router connectivity problems

In this chapter, you will learn about the various configurable components of the Cisco router and how to manipulate them. Basic router configuration and administrative tasks will be described, and the CDP protocol and its configuration will be introduced. In addition, you will learn how to configure and test IP. Finally, you will understand the steps involved in troubleshooting a Cisco router when there are connectivity problems.

ROUTER SETUP AND STARTUP

A router follows a specific boot process, but processes can vary. This section discusses the variety of startup options available during the boot process. In general, the boot process follows these steps:

1. Test hardware (POST).
2. Load bootstrap.
3. Locate and load Cisco IOS.
4. Locate and load router configuration file.

Figure 7-1 illustrates a simplified version of the basic flow of the boot process. The steps in the flow chart are discussed in greater detail in the following subsections.

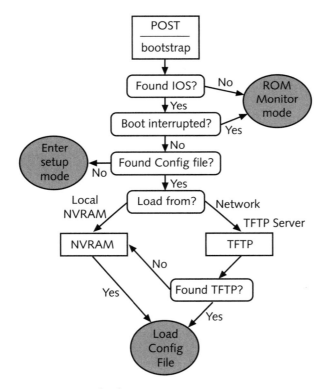

Figure 7-1   The boot process

POST

Read-only memory (ROM) in a router typically contains the **power-on self-test (POST)**, the bootstrap program, and often a version of the operating system. Most types of computer equipment do perform some type of POST immediately after being turned on. POST is a diagnostic test that determines if the hardware is operating correctly. During the POST, the bootstrap program, also called the **ROM Monitor**, checks basic operations of the attached hardware, including CPU, memory, and interfaces. The ROM Monitor checks the **configuration register** for instructions regarding how to load the Cisco IOS. Every Cisco router has a 16-bit configuration register, which is stored in NVRAM. This register allows you to control several boot functions, including:

- Forcing the system into the bootstrap program
- Enabling or disabling the console Break function
- Setting the console terminal baud rate
- Loading the IOS from ROM
- Loading the IOS from a TFTP server

You can examine the configuration register by typing "show version" at the enable mode prompt. The default is to load the IOS from flash memory. Figure 7-2 displays the output of the show version command.

Figure 7-2 Output from the show version command

The last line of this file should read "Configuration register is…" followed by a hexadecimal code. The last four binary digits of that code specify how your system will boot. Table 7-1 describes the meaning of the various combinations of the last four digits.

Table 7-1   Configuration register codes

Enter this:	Last four digits binary	Description
0x0000	0000	Enter ROM Monitor mode
0x0001	0001	Boot helper image from ROM (RxBoot mode)
0x2000 – 0xF	0010 – 1111	Check NVRAM for boot system commands; load IOS from flash if nothing else specified

Monitor Mode

You can set the router to enter **ROM Monitor mode** during the boot process by modifying the configuration register. The router also will enter ROM Monitor mode if it cannot find an IOS image during the boot process. The prompt for ROM Monitor mode is the greater than (>) symbol or, on the Cisco 1003, 1600, 2600, 3600, 4500, 7200, and 7500, the prompt is rommon>.

 On Cisco 2000, 2500, 3000, and 4000 series routers, you can press the Ctrl+Break keys within the first 60 seconds of the boot process to enter ROM Monitor mode.

You can use ROM Monitor mode to configure your router manually. You must provide each command in the correct syntax in order to configure the router. Also, you can initiate the automated startup process by typing "startup" at the prompt.

To configure your system to enter ROM Monitor mode, you can enter the following command at the global configuration prompt:

```
config-register 0x0
```

To configure your system to boot the helper image from ROM and enter RXBoot mode, you must enter the following command at the global configuration prompt:

```
config-register 0x1
```

To confirm your changes, go to the enable mode or user EXEC mode prompt, and then type "show version". The last line, depending on your previous actions, should have "(will be 0x0 at next reload)" or "(will be 0x1 next reload)." You can reboot using the reload command. When the router reboots, the ROM Monitor will load the IOS as specified in the configuration register.

Be careful when modifying the configuration register. Using ROM Monitor mode will not cause problems, but entering random hexadecimal commands above 0x2 may present a variety of problems. Modifying your configuration in this manner is only advisable when there is no other course of action.

If you see a series of seemingly random characters when you boot your router, change the baud rate on your terminal. Typically, the correct setting is 9600; however, when troubleshooting the system startup, you should try 2400 and other baud settings if 9600 does not work.

Cisco IOS

As mentioned, the Cisco IOS is usually loaded from flash memory. Figure 7-3 displays the output from a Cisco 2500 series router during bootup under this default condition.

System Bootstrap, Version 11.0(10c), SOFTWARE
Copyright (c) 1986-1996 by cisco Systems
2500 processor with 6144 Kbytes of main memory

%SYS-4-CONFIG_NEWER: Configurations from version 12.0 may not be correctly understood.
F3: 7379840+96124+568408 at 0x3000060

      Restricted Rights Legend

Use, duplication, or disclosure by the Government is
subject to restrictions as set forth in subparagraph
(c) of the Commercial Computer Software - Restricted
Rights clause at FAR sec. 52.227-19 and subparagraph
(c) (1) (ii) of the Rights in Technical Data and Computer
Software clause at DFARS sec. 252.227-7013.

      cisco Systems, Inc.
      170 West Tasman Drive
      San Jose, California 95134-1706

Cisco Internetwork Operating System Software
IOS (tm) 2500 Software (C2500-D-L), **Version 12.0**(4)T, RELEASE SOFTWARE (fc1)   ← This is IOS version 12.0
Copyright (c) 1986-1999 by cisco Systems, Inc.
Compiled Wed 28-Apr-99 15:15 by kpma
Image text-base: 0x0303CD7C, data-base: 0x00001000

cisco 2500 (68030) processor (revision L) with 6144K/2048K bytes of memory.
Processor board ID 03005087, with hardware revision 00000000
Bridging software.
X.25 software, Version 3.0.0.
2 Ethernet/IEEE 802.3 interface(s) ←   ⎫ There are 2 Ethernet
2 Serial network interface(s)   interfaces and 2 Serial
32K bytes of non-volatile configuration memory.   ⎭ interfaces on this router
8192K bytes of processor board System flash (Read ONLY)

Press RETURN to get started!

Figure 7-3   Output from the Cisco 2500 series router on bootup

If you want to see information about your router's flash memory, type "show flash" from the enable mode prompt. Figure 7-4 displays the output from the show flash command.

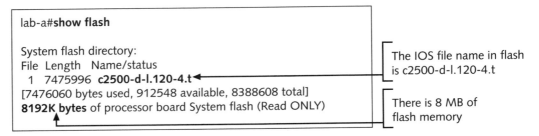

```
lab-a#show flash

System flash directory:
File  Length   Name/status
  1   7475996  c2500-d-l.120-4.t
[7476060 bytes used, 912548 available, 8388608 total]
8192K bytes of processor board System flash (Read ONLY)
```

The IOS file name in flash is c2500-d-l.120-4.t

There is 8 MB of flash memory

Figure 7-4   Output from the show flash command

A **Trivial File Transfer Protocol (TFTP) server** is a computer, such as a PC, UNIX workstation, or laptop that is running TFTP server services. This allows the Cisco router to transfer the IOS image, as well as other files, to the TFTP server via the Trivial File Transfer Protocol (TFTP). The TFTP protocol is a simple connectionless protocol that is less complex than FTP.

Cisco routers support the following fallback options for loading the IOS:

- If the IOS is configured to load from a TFTP server, but that server cannot be located, the IOS is loaded from flash memory.

- If the IOS cannot be found in flash or on a TFTP server, a minimal version of the IOS is loaded from ROM. The version of the IOS in ROM may be an older version of the IOS than the one currently running.

Booting from TFTP

You can force the router to load its IOS from a TFTP server by putting boot system commands into the configuration file. As long as the configuration register is set to 0x2, the ROM Monitor will look for these commands in NVRAM during the bootup process. Even if you do not want to load the IOS from a TFTP server you should maintain an additional backup copy of the IOS on a TFTP server in case something happens to the IOS on the router. Because the IOS is maintained in flash memory by default, to copy the IOS to a TFTP server, issue the following command from the enable mode:

```
copy flash tftp
```

Next, the IOS will prompt you to enter the source filename, which you can find using either the show version or show flash commands. You will then be asked for the IP address of the TFTP server. Finally, you will be prompted for the destination filename, which is usually the same as the source filename.

A typical IOS filename might look like this: igs-j-l.111-5. The default filename for the destination file is the same as the name of the source file. If you want to enable your system to boot the flash file from the TFTP server, issue the following command from **global configuration mode**:

```
boot system tftp igs-j-l.111-5
```

The boot system ROM command will force the router to boot into ROM.

This command assumes that the IOS filename is igs-j-l.111-5. This command will be broadcast so that a computer running TFTP software will respond. After you have inserted this command, you can type "show running-config" to see that the line has been entered in your configuration file. You should see "boot system tftp igs-j-l.111-5 255.255.255.255" on the terminal screen. To use the TFTP server, your system must have IP correctly configured for one of its interfaces, because TFTP is one of the many protocols associated with the TCP/IP suite.

You can enter as many boot system tftp commands as you would like for redundancy. This ensures that your system can boot from a TFTP server, even if the primary server is not available. When you view your configuration after entering multiple boot system tftp commands, you will see multiple boot system lines in the configuration. To remove any given line, type "no boot system tftp", followed by the IOS filename at the global configuration prompt. Remember, if you want these modifications to be applied to your startup configuration, you must type the following at the privileged EXEC mode prompt to ensure that your changes are applied to the startup configuration in NVRAM:

```
copy running-config startup-config
```

 If you want to clear the Cisco IOS in your flash memory, you can type, "erase flash" at the privileged EXEC mode prompt. Be extremely careful with this command, as it wipes out the working IOS on the router. Be sure to back up your configuration to a TFTP server before using this command.

Upgrading the IOS

Before you load a flash file to your router, use the show flash command to ensure that there is enough free memory to load the new Cisco IOS software. The system will tell you how much memory is used and how much is free. You may have to erase the existing flash memory before writing onto it due to space limitations.

 If you abort the copying process in the middle of copying a new flash memory, your existing flash memory will still be active, assuming that you have not erased it already.

Any time you are planning to upgrade or modify the IOS, you should back up your current IOS to a TFTP server. You can use the show flash or show version commands to learn the name of the flash file that you are using and then copy that file to the TFTP server. TFTP software is available for a variety of platforms such as UNIX, Windows NT, Windows 95/98, and MS-DOS/Windows. You can download TFTP server software from the Cisco Web site at *www.cisco.com*.

RXBoot Mode

RXBoot mode is another configuration mode that you can enter when changes to your system make it impossible to boot from the flash memory and you cannot locate a valid IOS image. The prompt from RXBoot mode is the hostname of your router followed by "boot" in parentheses. For example, if your router's name is router2, the prompt would be router2(boot). RXBoot mode provides a limited set of the Cisco IOS commands from ROM to allow you to configure the router. The commands that are accepted are a subset of those used in the normal user EXEC and privileged EXEC mode.

Cisco Catalyst 1900 IOS and Configuration Management

If you would like to upgrade or restore the IOS via TFTP, the command syntax is **copy tftp://tftp_server_address/IOS_file/ opcode**. The opcode command tells the device to load the file into flash memory. For example, assume that you had a backup of your switch configuration saved as cat1900en_9_01.bin on the TFTP server 192.168.1.220. You would use the following command from the enable mode prompt (assuming your switch is named Rm410HL):

```
Rm410HL#copy tftp://192.168.1.220/cat1900_9_01.binopcode
```

To backup the configuration settings for your Catalyst 1900 switch, you copy the contents of NVRAM to a TFTP server. The command syntax is **copy nvram tftp://tftp_server_address/config_file_name**. Therefore, if you want to make a backup copy of your switch configuration and you want to name it "rm410HLconfig", on a TFTP server, you would enter the following command:

```
Rm410HL#copy nvram tftp://192.168.1.220/rm410HLconfig
```

If you later need to restore the configuration of your switch from the TFTP server, you would change the order of the command slightly to show that the file was to be copied into NVRAM. To restore the configuration file that was backed up in the previous command, enter this command:

```
Rm410HL#copy tftp://192.168.1.220/rm410HLconfig nvram
```

If you decide that you don't want the configuration file, you can delete it with this command:

```
Rm410HL#delete nvram
```

That command will reset your switch to its factory default settings and you will be asked to confirm that change.

Router Configuration Files

The router configuration file that is used during the boot process is called the *startup-config*. Sometimes this file is referred to as the backup configuration because it is the saved version of the configuration file. Any time you want to revert to the settings in your startup-config, you can reboot the system by powering off and on the router or by issuing the reload command. As long as you haven't saved the running configuration on top of the startup configuration, the running configuration in RAM will be dumped when you reload, and the saved version in NVRAM will be loaded into RAM. It is important to note that when you copy over the startup configuration in NVRAM, that file is replaced. However, when you copy to the running configuration in RAM, the files are blended. In addition, there is no erase run command. If you want to get rid of the running configuration, you must reload either by command or by turning the router off and on.

If you would like to view the contents of the startup-config, you can type "show startup-config" or just "sh star" at the enable prompt. If you would like to see your working or running configuration, type "show running-config" or just "sh ru" at the enable prompt. The important copy commands as well as some other configuration commands are shown in Table 7-2.

7

Table 7-2   Important router copy commands

Command from Enable Mode	Description
copy running-config tftp	Copies the running configuration located in RAM to a TFTP server.
copy startup-config tftp	Copies the startup configuration located in NVRAM to a TFTP server.
copy tftp running-config	Copies the configuration from the TFTP server to the running configuration. The reconfiguration of the router is immediate when this command is issued. The running-config is not replaced. The files are blended.
copy tftp startup-config	Copies the configuration from the TFTP server to the startup configuration. The startup-config is replaced with the one from the TFTP server.
copy run start	Copies the working configuration file in RAM to the startup configuration file in NVRAM. Replaces the startup configuration file.
copy start run	Copies the startup configuration file in NVRAM to the running configuration in RAM. Does not replace the file in RAM; the files are blended.
copy flash tftp	Copies the IOS in flash memory to a TFTP server.
copy tftp flash	Copies the IOS from a TFTP server to flash memory.
configure terminal	Used to specify that you would like to configure your settings manually from the console terminal.
configure memory	Used to specify that you would like to pull your configuration information from NVRAM.

Table 7-2   Important router copy commands (continued)

Command from Enable Mode	Description
configure network	Indicates that you would like to load your working configuration from a TFTP server.
configure overwrite-network	Indicates that you would like to overwrite the existing NVRAM with the configuration information stored on the TFTP server.
erase startup-config	Erases the current startup configuration. When you reboot the computer, you will be prompted to enter the automated setup program.

This table lists the most important commands. If you are curious about additional commands, type "copy ?" at the enable prompt.

 Notice there is no copy command that copies between flash and a running or startup configuration file. It is important to think of the IOS and configuration files as separate. The IOS is a relatively large file that is the entire operating system whereas the configuration files are very small and modify the operation of the router.

Methods for Making Changes

When changes to the router's configuration or boot process are required, the administrator should follow a logical process for making those changes. Remember that changes usually can be implemented and tested without saving those changes to the startup configuration. This is because changes to the running configuration take place immediately. Almost everything can be done in working memory (running-config). When you are satisfied that the changes are correct, you can copy the running configuration to the startup configuration. These basic steps can be used for implementing changes:

1. Make changes as desired to the configuration.

2. Examine those changes.

3. Determine if the changes meet the desired result.

4. Remove the changes if they do not meet the desired result, or simply reboot the router.

5. Copy the changes from the running configuration to the startup configuration when they do meet the desired result.

If the administrator makes changes that should be tested by rebooting the router, then he or she can copy the Cisco IOS and startup configuration to a TFTP server first. This way, if the changes do not meet the desired result, those files can be copied back to the router from the TFTP server.

CDP

The **Cisco Discovery Protocol (CDP)** is a Cisco proprietary Data Link layer protocol that shares configuration information between Cisco devices that are connected locally to each other. All Cisco devices, including routers, switches, and access servers, can use CDP to discover each other and learn about the configurations of other devices. Using CDP can help you quickly determine the network topology.

With CDP, you can discover other devices on the same LAN segment and those connected over a serial interface. Figure 7-5 illustrates the CDP feedback after the show cdp neighbor command has been issued.

```
route#show cdp neighbor
Capability codes:   R- Router, T - Tran bridge, B - Source Route Bridge
                    S - Switch, H - Host, I - IGMP, r - Repeater

Device ID        Local Interface   Holdtme   Capability   Platform   Port ID
ROUTER1          Ser 1             170       R            2500       Ser 1
ROUTER2          Ser 0             170       R            4000       Ser 0
```

Figure 7-5 Show CDP neighbor command

The show cdp neighbor command supports the following options:

- Ethernet: To learn more about Ethernet interfaces attached to neighbors
- Null: To learn more about interfaces of a neighbor that does not have an address assigned
- Serial: More information about neighbors connected to serial interfaces.
- Detail: Detailed information about the CDP neighbor and all attached devices. This detailed information includes device identification, remote interface type, and remote IP address.

CDP was designed to be a low-overhead protocol. CDP broadcasts information every 60 seconds by default. You can modify the length of time between updates by using the cdp timer command. The CDP command is the same for routers and Cisco IOS enabled switches. For example, to change CDP to update every 120 seconds, type:

```
router(config)#cdp timer 120
```

The CDP information is only held a set length of time, which is 180 seconds by default. You can modify the length of time that the CDP information is held by issuing the cdp holdtime command. For example, to configure CDP packets to be discarded after one minute, type:

```
router(config)#cdp holdtime 60
```

After 60 seconds, the CDP information is discarded, given the preceding example. By default, CDP is enabled on all Cisco devices, but you modify CDP broadcasts on the network. To turn off CDP on the entire router, use the no cdp run command at the global configuration prompt. If you want to disable cdp information from being sent on a given interface, change to the interface configuration mode prompt, and then issue the no cdp enable command. For example, to remove CDP broadcasts from your Ethernet0 interface, enter the following from enable mode:

```
router#config +
router(config)#interface Ethernet0
router(config-if)#no cdp enable
```

You can use the show cdp interface command in enable mode to retrieve the statistics that CDP will report on the local router's interfaces.

 As an administrator, you can learn about a network's topology by using the telnet command in combination with the show cdp neighbor or show cdp neighbor detail command. Simply telnet into one of the virtual terminals and issue the cdp commands that you would use locally to determine attached Cisco devices.

IP ON THE ROUTER

If the router is initially configured using the extended setup program, you will be asked if you would like to enable IP on your router. If you answer yes, you will be prompted to configure IP on each of the interfaces that you wish to set up. If you answer no, you can either run setup again later, or you can configure the interfaces manually.

To manually configure IP on an interface, you must first change to interface configuration mode. Then, you can use the ip address command to configure an IP address for your specific interface. For example, if you want to configure the IP address 192.168.1.1 with the default Class C subnet mask for the Ethernet interface, type the following from enable mode:

```
Router#config t
Router(config)#int E0
Router(config-if)#ip address 192.168.1.1 255.255.255.0
Router(config-if)#no shutdown
```

Notice that the subnet mask was included in the IP address command. The command would be incomplete without the subnet mask. You can also add the command secondary to an ip address command and configure the address as a second IP address for the interface. Also notice the addition of the no shutdown command. This command will enable the interface. In the event you are configuring a serial interface as a **DCE (data communication equipment)**, you will also need to add the clockrate (bandwidth in bits per second) command.

If you want to change the way the subnet mask is shown when you view statistics about an interface, type "term ip netmask-format" at the enable mode prompt. You will have to choose decimal, bit-count, or hexadecimal to complete the command; the default is decimal. If you choose bit-count, the mask is displayed in CIDR format.

IP ON THE SWITCH

An IP address is not necessary on a switch like the Catalyst 1900 because switches, as you know from previous discussions, operate mainly on Layer 2 (MAC addresses). However, you may wish to configure an IP address for your switch so that you can manage it over the network via Telnet or some other management software. Also, you may need to configure an IP address for your switch if you wish to implement VLANs on your network (a concept covered in a later chapter).

By default, Cisco switches are not configured with IP addresses. In order to set an IP address, you must enter Global Configuration mode by typing **configure terminal** (or one of its abbreviations). Then, you can configure the IP address and default gateway using these commands:

```
Rm410HL(config)#ip address 192.168.1.204 255.255.255.0

Rm410HL(config)#ip default-gateway 192.168.1.1
```

IP CONNECTIVITY

Once you configure the router for IP, you should test for connectivity. There are several tools that can help you verify this connectivity. These tools apply to various layers of the OSI model, as described in Table 7–3.

Table 7-3   Testing connectivity by layer

Tool	OSI Layer	TCP/IP Layer
Telnet	Application layer	Application layer
Ping	Network layer	Internetwork layer
Trace	Network layer	Internetwork layer
Show ip route	Network layer	Internetwork layer
Show interface	Data Link and Physical layers	Network Interface layer

When testing connectivity, if you cannot get a connection at a higher layer, check the connectivity of a lower layer. For example, if you cannot get a telnet connection, you should attempt to ping the host to which you are trying to connect.

Telnet

Telnet is a utility that connects at the highest layer of the OSI model and provides remote access to other devices. Cisco routers allow telnet connections via their virtual terminal ports. If you can establish telnet connectivity to a router, you have established that it is available on the network and that you have connectivity at all layers. After you establish telnet connectivity, you can learn more about the configuration of the remote router by executing commands as if you were connected to the router locally.

 If you accidentally initiate a connection with another router from your locally attached router, you can stop the process by pressing Ctrl+Shift+6. This key combination can be used to stop any command from running. You can also use the logout command at the user EXEC or privileged EXEC mode prompt. This will log you out of the remote router but maintain the connection with your local router.

IP Host Names

When telnetting to a remote router or host, the IP address of the host must follow the telnet command. Rather than using IP addresses, it is easier to refer to a remote host or router using a name. Sometimes, you cannot gain connectivity because the host name that you are trying to connect with is entered in a table incorrectly. For example, suppose you are trying to telnet into router15, but the address for router15 is configured incorrectly on your system. To determine what addresses to names are mapped on your router, check the name table by issuing the following command:

```
router#show hosts
```

You will then see a list of the names configured on your router. If you would like to add an entry to your hosts file for name resolution, you must go to global configuration mode. For example, if you want to add an entry telling your router that router15 is at IP address 192.168.5.1, type:

```
router(config)#ip host router15 192.168.5.1
```

If you want to later remove that entry, type:

```
router(config)#no ip host router15 192.168.5.1
```

If you find that one of the entries in your host table is incorrect, you can remove it and enter the correct mapping. You can also allow a name server to handle the IP address to name resolution. For example, if you want to specify that a name server with IP address 172.33.44.1 be used by the router for name resolution, enter the command:

```
router(config)#ip name-server 172.33.44.1
```

Then, when a friendly name is used, the name server will be consulted to provide name resolution for the router. In this example, if you type "ping router3", the router will ping the IP address of router3 based on the name resolution in the table located on the device with the IP address 172.33.44.1. Using a name server provides name resolution from one location, making a table configuration on each device unnecessary.

Ping and Trace

If you can't get connectivity at the Application layer, try connectivity at the Internetwork layer. Ping and trace are available from the user EXEC and privileged EXEC mode. Ping and trace verify connectivity at the Internetwork layer of the TCP/IP model. Both commands use ICMP messages to verify that the destination host is reachable, and if not, give possible reasons for the problem. Ping sends a packet to the destination and waits for a response. By default, the ping utility with Cisco routers is configured to send five packets to the target. Ping can return the following replies:

- !: Successful receipt of the ICMP echo
- .: Request timed out
- U: Destination was unreachable
- C: Congestion experienced
- I: Ping interrupted
- ?: Packet type unknown
- &: Packet TTL exceeded

The information returned from ping (in addition to the replies listed above) includes the quantity of ICMP packets sent; the timeout duration; the transfer success rate; and the minimum, average, and maximum roundtrip times for the ICMP packets sent.

If you simply type "ping" and then press the Return key at the enable mode prompt, you will be able to enter your ping command step by step. You also will be able to control the protocol type (for example IPX rather than IP), the size of the ping packet, the number of packets sent, and other options. Using the ping command alone is referred to as **extended mode ping**. Extended mode ping can only be accessed from the privileged mode prompt.

Ping is a quick way to determine if there is network layer connectivity. If ping indicates a problem with connectivity, using trace may provide a better clue as to the source of the connectivity problem. The trace command is similar to the ping command, except that the replies are requested at each hop along the way to the destination. Trace sends multiple ICMP packets with progressively higher time-to-live counters (TTL) until the packet reaches the destination. If there are three routers between the destination and the source of the trace, there will be four replies to the message—one for each hop along the way and one when the trace reaches the final destination. The trace command is useful for determining where in the process the communication is breaking down. The following responses can be returned by a trace:

- !H: Indicates that a router received, but didn't forward, the ICMP echo request

- P: Protocol unreachable

- N: Network unreachable

- U: Port unreachable

- *: Request timed out

IP Route

If you cannot get connectivity using ping or trace, you should check your routing table. If the routing table is sending communications out of the wrong interface, or if there is no entry in the routing table that will handle routing to the target network, it will cause your higher-level connectivity to fail. You can issue the show ip route command from the enable mode prompt. This command displays the routing table. Typically, routing tables are dynamically created when routing protocols are configured on the router. If you want to, you can use the ip route command from the global configuration mode to statically enter routes in the routing table. Very often a routing table will consist of routes learned both through dynamic and static means. Routing is covered in more detail in Chapter 8.

Checking the Interface

One of the biggest mistakes made when troubleshooting is not checking the interfaces on the router. If the interfaces are down, packets cannot be delivered. Router interfaces go down for a variety of reasons including incorrect IP configuration and cable problems. You can use the show ip interface command to view the configuration of IP on your interfaces and to check the status of the interface.

You can check the configuration of a specific interface from the enable mode prompt with the show interface command. For example, if you wanted to check the statistics for Serial0, type:

```
router#show int s0
```

The first line reports the status of the interface. There are two elements to the first line: The first reports the physical status of the interface, and the next reports the status of the line protocol. If the interface and protocol are fully functional, you will see the following information:

```
Serial0 is up, line protocol is up
```

That report means that both the interface and line protocol are functioning properly. In other words, the interface is functioning at both the physical and data link layer. You also may see one of the following replies:

- Serial0 is up, line protocol is down: The interface is not receiving any network data or **keepalive frames,** but the physical interface is up and operational. This typically indicates that there is a problem with the configuration of the router. Check the running configuration using the show run command. Make sure routing protocols and static routing commands have been properly configured. Also make sure that the IP address for the interface was entered correctly. On serial interfaces, you will also get this report if the router your router is connected to through this interface is down. In other words, the remote attached router can push your router interface down.

- Serial0 is administratively down, line protocol is down: This indicates that the interface is disabled on the router. This usually occurs when you are not using the interface and there is no cable attached to it.

- Serial0 is up, line protocol is administratively down: This indicates that you need to use the no shutdown command on this interface to bring the interface back up. This typically happens when configurations are copied to the router from a file or TFTP server.

- Serial0 down, line protocol is down: This indicates that there is a physical problem with the serial interface on the router. Check the cable.

 Different types of interfaces can show different types of reports. For example, a Token Ring interface reports down when there is no electrical carrier signal present.

Figure 7-6 displays the output from the show interfaces command. Some of the less important output is not shown for space considerations.

```
lab-a#show interfaces
Ethernet0 is up, line protocol is up◄
  Hardware is Lance, address is 0000.0c8e.b490 (bia 0000.0c8e.b490)
  Internet address is 192.5.5.1/24
  MTU 1500 bytes, BW 10000 Kbit, DLY 1000 usec,
    reliability 255/255, txload 1/255, rxload 1/255
  Encapsulation ARPA, loopback not set
  Keepalive set (10 sec)
  ARP type: ARPA, ARP Timeout 04:00:00
  Last input never, output 00:00:03, output hang never
  Last clearing of "show interface" counters never
  Queueing strategy: fifo
  Output queue 0/40, 0 drops; input queue 0/75, 0 drops
  5 minute input rate 0 bits/sec, 0 packets/sec
  5 minute output rate 0 bits/sec, 0 packets/sec
Serial0 is down, line protocol is down◄
  Hardware is HD64570
  Internet address is 201.100.11.1/24
  MTU 1500 bytes, BW 1544 Kbit, DLY 20000 usec,
    reliability 255/255, txload 1/255, rxload 1/255
  Encapsulation HDLC, loopback not set
  Keepalive set (10 sec)
  Last input never, output never, output hang never
  Last clearing of "show interface" counters never
  Queueing strategy: fifo
  Output queue 0/40, 0 drops; input queue 0/75, 0 drops
  5 minute input rate 0 bits/sec, 0 packets/sec
  5 minute output rate 0 bits/sec, 0 packets/sec
    0 packets input, 0 bytes, 0 no buffer
    Received 0 broadcasts, 0 runts, 0 giants, 0 throttles
    0 input errors, 0 CRC, 0 frame, 0 overrun, 0 ignored, 0 abort
    15 packets output, 3198 bytes, 0 underruns
    0 output errors, 0 collisions, 2 interface resets
    0 output buffer failures, 0 output buffers swapped out
    0 carrier transitions
    DCD=up  DSR=up  DTR=down  RTS=down  CTS=up
Serial1 is administratively down, line protocol is down◄
  Hardware is HD64570
  MTU 1500 bytes, BW 1544 Kbit, DLY 20000 usec,
    reliability 255/255, txload 1/255, rxload 1/255
  Encapsulation HDLC, loopback not set
  Keepalive set (10 sec)
  Last input never, output never, output hang never
```

Interface E0 is fully functional. Frames can be sent and received on this interface.

S0 is not functional. In this case, the serial interface on the router attached to this router is down. If one end of a point-to-point link is down, it will "push" the attached up interface on the next router down.

The S1 interface is not functional. In this case, there is no cable attached to S1 as it is not being used.

Figure 7-6 Output from the show interfaces command

Clear Counters

The router keeps detailed statistics regarding data passing across its interfaces. Before using the show interface command, you may want to clear the existing interface information. You can clear these statistics **(counters)** on the interface by using the clear interface or clear counters command. To clear the counters for interface E0, type the following:

```
router#clear interface E0
```

If you want to clear the counters on all attached interfaces, use the clear counters command.

Debug

One of the most powerful tools you can use to obtain information from your router is the debug command. This tool is only available from privileged EXEC mode. Debug has numerous subcommands that allow you to troubleshoot particular protocols. If you would like to see all of the debugging counters available, you can use the debug all command. However, the debug all command will seriously affect router performance, so you should avoid experimenting with debug on a production router. Output from the debug all command is displayed in Figure 7-7.

With debug, you can also check for specific types of traffic on the wire. For example, if you want to perform general IP packet debugging, type the following:

```
router#debug ip packet
```

Details regarding IP packets received by the router will display. Again, the debug command is powerful, but also resource intensive and should not be run for extended periods of time due to its negative impact on router performance. Use the debug command only when necessary to check network traffic; use the no debug command to disable debugging when you are finished. For example, to turn off debugging for broadcast traffic, you would type:

```
router#no debug ip packet
```

You can also type "no debug all" or "undebug all". Additional debug commands are introduced in later chapters.

7

```
RouterB#debug all
This may severely impact network performance. Continue? [confirm]

All possible debugging has been turned on
RouterB#
IP: s=172.22.3.1 (Serial1), d=255.255.255.255, len 76, rcvd 2
UDP: rcvd src=172.22.3.1(520), dst=255.255.255.255(520), length=52
RIP: received v1 update from 172.22.3.1 on Serial1
      172.22.4.0 in 1 hops
      172.22.5.0 in 2 hops
RIP: Update contains 2 routes
SERVICE_MODULE(0): lxt441 interrupt 1 status A7 loop 0
SERVICE_MODULE(0): lxt441 interrupt 1 status 87 loop 0
SERVICE_MODULE(0): lxt441 interrupt 1 status A7 loop 0
SERVICE_MODULE(0): lxt441 interrupt 1 status 87 loop 0
Serial1: HDLC myseq 6631, mineseen 6631, yourseen 6580, line up
SERVICE_MODULE(0): lxt441 interrupt 1 status A7 loop 0
SERVICE_MODULE(0): lxt441 interrupt 1 status 87 loop 0
SERVICE_MODULE(0): lxt441 interrupt 1 status A7 loop 0
SERVICE_MODULE(0): lxt441 interrupt 1 status 87 loop 0
RIP: sending v1 update to 255.255.255.255 via Ethernet0 (172.22.2.1)
      subnet  172.22.3.0, metric 1
      subnet  172.22.4.0, metric 2
      subnet  172.22.5.0, metric 3
RIP: Update contains 3 routes
IP: s=172.22.2.1 (local), d=255.255.255.255 (Ethernet0), len 55, sending broad/m
ulticast
RIP: sending v1 update to 255.255.255.255 via Serial1 (172.22.3.2)
      subnet  172.22.2.0, metric 1
RIP: Update contains 1 routes
IP: s=172.22.3.2 (local), d=255.255.255.255 (Serial1), len 67, sending broad/mul
ticast
SERVICE_MODULE(0): lxt441 interrupt 1 status A7 loop 0
SERVICE_MODULE(0): lxt441 interrupt 1 status 87 loop 0
Serial0: attempting to restart
Serial1: HDLC myseq 6632, mineseen 6632, yourseen 6581, line up
IP: s=172.22.5.1 (Ethernet0), d=255.255.255.255, len 106, rcvd 2
UDP: rcvd src=172.22.5.1(520), dst=255.255.255.255(520), length=72
RIP: ignored v1 update from bad source 172.22.5.1 on Ethernet0
SERVICE_MODULE(0): lxt441 interrupt 1 status A7 loop 0
SERVICE_MODULE(0): lxt441 interrupt 1 status 87 loop 0
SERVICE_MODULE(0): lxt441 interrupt 1 status A7 loop 0
SERVICE_MODULE(0): lxt441 interrupt 1 status 87 loop 0
SERVICE_MODULE(0): lxt441 interrupt 1 status A7 loop 0
SERVICE_MODULE(0): lxt441 interrupt 1 status 87 loop 0
Serial1: HDLC myseq 6633, mineseen 6633, yourseen 6582, line up
All possible debugging has been turned off
RouterB#
```

The debug all command warns you that issuing this command could cause severe network congestion. This command should only be used for a short period of time as a troubleshooting tool.

Figure 7-7   Debug all command output

CHAPTER SUMMARY

- When the router boots, it follows a set routine.

- Although the router's boot process can vary, the typical boot process follows this sequence: First, the router checks all of its internal hardware components during a process called the POST (power-on self-test). Next, the router loads the basic configuration routine known as the bootstrap program. Then, the bootstrap attempts to locate the Cisco IOS, which, in turn, loads the router configuration file.

- If the Cisco IOS is set to load from a TFTP server, but the TFTP server cannot be located, then the IOS will boot from flash memory.

❐ If the IOS cannot be found in flash memory or on the TFTP server, then a limited version will boot from ROM.

❐ If the Cisco IOS is set to load a configuration file from a TFTP server, but the file or server is not available, the configuration file will be loaded from NVRAM. However, if a configuration file is not available in NVRAM or on a TFTP server, then the automated setup routine will be initialized.

❐ The Cisco Discovery Protocol (CDP) is proprietary to Cisco devices. This protocol shares information between Cisco devices about other local Cisco devices.

❐ CDP uses broadcasts to update neighbors every 60 seconds by default (the update time interval is configurable).

❐ Devices share information about their interface configurations and connections to other devices.

❐ IP configuration on Cisco switches and routers is similar: the command syntax is ip address [IP address] [subnet mask].

❐ When you configure an address for a router interface, you must be in interface configuration mode (config-if).

❐ When you configure an IP address for a Catalyst 1900 switch, you need only be in global configuration mode. These switches don't require IP addresses, you need only configure one if you intend to remotely manage the switch.

❐ You can verify router connectivity to other systems by using telnet to determine if there is Application layer connectivity.

❐ If you cannot get connectivity at the Application layer, try trace and ping. Then, check your routing table with the show ip route command to determine if there is a problem with the Network layer.

❐ One of the most important troubleshooting commands is the show interface command. If your interfaces are not up, you cannot route packets.

Key Terms

Cisco Discovery Protocol (CDP) — A Cisco proprietary Data Link layer protocol that shares configuration information between Cisco devices that are locally connected.

configuration register — A feature in Cisco routers that is stored in NVRAM and allows the administrator to control several boot functions.

counters — Detailed statistics kept by a router about data passing across its interface.

DCE (data communication equipment) — Equipment that performs some type of signal conversion between the terminal device and the transmission facility. Usually the DCE is part of the telco provider's equipment.

extended mode ping — When you type the word "ping" at the privileged EXEC prompt, and then press the Return or Enter key, you will be presented with ping options. Extended mode ping options include the destination address of the ping, the protocol, repeat count, and datagram size.

global configuration mode — A router mode that allows you to manipulate most of the router's generic settings. The prompt for global configuration mode is router(config)#.

keepalive frames — Data frames sent between two hosts to ensure that the connection between those hosts remains open.

power-on self test (POST) — A diagnostic program in ROM that runs when the router is powered on. POST checks hardware availability.

ROM Monitor — A bootstrap program that runs during the power-on self-test and checks basic operations of hardware, including CPU, memory, and interfaces.

ROM Monitor mode — A router mode in which you can configure the router manually.

RXBoot mode — A configuration mode that can be entered when changes to a system make it impossible to boot from the flash memory and a valid IOS image cannot be located.

Trivial File Transfer Protocol (TFTP) servers — Computers, such as PCs, laptops, or UNIX workstations, that can be used to maintain Cisco IOS versions and Cisco router configuration files. TFTP is a protocol that is used to copy files back and forth from a computer running TFTP server services.

REVIEW QUESTIONS

1. If you want to see the hexadecimal boot setting for the configuration register, which command would you use? (Choose all that apply.)

   a. Router> sh int

   b. Router> sh ver

   c. Router#sh ver

   d. Router#sh int

2. When the trace command is used, multiple packets are sent to a remote destination with:

   a. progressively higher TTL values until a packet reaches the destination

   b. progressively lower TTL values until a packet is returned from the destination

   c. progressively smaller hop counts

   d. full routing tables

3. If you want to configure the values that ping uses and have access to extended mode ping options, which of the following represents the appropriate prompt and the command you would type before pressing the Return key?

   a. router#ping

   b. router#ping ex md

   c. router#ping motd

   d. router> ping

   e. router#ping –e

   f. router> ping –e

4. What is usually stored in NVRAM? (Choose all that apply.)

   a. Configuration register

   b. Backup copy of the IOS

   c. Limited version of the IOS

   d. Configuration file

5. Which of the following connectivity utilities use ICMP messages for troubleshooting the connection? (Choose all that apply.)

   a. Ping

   b. Telnet

   c. Trace

   d. Ip route

   e. Show version

6. Which layer of the OSI model contains the telnet utility?

   a. Application

   b. Network

   c. Data Link

   d. Physical

   e. Transport

7. Which of the following information is *not* visible after you issue a ping?

   a. Quantity of ICMP packets sent

   b. Timeout duration

   c. Success rate

   d. MAC address

   e. Roundtrip times

7

8. If the packet type is unknown, what does ping report?

    a. !

    b. .

    c. ?

    d. U

9. Which of the following commands are considered incomplete or will not be recognized by the router's IOS? (Assume that the Return key is pressed immediately after the command.) (Choose all that apply.)

    a. router> ping 192.168.1.1

    b. router#ping

    c. router> ping

    d. router#config

    e. router> config

10. Which of the following maps the route from HostA to HostB across the Internet to an unknown destination?

    a. Show ip route

    b. Ping

    c. Trace

    d. Finger

11. If the configuration register is set to 0x2102, where will the system look for boot instructions?

    a. Flash

    b. NVRAM

    c. RAM

    d. ROM

12. If there are no specific instructions to the contrary, where does the system attempt to load the IOS from?

    a. ROM

    b. RAM

    c. NVRAM

    d. Flash

13. If you want to see information about other Cisco devices attached to your router, which of the following commands would you use?

    a. show cisco neighbor

    b. show cdp neighbor

    c. show cdp config

    d. initiate cdp scan

14. CDP is enabled by default on Cisco devices. True or False?

15. Which of the following is the first step in the router boot process?

    a. Locate and load Cisco IOS

    b. Load bootstrap

    c. Locate and load router configuration file

    d. POST

16. Which of the following occurs after the loading of the bootstrap?

    a. Test hardware

    b. Configuration register is examined to determine from where to load the IOS

    c. Locate and load router configuration file

    d. POST

17. What is another name for the privileged EXEC mode?

    a. Enable secret mode

    b. Enable mode

    c. Login mode

    d. User mode

18. By default, what will happen if the IOS cannot be found in flash memory?

    a. The router attempts to load a minimal copy from ROM.

    b. The router uses CDP.

    c. The router contacts an HTTP server.

    d. The router automatically shuts down.

19. If the router is configured to load the IOS from a TFTP server, where will the router look next for the IOS?

    a. ROM

    b. Flash

    c. FTP server

    d. HTTP server

    e. CDP

20. Which command could you use to back up the IOS to a TFTP server?

    a. copy IOS tftp

    b. copy flash tftp

    c. copy rom tftp

    d. copy running-config tftp

7

21. If you want to see information about other Cisco devices attached to your router, including their IP addresses, which of the following commands would you use?

    a. show cisco neighbor

    b. show cdp neighbor

    c. show cdp neighbor detail

    d. show cdp neighbor Ethernet

22. What is the command to erase the configuration file on a Cisco 1900 series switch?

    a. erase start

    b. delete start

    c. disable nvram

    d. delete nvram

23. The show interfaces command displays the following output: Ethernet0 is up, line protocol is administratively down. What do you infer?

    a. There is no cable attached to the Ethernet0 interface on the router.

    b. The no shutdown command needs to be configured on the Ethernet0 interface.

    c. Incompatible routing protocols have been configured on the router.

    d. There is a physical problem with the Ethernet0 interface on the router.

24. What is the purpose of a hosts file on a router?

    a. To allow you to use hostnames instead of IP addresses when referring to network devices

    b. To facilitate ARP on the router

    c. To allow routers to see other devices on the network

    d. To block unwanted hosts from using the router

25. Which of the following commands will display the routing table for a Cisco router?

    a. show route

    b. show ip route

    c. show routing table

    d. show table

CASE PROJECTS

1. Lisa and Moe are discussing the CDP protocol. They know it was developed by Cisco and is not part of any protocol suite with which they are familiar. What can you tell them about CDP? Specifically, what is the purpose of this protocol? With which OSI layer is it associated? Is it enabled by default? What is the update interval? How do you turn it on and off of a router? How do you turn it on and off of a single interface on a router? Why might you want to turn it off?

2. Moe and Jennifer have configured a router for a client. With the network administrator's help, they have connected it to the client's network. Unfortunately, it isn't working. They have called you for guidance. What troubleshooting steps do you recommend?

3. While configuring a client's router, Moe types the erase flash command. What are the consequences of this action? What steps will the router go through when it boots if the router is not configured to boot from a TFTP server?

4. Moe is embarrassed about erasing the router's flash memory. Lisa thinks the company has a backup flash file on a TFTP server. They've got you on the phone, and they want you to step them through the procedure to recover the router's operating system. The IOS filename is igs-j-l.111-5.

7

8

ROUTING PROTOCOLS

After reading this chapter and completing the exercises, you will be able to:

♦ Differentiate between nonroutable, routed, and routing protocols

♦ Define Interior Gateway Protocols, Exterior Gateway Protocols, distance-vector routing protocols, and link-state routing protocols

♦ Explain the concepts of count-to-infinity, split horizon, split horizon with poison reverse, and hold-down timers

♦ Describe, configure, and monitor the interior routing protocols RIP and IGRP

♦ Explain static routing and administrative distance

♦ Configure static routing and default routes

This chapter explains the concepts of nonroutable, routed, and routing protocols, which will be defined with a discussion of major protocols in each category. The distinction between distance-vector and link-state routing protocols is also examined. In addition, you learn the proper way to configure and monitor the routing protocols Routing Information Protocol (RIP) and Interior Gateway Routing Protocol (IGRP) on Cisco routers. Finally, the concepts and techniques needed to configure static routing and default routes are presented.

NONROUTABLE PROTOCOLS

In the early days of networking, networks were small collections of computers tied together for the purpose of sharing expensive peripherals such as high-end laser printers. Few companies could afford to link all their computers together on a local area network (LAN). Instead, using coaxial cable, computers were hooked together in workgroups. Figure 8-1 shows a typical early network.

Figure 8-1   Early network model using coaxial cable

Early networks were sometimes configured as **peer-to-peer networks**, in which computers communicate with and provide services to their "peers." Peer-to-peer networks do not pass packets between multiple networks. All communication occurs on the one network segment where the peer-to-peer network exists.

Due to the localized nature of traffic on a peer-to-peer network, network source and destination information is not needed and would produce unnecessary overhead. Instead, peer-to-peer networks can use small and efficient nonroutable protocols.

Several **nonroutable protocols** exist in today's networking world, but NetBEUI, short for NetBIOS Enhanced User Interface, is the most common. NetBEUI ships with all Microsoft Windows operating systems. In small, peer-to-peer networks, NetBEUI is easy to configure and use. Since it is very small, it is fast and efficient.

Unfortunately, NetBEUI cannot scale into large internetworks because it cannot hold Network layer information in its frame header. Without this information, packets cannot be routed between multiple network segments. Therefore, if you try to use NetBEUI— or any nonroutable protocol—in a network with multiple networks, communication between the networks will fail.

ROUTED PROTOCOLS

Routed protocols have packet headers that can contain Network layer addresses. Routed protocols were developed to support networks consisting of multiple networks or subnetworks. Figure 8-2 shows a typical **internetwork** within which routed protocols, such as TCP/IP or IPX/SPX, are used.

Figure 8-2   Common internetwork

In this sample internetwork, Host Alpha can communicate with Host Bravo only if Host Alpha uses a protocol that can add Network layer addressing to each packet header. With this Network layer addressing, information from Alpha can traverse the internetwork from Network 1 to Network 4. Without the Network layer information, all packets are only able to communicate within Network 1. **Transmission Control Protocol/Internet Protocol (TCP/IP)** and **Internetwork Packet Exchange/Sequence Packet Exchange (IPX/SPX)** are two protocols that can carry Network layer information. Thus, routers can route them through the internetwork.

For routed protocols to work on a network, every device (computer, printer, and router interface port) must be configured with a unique IP or IPX address. These Network layer **logical addresses**, described in Chapter 3, allow TCP/IP or IPX/SPX packets to be routed throughout the internetwork. Figure 8-3 shows the sample network with IP addresses assigned to each device.

Figure 8-3   Common internetwork with IP addresses

ROUTING PROTOCOLS

For proper network connectivity, you need more than just routed protocols on large internetworks. In order for routers to find the correct path for routed protocols, they use routing protocols to build routing tables that specify where every network in the internetwork is located. The administrator can also build routing tables statically; static routing is described later in this chapter. **Routing protocols** are protocols used by routers to make path determination choices and to share those choices with other routers. Table 8-1 shows a conceptual routing table that RouterB in Figure 8-3 would use to route a TCP/IP packet from Network 1 to Network 4.

Table 8-1   Conceptual route table

Network	Path	Distance
Network 2	Available via RouterB	directly connected
Network 3	Available via RouterA	1 hop
Network 4	Available via RouterC	2 hops

This table shows that RouterB can reach any of the networks in the internetwork. The Distance column refers to hop count as the single metric used in this routing table.

Hop count is the number of routers a packet must pass through to reach a particular network. A **metric** is a value used to define the suitability of a particular route. In other words, routers use metrics to determine which routes are better than other routes.

 In the internetwork shown in Figure 8-3, routing metrics are simple because of the single path nature of the internetwork. The route to Network 4 from RouterB will be via RouterA and RouterC; there is no better path available.

An **autonomous system (AS)**, which uses Interior Gateway Protocols as routing protocols, is a group of routers under the control of a single administration. Figure 8-4 shows Big Tin Inc.'s AS.

To Internet service provider (ISP)

Autonomous system 81

Figure 8-4   Big Tin Inc.'s AS

Big Tin Inc. has an autonomous system consisting of the four routers under the control of local network engineers. In general, AS systems run a single routing protocol.

Routing protocols come in two major categories: **Interior Gateway Protocols (IGPs)** are the routing protocols used within an AS, and **Exterior Gateway Protocols (EGP)** are routing protocols used to route information between multiple autonomous systems.

Routing Information Protocol (RIP), **Interior Gateway Routing Protocol (IGRP)**, **Enhanced Interior Gateway Routing Protocol (EIGRP)**, and **Open Shortest Path First (OSPF)** are examples of IGPs. RIP and IGRP are distance-vector routing protocols, and OSPF is a link-state routing protocol; these two categories are discussed in the following section. EIGRP is a hybrid routing protocol developed by Cisco to overcome some of the limitations associated with IGRP in particular and distance-vector routing protocols in general. As a hybrid routing protocol, EIGRP combines the best attributes of both distance-vector and link-state routing protocols. Additionally, EIGRP, when used with the no auto summary command, can support variable length subnet masking (VLSM). The use of variable length subnet masks within a single network number is beyond the scope of this book; it is covered in detail in studies for the CCNP Routing exam. EIGRP, like IGRP, is Cisco proprietary and can only be used between Cisco routers.

Border Gateway Protocol (BGP) and **Exterior Gateway Protocol (EGP)** are examples of EGPs. EGPs are the other category of routing protocols and are generally covered in depth in a CCNP Routing course. In this book, all discussions will focus on RIP and IGRP—both of which are basic IGPs.

Two Types of IGP Routing Protocols

Interior Gateway Routing protocols are subdivided into two major types of routing protocols: **distance-vector** and **link-state**. These protocol types accomplish the same job-determining routes within an autonomous system, but they do so via different mechanisms.

Distance-Vector Routing Protocols

Distance-vector routing protocols broadcast their entire routing table to each neighbor router at predetermined intervals (the actual interval rate depends on the distance-vector routing protocol in use, but varies between 30 and 90 seconds). Figure 8-5 shows how this process occurs.

Figure 8-5   Distance-vector routing protocol process

As the updates propagate throughout the network, RouterC will only receive information about RouterB's routing table via RouterA. This is sometimes referred to as **routing by rumor**. It also is one of the main problems with distance-vector routing protocols. If RouterB and RouterA have an update interval of 30 seconds, RouterC will not learn about network topology changes (changes in router interface states or route metrics) on RouterB for up to a minute. Figure 8-6 shows the types of problems this slow time to **convergence** (a state where all routers on the internetwork share a common view of the internetwork routes) can cause.

Time 2: RouterB reaches its update interval and sends to RouterA a route table that marks the network on E0 as unavailable.

Time 3
RouterA's route
table

Time 3: RouterA incorporates the changes it receives from RouterB and, once its update interval is reached, propagates those changes to RouterC.

Time 2
RouterB's route
table

RouterA

RouterB

RouterC

E0

E0

Time 1

Time 1: RouterB loses connectivity to the Ethernet network available via E0.

Figure 8-6   Distance-vector convergence example

Figure 8-6 shows that the time it will take the network to converge depends on the amount of time between update intervals on RouterB and RouterA. In this sample network, given its small size, the amount of time to converge would be fairly minimal. Still, for a short amount of time, RouterC mistakenly believes the Ethernet network attached to RouterB is viable and continues routing packets addressed to hosts on that network.

Problems, such as routing loops, can occur with distance-vector protocols if control measures are not put in place. **Routing loops** are often referred to as **count-to-infinity** problems because loops, without preventive measures (described next), will cause packets to bounce around the internetwork for an infinite amount of time. Figure 8-7 illustrates the types of problems that can occur with routing loops.

In this internetwork, true loops are not possible because of the linear nature of the network design. Still, the scenario presented in Figure 8-7 shows that the internetwork could, without proper precautions, readvertise a route that was in actuality not accessible. To prevent these problems, techniques such as defining a maximum, split horizon, split horizon with poison reverse, and hold-down timers are used to reduce the chances that incorrect routing table information will be propagated.

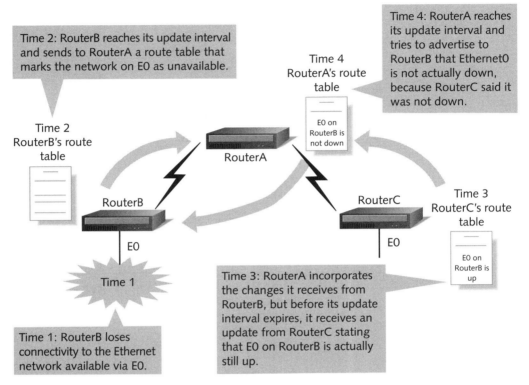

Figure 8-7   Distance-vector convergence problems

Defining a maximum is one of the easiest ways to limit count-to-infinity problems. If you assign a packet a maximum hop count, it cannot bounce infinitely around the internetwork. RIP, one of the most common distance-vector protocols, defines a maximum hop count of 15. Therefore, if a routing loop did occur on a RIP internetwork, the packet would only travel through 15 routers before the packet exceeded its TTL and was dropped. In other words, the 16th router that the packet tried to cross on a RIP internetwork would see that the packet had exceeded its TTL and would drop the packet. In the internetwork illustrated in the above figure, packets could potentially bounce around infinitely. For the RIP (version 1) routing protocol, hop count is the sole metric used to determine the relative desirability of a particular path.

Split horizon and **split horizon with poison reverse** are two other common ways to prevent routing loops when using distance-vector routing protocols. Split horizon controls what information a router will send out through a particular interface. In short, a router will not send information back through an interface about a route that it originally learned about through that same interface. For example, if RouterA in Figure 8-7 uses split horizon, it will not accept the update regarding E0 on RouterB from RouterC at Time 4 (Time 4 in Figure 8-7 represents the time when RouterC's update interval expires and RouterC sends out its update table). It won't accept it because that update would need to be sent out of the interface from which RouterA originally learned that E0 on RouterB was down. If RouterA uses split horizon with poison reverse, it not only refuses to accept RouterC's update regarding E0 on RouterB, but it also responds to RouterC's attempted update. RouterA will tell RouterC that the route to E0 on RouterB is no longer available by indicating that the hop count has been exceeded. In other words, it poisons the erroneous route advertised by RouterC so that no other router will see this as a viable route.

Another common technique used to stop routing loops is the **hold-down timer**. Hold-down timers allow a router to place a route in a state where it will not accept any changes to that route. If RouterA uses hold-down timers in Figure 8-7, the update from RouterC is ignored because the route would be in "hold-down" for a period of time after it was marked down. During this hold-down period, the router will not accept an update if it has a less favorable metric. It will accept an update and release the timer if the update has a more favorable metric. This prevents improper route information from being propagated throughout the internetwork. Hold-down timers are configurable by the network administrator.

Link-State Routing Protocols

Link-state routing protocols are the second type of routing protocols you can use to exchange route information between routers in an autonomous system. They behave very differently from distance-vector routing protocols. Routers configured with a link-state routing protocol use **link-state advertisements (LSAs)** to inform neighbor routers on the internetwork. However, instead of sending their entire routing tables, the LSAs contain only the local links for the advertised router. The **Shortest Path First (SPF) algorithm** uses the link information to compute the routes. So, router CPU resources are used instead of bandwidth.

Link-state packets (LSPs), packets used to send out LSAs, allow every router in the internetwork to share a common view of the **topology** of the internetwork. Figure 8-8 shows how a router configured with a link-state routing protocol **floods** or broadcasts LSPs to the network so that every other router on the internetwork has a common view of the topology of the internetwork.

In the example in Figure 8-8, the network quickly reaches a state of convergence due to the flooding of link-state packets. This is one huge advantage link-state routing protocols have over distance-vector routing protocols. Also, later updates by the routers in the internetwork will be **triggered updates**. These updates occur due to network topology changes, not periodic routing table advertisements. In other words, RouterB will only flood the internetwork with LSPs if a change occurs to its routing table. This announcement contains only the changes in the routing table, not the entire routing table. This conserves bandwidth on the internetwork links.

Time1: RouterB at startup floods the network with link-state packets and informs RouterA and RouterC of its link-state packets. Convergence time is drastically reduced, as compared to distance-vector routing protocols.

Time 1
RouterB's
route table

RouterA

RouterB

RouterC

EO

EO

Figure 8-8   Link-state advertisements

There are some drawbacks to using link-state routing protocols. Due to the complexity of the Shortest Path First algorithm and the need to hold a view of the entire internetwork topology, routers using link-state protocols must be configured with more memory and processing power than those using distance-vector routing protocols. In addition, link-state routing protocols such as OSPF are much more complicated to configure on the routers. This is why, for smaller scale internetworks, distance-vector routing protocols such as RIP and IGRP are typically used instead of OSPF.

Table 8-2 summarizes the key characteristics associated with distance-vector and link-state routing protocols.

Now that you have been introduced to the theory behind routing protocols, you need to learn how to actually configure specific protocols on Cisco routers. RIP and IGRP, both distance-vector protocols, are the two main protocols covered on the Cisco Certified Network Associate (CCNA) exam. In the next two sections, you will learn how to configure each protocol.

Table 8-2   Major characteristics of distance-vector and link-state routing protocols

Distance-vector	Link-state
Periodically broadcasts entire routing table to neighbor routers	Broadcasts links to all neighbor routers in the AS on start up; all other routing table updates contain only updated routes; updates only occur when a network topology change occurs
Slow to converge	Fast to converge due to link-state advertisements
Prone to routing loops because of routing by rumor nature	Less prone to routing loops because all other routers share a common view of the network
Easy to configure and administer	Harder to configure; requires greater memory and processing power on each router
Consumes relatively more bandwidth	Consumes relatively less bandwidth

ROUTING INFORMATION PROTOCOL

8

The first Interior Gateway Protocol you must know how to configure is RIPv1 (RIP version 1). There is another version of RIP, which is more sophisticated, but it is beyond the scope of the CCNA exam. When discussing RIP in the context of the CCNA exam, you should assume RIPv1. RIP is a distance-vector routing protocol that broadcasts entire routing tables to neighbors every 30 seconds, out of every interface. RIP uses hop count as its sole metric. As a result, RIP lacks the capability to factor in link speed or congestion between routers, which means that the shortest path between two points is not always the fastest. As previously mentioned, RIP has a maximum hop count of 15. As a result, RIP does not work in large internetworks. RIP has the following attributes:

- It is a distance-vector routing protocol.
- It has a maximum hop count of 15.
- Hop count is the only metric available for path selection.
- It broadcasts the entire routing table to neighbors every 30 seconds.
- It is capable of load balancing.
- It is easy to configure.

In addition, RIP is susceptible to all the problems normally associated with distance-vector routing protocols. It is slow to converge and forces routers to learn network information only from neighbors. Still, RIP is popular because it is easy to configure.

To install RIP on a Cisco router using TCP/IP, you must perform the following two tasks:

- Enable RIP
- Configure RIP routing for each major network you wish to advertise

You need only to configure major network numbers with RIP because RIP does not maintain subnet mask information within the routing tables it produces. As you go through the following text, remember that there are actually two versions of RIP. The CCNA exam focuses on RIP version 1, which does not pass subnet mask information with its routing table updates.

Enabling RIP Routing

For the following discussion of RIP, we will use the network in Figure 8-9. In the discussion, for brevity, we will only focus on enabling RIP on RouterB. You can assume that RIP has already been configured on RouterA and RouterC.

Figure 8-9   Sample IP network

To start configuring RIP, you must first enter privileged mode and then global configuration mode on your router. Once you type the enable command and config terminal command to enter global configuration mode, router output similar to that in Figure 8-10 should appear.

Once in global configuration mode, you must enable RIP with the router rip command. The command to enable RIP is displayed in Figure 8-11.

Configuring RIP Routing for Each Major Network

Figure 8-11 also displays the commands necessary to turn RIP routing on for a particular major network. The network *[network #]* command in Figure 8-11 turns RIP routing on for the major class B network 172.22.0.0. If you have multiple major networks configured on a router, an individual network *[network #]* command must be issued for each separate network.

After you have enabled RIP routing globally and configured each major network that the router will advertise with RIP updates, RIP is fully configured on the router. After the update interval of 30 seconds passes on each router, RouterB will eventually learn of all

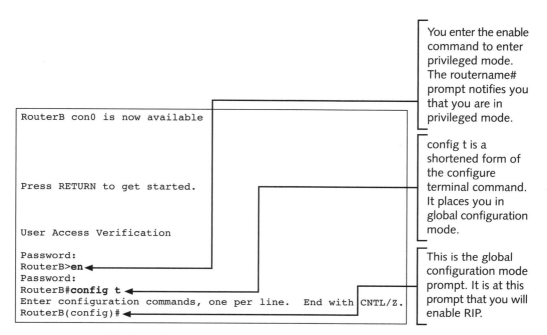

Figure 8-10   Global configuration mode

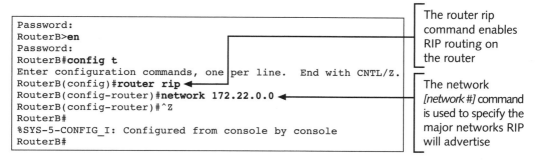

Figure 8-11   Configuring RIP

networks. You use the show ip route command to display the routing table. Figure 8-12 shows the output from the show ip route command on RouterB.

The output in Figure 8-12 illustrates an extremely important concept called administrative distance. **Administrative distance** is a value used to determine the reliability of a particular route. Administrative distances range from 0–255. The larger the number, the less reliable the connection is considered to be. The more reliable connection will always be favored over the less reliable and will therefore be installed as a route in the IP routing table of the router. Table 8-3 shows common routing protocols and their administrative distances.

The value 120 shown in the routing table in Figure 8-12 after subnet 172.22.4.0 and 172.22.5.0 is the administrative distance for RIP. A metric of 1 (1 hop) is listed after the 120 for the 172.22.4.0 entry and a metric of 2 (2 hops) is listed after the 120 for the 172.22.5.0 entry. Remember, RIP uses hops as its sole metric.

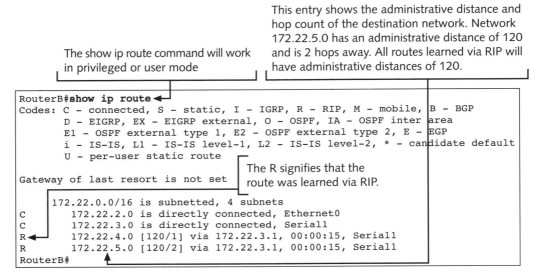

Figure 8-12 Output from the show ip route command

Table 8-3   Administrative distances

Route Learned via:	Administrative Distance
Directly connected network	0
Static route	1
EIGRP	90
IGRP	100
OSPF	110
RIP	120
Unknown	255

If a route is being discovered using both RIP and a directly connected interface, the route available via the directly connected interface will be the preferred route because it has a lower administrative distance. Likewise, if both IGRP and RIP advertise a route for a particular network, the IGRP route will be used because it is considered more reliable due to its lower administrative distance.

Show ip protocol and debug ip rip Commands

You can use the show ip protocol and debug ip rip commands to monitor RIP. You can type the show ip protocol command in either user mode or privileged mode. When you type this command, you will receive output similar to that shown in Figure 8-13.

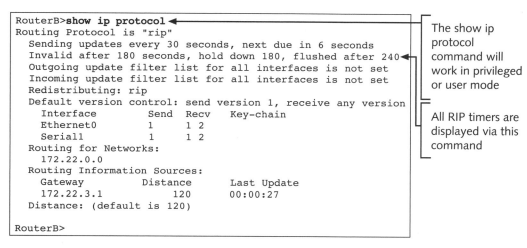

```
RouterB>show ip protocol
Routing Protocol is "rip"
  Sending updates every 30 seconds, next due in 6 seconds
  Invalid after 180 seconds, hold down 180, flushed after 240
  Outgoing update filter list for all interfaces is not set
  Incoming update filter list for all interfaces is not set
  Redistributing: rip
  Default version control: send version 1, receive any version
    Interface        Send  Recv   Key-chain
    Ethernet0        1     1 2
    Serial1          1     1 2
  Routing for Networks:
    172.22.0.0
  Routing Information Sources:
    Gateway         Distance      Last Update
    172.22.3.1          120       00:00:27
  Distance: (default is 120)

RouterB>
```

The show ip protocol command will work in privileged or user mode

All RIP timers are displayed via this command

Figure 8-13   Output from the show ip protocol command

In Figure 8-13, you can see the timers associated with RIP. RIP updates on TCP/IP networks, as stated previously, occur every 30 seconds. A route is considered invalid if six consecutive update intervals pass without an update from that route. The hold-down time of 180 seconds allows the router to stabilize its routing table to help prevent routing loops when a network path does go down. Finally, the **flush interval** is the time at which a route will be totally removed from the routing table if no updates are received.

The debug ip rip command, like all debug commands, should only be used when troubleshooting RIP. This command displays real-time rip updates being sent and received and places very high processing demands on your router, which could affect network performance. Figure 8-14 shows the output of the debug ip rip command.

As previously mentioned, RIP, like most distance-vector routing protocols is slow to converge. If RouterC in Figure 8-9 loses its connection to subnet 172.22.5.0 on Ethernet0, RouterB will learn about the route status changing. However, it could take at least a minute for the changes to propagate throughout the network (30 seconds maximum for the update interval on RouterC and RouterA). Once RouterB learns of the change in status for network 172.22.5.0, it marks the route as being possibly down and initiates a hold-down timer. You can type the show ip route command on RouterB to display this change in status. Figure 8-15 shows the results of the show ip route command after Ethernet0 on RouterC becomes inaccessible.

```
RouterB>en
Password:
RouterB#debug ip rip ◄
RIP protocol debugging is on
RouterB#
RIP: received v1 update from 172.22.3.1 on Serial1
     172.22.4.0 in 1 hops
     172.22.5.0 in 2 hops
RouterB#
RIP: sending v1 update to 255.255.255.255 via Ethernet0 (172.22.2.1)
     subnet  172.22.3.0, metric 1
     subnet  172.22.4.0, metric 2
     subnet  172.22.5.0, metric 3
RIP: sending v1 update to 255.255.255.255 via Serial1 (172.22.3.2)
     subnet  172.22.2.0, metric 1
RIP: ignored v1 update from bad source 172.22.5.1 on Ethernet0
RIP: received v1 update from 172.22.3.1 on Serial1
     172.22.4.0 in 1 hops
     172.22.5.0 in 2 hops
RouterB#
RIP: sending v1 update to 255.255.255.255 via Ethernet0 (172.22.2.1)
     subnet  172.22.3.0, metric 1
     subnet  172.22.4.0, metric 2
     subnet  172.22.5.0, metric 3
RIP: sending v1 update to 255.255.255.255 via Serial1 (172.22.3.2)
     subnet  172.22.2.0, metric 1
RIP: ignored v1 update from bad source 172.22.5.1 on Ethernet0
RouterB#no debug ip rip ◄
RIP protocol debugging is off
RouterB#
```

The debug ip rip command only works in privileged mode

The no debug ip rip command turns RIP debugging off

Figure 8-14 Output from the debug ip rip command

The route to subnet 172.22.5.0 is in hold down and marked as possibly down

```
RouterB#show ip route
Codes: C - connected, S - static, I - IGRP, R - RIP, M - mobile, B - BGP
       D - EIGRP, EX - EIGRP external, O - OSPF, IA - OSPF inter area
       E1 - OSPF external type 1, E2 - OSPF external type 2, E - EGP
       i - IS-IS, L1 - IS-IS level-1, L2 - IS-IS level-2, * - candidate default
       U - per-user static route

Gateway of last resort is not set

     172.22.0.0/16 is subnetted, 4 subnets
C       172.22.2.0 is directly connected, Ethernet0
C       172.22.3.0 is directly connected, Serial1
R       172.22.4.0 [120/1] via 172.22.3.1, 00:00:19, Serial1
R       172.22.5.0/24 is possibly down, ◄
          routing via 172.22.3.1, Serial1
```

Figure 8-15 Output from the show ip route command

Eventually, the route will be flushed from the route table. Still, with a hold–down time of 180 seconds and a flush timer of 240 seconds, the time it takes for the internetwork to converge can become excessive. If you issue the show ip route command after the route has been flushed from the routing table, you will get the router output displayed in Figure 8-16.

The route to subnet 172.22.5.0 has been removed from the route table

```
RouterB#show ip route
Codes: C - connected, S - static, I - IGRP, R - RIP, M - mobile, B - BGP
       D - EIGRP, EX - EIGRP external, O - OSPF, IA - OSPF inter area
       E1 - OSPF external type 1, E2 - OSPF external type 2, E - EGP
       i - IS-IS, L1 - IS-IS level-1, L2 - IS-IS level-2, * - candidate default
       U - per-user static route

Gateway of last resort is not set

     172.22.0.0/16 is subnetted, 3 subnets
C       172.22.2.0 is directly connected, Ethernet0
C       172.22.3.0 is directly connected, Serial1
R       172.22.4.0 [120/1] via 172.22.3.1, 00:00:10, Serial1
RouterB#
```

Figure 8-16 New output from the show ip route command

Note that RIP relies on hop count as its single metric. In the network in Figure 8-17, a router configured to use RIP would always route packets to the subnet 172.22.5.0 via the 56-Kbps link between RouterB and RouterC because of the hop count of one.

Figure 8-17 RIP problems caused by hop count reliance

As this network is configured, it may actually be faster to route packets along the T1 lines. This route, with a hop count of two, will not be used by RIP as the best route even though it may be faster. To combat this problem associated with distance-vector protocols such as RIP, Cisco developed its own proprietary distance-vector protocol: IGRP.

INTERIOR GATEWAY ROUTING PROTOCOL

IGRP is a proprietary distance-vector routing protocol created by Cisco to solve some of the problems associated with RIP. A larger hop count metric allows IGRP to be used on larger networks. In fact IGRP supports a hop count of 255, although 100 is the default if hop count is configured to be used as a metric. If, for example, IGRP is configured to use hops as a metric and 255 hops is the value configured, on the 256th hop, IGRP will return an ICMP destination network unreachable message. In some situations you may actually want to reduce IGRP's hop count to speed convergence and route processing. The metric maximum-hops command allows you to set the maximum hop count for IGRP. You should set the hop count to the maximum number of routers within your network if you are going to use hops with IGRP.

IGRP does not use hops as a metric by default. The default metrics for IGRP are bandwidth and delay only. IGRP can also be configured to use load and reliability metrics. The metrics that can be configured for IGRP are listed below:

- Hops: Number of routers between source and destination networks
- Load: The load on a link in the path
- Bandwidth: The speed of the link (default)
- Reliability: Measures reliability with a scale of 0 to 255
- Delay: The delay on the medium (default)
- MTU: The size of the datagram

Remember, by default, IGRP computes the best available route using only bandwidth and delay, but it can be configured to use most of the metrics mentioned previously. The ability to use bandwidth as a factor in the route selection process, along with reliability and delay, allows IGRP to make more intelligent route choices than RIP. IGRP also has the ability to use multiple, different cost paths to allow for redundancy and load balancing. IGRP can support up to four different cost paths.

Configuring IGRP on a Cisco router using TCP/IP is a simple process accomplished with the router igrp [autonomous system #] and network [network #] commands. Autonomous system numbers are public if the autonomous system exchanges routing information with other autonomous systems on the Internet. They are private if the routing is invisible to the Internet. The IANA (Internet Assigned Numbers Authority) assigns the numbers. The autonomous system number must be configured the same on all routers that need to share routing table information. IGRP routers will not share table information with other IGRP routers that are not in the same autonomous system. Figure 8-18 shows the router commands necessary to configure IGRP.

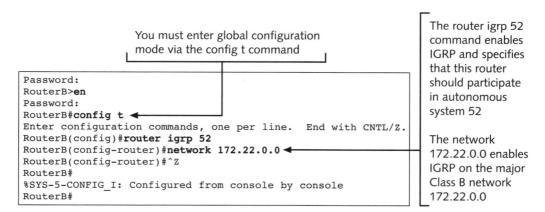

Figure 8-18   Commands used to configure IGRP

Once IGRP is configured throughout the internetwork, you can issue the show ip route command to monitor all available IGRP routes. Figure 8-19 shows the results of this command.

8

The Cisco IOS by default displays the subnet mask as a / (forward slash) followed by the number of bits in the mask. A /16 subnet mask indicates that a Class B network is being used.

```
RouterB#show ip route
Codes: C - connected, S - static, I - IGRP, R - RIP, M - mobile, B - BGP
       D - EIGRP, EX - EIGRP external, O - OSPF, IA - OSPF inter area
       E1 - OSPF external type 1, E2 - OSPF external type 2, E - EGP
       i - IS-IS, L1 - IS-IS level-1, L2 - IS-IS level-2, * - candidate default
       U - per-user static route

Gateway of last resort is not set

     172.22.0.0/16 is subnetted, 4 subnets
C        172.22.2.0 is directly connected, Ethernet0
C        172.22.3.0 is directly connected, Serial1
I        172.22.4.0 [100/10476] via 172.22.3.1, 00:00:20, Serial1
I        172.22.5.0 [100/10576] via 172.22.3.1, 00:00:20, Serial1
RouterB#
```

Routes learned via IGRP are displayed for each subnetwork.

The routes for RIP are no longer displayed because IGRP has a lower administrative distance and therefore a more reliable route.

In this example, the [100/10576] signifies the administrative distance and metric. The route to subnet 172.22.5.0 via 172.22.3.1 has an administrative distance of 100 (lower than RIP's 120 administrative distance) and a metric of 10576 (figured using the bandwidth and delay metrics by default).

Figure 8-19   The show ip route command with IGRP

If you wish to see the IGRP timers, you can type the show ip protocol command. It will present output similar to that found in Figure 8-20.

IGRP sends out routing table updates every 90 seconds. Compared to RIP, this reduces the amount of broadcast traffic used to maintain routing tables. In Figure 8-20, you can see that the router is running multiple routing protocols, RIP and IGRP. In the real world, you would normally not configure your routers to run both RIP and IGRP on the same router on a permanent basis. Doing so would waste network bandwidth for RIP updates that would always be considered inferior to IGRP updates and therefore not be placed in the routing table. However, redistributing RIP routes in an IGRP network may be necessary on a temporary basis when companies or organizations merge and different communications facilities must be joined or interconnected.

IGRP sends updates every
90 seconds

```
RouterB#show ip protocol
Routing Protocol is "rip"
  Sending updates every 30 seconds, next due in 21 seconds
  Invalid after 180 seconds, hold down 180, flushed after 240
  Outgoing update filter list for all interfaces is not set
  Incoming update filter list for all interfaces is not set
  Redistributing: rip
  Default version control: send version 1, receive any version
    Interface        Send  Recv   Key-chain
    Ethernet0         1     1 2
    Serial1           1     1 2
  Routing for Networks:
    172.22.0.0
  Routing Information Sources:
    Gateway          Distance        Last Update
    172.22.3.1          120          00:00:12
  Distance: (default is 120)

Routing Protocol is "igrp 52"
  Sending updates every 90 seconds, next due in 68 seconds
  Invalid after 270 seconds, hold down 280, flushed after 630
  Outgoing update filter list for all interfaces is not set
  Incoming update filter list for all interfaces is not set
  Default networks flagged in outgoing updates
  Default networks accepted from incoming updates
  IGRP metric weight K1=1, K2=0, K3=1, K4=0, K5=0
  IGRP maximum hopcount 100
  IGRP maximum metric variance 1
  Redistributing: igrp 52
  Routing for Networks:
    172.22.0.0
  Routing Information Sources:
    Gateway          Distance        Last Update
    172.22.3.1          100          00:00:36
  Distance: (default is 100)

RouterB#
```

Figure 8-20   The show ip protocol command with IGRP

A final command available to monitor IGRP is the debug ip igrp command. Figure 8-21 shows the correct syntax for typing the command and some common router output from the command.

The debug ip igrp command has two subcommands

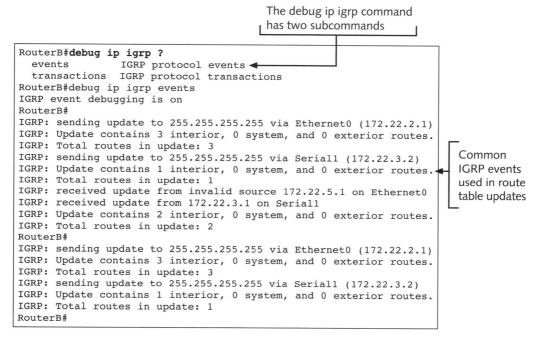

```
RouterB#debug ip igrp ?
  events          IGRP protocol events
  transactions  IGRP protocol transactions
RouterB#debug ip igrp events
IGRP event debugging is on
RouterB#
IGRP: sending update to 255.255.255.255 via Ethernet0 (172.22.2.1)
IGRP: Update contains 3 interior, 0 system, and 0 exterior routes.
IGRP: Total routes in update: 3
IGRP: sending update to 255.255.255.255 via Serial1 (172.22.3.2)
IGRP: Update contains 1 interior, 0 system, and 0 exterior routes.
IGRP: Total routes in update: 1
IGRP: received update from invalid source 172.22.5.1 on Ethernet0
IGRP: received update from 172.22.3.1 on Serial1
IGRP: Update contains 2 interior, 0 system, and 0 exterior routes.
IGRP: Total routes in update: 2
RouterB#
IGRP: sending update to 255.255.255.255 via Ethernet0 (172.22.2.1)
IGRP: Update contains 3 interior, 0 system, and 0 exterior routes.
IGRP: Total routes in update: 3
IGRP: sending update to 255.255.255.255 via Serial1 (172.22.3.2)
IGRP: Update contains 1 interior, 0 system, and 0 exterior routes.
IGRP: Total routes in update: 1
RouterB#
```

Common IGRP events used in route table updates

Figure 8-21   Output from the debug ip igrp command

STATIC ROUTING

Although routing protocols are easy to configure and maintain, many times they are unnecessary. Some networks are so small that using a routing protocol creates unnecessary traffic and an inefficient use of router processor resources. In addition, some networks may have only one route out and therefore can be configured with a single static route. Routers with only one route out are also known as **stub routers**. Stub routers are usually the last router in a chain. Networks with one route to the Internet are called **stub networks**. **Static routes** are configured by a network administrator using the ip route command as shown in the next section.

Adding Static Routes

Figure 8-22 shows the routing table for RouterC. As previously mentioned, this table can be dynamically configured using routing protocols such as RIP and IGRP or the table can be built statically using ip route commands. Although static routing gives the

8

administrator full control as to how packets will be routed, the disadvantage of using static routing is the initial manual configuration and the possible reconfiguration if routes are changed. Notice that for all interfaces that are physically attached to RouterC, the route to the network is through a local interface on the router. However, for packets destined to network 172.32.1.0, RouterC must forward them to RouterD. As you can see, RouterC is configured to send the packets to the 172.32.2.1 interface on RouterD because that is the next hop for the packet from the perspective of RouterC.

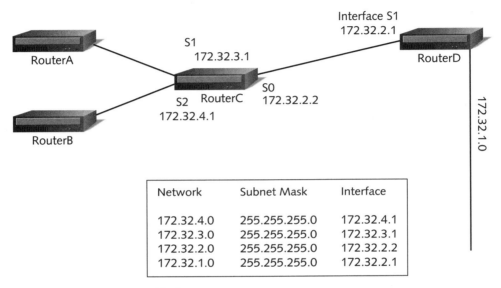

Figure 8-22   Routing table for RouterC

The commands that would be necessary to statically construct the proper routes for the routing table on RouterD to reach all the shown networks are shown below. To statically configure a route, you must type the destination network identifier, subnet mask, and the IP address of the interface of the next hop in the path. The syntax for the ip route command is **ip route [*destination network address*] [*destination network mask*] [*ip address next hop interface*][*administrative distance*]**. The administrative distance is optional. You only have to add an administrative distance if you want to change the default administrative distance of 1 (see Table 8-3). The following entries for RouterD would allow it to route to all the networks in Figure 8-22:

- RouterD# config t

- RouterD(config)# ip route 172.32.3.0 255.255.255.0 172.32.2.2

- RouterD(config)# ip route 172.32.4.0 255.255.255.0 172.32.2.2

The two entries for networks attached to RouterC are headed for the same interface. RouterD must move those packets destined for networks on the remote side of RouterC to the interface on RouterC that is connected to RouterD. Static routes to 172.32.2.0 and

172.32.1.0 are unnecessary because RouterD has directly connected interfaces to those two networks.

Static routes are very powerful as they allow administrators complete control over path selection. In addition, they use less bandwidth, less memory and fewer CPU resources than routing protocols.

Changing Administrative Distance

The IP route command also allows you to configure an administrative distance, which, as discussed previously, is a value used by the router to select the best route to a destination when there are two or more different routes to the same destination being reported from more than one source—for example from RIP, IGRP, and from a static entry. The default administrative distances were listed earlier in the chapter in Table 8-3.

Static routes have a much lower default metric than routes learned by **dynamic routing protocols** because a static route is considered to be a preferred route since someone took the trouble to enter it. Of course, if you want the static route to be used as a back up route to one learned via a dynamic routing protocol, be sure to set the administrative distance of the static route higher than that of the default dynamic routing protocol. Remember, unless you add an administrative distance value to the end of your ip route command, the administrative distance will be 1. For example, to set an administrative distance of 150 for the static entry to network 192.168.5.0, type:

```
router(config)#ip route 192.168.5.0 255.255.255.0
192.168.4.2. 150
```

If you want the static route entry to survive an interface shutdown, be sure to add the word "permanent" at the end of the line. For example, an interface, such as E0, can be shut down by typing the shutdown command. The following commands could be used to shut down E0:

- `router#configure t`
- `router(config)#int E0`
- `router(config-if)#shutdown`

If you want your static route mappings to remain, even if an interface is shut down, you must add "permanent" to the end of the ip route command—otherwise the route will be deleted from the routing table when the interface is shut down.

Configuring a Default Route

When you connect a router to the Internet, as a practical matter, you cannot and would not want to enter all of the possible networks that are beyond your network. The table would be massive and difficult to maintain. Once you have the routing table setup to handle all of the networks that you care to configure and you want all other packets to go to a specific location (usually a router that connects to the Internet), you can enter a **default route** for your router. When you do, all packets that are not defined specifically in your routing table will go to the specified interface for the default route. A default route is a type of static route that the administrator configures. Without a default route, all packets addressed to destinations on networks not specifically listed in the routing table will not reach their destinations. This is why most network administrators use a combination of dynamic routing protocols and static routes to maintain the routing tables on their routers. In the case of stub networks, very often only static routing is used. When IP routing is enabled, you can use the ip default-network command or the ip route 0.0.0.0 0.0.0.0 command to configure a default route. The way in which routing protocols propagate the default route information varies for each protocol and is beyond the scope of this text and the CCNA exam.

The ip default-network command is typically configured on the routers that connect to a single router with a static default route. Look at Figure 8-22 again. This time, assume that Router D connects to the Internet and that Routers A, B, and C are part of the internal network. If you are in charge of configuring Routers A, B and C and you want to ensure that all packets that are destined for any external network are routed properly, enter the following command on Routers A, B, and C:

```
RouterA(config)# ip default-network 172.32.1.0
```

Router A and Router B would use RouterC interfaces as their default gateways. Router C could use interface 172.32.2.1 as its default gateway. This means that it would be up to Router D to route packets to the Internet for all internal hosts. To allow Router D to route these packets, you would need to configure a default route as described below.

A default route uses the following format:

```
RouterD(config)# ip route 0.0.0.0 0.0.0.0 [next hop
router ip address] [administrative distance]
```

The zeroes in the command represent any destination network with any mask. Default routes are sometimes called **quad zero routes**. A default route is used only if no other route to a network exists in the routing table. In short, a router configured with a default route sends packets destined to a network it does not have a route for to the specified next hop router. Figure 8-23 shows a network where a default route would be ideal.

Figure 8-23   Default route example

As the figure shows, RouterA only has one way out to the Internet. The ISP router could therefore be set as the next hop router for all routes for which RouterA did not have a route. To accomplish this, the following command would be added to RouterA:

```
RouterA(config)# ip route 0.0.0.0 0.0.0.0 192.168.12.1
```

With the addition of this static default route, any packet destined for a network that RouterA does not have an explicit route for in its routing table will be forwarded to the ISP router.

CHAPTER SUMMARY

- ❏ Protocols vary in their functions. Some protocols are designed to be used in small networks without the need for Network layer addressing. These protocols are described as nonroutable protocols.

- ❏ The most common nonroutable protocol is NetBEUI.

- ❏ Other protocols were designed with the ability to move between multiple networks via Network layer addressing. These protocols are routed protocols.

- ❏ The most common routed protocol suite is TCP/IP.

- ❏ Protocols must be available that can find the best path throughout an internetwork and relay that information to routers. Routing protocols serve this function on modern networks.

- ❏ Routing protocols are classed in two major groups: Interior Gateway Protocols and Exterior Gateway Protocols.

- ❏ Interior Gateway Protocols are routing protocols that function within a single autonomous system. Exterior Gateway Protocols function as routing protocols between autonomous systems.

- ❏ Interior routing protocols are further divided into distance-vector routing protocols and link-state routing protocols.

- ❏ These two types of Interior Gateway Protocols use very different methods to determine the best path in an internetwork.

- ❏ Distance-vector protocols periodically broadcast entire routing tables to neighbor routers.

- ❏ Link-state protocols broadcast link updates to neighbor routers on the internetwork upon startup and when network topology changes.

- ❏ Two common distance-vector IGPs are the Routing Information Protocol and the Interior Gateway Routing Protocol.

- ❏ RIP is an easy-to-configure routing protocol that uses hop count as its sole metric. RIP has a hop count limit of 15. RIP uses split horizon, split horizon with poison reverse, and hold-down timers to help limit routing loops.

8

❑ IGRP is also a distance-vector routing protocol. IGRP has a maximum hop count of 255. IGRP is not limited to using hop count as its sole metric. IGRP can also use load, bandwidth, reliability, and delay when determining best path. IGRP uses only bandwidth and delay by default.

❑ Static routes are used to conserve bandwidth and lower memory and CPU load on a router while still allowing for correct routing table creation.

❑ Static routes give administrators control and flexibility in path selection in a network.

KEY TERMS

administrative distance — A value used to determine the reliability/desirability of a particular routing table update.

autonomous system (AS) — A group of routers under the control of a single administration.

Border Gateway Protocol (BGP) — An exterior gateway protocol used to route between multiple autonomous systems.

convergence — The point at which all routers on a network share a similar view of the network.

count-to-infinity — A routing loop whereby packets bounce infinitely around an internetwork.

default route — A static route that directs all traffic not specified anywhere else in the routing table to a particular route. Same as quad zero route.

defining a maximum — A technique used with distance-vector routing protocols to prevent packets from bouncing infinitely throughout an internetwork.

distance-vector routing protocol — A routing protocol that functions by broadcasting the entire routing table periodically to all connected neighbors; examples include RIP and IGRP.

dynamic routing protocol — A protocol that builds the routing table automatically. Examples include RIP and IGRP.

Enhanced Interior Gateway Routing Protocol (EIGRP) — A proprietary Cisco distance-vector protocol developed to overcome some of the limitations associated with distance-vector protocols. EIGRP is considered a hybrid routing protocol.

Exterior Gateway Protocol (EGP) — A gateway protocol used to route between multiple autonomous systems.

flood — The process of broadcasting packets onto a network.

flush interval — The time at which a route is totally removed from the routing table.

hold-down timers — A technique used to stop routing loops in which updates from an inferior source are not allowed for a certain interval. Used by routers to stabilize routing tables and to prevent erroneous routing table updates.

hop count — A count of the number of routers a packet must pass through in order to reach a destination network.

Interior Gateway Protocol (IGP) — A gateway protocol used to route within one autonomous system.

Interior Gateway Routing Protocol (IGRP) — A proprietary Cisco distance-vector routing protocol that uses delay and bandwidth as its default metrics.

internetwork — Multiple networks connected by routers.

Internetwork Packet exchange/Sequence Packet exchange (IPX/SPX) — A routed protocol stack developed by Novell for use with the Netware network operating system.

link-state advertisement (LSA) — A routing information packet used by link-state routing protocols to advertise their local network link information to neighbor routers in an internetwork.

link-state packets (LSP) — Packets used to send out link-state advertisements.

link-state routing protocols — Routing protocols that function via link-state advertisements using link-state packets to inform all routers on the internetwork of route tables. OSPF is the most common link-state routing protocol.

logical addresses — Layer 3 addresses (also referred to as Network layer addresses) that allow routed protocols to determine which network a particular host is on.

metric — A value used to define the suitability or desirability of a particular route.

nonroutable protocols — Protocols that do not contain Network layer addressing and therefore cannot pass between multiple networks.

Open Shortest Path First (OSPF) — A link-state routing protocol based upon open (nonproprietary) standards.

peer-to-peer networks — Small networks, normally consisting of fewer than 10 computers, in which each computer can give and receive network services.

quad zero route — *See* default route.

routed protocols — Protocols that do contain Network layer addressing and therefore can pass between multiple networks.

routing by rumor — The learning of routes through second-hand information, and not directly from the router experiencing the change. Routing by rumor is characteristic of distance-vector routing protocols.

routing loops — A network state in which packets are continually forwarded from one router to another in an attempt to find the destination network.

Routing Information Protocol (RIP) — A distance-vector routing protocol that uses hop count as its only metric.

routing protocols — Protocols used by routers to define and exchange routing table information in an internetwork.

Shortest Path First (SPF) algorithm — A complex algorithm used by link-state routing protocols to determine the best path in an internetwork.

split horizon — A technique used by routers to prevent routing loops. In short, a router will not send an update for a route via an interface from which it originally received knowledge of that route.

8

split horizon with poison reverse — A split horizon in which the router responds to attempts to update a route with an update that marks the route in contention as unreachable.

static routes — A route manually added by a network administrator to the routing table of a router.

stub network — A network with only one route to the Internet.

stub router — A router that is last in a chain of routers. There is only one path for all hosts connected to this router to get to the outside world.

Transmission Control Protocol/Internet Protocol (TCP/IP) — Routed protocol stack developed in the late 1960s for use on the precursor to the Internet; protocol stack of the modern-day Internet.

triggered updates — Occur due to network topology changes, not periodic route table advertisements.

topology — The physical or logical structure of a network.

REVIEW QUESTIONS

1. Which of the following is necessary to add IGRP to a router? (Choose all that apply.)

   a. router rip

   b. router igrp [*autonomous system #*]

   c. network [*major network #*]

   d. router network igrp

2. What is the administrative distance of RIP?

   a. 100

   b. 110

   c. 120

   d. 90

3. Link-state routing protocols _____. (Choose all that apply.)

   a. use link-state advertisements to notify neighbor routers of route changes

   b. send routing tables to neighbors

   c. reach convergence faster than distance-vector routing protocols

   d. determine the best path via the hop count algorithm

4. RIP has a maximum hop count of _____.

   a. 255

   b. 16

   c. 15

   d. 254

5. Which command enables RIP on a router?

   a. router network RIP

   b. router rip

   c. router igrp

   d. router ospf

6. Which command will show the IP routing table of a router?

   a. show ip route

   b. show ip protocol

   c. debug ip igrp events

   d. show run

7. Nonroutable protocols are able to pass packets among multiple networks. True or False?

8. IGRP can use which of the following as metrics? (Choose all that apply.)

   a. hop count

   b. bandwidth

   c. delay

   d. split horizon

9. Which of the following is a routed protocol? (Choose all that apply.)

   a. NetBEUI

   b. TCP/IP

   c. IPX/SPX

   d. RIP

10. Which of the following helps to prevent routing loops? (Choose all that apply.)

    a. split horizon

    b. count-to-infinity

    c. hold-down timers

    d. split horizon with poison reverse

11. At which router prompt can you use the router rip and router igrp [*autonomous system*] commands?

    a. RouterB#

    b. RouterB>

    c. RouterB(config)#

    d. RouterB(config-router)#

8

12. At which router prompt can you issue the network [*network #*] command?

    a. RouterB#

    b. RouterB>

    c. RouterB(config)#

    d. RouterB(config-router)#

13. The debug ip rip command can be used in user mode and privileged mode. True or False?

14. Which of the following routing protocols can route between autonomous systems? (Choose all that apply.)

    a. IGRP

    b. RIP

    c. BGP

    d. EGP

15. What type of routing protocol is used within autonomous systems?

    a. Exterior Gateway Protocols

    b. TCP/IP

    c. NetBEUI

    d. Interior Gateway Protocols

16. RIP and IGRP both advertise a route to a particular network. Which route will be added to the routing table?

    a. the RIP route

    b. the IGRP route

    c. NetBEUI

    d. BGP-enhanced IGRP

17. What command is used to display RIP timers?

    a. show ip route

    b. show run

    c. debug ip rip

    d. show ip protocol

18. What two commands are needed to configure RIP on a router? (Choose all that apply.)

    a. network rip

    b. router rip

    c. router network rip

    d. network [*network #*]

19. A metric is a variable used to determine the suitability of a route. True or False?

20. A major drawback of link-state routing protocols is:

   a. routing by rumor

   b. increased memory and processing required on routers

   c. slow time to convergence

   d. inability to adapt to network topology changes

21. Which of the following commands would enable a routing protocol that is only concerned with hop count?

   a. router# router igrp

   b. router(config)# router igrp

   c. router# router rip

   d. router(config)# router rip

   e. router# router ospf

22. Which of the following are true about administrative distance? (Choose all that apply.)

   a. The higher the administrative distance, the more desirable the route.

   b. Administrative distances are used with static routes.

   c. The default administrative distance for RIP is 120.

   d. The default administrative distance for static routes is higher than those for dynamic routes.

   e. The default administrative distance for a connected network is lower than for the default route of IGRP.

23. What does the number 240 stand for in the following command?

   Router(config)# ip route 192.168.1.0 255.255.255.0 240

   a. Number of masked bits

   b. Decimal subnet mask

   c. Number of hops

   d. Administrative distance

   e. Autonomous network number

24. If you want to monitor real-time RIP traffic, which command would you type?

   a. router> router rip

   b. router# router rip

   c. router# show rip

   d. router(config)# show rip

   e. router# debug ip rip

8

25. Which of the following does RIP support? (Choose all that apply.)

   a. Load balancing

   b. Link reliability metric

   c. Bandwidth metric

   d. Load

CASE PROJECTS

1. Winslow Networks has been hired by Big Tin Inc. to redesign Big Tin's network. Currently, the network consists of 14 routers with a potential growth of 3 routers in the next four months. Moe suggests the company implement RIP for internetwork routing since it is so popular and easy to configure. Is this the best possible solution for Big Tin Inc.? Justify your answers.

2. Hogan's, an international food services conglomerate, wishes to implement wide area network links between their 25 plants spread across 13 countries. You have been brought in to act as a consultant on the project. Hogan's wishes for convergence to be as quick as possible, and, due to slow WAN links in some undeveloped countries, must reduce routing table updates to the absolute minimum to conserve bandwidth. Hogan's suggests using a distance-vector routing protocol because of their relative simplicity. Create a network design using the distance-vector protocol you feel will meet Hogan's needs. What metrics are used by default? Which metrics can and should be configured? Justify your answer.

3. Moe and Jennifer are configuring RIP on a client's router, and they want your help. The network number is 204.207.5.0. There are three interfaces on the router. The IP addresses for those interfaces are 204.207.5.97, 204.207.5.113, and 204.207.5.82. The subnet mask is 255.255.255.240. The hostname for the router is "newyork." What mode should Moe and Jennifer be in to use the router rip command? What will the prompt look like? How will the prompt change after the router rip command is issued? Jennifer has written the following commands for entry next:

   network 204.207.5.96

   network 204.207.5.112

   network 204.207.5.80

   What do you tell her?

9

IPX/SPX

**After reading this chapter and completing the exercises,
you will be able to:**

♦ Describe the IPX/SPX protocol stack and map its major protocols
to the OSI model

♦ Identify the parts of an IPX/SPX network address

♦ Define the Data Link layer frame formats supported by NetWare
and the Cisco IOS

♦ Describe the function of Service Advertisement Protocol advertisements and the processes Cisco routers use when dealing with SAP
advertisements

♦ Configure IPX/SPX on a router

♦ Monitor IPX/SPX on a router

In a perfect world, network administrators would run a single protocol stack
that worked flawlessly with network operating systems from all vendors. In
the real world (right now anyway), you must normally run at least two protocol stacks to get the functionality that your network needs. For instance,
many networks using Novell's NetWare products run both the IPX/SPX and
TCP/IP protocol stacks. Up until this point, you have focused on TCP/IP as
the protocol stack of choice for use on all internetworks. In this chapter, you
will learn about IPX/SPX as an internetworking protocol stack.

IPX/SPX PROTOCOL STACK

IPX/SPX was originally derived by Novell from the Xerox Network Systems protocol stack, and its role as a networking protocol stack expanded quickly as Novell's NetWare became the standard network operating system in many organizations during the late 1980s and early 1990s. Then, in the mid-1990s, the Internet took hold and TCP/IP became the protocol of choice among networking professionals. Still, in order for some NetWare-aware applications to run correctly, many organizations must continue to run IPX/SPX. Therefore, even though NetWare has been able to use TCP/IP for some time now and runs it natively under NetWare 5 or higher, network administrators find themselves dealing with many multiprotocol networks using TCP/IP and IPX/SPX.

As is evident in Figure 9-1, the IPX/SPX protocol stack does not follow the seven-layer OSI model exactly. Instead, like most modern protocol stacks, it maps loosely to the model.

Figure 9-1   IPX/SPX protocol stack

Internetwork Packet Exchange (IPX), **Sequenced Packet Exchange (SPX)**, **Service Advertisement Protocol (SAP)**, **NetWare Core Protocol (NCP)**, **Routing Information Protocol (RIP)**, and **NetWare Link Services Protocol (NLSP)** are several of the main protocols in the IPX/SPX protocol stack. They perform the following functions:

- IPX is a connectionless, predominantly layer 3 protocol, although, as you can see in Figure 9-1, it does spill over into some layer 4 functions. It is responsible for finding the best path through a multipath IPX network. IPX is similar in function to the IP protocol found in the TCP/IP protocol stack. It can use RIP and NLSP to determine the best path among multiple paths through the internetwork.

- SPX, a connection-oriented layer 4 protocol, provides guaranteed delivery services for the connectionless IPX protocol. SPX is similar in function to TCP in the TCP/IP protocol stack.

- SAP, which operates at layers 5, 6, and 7, advertises services running on IPX/SPX servers and helps clients locate network services.

- NCP facilitates client/server interaction on a NetWare network. NCP handles basic file and print sharing, authentication services, and directory services. NCP functions at layers 4, 5, 6, and 7 of the OSI model.

- IPX RIP is an integrated distance vector routing protocol (see Chapter 8 for details on distance vector routing protocols). It uses **ticks** (1/18 of a second time counts used to determine the desirability of a particular route) and hop count as metrics. These metrics determine the best path within an IPX/SPX internetwork. The RIP used in IPX/SPX sends out routing table updates every 60 seconds and uses ticks as its main metric (hop count is used to break ties). RIP functions at layer 3 of the OSI model.

- NLSP is a link state routing protocol designed by Novell as the successor to RIP. Like RIP, NLSP functions at layer 3 of the OSI model.

9

IPX/SPX ADDRESSING

IPX/SPX addressing, when compared with TCP/IP addressing, is actually quite simple. **IPX/SPX addresses** are 80-bit addresses that use a network.node format. The network portion of the address consists of up to 32 bits displayed as eight hexadecimal digits. The network administrator assigns the network portion of the address. The node portion on the address is the 48-bit physical MAC address of a node. It is displayed as 12 hexadecimal digits. The fact that IPX/SPX uses the MAC address as part of the logical address means that address resolution, such as ARP, is unnecessary. The following example shows an IPX/SPX address:

200.0020.7811.4a62

The assigned network address is 200, while 0020.7811.4a62 represents the node portion of the address (and therefore the MAC address of the node). The MAC address starts with the rightmost bits and goes for 48 bits, or 12 hexadecimal digits. The network number will always start with the leftmost bits and can be 32 bits in length. Usually, leading zeroes in the network portion of the address are not displayed.

The above example shows an important concept relating to IPX/SPX addressing. The network portion of the address can be up to 32 bits, but it is not required to fill the entire 32-bit space to be valid. Our example shows a node with the MAC address of 0020.7811.4a62 on the IPX/SPX network 200.

The arbitrary manner of assigning IPX/SPX network numbers makes determining the network number on an IPX/SPX segment a daunting task. Asking the network administrator for the segment's network number is the easiest and, therefore, the recommended method for finding out the network number. If you have physical access to a router that has an interface port on the segment on which you want to determine the network number, you can use the IOS command show ipx interface to find the network number. Lastly, you can use the show cdp neighbors command from an adjacent router to determine the network numbers of neighboring routers.

IPX/SPX DATA LINK LAYER FRAME TYPES

In order for all nodes on an IPX/SPX network to communicate, they must share a common Data Link layer frame **encapsulation**, which is the process of wrapping Protocol Data units from upper layers with headers and, at the Data Link layer, with trailer information. If two computers do not share this encapsulation, they cannot communicate because their data packets use a different form of Data Link layer header. Also, in order for Cisco routers to participate in IPX/SPX networks, their interfaces must use the same encapsulation type as the networks to which they are attached. The most common Data Link layer frame formats and their characteristics are listed in Table 9-1.

Table 9-1   Data link layer encapsulations

Novell Frame Format Designation	Used by Networks Running:
802.3 (Ethernet Raw)	NetWare 3.11 or lower
802.2	NetWare 3.12 or higher
Ethernet_II	Both IPX/SPX and TCP/IP
Ethernet_snap	IPX/SPX, TCP/IP, and AppleTalk

Although the above formats and designations are easy to comprehend and use, confusion arises due to the terminology the Cisco IOS uses for frame formats. Table 9-2 shows the Novell Ethernet frame format designations and the associated Cisco encapsulation terminology. Later in this chapter, you use the Cisco encapsulation terms to set frame encapsulation on a router's interface ports.

Table 9-2   Cisco encapsulation terminology

Novell Ethernet Frame Format Designation	Cisco Encapsulation Terminology
802.3 (Ethernet Raw)	novell-ether (default setting on Ethernet)
802.2	sap
Ethernet_II	arpa
Ethernet_snap	snap

IPX/SPX networks running in a wide-area network environment often cross serial interfaces. When it crosses the interfaces, it is encapsulated in the Cisco default serial encapsulation of HDLC. This is because Novell doesn't specify a default serial Data Link format. Because of this default, the category "serial" does not appear in either Table 9-1 or 9-2.

Other frame formats supported by IPX/SPX and the Cisco IOS are displayed in Table 9-3.

All nodes on an IPX/SPX network (including all router ports) must be configured with the same Data Link layer frame encapsulation. Otherwise, the nodes cannot communicate with one another. In essence, two nodes using different frame formats speak two different and totally incompatible languages. You can fix this problem by ensuring that all nodes on your IPX/SPX network use the same Data Link layer frame type.

Table 9-3 Other supported frame types

Other Novell Frame Formats	Cisco Encapsulation Terminology
Token_ring	sap
Token_ring_snap	snap
FDDI_snap	snap
FDDI_802.2	sap
FDDI_raw	novell-fddi

9

SAP ADVERTISEMENTS

SAP advertisements on an IPX/SPX network allow servers to "advertise" running services such as print services, directory services, and file-sharing services to network clients. Clients also use SAP advertisements to request a list of services from a server's SAP table, which contains a list of all services available on a network segment. For example, in Figure 9-2, the SAP table for NetWare Server A includes all services that it currently provides, plus all services provided by NetWare Server B.

NetWare servers take SAP broadcasts, which occur every 60 seconds by default, and build SAP tables. Therefore, all servers on a segment learn about all services provided by their peers on that segment. Clients can request SAP information from any server, and that server, if SAP broadcasts are working correctly, should be able to provide the client with a list of all services on the local segment.

The **Get Nearest Server (GNS)** request used by clients at startup allows them to find the nearest running NetWare server. The GNS request takes the form of a SAP broadcast. As a result, if the segment has a local NetWare server, the nearest server responds with its location and available services. Again, using Figure 9-2 as an example, if the IPX/SPX client issues a GNS request, either NetWare Server A or NetWare Server B responds to the request (the closest server to the client would respond first). SAP advertisements become slightly complicated when routers get involved.

Figure 9-2   SAP example

In a true NetWare network, both servers would also provide directory services to clients on this segment.

Since SAP broadcasts occur every 60 seconds by default, they would quickly overwhelm most WAN links if all SAP broadcasts by all servers were forwarded through routers. However, SAP broadcasts are such an integral part of IPX/SPX communications that a method is needed to pass the information contained in SAP broadcasts without passing the broadcasts themselves. Routers—which by default block broadcasts in order to reduce unnecessary traffic—accomplish this task by building and using SAP tables. Thus, routers can respond to SAP requests if no NetWare server is available on a local segment.

Figure 9-3 shows a network where the IPX/SPX client on network 200 has no access to a local NetWare server. If the client sends out a GNS request, RouterB will respond to the request with the information in its SAP table.

Figure 9-3   Router SAP example

In Figure 9-4, RouterB informs the client that the nearest NetWare server is Server A on network 300.

All SAP requests by IPX/SPX clients on network 200 initiate a response by RouterB. RouterB also informs all other routers of its SAP table via a directed message sent every 60 seconds. Router SAP tables eliminate the need for large numbers of SAP broadcasts to traverse the internetwork. The number and type of SAP entries in a router's table and the types of entries propagated to other routers can be controlled via access lists known as SAP filters. SAP filters are discussed in Chapter 10 of this text.

Figure 9-4   Router response to SAP requests

CONFIGURING IPX/SPX

Configuring IPX/SPX on Cisco routers is a multistep process. First, you must enter global configuration mode and enable IPX routing. Then, if your network has multiple paths, you should enable multiple paths for IPX routing with the ipx maximum-paths *[# of paths]* command. You would replace the *# of paths* variable with the number of possible paths in your IPX network (up to a total of 512 paths). This command is a **load balancing** command. Load balancing basically consists of distributing network traffic evenly across multiple channels so that no single channel will be overloaded. If you enable maximum-paths with a value greater than one, the router will load balance between the two paths or between the number of paths designated, as long as the ticks and hops are the same on the multiple routes. Finally, you must configure IPX network numbers and encapsulation types on each interface.

The default value for maximum-paths is one. In other words, load balancing is disabled by default.

The first step in configuring IPX requires that you log in to your router and enter global configuration mode. The process is detailed in Figure 9-5.

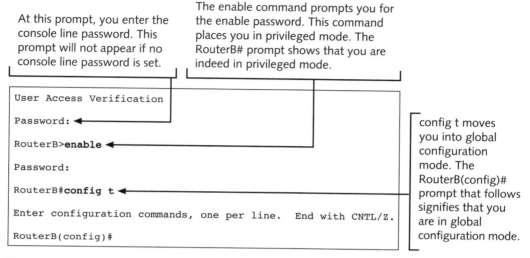

At this prompt, you enter the console line password. This prompt will not appear if no console line password is set.

The enable command prompts you for the enable password. This command places you in privileged mode. The RouterB# prompt shows that you are indeed in privileged mode.

```
User Access Verification
Password:
RouterB>enable
Password:
RouterB#config t
Enter configuration commands, one per line.  End with CNTL/Z.
RouterB(config)#
```

config t moves you into global configuration mode. The RouterB(config)# prompt that follows signifies that you are in global configuration mode.

Figure 9-5   Entering global configuration mode

Once you see the routername(config)# prompt, you are in global configuration mode. The config t (short for configure terminal) command places you in this mode. To configure IPX routing, you enter the ipx routing command. Figure 9-6 shows the commands necessary to enable IPX routing.

```
RouterB(config)#ipx routing
RouterB(config)#^Z
RouterB#
%SYS-5-CONFIG_I: Configured from console by console
RouterB#
```

The ipx routing command, typed at global configuration mode, enables IPX routing on the router.

Figure 9-6   Enabling IPX routing

You can verify that ipx routing has been added to the configuration by trying the show run command. This command produces the output found in Figure 9-7.

If you properly add ipx routing, the ipx routing entry will be added to the running configuration. The configuration in Figure 9-7 also contains a TCP/IP address because this is a multiprotocol network. To save the configuration changes, you should issue the copy run start command. This ensures that the running configuration is copied into the startup configuration.

```
RouterB#show run
    Building configuration...

    Current configuration:
    !
    version 11.1
    service udp-small-servers
    service tcp-small-servers
    !
    hostname RouterB
    !
    enable secret 5 $1$RHhg$ngXce3OBeC7GprpPjtqsP1
    !
    ipx routing 0060.474f.6506  ◄─────────────────
    !
    interface Ethernet0
    ip address 172.22.2.1 255.255.255.0
    !
    interface Serial0
    no ip address
    !
    interface Serial1
    ip address 172.22.3.2 255.255.255.0
    !
    router rip
    network 172.22.0.0
    !
    no ip classless
    !
    !
    !
    !
    line con 0
    password password
    login
    line vty 0 4
    password password
    login
    !
    end

RouterB#
```

The ipx routing entry in the running configuration shows that IPX routing is on. The hexadecimal number following the ipx routing entry is the MAC address of the configured interface.

Figure 9-7   Verifying IPX routing

 IP routing is enabled by default on all Cisco routers. If for some reason IP routing is ever turned off on a router, you can enable it with the ip routing command.

As previously mentioned, if you have a network consisting of multiple paths, you should use the ipx maximum-paths command to enable load balancing. Figure 9-8 shows a network where the ipx maximum-paths value for RouterB should be set to 2 because the router has two equal distance and cost paths that are usable.

Figure 9-9 shows the commands necessary to complete this task on the router.

Figure 9-8   Multipath IPX network

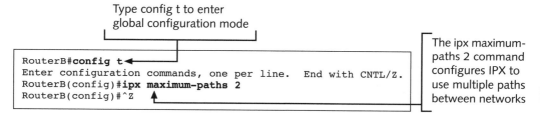

Type config t to enter
global configuration mode

The ipx maximum-
paths 2 command
configures IPX to
use multiple paths
between networks

```
RouterB#config t
Enter configuration commands, one per line.  End with CNTL/Z.
RouterB(config)#ipx maximum-paths 2
RouterB(config)#^Z
```

Figure 9-9   Configuring ipx maximum-paths

If you enter the show run command after enabling multiple paths, the ipx maximum–paths statement is visible. Figure 9-10 shows the output from typing the show run command.

```
RouterB#show run
Building configuration...

%SYS-5-CONFIG_I: Configured from console by console
Current configuration:
!
version 11.1
service udp-small-servers
service tcp-small-servers
!
hostname RouterB
!
enable secret 5 $1$RHhg$ngXce3OBeC7GprpPjtqsP1
!
ipx routing 0060.474f.6506
ipx maximum-paths 2
!
interface Ethernet0
 ip address 172.22.2.1 255.255.255.0
!
interface Serial0
 no ip address
!
interface Serial1
 ip address 172.22.3.2 255.255.255.0
!
 --More—
```

The router is now
configured to route
using multiple paths

Figure 9-10   Show run output after ipx maximum-paths 2 command

The More statement at the end of this output in Figure 9-10 denotes that you need to hit the Spacebar to display additional lines. For the sake of brevity, the extra output is not displayed in this example. You will notice, however, that the show run output now has the ipx maximum-paths 2 statement added. The paths statement is changed to 2 because in the example network, the router has two equal cost and distance paths available for it to use. To make this change permanent, you must issue the copy run start command. It is important to note that the only required command to enable IPX routing on a router is the ipx routing command; the ipx maximum-paths command is optional.

Once you configure IPX routing globally on a router, you must enable IPX/SPX on each individual interface. Configuring IPX on an interface is a two-step process:

1. First, you must assign an IPX network number to an interface.

2. Then, you configure an encapsulation on an interface.

Configuring encapsulation becomes necessary only if you wish to use an encapsulation type that is different from the default. The default for all Ethernet interfaces is novell-ether (which translates to frame type 802.3). The default for all serial interfaces is **High-level Data Link Control (HDLC)**. Since many modern NetWare networks consist of 4.11 servers with a default frame type of 802.2, you will likely need to change the encapsulation on most of the Ethernet ports on a router. The 802.2 frame type corresponds to the Cisco encapsulation term "sap".

We now begin the actual configuration of interfaces. Throughout the following example, all command inputs and router outputs use Figure 9-11 as a reference; all commands occur on RouterB.

Figure 9-11   IPX network

In order to begin interface configuration, you must log in to the router, enter privileged mode, and then enter global configuration mode. Figure 9-12 shows how you enter global configuration mode.

At this prompt, you enter the line console password. This prompt will not appear if the line console password is not set.

The enable command prompts you for the enable password. This command places you in privileged mode. The RouterB# prompt shows that you are indeed in privileged mode.

config t moves you into global configuration mode. The RouterB(config)# prompt that follows signifies that you are in global configuration mode.

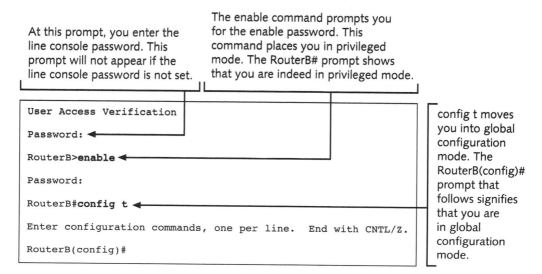

```
User Access Verification
Password: ◄
RouterB>enable ◄
Password:
RouterB#config t ◄
Enter configuration commands, one per line.  End with CNTL/Z.
RouterB(config)#
```

Figure 9-12   Entering global configuration mode

9

To configure an interface, you need to switch to interface configuration mode. The interface command can be used to switch to a particular interface. In this example, referring back to Figure 9-6, you wish to configure IPX/SPX on the Ethernet0 interface of RouterB. Figure 9-13 shows how you enter configuration mode for interface Ethernet0.

At global configuration mode prompt, you type interface [*interface type*/#] to access interface configuration mode

```
RouterB(config)#int e0 ◄
RouterB(config-if)#
```

Figure 9-13   Entering interface configuration mode

The int e0 (short for interface ethernet0) command moves you into the interface configuration mode. The RouterB(config-if)# prompt allows you to distinguish that you are currently in interface configuration mode. At this point, you configure the IPX network number and type of encapsulation. Figure 9-14 shows the commands necessary to accomplish this task.

Once in interface configuration mode, the ipx command followed by the ? results in a Help screen that lists all available commands

The network command is the command used to configure an IPX network number on an interface

```
RouterB(config)#int e0
RouterB(config-if)#ipx ?◄
access-group               Enable IPX accounting on this interface
accounting
advertise-default-route-only  Only advertise the IPX/RIP default route out onto this network
bandwidth-percent          Set EIGRP bandwidth limit
compression                Select IPX compression commands
delay                      Set a Novell delay on the interface, in 'ticks'
down                       Bring an IPX network administratively down
encapsulation              Novell encapsulation
gns-reply-disable          Disable Get Nearest Server replies on this interface
gns-response-delay         Delay in answering GNS on this interface
hello-interval             Configures IPX EIGRP hello interval
helper-address             Forward broadcasts to a specific address
helper-list                      Filter helpered IPX packets on input
hold-down                  Configures IPX EIGRP routes hold down time
hold-time                  Configures IPX EIGRP hold time
input-network-filter       Filter incoming routing updates
input-sap-filter           Filter services learned from the Service Advertising Protocol
ipxwan                           Configure IPXWAN on this interface
link-delay                 Set an IPX link delay on the interface, in microseconds
netbios                          Setup IPX NetBIOS filters and caching on this interface
network                    Assign an IPX network & enable IPX routing◄
nlsp                             Select NLSP commands
output-gns-filter          Filter services reported in response to Get Nearest Server
output-network-filter      Filter outgoing routing updates
output-rip-delay           Interpacket delay for RIP updates
output-sap-delay           Interpacket delay for SAP updates
output-sap-filter          Filter services reported via SAP
pad-process-switched-packets  Pad odd-length packets on output (process-switched only)
ppp-client                 Configure interface for PPP client mode
rip-max-packetsize         Maximum size of RIP packets being sent on interface
rip-multiplier             Multiple of RIP update interval for aging of RIP routes
route-cache                Enable fast switching
router-filter                    Filter sources of routing updates
router-sap-filter          Select source router and service type of SAP updates
sap-incremental            Send incremental SAP updates - for IPX EIGRP networks only
sap-interval               Set SAP update period
sap-max-packetsize               Maximum size of SAP packets being sent on interface
sap-multiplier             Multiple of SAP update interval for aging of SAP routes
split-horizon              Perform split horizon
spx-idle-time              Set an SPX idle time on the interface, in seconds
spx-spoof                  Spoof SPX keepalives packets
throughput                 Set IPX link throughput in bit per second
triggered-rip-delay        Interpacket delay for triggered RIP updates
                                 (override output-rip-delay for triggered updates only)
triggered-sap-delay        Interpacket delay for triggered SAP updates
                                 (override output-rip-delay for triggered updates only)
type-20-propagation        Forward IPX type 20 propagation packets
update-time                Set IPX routing update timer
watchdog-spoof             Answer Server Watchdog packets for Client machines
```

Figure 9-14 Configuring an IPX network number

You enter the network portion of the command next and specify the IPX network number assigned by the network administrator to this segment. Figure 9-15 shows the commands necessary to add 200, the IPX network number, to an interface.

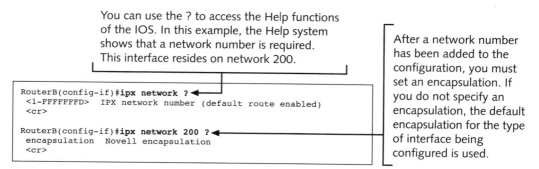

You can use the ? to access the Help functions of the IOS. In this example, the Help system shows that a network number is required. This interface resides on network 200.

After a network number has been added to the configuration, you must set an encapsulation. If you do not specify an encapsulation, the default encapsulation for the type of interface being configured is used.

```
RouterB(config-if)#ipx network ?
<1-FFFFFFFD>  IPX network number (default route enabled)
<cr>

RouterB(config-if)#ipx network 200 ?
encapsulation  Novell encapsulation
<cr>
```

Figure 9-15   Configuring an interface for IPX

The next major item that must be configured is the encapsulation type. You enter the encapsulation portion of the command followed by the encapsulation type. If you forget the Cisco IOS terminology for each Novell frame encapsulation type, you can use the context-sensitive ? command to display all possible options. Figure 9-16 shows output that lists the encapsulation types supported by the IOS.

```
RouterB(config-if)#ipx network 200 encapsulation ?
arpa          Novell Ethernet_II
hdlc          HDLC on serial links
novell-ether  Novell Ethernet_802.3
novell-fddi   Novell FDDI RAW
sap           IEEE 802.2 on Ethernet, FDDI, Token Ring
snap          IEEE 802.2 SNAP on Ethernet, Token Ring, and FDDI
RouterB(config-if)#
```

The ? command lists the available encapsulation types

Figure 9-16   Identifying available encapsulation types

In Figure 9-11, port E0 resides on a segment using the 802.2 frame type. Therefore, it must be configured with sap encapsulation. Figure 9-17 displays the commands necessary to perform this task.

If you are unsure if a command is complete, placing the ? command at the end of a line will list all command options still available. In this example, you see that a command called secondary is available. Secondary interfaces will be discussed later in this chapter.

```
RouterB(config-if)#ipx network 200 encapsulation sap ?
secondary  Make this network a secondary network
<cr>

RouterB(config-if)#ipx network 200 encapsulation sap
RouterB(config-if)#
```

The completed command enables IPX routing for network 200 with an encapsulation of sap for this particular interface

Figure 9-17   Configuring encapsulation on an IPX interface

9

Your final command, ipx network 200 encapsulation sap, configures Ethernet0 to reside on IPX network 200 using 802.2 encapsulation. If all the routers in Figure 9-11 were configured as indicated in this chapter, IPX/SPX communications would now be possible across the internetwork.

The Secondary Command

On occasion, you may need to configure multiple networks using multiple frame types on a single router interface. For instance, in Figure 9-18, E0 on RouterB must support IPX network 200 using 802.2 encapsulation and IPX network 2f using Ethernet_II encapsulation.

Figure 9-18   Multiple IPX networks per interface

You can accomplish this support by using the secondary command, or by adding multiple networks and encapsulations through subinterfaces. (Subinterfaces are discussed in the next section.) Using the secondary command, you can add IPX network 2f as a secondary network on the interface Ethernet0. The router output in Figure 9-19 displays proper use of this command.

Typing the show run command allows you to see that a secondary network and encapsulation type have been added to port Ethernet0. Figure 9-20 shows the output from typing the show run command after configuring the secondary network and encapsulation.

You must first enter interface configuration mode for the interface to which you wish to add the secondary network and encapsulation

This command will add IPX routing for network 2f with an encapsulation of arpa on a second virtual interface. With this command, the single physical Ethernet0 interface can support two different networks and two different frame types.

Pressing the Cntl-Z combination takes you out of configuration mode and drops you into privileged mode

```
RouterB(config)#int e0
RouterB(config-if)#ipx network 2f encapsulation arpa secondary
RouterB(config-if)#^Z
RouterB#
```

Figure 9-19   Configuring secondary networks and encapsulations on an IPX interface

```
RouterB#show run
    Building configuration...

    Current configuration:
    !
    version 11.1
    service udp-small-servers
    service tcp-small-servers
    !
    hostname RouterB
    !
    enable secret 5 $1$RHhg$ngXce3OBeC7GprpPjtqsP1
    !
    ipx routing 0060.474f.6506
    ipx maximum-paths 2
    !
    interface Ethernet0
    ip address 172.22.2.1 255.255.255.0
    ipx network 200 encapsulation SAP
    ipx network 2F encapsulation ARPA secondary
    !
    interface Serial0
    no ip address
            --More—
```

Ethernet0 is now configured to route IPX on two different networks using two different encapsulation types

Figure 9-20   Show run output displaying secondary network and encapsulation

Subinterfaces

The secondary command does have two problems associated with it. First, you can only add one secondary network and encapsulation per interface. If you need more, the secondary command will not work for you. In addition, the secondary command may not be included in future versions of the Cisco IOS. Thus, Cisco recommends the use of subinterfaces. **Subinterfaces**, which are virtual interfaces associated with a physical interface, provide a means to add a practically unlimited number of networks and encapsulations.

(The actual number of subinterfaces that can be configured on a physical interface is in the billions.) Figure 9-21 displays the commands necessary to enter subinterface configuration mode.

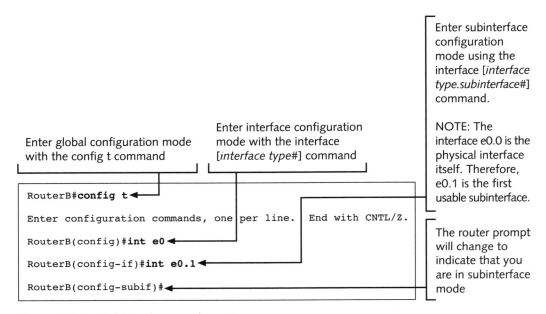

Enter subinterface configuration mode using the interface [*interface type.subinterface#*] command.

NOTE: The interface e0.0 is the physical interface itself. Therefore, e0.1 is the first usable subinterface.

Enter interface configuration mode with the interface [*interface type#*] command

Enter global configuration mode with the config t command

The router prompt will change to indicate that you are in subinterface mode

Figure 9-21   Subinterface configuration

The router output in Figure 9-22 shows the addition of the IPX network 2f using Ethernet_II encapsulation via the use of a subinterface.

The int e0.1 command switches you to subinterface configuration mode. This mode is denoted by the RouterB(config-subif)# prompt.

Figure 9-22   Subinterface configuration with the subinterface method

You can verify that the subinterface has been added with the show run command. Figure 9-23 shows the output from the show run command.

```
RouterB#show run
Building configuration...

Current configuration:
!
version 11.1
service udp-small-servers
service tcp-small-servers
!
hostname RouterB
!
enable secret 5 $1$RHhg$ngXce3OBeC7GprpPjtqsP1
!
ipx routing 0060.474f.6506
ipx maximum-paths 2
!
interface Ethernet0
ip address 172.22.2.1 255.255.255.0
ipx network 200 encapsulation SAP
!
interface Ethernet0.1
ipx network 2F encapsulation ARPA
!
interface Serial0
no ip address
--More—
```

A virtual interface Ethernet0.1 has been added to the running configuration

Figure 9-23   Show run command output after adding a subinterface

Directly below the Ethernet0 configuration information, the Ethernet0.1 subinterface information shows that IPX network 2f with Ethernet_II encapsulation has been added. If you needed to add another network and encapsulation, you would add it to subinterface Ethernet0.2.

Configuration of interfaces constitutes the second in a series of steps necessary for configuration of IPX/SPX on a router. Each interface should be assigned a network number and encapsulation type to ensure that IPX/SPX communication can occur.

MONITORING IPX/SPX

A variety of IOS commands allow you to monitor the performance of IPX/SPX on your routers. Useful commands include show ipx route, show ipx interface, show ipx servers, debug ipx (various subcommands exist for this command), and the extended ping command.

The first monitoring command, show ipx route, displays the current IPX routing tables contained on a router. Using Figure 9-24 as the sample network, Figure 9-25 shows the routing table for RouterA. The table details how RouterA learns of IPX network 200 and 2f via RIP updates from RouterB. Remember that the RIP used by IPX/SPX is not the same as RIP configured for TCP/IP.

Figure 9-24   Multiple IPX networks per interface

The R at the beginning of each route entry signifies that the router learned the route via a RIP update. The C signifies that network 300 is directly connected via the Serial0 interface.

This route table shows that RouterA learned of a route to networks 2f and 200 that has an administrative distance of 7 and is 1 hop away (the 07 equals administrative distance, and the 01 represents the number of hops, or routers, a packet must pass through to get to the destination network).

```
RouterA#show ipx route
Codes: C - Connected primary network,    c - Connected secondary network
   S - Static, F - Floating static, L - Local (internal), W - IPXWAN
   R - RIP, E - EIGRP, N - NLSP, X - External, A - Aggregate
   s - seconds, u - uses

3 Total IPX routes. Up to 1 parallel paths and 16 hops allowed.

No default route known.

C        300 (HDLC),         Se0
R         2F [07/01] via     300.0060.474f.6506,    49s, Se0
R        200 [07/01] via     300.0060.474f.6506,    49s, Se0
RouterA#
```

Figure 9-25   Output from show ipx route command

You can use the show ipx traffic command to display the amount of IPX traffic a router has sent and received. Figure 9-26 contains typical router output you may receive from the show ipx traffic command.

RouterB has sent 625 broadcasts and 9 RIP updates. No broadcast or RIP updates have been received. On a production network, this may indicate a problem with a neighbor router. In this case, RouterA, the closest neighbor to RouterB, had its DCE/DTE cable to RouterC removed.

```
RouterB>show ipx traffic
System Traffic for 0.0000.0000.0001 System-Name: RouterB
Rcvd:   2 total, 2 format errors, 0 checksum errors, 0 bad hop count,
        2 packets pitched, 0 local destination, 0 multicast
Bcast:  0 received, 625 sent
Sent:   625 generated, 0 forwarded
        0 encapsulation failed, 0 no route
SAP:    0 SAP requests, 0 SAP replies, 0 servers
        0 SAP advertisements received, 0 sent
        0 SAP flash updates sent, 0 SAP format errors
RIP:    0 RIP requests, 0 RIP replies, 3 routes
        0 RIP advertisements received, 604 sent
        9 RIP flash updates sent, 0 RIP format errors
Echo:   Rcvd 0 requests, 0 replies
        Sent 0 requests, 0 replies
        0 unknown: 0 no socket, 0 filtered, 0 no helper
        0 SAPs throttled, freed NDB len 0
Watchdog:
        0 packets received, 0 replies spoofed
Queue lengths:
        IPX input: 0, SAP 0, RIP 0, GNS 0
        SAP throttling length: 0/(no limit), 0 nets pending lost route reply
        Delayed process creation: 0
EIGRP:  Total received 0, sent 0
        Updates received 0, sent 0
        Queries received 0, sent 0
        Replies received 0, sent 0
        SAPs received 0, sent 0
NLSP:   Level-1 Hellos received 0, sent 0
        PTP Hello received 0, sent 0
        Level-1 LSPs received 0, sent 0
        LSP Retransmissions: 0
        LSP checksum errors received: 0
        LSP HT=0 checksum errors received: 0
        Level-1 CSNPs received 0, sent 0
        Level-1 PSNPs received 0, sent 0
        Level-1 DR Elections: 0
        Level-1 SPF Calculations: 0
        Level-1 Partial Route Calculations: 0
RouterB>
```

Figure 9-26   Show IPX traffic command output

Another useful monitoring command is the show ipx interface command. This command will display all IPX interfaces and their configurations, or you can specify a single interface. For example, if you want to monitor IPX on Ethernet0, you use the show ipx interface e0 command. Figure 9-27 shows the result of this command on RouterB.

This command will display all IPX
parameters associated with this interface

```
RouterB>show ipx interface e0
    Ethernet0 is up, line protocol is up
    IPX address is 200.0060.474f.6506, SAP [up] line-up, RIPPQ: 0, SAPPQ: 0
    Delay of this IPX network, in ticks is 1 throughput 0 link delay 0
    IPXWAN processing not enabled on this interface.
    IPX SAP update interval is 1 minute(s)
    IPX type 20 propagation packet forwarding is disabled
    Incoming access list is not set
    Outgoing access list is not set
    IPX helper access list is not set
    SAP GNS processing enabled, delay 0 ms, output filter list is not set
    SAP Input filter list is not set
    SAP Output filter list is not set
    SAP Router filter list is not set
    Input filter list is not set
    Output filter list is not set
    Router filter list is not set
    Netbios Input host access list is not set
    Netbios Input bytes access list is not set
    Netbios Output host access list is not set
    Netbios Output bytes access list is not set
    Updates each 60 seconds, aging multiples RIP: 3 SAP: 3
    SAP interpacket delay is 55 ms, maximum size is 480 bytes
    RIP interpacket delay is 55 ms, maximum size is 432 bytes
    IPX accounting is disabled
    IPX fast switching is configured (enabled)
    RIP packets received 0, RIP packets sent 548
    SAP packets received 0, SAP packets sent 4
RouterB>
```

Figure 9-27   Output from the show ipx interface e0 command

The final show command—show ipx servers—allows you to view all IPX servers on a network. It takes entries from a router's SAP tables and builds a list of all available services. Network administrators use this command to verify that their NetWare servers are advertising the services that have been configured for clients to access.

The debug ipx command gives network administrators the ability to do real-time monitoring of IPX traffic across a router. Like the debug ip command, the debug ipx command can produce an enormous amount of router overhead. Debug ipx is so powerful that it is only accessible in privileged mode. You should only use this command for troubleshooting; do not leave it on continuously. If the debug ipx command is on continuously, it is possible that your router may not be able to handle the normal routing of packets. This results in dropped packets and inconsistent network performance.

The router output that follows uses the context-sensitive Help features to display all possible options for the debug ipx command. The final subcommand, debug ipx routing activity, turns on debugging for RIP routing updates and NLSP routing updates. Figure 9-28 shows how to correctly type this command on a router.

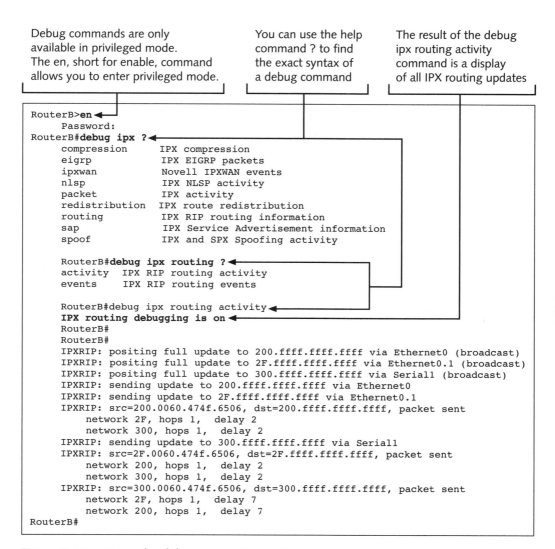

Debug commands are only available in privileged mode. The en, short for enable, command allows you to enter privileged mode.

You can use the help command ? to find the exact syntax of a debug command

The result of the debug ipx routing activity command is a display of all IPX routing updates

```
RouterB>en
    Password:
RouterB#debug ipx ?
    compression    IPX compression
    eigrp          IPX EIGRP packets
    ipxwan         Novell IPXWAN events
    nlsp           IPX NLSP activity
    packet         IPX activity
    redistribution IPX route redistribution
    routing        IPX RIP routing information
    sap            IPX Service Advertisement information
    spoof          IPX and SPX Spoofing activity

RouterB#debug ipx routing ?
    activity   IPX RIP routing activity
    events     IPX RIP routing events

RouterB#debug ipx routing activity
IPX routing debugging is on
RouterB#
RouterB#
IPXRIP: positing full update to 200.ffff.ffff.ffff via Ethernet0 (broadcast)
IPXRIP: positing full update to 2F.ffff.ffff.ffff via Ethernet0.1 (broadcast)
IPXRIP: positing full update to 300.ffff.ffff.ffff via Serial1 (broadcast)
IPXRIP: sending update to 200.ffff.ffff.ffff via Ethernet0
IPXRIP: sending update to 2F.ffff.ffff.ffff via Ethernet0.1
IPXRIP: src=200.0060.474f.6506, dst=200.ffff.ffff.ffff, packet sent
    network 2F, hops 1,  delay 2
    network 300, hops 1,  delay 2
IPXRIP: sending update to 300.ffff.ffff.ffff via Serial1
IPXRIP: src=2F.0060.474f.6506, dst=2F.ffff.ffff.ffff, packet sent
    network 200, hops 1,  delay 2
    network 300, hops 1,  delay 2
IPXRIP: src=300.0060.474f.6506, dst=300.ffff.ffff.ffff, packet sent
    network 2F, hops 1,  delay 7
    network 200, hops 1,  delay 7
RouterB#
```

Figure 9-28   Using the debug ipx routing activity command

Debugging helps you determine what routes are being sent to neighboring routers. To turn off IPX debugging, you issue the no debug ipx routing activity command. The no debug all command and the undebug all command will turn off all debugging.

The extended ping command, available only in privileged mode, allows users to ping IPX addresses across the network. To determine the IPX address of a destination router port, you can use the show ipx interface command at the destination router. The show cdp neighbor detail command also lists the IPX address of neighbor routers. Figure 9-29 shows the use of the extended ping command. Note that an exclamation point signifies a successful response to the ping request.

The extended ping command,
available only in privileged mode,
can be used to ping IPX addresses

```
RouterB#ping
Protocol [ip]: ipx
Target IPX address:300.0000.0c8d.e633
Repeat count [5]:
Datagram size [100]:
Timeout in seconds [2]:
Verbose [n]:
Novell Standard Echo [n]:
Type escape sequence to abort.
Sending 5, 100-byte IPX cisco Echoes to 300.0000.0c8d.e633, timeout is 2
seconds

!!!!!
Success rate is 100 percent (5/5), round-trip min/avg/max = 36/36/36 ms
RouterB#
```

Figure 9-29   Extended ping command

Just like a typical ping, the extended ipx ping verifies that IPX address 300.0000.0c8d.e633 exists and is functional.

CHAPTER SUMMARY

◻ The IPX/SPX protocol stack, like TCP/IP, contains many separate protocols that work together to accomplish the task of network communication.

◻ Layer 3 protocols in the IPX/SPX protocol stack include IPX, RIP, and NLSP.

◻ Layer 4 protocols such as SPX provide connection-oriented services for the connectionless IPX.

◻ As with most protocol stacks, upper-layer protocols such as NCP and SAP exist in IPX/SPX to support particular client/server functions. In particular, SAP allows servers to broadcast available services and clients to request services. The GNS request is an example of a SAP request.

◻ IPX/SPX addresses are 80-bit addresses in a network.node format. Thirty-two bits of the address are reserved for the network portion of the address. Network administrators assign this portion of the address. The MAC address becomes the node portion, consisting of 48 bits. IPX/SPX addresses usually appear in hexadecimal.

◻ Novell specifies four Data Link layer formats: 802.3, 802.2, and Ethernet_II, and Ethernet_snap. The Cisco IOS refers to these formats as novell-ether, sap, arpa, and snap.

◻ Novell-ether is the default on Cisco routers and does not have to be explicitly configured.

◻ Servers and routers use SAP advertisements to build SAP tables of all IPX/SPX services on the network.

◻ SAP broadcasts occur every 60 seconds by default. Routers do not, by default, pass SAP broadcasts. Instead, each router builds a SAP table from all SAP advertisements it sees and passes that table to its IPX/SPX-enabled neighbor routers every 60 seconds. This process reduces the number of broadcasts that would otherwise have to be passed over slow WAN links.

◻ Network administrators use two steps in configuring IPX/SPX on a router: (1) enable IPX routing with the ipx routing command, and (2) enable IPX on each interface with the ipx network [*network #*] encapsulation [*encapsulation keyword*] command.

◻ If necessary, the ipx maximum-paths command can be used to enable load balancing on an IPX network. By default, load balancing is not configured.

◻ Common IPX monitoring commands include show ipx route, show ipx interface, show ipx servers, debug ipx (various subcommands exist for this command), and the extended ping command.

9

KEY TERMS

encapsulation — The process of wrapping Protocol Data Units from upper-layer protocols into a Data Link layer format; common frame types are 802.3, 802.2, and Ethernet_II.

Get Nearest Server (GNS) — A SAP request sent by clients; attempts to locate the nearest NetWare server.

High-level Data Link Control (HDLC) — The default Data Link layer encapsulation for all Cisco serial interfaces.

Internetwork Packet Exchange (IPX) — Predominantly a layer 3 protocol used by the IPX/SPX protocol stack for routing packets along the shortest path in an IPX internetwork.

Internetwork Packet Exchange/Sequenced Packet Exchange (IPX/SPX) — Protocol stack developed by Novell from the Xerox Network System protocol stack.

IPX/SPX addresses — Eighty-bit addresses consisting of a 32-bit network portion and a 48-bit node portion; the network administrator arbitrarily assigns the network portion. The MAC address of the node makes up the node portion of the address; addresses normally appear in hexadecimal format.

load balancing — The ability of a router to distribute packets among multiple same cost paths.

NetWare Core Protocol (NCP) — Upper-layer protocol that handles most of the client/server interaction on a Novell NetWare network.

NetWare Link Services Protocol (NLSP) — Layer 3, link state routing protocol built into the IPX/SPX protocol stack.

Routing Information Protocol (RIP) — Layer 3, distance vector routing protocol built into the IPX/SPX protocol stack; not the same RIP found in TCP/IP; sends out routing table updates every 60 seconds.

Sequenced Packet Exchange (SPX) — Layer 4, connection-oriented protocol used to provide guaranteed delivery services to IPX.

Service Advertisement Protocol (SAP) — Upper-layer protocol used by IPX/SPX servers to advertise available services; also used by clients to discover what services are available on the local segment.

subinterfaces — Logical interfaces used to add multiple networks and multiple frame types to a single physical interface; a replacement for the older secondary command.

ticks — $\frac{1}{18}$-second time counts used to determine the desirability of a particular route.

REVIEW QUESTIONS

1. If you are running the 802.2 frame type on your network, which Cisco encapsulation type would you define on your router ports?

   a. arpa

   b. snap

   c. sap

   d. novell-ether

2. Which layer 3 protocol in the IPX/SPX protocol stack is connectionless and finds the best path to route packets throughout an internetwork?

   a. IPX

   b. SPX

   c. NCP

   d. SAP

3. Which command would you enter in global configuration mode to turn on IPX routing?

   a. route ipx

   b. show ipx route

   c. routing ipx

   d. ipx routing

4. How often are SAP advertisements broadcast by default?

   a. every 30 seconds

   b. every 60 seconds

   c. never

   d. one per client GNS request

5. Which monitoring command displays IPX routing tables for a router?

   a. extended ping

   b. show ipx traffic

   c. show ipx interface

   d. show ipx route

6. If you are running IPX over a serial interface, what is the default encapsulation setting?

   a. hdlc

   b. novell–ether

   c. serial

   d. snap

7. Which of the following shows the correct command sequence for adding the network 3f with Ethernet_II encapsulation to a subinterface of Ethernet0?

   a. int e0.1, ipx network 3f encap arpa sec snap

   b. int e0, ipx network 3f encap arpa

   c. int e0.1, ipx network 3f encap arpa

   d. int e0.1, encap arpa

8. Which of the following monitoring commands displays information concerning the number and types of IPX packets sent and received?

   a. show ipx route

   b. show ipx traffic

   c. debug ipx routing activity

   d. show ipx interface

9. The RIP protocol found in IPX/SPX broadcasts routing table information every _____.

   a. 60 seconds

   b. 35 seconds

   c. 2 minutes

   d. 30 seconds

9

10. In the address 2bc4.0020.7811.4a62, which portion is the network and which portion is the node address? (Choose all correct answers.)

    a. network 2bc4.0020

    b. node 0020.7811.4a62

    c. network 0020.7811.4a62

    d. network 2bc4

11. Which of the following is the default frame encapsulation type on Ethernet interfaces?

    a. 802.3

    b. arpa

    c. novell–ether

    d. snap

12. What command would you use to enable load balancing between three possible routes on an IPX/SPX network?

    a. ipx routing

    b. ipx maximum–paths 3

    c. ipx maximum 3

    d. route ipx maximum–paths 3

13. Which of the following correctly shows the sequence of commands to add IPX network 300 with 802.2 encapsulation to interface Ethernet0?

    a. int e0, encap arpa, ipx network 300

    b. int e0, ipx network 300 encap arpa

    c. int e0.1, ipx network 300 encap sap

    d. int e0, ipx network 300 encap sap

14. You can add a second IPX network and encapsulation to a physical interface with the secondary command. True or False?

15. The routing protocols built into IPX/SPX are _____. (Choose all that apply.)

    a. OSPF

    b. NLSP

    c. RIP

    d. IGRP

16. Cisco routers cannot respond to GNS requests from IPX/SPX clients. True or False?

17. Which of the following router prompts signifies subinterface configuration mode?

    a. RouterB(config-subif)#

    b. RouterB(config-if)#

c. Router(config)#

d. Router#

18. Servers and routers use which of the following protocols to send out tables of available IPX/SPX services?

a. RIP

b. NLSP

c. SAP

d. SNAP

19. What is the Cisco IOS terminology for Ethernet_snap encapsulation?

a. novell-ether

b. sap

c. arpa

d. snap

20. From which of the following router prompts can you issue the extended ping command for ipx?

a. RouterB>

b. RouterB(config)#

c. RouterB#

d. RouterB(ping)#

21. The show interface command for an Ethernet interface shows the Cisco encapsulation type as novell-ether. What Novell encapsulation type does this represent?

a. 802.2

b. sap

c. 802.3

d. Ethernet_II

22. Which of the following items are used as metrics in IPX RIP? (Choose all that apply.)

a. bandwidth

b. ticks

c. hop count

d. delay

23. A router configured for IPX/SPX receives a GNS request on a segment that does not have a Novell server. What does the router do with the request?

a. The router discards the request because it is a broadcast.

b. The router broadcasts the request out to all of its interfaces.

c. The router forwards the request to the closest Novell server.

d. The router attempts to answer the request with entries from its SAP table.

24. Which protocol in the IPX/SPX protocol stack handles basic file and print sharing, authentication services, and directory services?

a. NCP

b. NLSP

c. SAP

d. IPX

25. A tick is _____.

a. 30 seconds

b. 1/30th of a second

c. 60 seconds

d. 1/18th of a second

CASE PROJECTS

1. Parmer and Smith Inc. have hired you and your team to configure their new network infrastructure. They are currently running both Netware 3.12 servers and Netware 4.11 servers. After the upgrade of their routers, no one can access resources on the Netware 3.12 or 4.11 servers. What could be causing this problem? Lisa suspects a frame type mismatch between the router and the servers. Do you agree with her? Why or why not?

2. Drake and Associates needs someone to troubleshoot communications problems within their predominantly IPX network. What commands could you use on their Cisco routers to monitor and troubleshoot their network? Also, briefly describe what each monitoring and troubleshooting command tells you about the network.

3. A customer is considering upgrading his network to Cisco routers and equipment. Before he does this, he wants to learn how Cisco routers deal with SAP tables and SAP updates. Create a short memo that details how Cisco routers deal with SAP tables and SAP updates.

10

ACCESS LISTS

After reading this chapter and completing the exercises, you will be able to:

♦ Describe the usage and rules of access lists

♦ Establish standard IP access lists

♦ Produce extended IP access lists

♦ Develop standard IPX access lists

♦ Create extended IPX access lists

♦ Define IPX SAP filters

♦ Apply access lists to interfaces

♦ Monitor and verify access lists

In this chapter, you will learn how to create and apply access lists to control both traffic flow and network security. In the process, you will review the use and rules of access lists. Then, you will be introduced to the creation of standard and extended IP access lists. In addition, you will read about how to create IPX standard access lists, extended IPX access lists, and SAP filters. After learning the proper techniques for creating access lists, you will review how to apply such lists to router interfaces. Finally, you will learn how to monitor and verify access lists.

ACCESS LISTS: USAGE AND RULES

Network traffic flow and security influence the design and management of computer networks. Fortunately, access lists, which are built into the Cisco IOS, solve many of the problems associated with these two tasks. **Access lists** are permit or deny statements that filter traffic based on the source address, destination address, protocol type, and port number of a packet. They are available for IP, IPX, AppleTalk, and many other protocols.

Access List Usage

You can create a standard access list that examines a packet for the packet's source header information. For instance, RouterA can use an access list to deny access from Network 4 to Network 1; both networks are shown in Figure 10-1. If a packet from Network 4 arrives at the interface where you placed the access list, the router examines the packet and uses the access list to determine if it needs to discard the packet.

Figure 10-1   Sample network

With the following conceptual syntax, you create the standard access list to block access from Network 4 to Network 1:

> access-list 1 deny Network 4
>
> access-list 1 permit any

The access list ends with an **implicit deny any**, which blocks all packets that do not meet the requirements of the access list. Some administrators configure the deny any statement to make it more obvious, however, this is unnecessary. Access-list 1, if applied to the interface of RouterA connected to Network 1, blocks only the traffic coming from Network 4 to Network 1. If you wanted to deny traffic from Network 3 and Network 4, the conceptual access list syntax would then become the following:

> access-list 1 deny Network 3
>
> access-list 1 deny Network 4
>
> access-list 1 permit any

The previous access-list statements are not the exact Cisco IOS syntax for the access list command. Actual IOS syntax will be covered later in the chapter.

The final permit any statement is necessary because all access lists in the Cisco IOS end with an implicit deny any. If you apply the access list to the interface of RouterA that is connected to Network 1, it blocks traffic from Networks 3 and 4, while allowing all other network traffic to access Network 1.

With careful planning, you can create access lists that control which traffic crosses particular links, and which segments of your network will have access to others. In other words, you can control traffic flow and security. Security is enhanced because you can permit or deny particular networks access to parts of your network. In the example above, Network 4 may be a student network, and Network 1 may be an administrative network. The first list stops students from Network 4 from accessing any resources in Network 1, the administrative network.

 Although access lists can help with network security, they do not take the place of more advanced security measures, such as firewalls. Access lists, combined with dedicated firewalls at the edge of your network, provide the greatest security.

10

Problems with Access Lists

One of the most common problems associated with access lists is a lack of planning. Before you begin configuring access lists on your router, you must plan exactly what needs to be filtered and where it needs to be filtered. Careful planning prior to the configuration of lists can cut down on simple logic mistakes, which commonly occur when you do not think through the effects of your actions.

Another troublesome area is the sequential nature in which you must enter the list into the router. You cannot move individual statements once they are entered. When making changes, you must remove the list, using the no access-list [list number] command, and then retype the commands. Many network administrators simplify this time-consuming process by creating their access lists in a simple word processor, such as Notepad, and then copying and pasting the access list into the router configuration. Using this method, an administrator can create a perfect access list (free of typos) and then apply the list to any single router or a group of routers. This allows a type-once, use-many scenario that reduces errors and the time necessary to configure a router.

Finally, many new network administrators find themselves in trouble when they Telnet into a router and begin applying an access list. Access lists begin working the second they are applied to an interface. It is very possible that many new administrators will find themselves inadvertently blocked from the very router on which they are applying an access list. While this is not a serious problem when the router is in the same building as the administrator, it is a serious problem when the router is in another city and thus physically inaccessible.

Fortunately, the reload command can save you from a long car ride or an embarrassing phone call to a local administrator to explain the problem. With the reload command, an administrator can schedule the router to reload in a certain number of minutes, hours, or even days. For access list configuration, you probably want to schedule the reload to the granularity of minutes or hours. The syntax for the reload command is reload in *[hh:]mm* (reloads in a certain number of hours or minutes) or reload at *hh:mm [month day | day month]* (reloads at a certain time on a certain date). For example, before modifying or adding access lists to a remote router, an administrator could type the following command:

> RouterB#reload in 30

If an access list locks the administrator out, the router would reload in 30 minutes with a running-config that did not contain the access-list that blocked the administrator's access. Note, however, that in this case, the reload command will only work if you do not copy the running-config to the startup-config while working with the access lists. If you create and apply the lists and they have the intended results, you can cancel the scheduled reload with the reload cancel command.

Access List Rules

Regardless of the type of access list you create, standard or extended, you must follow certain rules. For instance, you must create and apply access lists sequentially. Also, as stated earlier, access lists always end with an implicit deny.

The following example shows the structure of a standard IP access list. The router applies each line in the order in which you type it into the access list:

> RouterA(config)#access-list 1 deny 172.22.5.2 0.0.0.0
>
> RouterA(config)#access-list 1 deny 172.22.5.3 0.0.0.0
>
> RouterA(config)# access-list 1 permit any

The previous example is a standard IP access list that denies the hosts 172.22.5.2 and 172.22.5.3, while allowing all other traffic. The list is applied sequentially from the top down as the router checks the packets arriving at the interface where this access list is applied, in order to check if the packets match the permit and deny statements.

In the process of applying access lists, the router first checks an arriving packet to determine if it matches the deny 172.22.5.2 0.0.0.0 statement. If it does, the router discards the packet. If it does not, the router applies the second statement, deny 172.22.5.3 0.0.0.0. If the packet matches the second statement, the router discards the packet. Once again, if the packet does not meet the rules of the first two lines, the router applies the final permit any statement, and the packet is forwarded through the interface.

If you want to add another deny line to this list, you can go back into global configuration mode and do so. Because all new lines are added to the end of the list, adding the line

RouterA(config)# access–list 1 deny 172.22.5.5 0.0.0.0 will produce the following list:

> access–list 1 deny 172.22.5.2 0.0.0.0
>
> access–list 1 deny 172.22.5.3 0.0.0.0
>
> access–list 1 permit any
>
> access–list 1 deny 172.22.5.5 0.0.0.0

The new line is appended to the end of access list 1. The router checks the packet against the first three statements. Once the packet matches one of the statements, the router discards or forwards it based on that match. Since the third statement says that all packets are permitted and can be forwarded, the existence of the fourth line has no effect; a packet from 172.22.5.5 would be forwarded before it ever reached the deny 172.22.5.5 0.0.0.0 statement. To fix this problem, you must remove the access-list completely and recreate it using the correct sequence.

If you wish to remove an access-list, you use the no access–list *[list #]* command. For example, to remove the above list, you enter global configuration mode and type the no access–list 1 command. Figure 10-2 shows the correct procedure for typing this command.

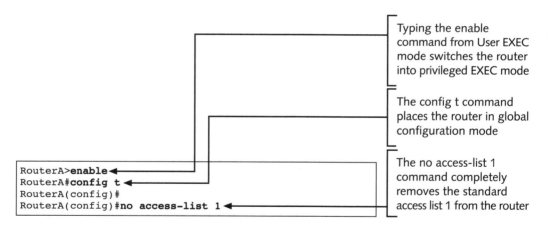

Figure 10-2   No access-list command

This command will remove the entire list. You cannot remove a particular line in an access list. As a general rule, you should place first in the list the lines with the most potential matches so that packets will not undergo unnecessary processing. You should also avoid unnecessarily long access lists. A very long access list will consume large sums of CPU processing time and could cause your router to act as a bottleneck on your network.

As previously mentioned, in order to ease the administrative load associated with access lists, Cisco recommends using a text editor to create them. You can then easily make changes to the list and apply it to the router configuration using copy and paste. You should place a no access–list *[list #]* command as the first line of the text file. This command allows you to completely remove an access list from a router. If you don't use this command, the lines of the access list in the text file will be appended to the end of the existing list when you paste it into the configuration.

After you create access lists, you must apply them to interfaces so they can begin filtering traffic. You apply a list as either an outgoing or an incoming filter. To determine how to apply the list, you have to look through the eyes of "The man in the router." Traffic coming in to the man in the router, through any of the interfaces, is considered **inbound** and needs to be filtered using incoming traffic filters, as shown in Figure 10-3.

Figure 10-3   The man in the router

You would apply the access list to an interface with the following command:

> ip access-group 1 in
> (the one in this example represents the access-list numbered 1)

Once traffic gets to the "The man in the router," he must push it out to one of the interfaces. Access lists to block his outward delivery must be applied as **outbound** filters. You would use this command to set an outbound access list filter:

> ip access-group 1 out
> (again, the 1 specifies that you are applying access list 1 to the interface)

The final rule that access lists must follow states that an interface cannot have more than one inbound or outbound list, per protocol, assigned to it. This means that a router can have no more than one inbound IP access list and one outbound applied at the same time. Multiple lists are allowed only if the lists are different protocols.

In summary, all access lists follow these rules:

- Routers apply lists sequentially in the order in which you type them into the router.

- Routers apply lists to packets sequentially, from the top down, one line at a time.

- Packets are processed only until a match is made and then they are acted upon based on the access list criteria contained in access list statements.

- Lists always end with an implicit deny. Routers discard any packets that do not match any of the access list statements.

- Access lists must be applied to an interface as either inbound or outbound traffic filters.

- Only one list, per protocol, per direction can be applied to an interface.

- Access lists are effective as soon as they are applied, however you must use the copy run start command to save your list after configuration if you want it to survive a router reload.

10

Now that you understand the basic rules of access lists, you need to understand specific types of access lists. The main types of access lists you will learn about are standard and extended IP and IPX lists.

STANDARD IP ACCESS LISTS

Standard IP access lists filter network traffic based on the source IP address only. Using a standard IP access list, you can filter traffic by a host IP, subnet, or a network address. In order to configure standard IP access lists, you must create the list and then apply it to an interface using the syntax following this paragraph. A detailed explanation of each item is contained in the subsequent bulleted list. The brackets in each command syntax are not part of the command; they group items that are replaced within each specific entry.

access-list *[list #] [permit | deny] [source address] [source wildcard mask]*

- *[list #]*: Standard IP access lists are represented by a number in the range of 1–99 (in IOS versions 11.2 and greater, they can also be represented by text names).

- *[permit | deny]*: Used to specify the nature of the access list line. It is either a permit or a deny statement.

- *[source address]*: The IP address of the source

- *[source wildcard mask]*: A **wildcard mask**, or **inverse mask**, applied to determine which bits of the source address are significant

Wildcard masks are one of the most important concepts in IP access lists. Routers use them to determine which bits in an address will be significant. Unlike subnet masks, 0s are placed in bit positions deemed significant, and 1s are placed in positions that are not significant. In other words, where there is a 0 in the mask, the corresponding bit in the incoming packet (either 0 or 1) must match the bit in the IP address in the access list. If there is no match, the packet passes to the next line in the access list. Consider the addresses and wildcard masks shown in Table 10-1.

Table 10-1 Wildcard mask examples

IP Address	Wildcard Mask	Result
172.22.5.2	0.0.0.0	All bit positions must match exactly. Therefore, the access list line will only be applied to host 172.22.5.2. For a match, the incoming packet must have an IP address of exactly 172.22.5.2.
172.22.5.0	0.0.0.255	Bit positions in the first three octets must match exactly, but the last octet can be any valid number. The access list line will apply to all hosts in the 172.22.5.0 subnet.
172.22.1.0	0.0.254.255	The first two octets must match exactly, as must the least significant bit position in the third octet, which in this case is a 1. The last octet can be any valid number. This mask would allow you to permit or deny odd subnets from the 172.22.0.0 major network because odd subnets will always have a 1 in the final bit position of the third octet. The example assumes a subnet mask of 255.255.255.0 for a Class B network.

To understand wildcard masking, you may find it helpful to examine the addresses in binary format. Consider the example in Figure 10-4, which shows a wildcard mask that forces the packet to match all four octets of the source address.

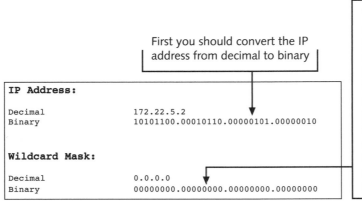

Figure 10-4 Wildcard masking example matching a single host

Since 0s represent significant bits, you can see that in Figure 10-4, a wildcard mask of 0.0.0.0 requires that the source address match exactly. The second example, in Figure 10-5, shows how you permit or deny an entire subnet.

First you should convert the IP address from decimal to binary

```
IP Address:

Decimal           172.22.5.0
Binary            10101100.00010110.00000101.00000000
Wildcard Mask:

Decimal           0.0.0.255
Binary            00000000.00000000.00000000.11111111
```

You can then convert the wildcard mask to binary. All bit positions occupied by a 0 in the wildcard mask are significant and must match when a packet is examined by the router for access list criteria. This wildcard mask requires that the first three octets match exactly. Since the final octet is all 1's, the final octet is not significant. It can be any valid value from 1 to 254.

Figure 10-5   Wildcard masking example matching a complete subnet

Again, if you remember that 0s represent significant bits, you see that the first three octets must match. The final octet of the wildcard mask consists of 1s and signifies that the value of the fourth octet is not significant.

It is relatively easy to decipher wildcard masks when an entire octet is either all 0s (zero) or all 1s (255). It is more difficult when some bits in an octet are 0s and some bits are 1s. This mixing of 0s and 1s in an octet is called **partial masking**.

The final example of wildcard masking is a bit tougher and requires examining two IP addresses to fully understand it. Figure 10-6 illustrates the first address, an odd subnet.

In this example, the first two octets must match exactly. Also, the final bit place in the third octet must match; it must be a 1! Therefore, an access list that states access-list 1 permit 172.22.1.0 0.0.254.255 will allow traffic from any odd-numbered subnet to pass. Even-numbered subnets are blocked because their last bit position in the third octet is a 0.

This wildcard mask requires that the first two octets and the final bit position of the third octet match the IP address in the access list. The values in the last octet are not significant. Since the final bit positions in the third octet of the IP address in the access list are turned on (set to 1), all packets that the access list will permit or deny must have a 1 in the final bit position of the third octet.

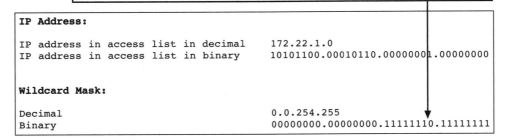

```
IP Address:

IP address in access list in decimal     172.22.1.0
IP address in access list in binary      10101100.00010110.00000001.00000000


Wildcard Mask:

Decimal                                  0.0.254.255
Binary                                   00000000.00000000.11111110.11111111
```

Figure 10-6   Wildcard masking example using partial masking

If you use a source of 172.22.1.0 and a wildcard mask of 0.0.254.255, any packet that the list will act upon must have a 1 in the least significant bit position of the third octet. If a packet with the IP address of 172.22.2.1 is examined by the access list in the previous paragraph, the router ignores it because the least significant bit of the third octet (see below) is a 0, not a 1. Figure 10-7 shows why this is true.

This wildcard mask requires that the first two octets and the final bit position of the third octet match the IP address in the access list. The values in the last octet are not significant. Since the final bit position in the third octet of the examined IP address and the IP address in the access list do not match (one is a 0 and the other is a 1), any line in an access list with a permit or deny 172.22.1.0 0.0.254.255 would not apply to the address 172.22.2.1. In fact, no even subnet could be affected because all even subnets would have a value of 0 in the last bit position of the third octet.

```
Decimal of examined IP address     172.22.2.1

Binary of examined IP address      10101100.00010110.00000010.00000001

IP address in access list:         10101100.00010110.00000001.00000000

Wildcard mask:                     00000000.00000000.11111110.11111111
```

Figure 10-7   Wildcard masking example without match

Since the least significant bit positions do not match, any address within the subnet 172.22.2.0 is out of the required range of the access list and is thus discarded (or ignored, depending on the function of the access list).

Standard IP Access List Examples

Standard IP access lists permit or deny packets based only upon the source address. These addresses can be a single host address, a subnet address, or a full network address. Consider the IP network in Figure 10-8:

Figure 10-8   Sample IP Network

Using the sample network in Figure 10-8, you can create a standard IP access list that blocks host 172.22.5.2 from accessing subnet 172.22.2.0. Figure 10-9 shows the commands you would enter on RouterB to accomplish this task.

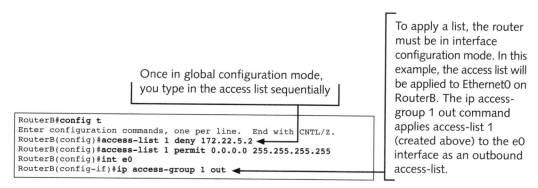

Once in global configuration mode, you type in the access list sequentially

To apply a list, the router must be in interface configuration mode. In this example, the access list will be applied to Ethernet0 on RouterB. The ip access-group 1 out command applies access-list 1 (created above) to the e0 interface as an outbound access-list.

```
RouterB#config t
Enter configuration commands, one per line.  End with CNTL/Z.
RouterB(config)#access-list 1 deny 172.22.5.2
RouterB(config)#access-list 1 permit 0.0.0.0 255.255.255.255
RouterB(config)#int e0
RouterB(config-if)#ip access-group 1 out
```

Figure 10-9   Creating a standard IP access list

In global configuration mode, you add each line of the access list sequentially and then apply it to an interface in order to cause it to take effect. In this example, the deny statement does not include a source wildcard mask because the default mask for standard IP access lists is 0.0.0.0, which is the exact mask needed in the example. It is also possible to replace the 0.0.0.0 255.255.255.255 entry, which represents all hosts and all networks, with the **any** keyword. Once the list is applied to RouterB's Ethernet0 interface, packets from 172.22.5.2 will be blocked from going out the interface.

Correct placement of a list is imperative. If the list were placed on RouterB's S1 interface as an inbound list, it would work with the sample network. However, if RouterB had another Ethernet interface, as shown in Figure 10-10, placing the access list on S1 would inadvertently block traffic to the second Ethernet interface, e1.

Figure 10-10   Sample IP network with two Ethernet interfaces on RouterB

Applying the previous list as an inbound access list on S1 blocks all traffic from host 172.22.5.2 to other ports on RouterB. Since you only want to block access to subnet 172.22.2.0, this is not the correct way to apply the list; you should apply the standard IP access list as close to the destination as possible. Otherwise, you will inadvertently block access to portions of your network.

To view the access lists defined on your router, use the show access-lists command. Since this is an IP access list, you could also use the show ip access-lists command. Figure 10-11 shows the correct procedures to type in both commands.

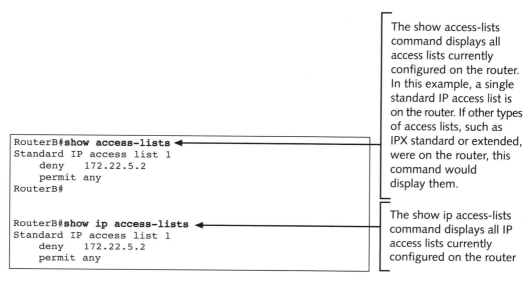

```
RouterB#show access-lists
Standard IP access list 1
    deny    172.22.5.2
    permit any
RouterB#


RouterB#show ip access-lists
Standard IP access list 1
    deny    172.22.5.2
    permit any
```

The show access-lists command displays all access lists currently configured on the router. In this example, a single standard IP access list is on the router. If other types of access lists, such as IPX standard or extended, were on the router, this command would display them.

The show ip access-lists command displays all IP access lists currently configured on the router

Figure 10-11   Show access-lists and show ip access-lists commands

RouterB has one standard IP access list defined on it. To view which interfaces have IP access lists set, use the show ip interface command. Your router will return a list of all interfaces and details about which access lists are applied, inbound and outbound. For the sake of brevity, only Ethernet0 is displayed in Figure 10-12.

10

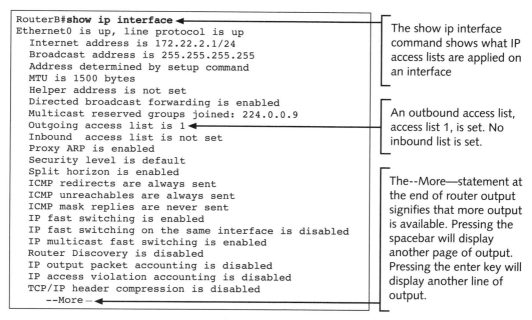

```
RouterB#show ip interface
Ethernet0 is up, line protocol is up
  Internet address is 172.22.2.1/24
  Broadcast address is 255.255.255.255
  Address determined by setup command
  MTU is 1500 bytes
  Helper address is not set
  Directed broadcast forwarding is enabled
  Multicast reserved groups joined: 224.0.0.9
  Outgoing access list is 1
  Inbound  access list is not set
  Proxy ARP is enabled
  Security level is default
  Split horizon is enabled
  ICMP redirects are always sent
  ICMP unreachables are always sent
  ICMP mask replies are never sent
  IP fast switching is enabled
  IP fast switching on the same interface is disabled
  IP multicast fast switching is enabled
  Router Discovery is disabled
  IP output packet accounting is disabled
  IP access violation accounting is disabled
  TCP/IP header compression is disabled
     --More--
```

The show ip interface command shows what IP access lists are applied on an interface

An outbound access list, access list 1, is set. No inbound list is set.

The--More—statement at the end of router output signifies that more output is available. Pressing the spacebar will display another page of output. Pressing the enter key will display another line of output.

Figure 10-12   Show ip interface command

If, for some reason, you decide that an access list needs to be removed from an interface, you can remove it with the no ip access-group [*list #*] command, as shown in Figure 10-13.

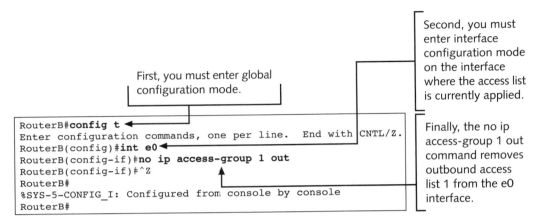

First, you must enter global configuration mode.

Second, you must enter interface configuration mode on the interface where the access list is currently applied.

Finally, the no ip access-group 1 out command removes outbound access list 1 from the e0 interface.

```
RouterB#config t
Enter configuration commands, one per line.  End with CNTL/Z.
RouterB(config)#int e0
RouterB(config-if)#no ip access-group 1 out
RouterB(config-if)#^Z
RouterB#
%SYS-5-CONFIG_I: Configured from console by console
RouterB#
```

Figure 10-13   Removing an ip access list from an interface

If you type the show ip interface command, it will show that access list 1 is no longer an outbound access list. Figure 10-14 displays the results of the show ip interface command after you type the no ip access-group 1 out command.

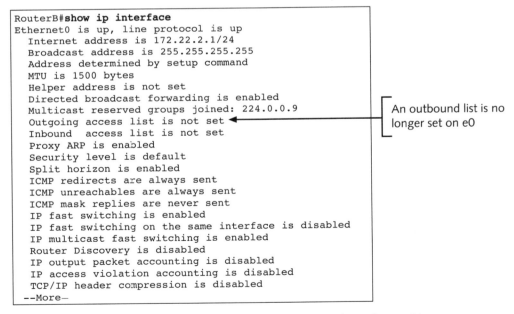

```
RouterB#show ip interface
Ethernet0 is up, line protocol is up
  Internet address is 172.22.2.1/24
  Broadcast address is 255.255.255.255
  Address determined by setup command
  MTU is 1500 bytes
  Helper address is not set
  Directed broadcast forwarding is enabled
  Multicast reserved groups joined: 224.0.0.9
  Outgoing access list is not set
  Inbound  access list is not set
  Proxy ARP is enabled
  Security level is default
  Split horizon is enabled
  ICMP redirects are always sent
  ICMP unreachables are always sent
  ICMP mask replies are never sent
  IP fast switching is enabled
  IP fast switching on the same interface is disabled
  IP multicast fast switching is enabled
  Router Discovery is disabled
  IP output packet accounting is disabled
  IP access violation accounting is disabled
  TCP/IP header compression is disabled
--More—
```

An outbound list is no longer set on e0

Figure 10-14   Show ip interface after removal of access list 1 from e0

Access lists are not effective until they are applied to an interface. If a list is created and not applied or if a list is applied and then the list itself is removed, the commands will be executed, but all traffic will be permitted in and out.

Now, assume that instead of blocking a single host from subnet 172.22.5.0, you want to block all traffic from this subnet to subnet 172.22.2.0, using a standard IP access list. Once again, you need to create the access list in global configuration mode and apply the access list to an interface in interface configuration mode. In this example, you will apply the list as an outbound filter on RouterB's Ethernet0 interface, as this is closest to the destination as possible. (Recall that Figure 10-8 shows the network that contains RouterB.) Both parts of the task can be accomplished at the same time; the router output in Figure 10-15 shows both the creation of the list and the application of the list as an outbound filter on Ethernet0.

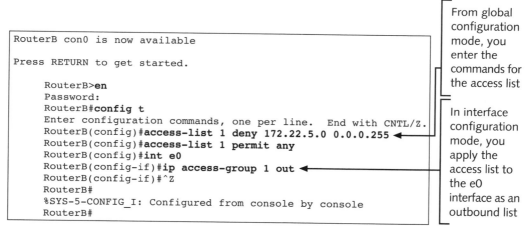

10

From global configuration mode, you enter the commands for the access list

In interface configuration mode, you apply the access list to the e0 interface as an outbound list

Figure 10-15   Creation and application of standard IP access list

You can use the show access-lists or show ip access-lists command and then the show ip interface command to verify that the list has been entered and applied correctly. Figure 10-16 shows the results of these two commands after the procedures in Figure 10-15 have been performed.

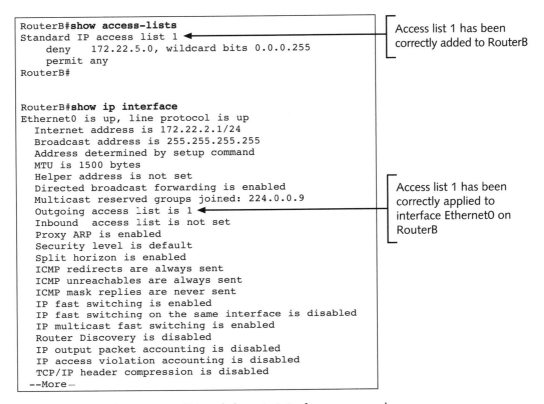

```
RouterB#show access-lists
Standard IP access list 1
    deny    172.22.5.0, wildcard bits 0.0.0.255
    permit any
RouterB#


RouterB#show ip interface
Ethernet0 is up, line protocol is up
   Internet address is 172.22.2.1/24
   Broadcast address is 255.255.255.255
   Address determined by setup command
   MTU is 1500 bytes
   Helper address is not set
   Directed broadcast forwarding is enabled
   Multicast reserved groups joined: 224.0.0.9
   Outgoing access list is 1
   Inbound  access list is not set
   Proxy ARP is enabled
   Security level is default
   Split horizon is enabled
   ICMP redirects are always sent
   ICMP unreachables are always sent
   ICMP mask replies are never sent
   IP fast switching is enabled
   IP fast switching on the same interface is disabled
   IP multicast fast switching is enabled
   Router Discovery is disabled
   IP output packet accounting is disabled
   IP access violation accounting is disabled
   TCP/IP header compression is disabled
--More—
```

Access list 1 has been correctly added to RouterB

Access list 1 has been correctly applied to interface Ethernet0 on RouterB

Figure 10-16   Show access-list and show ip interface commands

Finally, assume that you want to block access to the 172.22.2.0 subnet from all hosts on subnets 172.22.4.0 and 172.22.5.0. You can accomplish this task by entering the commands shown in Figure 10-17.

Again, you can use the show ip access-list or show access-list commands to verify that the access list was entered correctly. The show ip interface command will show all IP interfaces. If you wish to view a specific interface, you can use show ip interface *[interface#]*. For example, throughout these examples, you could have used the show ip interface e0 command to view just the Ethernet0 interface.

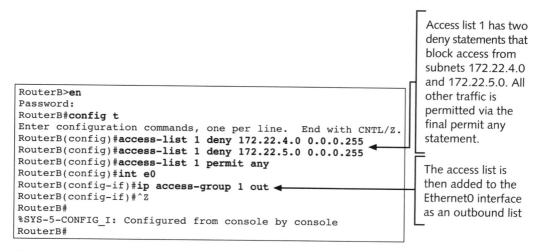

Access list 1 has two deny statements that block access from subnets 172.22.4.0 and 172.22.5.0. All other traffic is permitted via the final permit any statement.

The access list is then added to the Ethernet0 interface as an outbound list

```
RouterB>en
Password:
RouterB#config t
Enter configuration commands, one per line.  End with CNTL/Z.
RouterB(config)#access-list 1 deny 172.22.4.0 0.0.0.255
RouterB(config)#access-list 1 deny 172.22.5.0 0.0.0.255
RouterB(config)#access-list 1 permit any
RouterB(config)#int e0
RouterB(config-if)#ip access-group 1 out
RouterB(config-if)#^Z
RouterB#
%SYS-5-CONFIG_I: Configured from console by console
RouterB#
```

Figure 10-17   Access list that blocks multiple subnets

Monitoring Standard IP Access Lists

Three main commands are available for monitoring access lists on your router. The first two, show access-lists and show ip access-lists, display the exact syntax of all access lists and IP access lists, respectively. The show interfaces or show ip interface command is used to verify that an access list has been successfully applied to an interface. It is a good idea to run each of these commands after creating and applying access lists, to visually inspect and verify that statements were typed in correctly and that the lists will function as entered. Use the no access-list *[list #]* command to remove the list and the no ip access-group *[list #] [direction]* command to remove the application of the list.

EXTENDED IP ACCESS LISTS

As previously mentioned, standard IP access lists are limited to filtering by source IP addresses only. **Extended IP access lists**, on the other hand, can filter by source IP address, destination IP address, protocol type, and application port number. This granularity allows you to design extended IP access lists that permit or deny a single type of IP protocol, such as TCP, and then filter by a particular port of a particular protocol, port 21 or FTP, for example.

In order to configure extended IP access lists, you must create the list and then apply it to an interface using the following syntax (a detailed explanation of each item is contained in the subsequent bulleted list):

access-list *[list #] [permit | deny] [protocol] [source IP address] [source wildcard mask] [operator] [port] [destination IP address] [destination wildcard mask] [operator] [port] [log]*

10

- *[list #]*: Extended IP access lists are represented by a number in the range of 100–199 (in IOS versions 11.2 and greater, they can also be represented by text names).

- *[permit | deny]*: Used to specify the nature of the access list line. It is either a permit or a deny statement.

- *[protocol]*: The IP protocol to be filtered can be IP (which includes all protocols in the TCP/IP suite) TCP, UDP, ICMP, or others.

- *[source address]*: The IP address of the source

- *[source wildcard mask]*: A wildcard mask, or inverse mask, applied to determine which bits of the source address are significant

- *[destination address]*: The IP address of the destination

- *[destination wildcard mask]*: A wildcard mask, or inverse mask, applied to determine which bits of the destination address are significant

- *[operator]*: Can contain lt (less than), gt (greater than), eq (equal to), or neq (not equal to). It is used if an extended list filters by a specific port number.

- *[port]*: If necessary, the port number of the protocol to be filtered. Alternatively, a service using TCP such as www or ftp can be specified.

- *[log]*: Turns on logging of access list activity

Extended IP Access List Examples

Using Figure 10-18 as an example, this section discusses how to block host 172.22.5.2 from accessing Web services on server 172.22.2.2. The extended IP access list example shows how to block WWW access using the context-sensitive, built-in help features in the Cisco IOS that display all available IOS options.

The configuration begins when you type the enable command to enter privileged mode on RouterC. Typing "?" at the privileged mode prompt shows all available commands. Figure 10-19 displays all the commands you must type to create the extended IP access list. The figure also displays the different access list groupings and their number ranges.

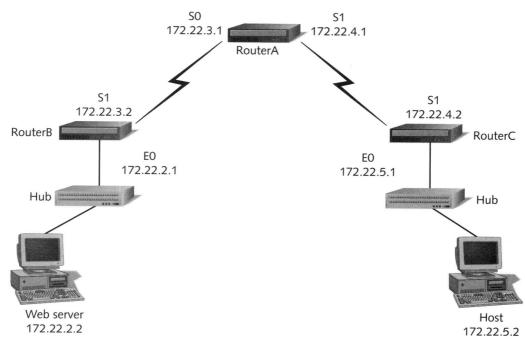

Figure 10-18   Sample IP network with a Web server

Unlike standard IP access lists, extended access lists do not have a default wildcard mask of 0.0.0.0. Therefore, you must specify the wildcard mask for the source IP address. You can use either the typical wildcard mask as previously defined, or, as in the example in Figure 10-20, you can use shortcuts. The **host** keyword is short for a wildcard mask of 0.0.0.0; in other words, the line will only be applied to packets that match the one source address specified with the host keyword. Figure 10-20 shows a continuation of the access list started in Figure 10-19; note the use of the host keyword. Notice also that the host keyword is placed before the IP address rather than after it like the wild-card mask would be.

Typing the ? command displays all commands available from this prompt. Notice that access-list is the second command on the list.

You then enter the access-list command to begin typing the access list. Again, the ? command reveals correct syntax for the command and possible number ranges for different access lists.

Since this list is an extended IP address, it will be designated with the number 100

```
RouterC>enable
Password:
RouterC#config t
Enter configuration commands, one per line. End with CNTL/Z.
RouterC(config)#? ◄
Configure commands:
  aaa                            Authentication, Authorization and Accounting.
  access-list                    Add an access list entry
  alias                          Create command alias
  arp                            Set a static ARP entry
  async-bootp                    Modify system bootp parameters
  banner                         Define a login banner
  boot                           Modify system boot parameters
  bridge                         Bridging Group.
  buffers                        Adjust system buffer pool parameters
  busy-message                   Display message when connection to host fails
  cdp                            Global CDP configuration subcommands
  chat-script                    Define a modem chat script
  clock                          Configure time-of-day clock
  config-register                Define the configuration register
  default-value                  Default character-bits values
  dialer-list                    Create a dialer list entry
  dnsix-dmdp                     Provide DMDP service for DNSIX
  dnsix-nat                      Provide DNSIX service for audit trails
  downward-compatible-config     Generate a configuration compatible with older
                                 software
  enable                         Modify enable password parameters
 --More —


RouterC(config)#access-list ? ◄
  <1-99>       IP standard access list
  <100-199>    IP extended access list
  <1000-1099>  IPX SAP access list
  <1100-1199>  Extended 48-bit MAC address access list
  <1200-1299>  IPX summary address access list
  <200-299>    Protocol type-code access list
  <700-799>    48-bit MAC address access list
  <800-899>    IPX standard access list
  <900-999>    IPX extended access list


RouterC(config)#access-list 100 ? ◄
```

Figure 10-19 Extended IP access list example

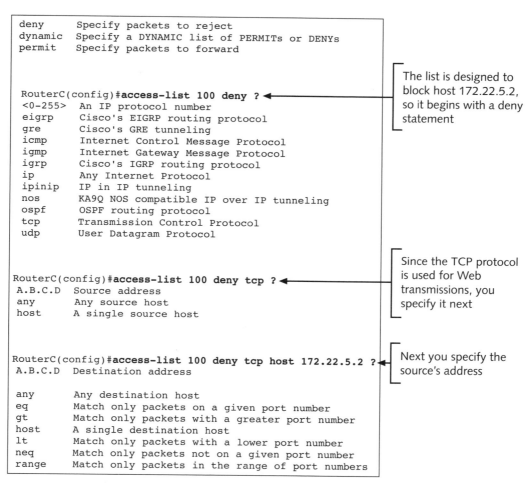

```
deny      Specify packets to reject
dynamic   Specify a DYNAMIC list of PERMITs or DENYs
permit    Specify packets to forward


RouterC(config)#access-list 100 deny ?
<0-255>  An IP protocol number
eigrp    Cisco's EIGRP routing protocol
gre      Cisco's GRE tunneling
icmp     Internet Control Message Protocol
igmp     Internet Gateway Message Protocol
igrp     Cisco's IGRP routing protocol
ip       Any Internet Protocol
ipinip   IP in IP tunneling
nos      KA9Q NOS compatible IP over IP tunneling
ospf     OSPF routing protocol
tcp      Transmission Control Protocol
udp      User Datagram Protocol


RouterC(config)#access-list 100 deny tcp ?
A.B.C.D  Source address
any      Any source host
host     A single source host


RouterC(config)#access-list 100 deny tcp host 172.22.5.2 ?
A.B.C.D  Destination address

any      Any destination host
eq       Match only packets on a given port number
gt       Match only packets with a greater port number
host     A single destination host
lt       Match only packets with a lower port number
neq      Match only packets not on a given port number
range    Match only packets in the range of port numbers
```

The list is designed to block host 172.22.5.2, so it begins with a deny statement

Since the TCP protocol is used for Web transmissions, you specify it next

Next you specify the source's address

10

Figure 10-19   Extended IP access list example (continued)

```
RouterC(config)#access-list 100 deny tcp host 172.22.5.2 host 172.22.2.2 ?
  eq           Match only packets on a given port number
  established  Match established connections
  gt           Match only packets with a greater port number
  log          Log matches against this entry
  lt           Match only packets with a lower port number
  neq          Match only packets not on a given port number
  precedence   Match packets with given precedence value
  range        Match only packets in the range of port numbers
  tos          Match packets with given TOS value
  <cr>
```

Figure 10-20   Extended IP access list example continued

At this point, you have specified your protocol and the source and destination addresses. You must now configure the operator and port. The example list should block WWW and therefore must contain an equal to operator and the WWW port number or name.

You place the port number or name and press enter to add the line to the access list

The next line you must add is a line that will permit all other IP traffic. If you do not, the implicit deny any at the end of the access list will block all other traffic. Notice that the any keyword is used twice; the first instance corresponds to any source, and the second corresponds to any destination.

```
RouterC(config)#access-list 100 deny tcp host 172.22.5.2 host 172.22.2.2 eq ?
  <0-65535>    Port number
    bgp          Border Gateway Protocol (179)
    chargen      Character generator (19)
    cmd          Remote commands (rcmd, 514)
    daytime      Daytime (13)
    discard      Discard (9)
    domain       Domain Name Service (53)
    echo         Echo (7)
    exec         Exec (rsh, 512)
    finger       Finger (79)
    ftp          File Transfer Protocol (21)
    ftp-data     FTP data connections (used infrequently, 20)
    gopher       Gopher (70)
    hostname     NIC hostname server (101)
    ident        Ident Protocol (113)
    irc          Internet Relay Chat (194)
    klogin       Kerberos login (543)
    kshell       Kerberos shell (544)
    login        Login (rlogin, 513)
    lpd          Printer service (515)
    nntp         Network News Transport Protocol (119)
    pop2         Post Office Protocol v2 (109)
    pop3         Post Office Protocol v3 (110)
    smtp         Simple Mail Transport Protocol (25)
    sunrpc       Sun Remote Procedure Call (111)
    syslog       Syslog (514)
    tacacs       TAC Access Control System (49)
    talk         Talk (517)
    telnet       Telnet (23)
    time         Time (37)
    uucp         Unix-to-Unix Copy Program (540)
    whois        Nicname (43)
    www          World Wide Web (HTTP, 80)



RouterC(config)#access-list 100 deny tcp host 172.22.5.2 host 172.22.2.2 eq www
RouterC(config)#access-list 100 permit ip any any
RouterC(config)#
```

Figure 10-20   Extended IP access list example continued (continued)

Once an extended IP access list is created, it must be applied to an interface, just like a standard list. The difference is the placement of the list. Standard IP access lists examine the source address only. As a result, you must place them as close to the destination as possible to avoid blocking traffic bound for another interface/network. On the other hand, extended IP access lists are able to filter based on source and destination. Therefore, they are placed as close to the source as possible.

In our sample network, the list is best placed as an inbound filter on the Ethernet0 interface of RouterC. Traffic from host 172.22.5.2 destined for the Web server at 172.22.2.2 will be blocked before it has a chance to even enter the network. Because of their placement, extended access lists create less traffic across the internetwork. Figure 10-21 displays the proper commands for adding the extended access list as an inbound list on interface Ethernet0.

```
RouterC(config)#int e0
RouterC(config-if)#ip access-group 100 in ◄───────
RouterC(config-if)#^Z
RouterC#
%SYS-5-CONFIG_I: Configured from console by console
RouterC#
```

Once in interface configuration mode, you use the ip access-group [list #] [in | out] command to add the list to the interface.

Figure 10-21   Applying an extended ip access list to an interface

If you wish to remove a list from an interface, you enter interface configuration mode and use the no ip access-group [list #] [in | out] command. Figure 10-22 shows this command.

```
RouterC#config t
Enter configuration commands, one per line.  End with CNTL/Z.
RouterC(config)#int e0
RouterC(config-if)#no ip access-group 100 in ◄──
RouterC(config-if)#^Z
RouterC#
%SYS-5-CONFIG_I:  Configured from console by console
RouterC#
```

Once in interface configuration mode, you use the no ip access-group [list #] [in\out] command to remove a list from the interface

Figure 10-22   Removing an extended ip access list from an interface

The "Established" Parameter

Very often, network administrators want to block all TCP/IP traffic outside their network from coming into their network. However, if you use deny statements to deny all traffic coming in, no one will be able to browse the Web, get email, ping, or other networking activities that involve a response to a request. For example, if you attempt to view the web page at *www.cisco.com*, a DNS server somewhere has to resolve *www.cisco.com* to an IP address and provide that address to your computer. This usually requires traffic from outside your network coming into your network. If all traffic coming in were blocked by an access list, DNS as well as other network activities that we take for granted could not be accomplished. The easiest way to get around this problem is to use an extended ip access list with the **established** parameter. Review the following access list line:

access-list 100 permit tcp any 15.0.0.0 0.255.255.255 established

This command would permit traffic from any host on any network to any destination on the 15.0.0.0 network, as long as the traffic was in response to a request initiated inside network 15.0.0.0. In other words, a TCP connection must already be established in order for the outside traffic to be let in.

Monitoring Extended IP Access Lists

The same commands used to monitor standard IP access lists are used to monitor extended IP access lists. If you wish to view the access lists configured on your router, you use the show access-lists or show ip access-lists commands. To see if the list has been applied to an interface, use the show interfaces or show ip interface command. Figure 10-23 shows the show ip access-lists commands.

```
RouterC#show ip access-lists
Extended IP access list 100
    deny tcp host 172.22.5.2 host 172.22.2.2 eq www
    permit ip any any (450 matches)
RouterC#
```

Extended access lists show the number of matches per line of the access list. The deny statement in list 100 has not been used in this example. No attempts have been made by host 172.22.5.2 to access the Web server.

450 packets have matched the permit ip any any statement

Figure 10-23   Show ip access-lists command

As shown in Figure 10-23, extended IP lists keep track of the number of packets that pass each line of an access list. These matches or counters can be reset to zero for troubleshooting purposes. To clear the counters, you issue the clear access-list counters *[list #]* command. Use the no access-list *[list#]* command to remove the list and the no ip access-group *[list#]* *[direction]* command to remove the application of the list.

```
RouterC#clear access-list counters 100
RouterC#show ip access-list
Extended IP access list 100
     deny tcp host 172.22.5.2 host 172.22.2.2 eq www
     permit ip any any (9 matches) ◄
RouterC#
```

Notice that the number of matches on access list 100 has dropped from the previous 450 matches in Figure 10-23 to 9 because the counters were cleared to 0 (zero)

Figure 10-24   Clear access-list counters command

STANDARD IPX ACCESS LISTS

Standard IPX access lists are very similar to their IP cousins, but they have one distinct difference. While standard IP access lists only filter based on source addresses, **standard IPX access lists** can filter based on source and destination nodes or networks. In all other respects, they act just like standard IP access lists. In order to configure standard IPX access lists, you must create the list and then apply it to an interface using the following syntax (a detailed explanation of each item is contained in the subsequent bulleted list):

access-list [list #] [permit | deny] [source network / node address] [destination network / node address]

- *[list #]*: Standard IPX access lists are represented by a number in the range of 800–899.

- *[permit | deny]*: Used to specify the nature of the access list line. It is either a permit or a deny statement.

- *[source network / node address]*: The IPX address of the source network or node

- *[destination network / node address]*: The IPX address of the destination network or node

Standard IPX Access List Examples

In order to visualize the placement and function of standard IPX access lists, you must have a reference network. Figure 10-25 shows the IPX network used in this section.

Assume that in the sample IPX network in Figure 10-25, you wish to block all traffic from IPX network 500 to IPX network 200. In addition, traffic flow between network 500 and network 300 must remain unaffected. Figure 10-26 shows how you create the access list using context-sensitive help.

10

Figure 10-25   Sample IPX Network

The -1 keyword stands for all IPX networks and all IPX nodes, just as the any keyword stands for all IP addresses in IP access lists. The final line in the access list is necessary because IPX access lists, like all access lists, end with an implicit deny any. Without the final line, you would block traffic between network 500 and networks 200 and 300.

Your next step is to apply the list to an interface. The ipx access-group command accomplishes this task.

Figure 10-26   Standard IPX access list configuration

Monitoring Standard IPX Lists

You can view IPX access lists with the show access-lists command or show access-lists *[list number]* command if you want to view one particular list. To see if the list has been successfully applied to an interface, use the show ipx interface command. Figure 10-27 shows the router output when you type this command. Use the no access-list *[list #]* command to remove the list and the no ipx access-group *[list #] [direction]* command to remove the application of the list.

```
RouterC#show access-lists
Extended IP access list 100
    deny    tcp host 172.22.5.2 host 172.22.2.2 eq www
    permit ip any any (450 matches)

Novell access list 800
    deny 500 200
    permit FFFFFFFF FFFFFFFF
RouterC#
```

The standard IPX access list has been created on the router. It denies traffic from network 500 to 200, but permits all other traffic.

Figure 10-27   Show access-lists command

EXTENDED IPX ACCESS LISTS

Extended IPX access lists allow you to filter based on source and destination network or node address, IPX protocol type, and IPX socket number. In order to configure extended IPX access lists, you must create the list and then apply it to an interface using the following syntax (a detailed explanation of each item is contained in the subsequent bulleted list):

access-list *[list#] [permit | deny] [protocol] [source network/node] [socket] [destination network/node] [socket]*

- *[list#]*: Extended IPX access lists are represented by a number in the range of 900–999.

- *[permit | deny]*: Used to specify the nature of the access list line. It is either a permit or a deny statement.

- *[protocol]*: IPX protocol. A −1 or the any keyword specifies all IPX protocols.

- *[source network/node address]*: The IPX address of the source network or node. The any keyword specifies any network/node address.

- *[socket]*: Similar to the port value in IP access lists. Points to a particular service. A zero or the all keyword specifies all sockets.

- *[destination network/node address]*: The IPX address of the destination network or node. The any keyword specifies any network/node address.

- *[socket]*: Similar to the port value in IP access lists. Points to a particular service. A zero or the all keyword specifies all sockets.

10

Extended IPX Access Lists Example

We can take our standard IPX access list and convert it to an extended list to show the correct format of an extended IPX access list. Figure 10-28 shows how you do this using context-sensitive help.

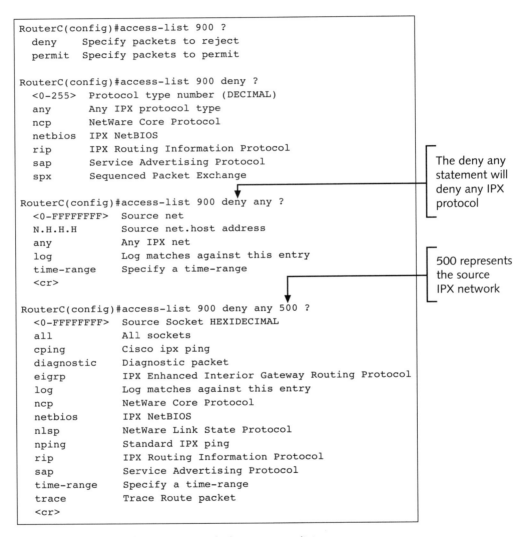

```
RouterC(config)#access-list 900 ?
  deny     Specify packets to reject
  permit   Specify packets to permit

RouterC(config)#access-list 900 deny ?
  <0-255>  Protocol type number (DECIMAL)
  any      Any IPX protocol type
  ncp      NetWare Core Protocol
  netbios  IPX NetBIOS
  rip      IPX Routing Information Protocol
  sap      Service Advertising Protocol
  spx      Sequenced Packet Exchange

RouterC(config)#access-list 900 deny any ?
  <0-FFFFFFFF>  Source net
  N.H.H.H       Source net.host address
  any           Any IPX net
  log           Log matches against this entry
  time-range    Specify a time-range
  <cr>

RouterC(config)#access-list 900 deny any 500 ?
  <0-FFFFFFF>  Source Socket HEXIDECIMAL
  all          All sockets
  cping        Cisco ipx ping
  diagnostic   Diagnostic packet
  eigrp        IPX Enhanced Interior Gateway Routing Protocol
  log          Log matches against this entry
  ncp          NetWare Core Protocol
  netbios      IPX NetBIOS
  nlsp         NetWare Link State Protocol
  nping        Standard IPX ping
  rip          IPX Routing Information Protocol
  sap          Service Advertising Protocol
  time-range   Specify a time-range
  trace        Trace Route packet
  <cr>
```

The deny any statement will deny any IPX protocol

500 represents the source IPX network

Figure 10-28   Configuring extended IPX access-lists

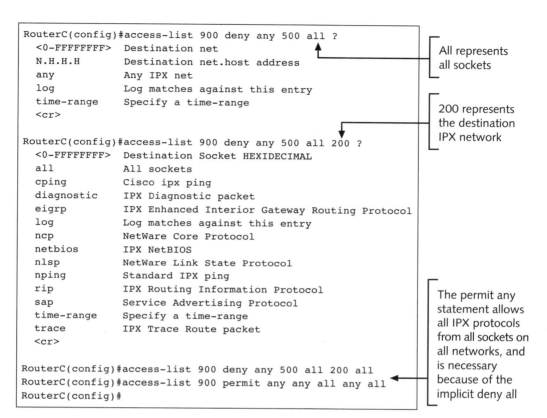

```
RouterC(config)#access-list 900 deny any 500 all ?
  <0-FFFFFFFF>  Destination net
  N.H.H.H       Destination net.host address
  any           Any IPX net
  log           Log matches against this entry
  time-range    Specify a time-range
  <cr>

RouterC(config)#access-list 900 deny any 500 all 200 ?
  <0-FFFFFFFF>  Destination Socket HEXIDECIMAL
  all           All sockets
  cping         Cisco ipx ping
  diagnostic    IPX Diagnostic packet
  eigrp         IPX Enhanced Interior Gateway Routing Protocol
  log           Log matches against this entry
  ncp           NetWare Core Protocol
  netbios       IPX NetBIOS
  nlsp          NetWare Link State Protocol
  nping         Standard IPX ping
  rip           IPX Routing Information Protocol
  sap           Service Advertising Protocol
  time-range    Specify a time-range
  trace         IPX Trace Route packet
  <cr>

RouterC(config)#access-list 900 deny any 500 all 200 all
RouterC(config)#access-list 900 permit any any all any all
RouterC(config)#
```

All represents all sockets

200 represents the destination IPX network

The permit any statement allows all IPX protocols from all sockets on all networks, and is necessary because of the implicit deny all

10

Figure 10-28   Configuring extended IPX access-lists (continued)

Monitoring Extended IPX Access Lists

Just as with all other access lists, the show access-lists command will display your extended IPX access lists along with all other access lists on the router. Figure 10-29 shows an example of this command. As with all previous lists discussed, use the no access-list *[list #]* command to remove the list and the no ipx access-group *[list #]* *[direction]* command to remove the application of the list.

```
RouterC#show access-lists
IPX standard access list 800
    deny 500 200
    permit FFFFFFFF FFFFFFFF

IPX extended access list 900
    deny any 500 all 200 all
    permit any any all any all

Extended IP access list 100
    deny tcp host 172.22.5.2 host 172.22.2.2 eq www
    permit ip any any (450 matches)
RouterC#
```

All access lists, including the extended IPX access list, are shown

Figure 10-29   Show access-lists command

IPX SAP FILTERS

IPX SAP filters limit SAP traffic in order to control what resources on the IPX network will be visible to IPX clients. This allows you to limit the "advertising" of particular servers and services to a particular IPX network segment. Since SAP advertisements are broadcast, limiting them reduces network traffic. For instance, you could block the server used for school administration from "advertising" to the router, which in turn blocks the propagation of administration server updates in other SAP tables.

IPX input SAP filters reduce the number of SAP entries that are placed into a router's SAP table. IPX output SAP filters reduce the number of entries in the SAP table that are passed to other connected routers (for an in-depth discussion of SAP and routers, review Chapter 9).

In order to configure IPX SAP filters, you must create the list and then apply it to an interface using the following syntax (a detailed explanation of each item is contained in the subsequent bulleted list):

access-list *[list #] [permit | deny] [source network/node] [service-type]*

- *[list#]*: IPX SAP filters are represented by a number in the range of 1000–1099.
- *[permit | deny]*: Used to specify the nature of the access list line. It is either a permit or a deny statement.
- *[source network/node address]*: The IPX address of the source network or node.
- *[service-type]*: IPX service such as print service, files services, or directory services for example.

IPX SAP Filter Example

In order to create an IPX SAP filter, you must first determine what SAP services you wish to block. Refer to the example in Figure 10-25. Assume that you want to create a SAP filter that blocks all SAP updates on network 200 from being advertised by

RouterB in its SAP table updates. Figure 10-30 shows how you do that using context-sensitive help.

```
RouterB(config)#access-list ?
    <1-99>       IP standard access list
    <100-199>    IP extended access list
    <1000-1099>  IPX SAP access list
    <1100-1199>  Extended 48-bit MAC address access list
    <1200-1299>  IPX summary address access list
    <200-299>     Protocol type-code access list
    <700-799>     48-bit MAC address access list
<800-899>      IPX standard access list
    <900-999>    IPX extended access list

RouterB(config)#access-list 1000 ?
    deny    Specify packets to reject
    permit  Specify packets to forward

RouterB(config)#access-list 1000 deny ?
    -1            Any IPX net
    <0-FFFFFFFF>  Source net
    N.H.H.H       Source net.host address

RouterB(config)#access-list 1000 deny 200 ?
    <0-FFFFFFFF>  Service type-code (0 matches all services)
    N.H.H.H       Source net.host mask
    <cr>

RouterB(config)#access-list 1000 deny 200 0
RouterB(config)#access-list 1000 permit -1 0
RouterB(config)#exit
RouterB#
%SYS-5-CONFIG_I: Configured from console by console
RouterB#
```

At this point, you must specify which network you wish to block

The final permit statement allows SAP updates from all other networks to be advertised

10

Figure 10-30   IPX SAP filter example

IPX SAP filters must be applied to interfaces just like all other access lists. To apply IPX SAP filters, you must use the ipx input-sap-filter *[list #]* or ipx output-sap-filter *[list #]* commands. Figure 10-31 shows the ipx input-sap-filter *[list #]* command.

The resulting list and application of that list would block all SAP updates from network 200 from being passed to other routers in the internetwork.

```
RouterB#config t
Enter configuration commands, one per line.  End with CNTL/Z.
RouterB(config)#int e0
RouterB(config-if)#ipx input-sap-filter 1000
RouterB(config-if)#exit
RouterB(config)#^Z
RouterB#
%SYS-5-CONFIG_I: Configured from console by console
RouterB#
```

From interface configuration mode, the ipx input-sap-filter command applies access list 1000 as an input filter

Figure 10-31   Applying an IPX SAP filter to an interface

Monitoring IPX SAP Filters

Like all other access lists, the show access-lists command displays all lists including all SAP filters defined on the router. To make sure the list was applied successfully to the interface, use the show ipx interface command. To remove the sap filter, use the no access-list *[list #]* command. To remove the application of a sap filter from an interface use the no ipx input-sap-filter *[list #]* or no ipx output-sap-filter *[list #]* command.

USING NAMED LISTS

In Cisco IOS versions 11.2 and above, you can use names instead of numbers to identify your lists. These are known as **named access lists**. You cannot use the same name for multiple lists. Even different list types cannot have the same name. For example, you could not specify a standard list named Cannon if you already had an extended list named Cannon. To name a standard ip access list, use the following syntax:

> RouterC(config)# ip access-list standard *[name]*

To name an extended ip access list, use the following syntax:

> RouterC(config)# ip access-list extended *[name]*

Once the list is named, the permit or deny statement is entered. The commands follow the same syntax as unnamed lists however; the beginning part of the command is not included. For example, the syntax for a deny or permit statement for a standard ip named list would look as follows:

> RouterC(config)# deny{*source [source-wildcard]* | *any*}

or

> RouterC(config)# permit{*source [source-wildcard]* | *any*}

To apply a standard ip named list to an interface, the syntax would be as follows:

> RouterC(config-if)# ip access-group *[name] [in* | *out]*

The naming feature allows you to maintain security by using an easily identifiable access list. It also removes the limit of 100 lists per filter type.

CHAPTER SUMMARY

- ❐ Access lists are one of the most important IOS tools for controlling network traffic and security.

- ❐ Access lists are created in a two-step process. First, you create the list in global configuration mode, using the specific syntax of the type of list you wish to create. Then, you apply the list to an interface in interface configuration mode to make it active.

❑ All access lists are created sequentially and applied sequentially to all packets that enter an interface where the list is applied.

❑ Access lists, by default, always end in an implicit deny any, which will drop any packet that does not meet an access list criteria.

❑ Only one access list per direction (inbound or outbound) per protocol can be applied to an interface.

❑ Standard IP access lists allow you to filter traffic based on the source IP address of a packet. They should be applied to an interface as close to the destination as possible to avoid accidentally blocking valid traffic.

❑ Extended IP access lists filter traffic based on source, destination, protocol type, and application type. They allow for more specific control over network traffic. They should be placed as close to the source as possible to keep unnecessary traffic from getting onto the internetwork.

❑ Standard IPX access lists are more complex than standard IP lists because they can incorporate destination addresses into filtering decisions; however, they behave nearly exactly the same.

❑ Extended IPX lists allow you to filter based on IPX protocol type and other IPX parameters.

❑ IPX SAP filters allow you to limit the amount of SAP traffic passed by your routers. All IPX lists should be placed as close to the source as possible.

❑ Ranges of numbers represent all access lists. Table 10-2, which follows, summarizes the numbers associated with each type of list you need to be familiar with in order to pass the CCNA exam.

Table 10-2 Access list number ranges

Access List Type	Number
Standard IP access lists	1–99
Extended IP access lists	100–199
Standard IPX access lists	800–899
Extended IPX access lists	900–999
IPX SAP filters	1000–1099

Key Terms

access lists — Permit or deny statements that filter traffic based on criteria such as source address, destination address, and protocol type.

any — A keyword used to represent all hosts or networks; replaces 0.0.0.0 255.255.255.255 in an access list.

established — A keyword that requires traffic to have originated inside the trusted network.

extended IP access lists — IP access lists that filter traffic by source IP address, destination IP address, protocol type, and port number.

extended IPX access lists — IPX access lists that filter traffic based on source and destination IPX nodes or networks, IPX protocol type, and IPX socket number.

host — A keyword for an extended IP list that specifies that an address should have a wildcard mask of 0.0.0.0.

implicit deny any — Blocks all packets that do not meet the requirements of the access list. Exists at the end of all lists.

inbound — A direction parameter used when applying an access list. Direction is into the router.

inverse mask — *See* **wildcard mask**.

IPX SAP filters — Access lists that filter SAP traffic on a network.

named access list — Access list that uses names instead of number ranges.

outbound — A direction parameter used when applying an access list. Direction is out of the router.

partial masking — When an octet in a wildcard mask contains a mix of binary 1's and 0's.

standard IP access lists — Filter traffic based on source IP address.

standard IPX access lists — Filter traffic based on source and destination IPX nodes or networks.

wildcard mask — Applied to IP addresses to determine if an access list line will act upon a packet. Zeros are placed in positions deemed significant, and ones are placed in nonsignificant positions.

REVIEW QUESTIONS

1. Which wildcard mask would apply an access list line to all packets from network 175.25.0.0?

   a. 255.255.255.0

   b. 255.255.0.0

   c. 255.254.0.0

   d. 0.0.255.255

2. Standard IP access lists filter traffic based on which of the following? (Choose all that apply.)

   a. destination IP address

   b. IP protocol

   c. port number

   d. source IP address

3. Wildcard masks use a _____ to signify which bits of an address are significant.

4. Standard IPX access lists filter traffic based on which of the following? (Choose all that apply.)

   a. IPX protocol

   b. source IPX address

   c. destination IPX address

   d. socket number

5. Which command shows only the IP access lists on a router?

   a. show access-lists

   b. show ipx access-lists

   c. show ip access-lists

   d. show interface

6. Which commands allow you to view the interfaces that have IP access lists applied to them? (Choose all that apply.)

   a. show interfaces

   b. show ip interface

   c. show ip traffic

   d. show ip counters

7. Which host and wildcard mask pair does the any keyword represent?

   a. 255.255.255.255 0.0.0.0

   b. 0.0.255.255 0.0.0.0

   c. 0.0.0.0 0.0.0.0

   d. 0.0.0.0 255.255.255.255

8. Which command is used to apply an IP access list to an interface?

   a. ip access-group *[list #] [in | out]*

   b. ip access-group permit 100

   c. ip access-group *[list #] [permit | deny]*

   d. show ip interface

9. Access lists are _____. (Choose all that apply.)

   a. used to filter traffic and control network security

   b. applied as either inbound or outbound filters

   c. sequential permit or deny statements

   d. built into the router's firmware

10

10. Standard IP access lists are represented by the _____ number range.

    a. 100–199

    b. 1–99

    c. 1000–1099

    d. 200–299

11. Extended IPX access lists are represented by the _____ number range.

    a. 900–999

    b. 800–899

    c. 1000–1099

    d. 1–99

12. Which command could be used to remove an access list from your router?

    a. no ip access-group in

    b. no ip access-list 1 in

    c. no access-list 1

    d. no ip access-list one

13. Extended IP access lists are represented by the _____ number range.

    a. 100–199

    b. 200–299

    c. 1000–1099

    d. 1–99

14. IPX SAP filters are represented by the _____ number range.

    a. 100–199

    b. 1–99

    c. 800–899

    d. 1000–1099

15. The show access-lists command displays _____.

    a. access lists applied to interfaces

    b. all access lists on the router

    c. only IP access lists on the router

    d. only IPX access lists on the router

16. At which of the following prompts would you create an access list?

    a. RouterC#

    b. RouterC>

    c. RouterC(config-if)#

    d. RouterC(config)#

17. At which of the following prompts would you apply an access list to an interface?

    a. RouterC#

    b. RouterC>

    c. RouterC(config-if)#

    d. RouterC(config)

18. Which of the following host and corresponding wildcard mask pairs represent the same value as host 172.29.2.2?

    a. 0.0.0.0   255.255.255.255

    b. 172.29.2.2   0.0.0.0

    c. 255.255.255.255   0.0.0.0

    d. 0.0.0.0   172.29.2.2

19. Standard IPX access lists are represented by the _____ number range.

    a. 1–99

    b. 800–899

    c. 900–999

    d. 1000–1099

20. A router can have one _____ access list and one _____ access list per protocol on each interface.

21. Which of the following is a benefit of using named lists?

    a. The syntax is identical to using numbered lists.

    b. There aren't as many lists allowed so it is easier to remember them.

    c. You are not constrained by the 100 lists per filter type limit.

    d. There are no benefits to using named lists.

22. What happens if a list is applied to an interface and then the list itself is removed?

    a. The commands will be executed and all traffic will be denied.

    b. The commands will be executed and all traffic will be permitted.

    c. The commands will not be executed and all traffic will be permitted.

    d. None of the above

23. What is true of the host keyword? (Choose all that apply.)

    a. It can only be used with extended ip lists.

    b. It can be used with standard and extended ip lists.

    c. It replaces the 0.0.0.255 wildcard mask.

    d. It replaces the 0.0.0.0 wildcard mask.

    e. It is placed before the IP address with which it is associated.

    f. It is placed after the IP address with which it is associated.

10

24. What is the purpose of the "established" parameter?

    a. to establish a connection between the sender and receiver

    b. to prevent any traffic into a network

    c. to prevent any traffic into a network that didn't originate from that network

    d. to permit all tcp traffic but not ip traffic into the established network

25. All access lists presented in this chapter, except standard ip lists, should be placed where?

    a. as close to the source as possible

    b. as close to the destination as possible

    c. as close to the serial interface as possible

    d. as close to the tftp server as possible

CASE PROJECTS

1. Freytech industries has hired you and your team at Winslow Networks to help with an important network project. They wish to block HTTP traffic from network 170.55.0.0 to their Web server at 164.106.105.3. Lisa suggests the following list:

   access–list 10 deny 170.55.0.0

   access–list 10 permit any

   What will Lisa's list do? Modify Lisa's list so that it will work for your client.

2. You have been asked to deliver a speech on the SAP traffic filtering capabilities of the Cisco IOS. Prepare a short outline that addresses why SAP filtering is important and the proper techniques for creating and applying SAP filters.

11

PPP AND ISDN

After reading this chapter and completing the exercises, you will be able to:

♦ Describe Cisco's PPP encapsulation

♦ Configure PPP encapsulation and its options

♦ Describe and enable PPP multilink

♦ Explain how to implement ISDN BRI on Cisco routers

♦ Configure an ISDN BRI connection

In Chapter 5 you received an overview of WAN technologies such as Frame Relay, X.25, and Integrated Services Digital Network (ISDN). You also learned about WAN connectivity terminology such as channel service unit/digital service unit (CSU/DSU), terminal adapter (TA), Central Office (CO), and Regional Bell Operating Companies (RBOC). WAN protocols, such as Point-to-Point Protocol (PPP) and High-level Data Link Control (HDLC), and WAN standards were also introduced. In this chapter, expanded coverage is given to PPP and ISDN. Finally, you will learn how to configure a Cisco router to support PPP and ISDN.

PPP

PPP is an Internet standard protocol defined in RFCs 2153 and 1661. The IETF defined PPP to provide point-to-point, router-to-router, host-to-router, and host-to-host connections. Because of the point-to-point physical configuration, PPP is considered a peer technology. PPP is commonly used over dial-up or leased lines to provide connections into IP networks. PPP also supports other Network layer protocols such as Novell IPX and AppleTalk. Due to its flexibility, PPP is the most widely used WAN connection method today.

SLIP was the predecessor to PPP; it only supported TCP/IP connections. In addition, SLIP offers no encryption, compression, or error correction. It is an analog protocol limited to 56 Kbps transmission. PPP overcomes all of SLIP's limitations. Other advantages offered by PPP are the capability to handle asynchronous as well as synchronous communication. PPP is also more efficient and supports more protocols and interfaces. PPP can be used over several different physical interfaces, including:

- Asynchronous serial

- ISDN synchronous serial

- High-Speed Serial Interface (HSSI)

Asynchronous serial connections are typically used with analog modems, which connect directly to the existing phone lines and outlets that are wired in residential areas throughout the United States. ISDN synchronous serial connections require the use of ISDN modem equipment in order to interface with the Integrated Services Digital Network (ISDN) provided by many public carriers. (ISDN is described in greater detail later in this chapter.) **High-Speed Serial Interface (HSSI)** is a type of serial device that was developed by Cisco and T3Plus Networking. It defines a serial connection that operates at speeds of up to 52 Mbps over distances of up to 15 meters (50 feet).

PPP in the Protocol Stack

Most WAN protocols operate at the Data Link layer of the OSI model. As mentioned, you can use PPP over both asynchronous and synchronous connections at the Physical layer of the OSI reference model. The Link Control Protocol is used at the Data Link layer to establish, configure, and test the connection. PPP also relies on Network layer services called **Network Control Protocols (NCPs)** at layer 3 of the OSI model. NCPs allow the simultaneous use of multiple network layer protocols and are required for each protocol that utilizes PPP. Examples of NCPs include **IP Control Protocol (IPCP)**, **IPX Control Protocol (IPXCP)**, and **AppleTalk Control Protocol (ATCP)**. Figure 11-1 illustrates the location of PPP in the protocol stack; notice that the NCPs function at the Network layer.

Figure 11-1   PPP in the protocol stack

Frame Format

PPP, like many WAN technologies, is based on the **High-level Data Link Control (HDLC)** protocol. The difference between PPP frames and HDLC frames is that PPP frames contain protocol and **Link Control Protocol (LCP)** fields, as shown in Figure 11-2. The Protocol field allows PPP to simultaneously support multiple protocols by allowing it to indicate which protocol it is encapsulating. PPP uses the LCP field to establish, configure, maintain, and terminate connections.

11

HDLC

Flag	Address	Control	Data	FCS	Flag

Cisco HDLC

Flag	Address	Control	Proprietary	Data	FCS	Flag

PPP

Flag	Address	Control	Protocol	LCP Data	FCS	Flag

LCP

Code	Identifier	Length	Data

Figure 11-2   HDLC and PPP packet structure

Figure 11-2 also shows the Cisco proprietary HDLC frame. Cisco HDLC has proprietary fields that support the encapsulation of multiple protocols. Cisco's HDLC is the default encapsulation type for serial interfaces on Cisco routers. The elements of the PPP frame are as follows:

- **Flag**: Binary sequence 01111110, which indicates the beginning of the frame

- **Address**: Binary sequence 11111111; since PPP is used to create a point-to-point connection, there is no need for PPP to assign an individual address for each host.

- **Control**: Binary sequence 00000011, which indicates that the transmission of user data will not be sequenced and is to be delivered over a connectionless link

- **Protocol**: Two bytes used to identify the protocol that is encapsulated

- LCP or **Data**: The LCP field is also known as the Data field. This location contains the LCP information and the data that has been encapsulated from the higher layers. The default size of this field is 1500 bytes, but PPP implementations can negotiate a larger size for this field. LCP is explained in greater detail in the following section.

- **Frame Check Sequence (FCS)**: Two bytes by default, but can be as large as four bytes; uses a cyclical redundancy check (CRC) to verify the integrity of the frame to ensure that it was not corrupted during transmission

- **Flag**: Binary sequence 01111110, which identifies the end of the data frame

LCP

LCP is described in RFCs 1548, 1570, 1661, 2153, and 2484. RFC 1661, which made RFC 1548 obsolete, describes PPP organization and methodology, including basic LCP extensions. RFC 1661 was later updated by RFC 2153, which explains PPP Vendor extensions. RFC 1570 and its update, RFC 2484, further expand the definition of LCP extensions. The LCP field of the PPP packet can contain many different pieces of information, including:

- **Asynchronous character map**: Allows PPP to encode its transmission properly for the recipient host

- **Maximum receive unit size**: Sets the receive buffer size for the LCP connection, typically 1500 bytes

- **Compression**: Data compression that can be performed on the PPP packet at the source and then uncompressed at the destination; typically improves the speed of data transfer over slow serial connections because less data has to traverse the connection

- **Authentication**: Can be enabled to require a password in order to establish the PPP connection; two authentication protocols are available—**Password Authentication Protocol (PAP)** and **Challenge Handshake**

Authentication Protocol (CHAP). Authentication is described in greater detail in the following section.

- **Magic number**: Aids in detecting links that are in the looped-back condition. When interfaces are looped-back, data that is sent out the interface is immediately received on that interface. Magic numbers are unique numbers added by the router to a packet, which allow it to detect a looped-back link. If the router receives a packet that contains its own unique magic number, it detects that the interface is looped back. Loopback is typically used for testing interfaces to ensure they are sending and receiving data. The **loopback command** can be run from the interface configuration prompt. Although good for testing, looped-back interfaces are undesirable in production environments. In a production environment, you can use the **down-when-looped** command from interface configuration mode, which will automatically shut down that interface when looping is detected.

- **Link Quality Monitoring (LQM)**: Checks the reliability of the link by monitoring the number of errors, latency between requests, connection retries, and connection failures on the PPP link

- **Multilink**: Allows multiple transmission devices to send data over separate physical connections. The benefit of multilink is that you can combine the bandwidth of two separate devices over one logical connection. For example, two 64-Kbps ISDN channels can be combined to provide an effective throughput of 128 Kbps. PPP will fragment, sequence, and reassemble these packets in order to provide faster throughput over multiple slow serial connections. Multilink is defined in RFC 1717, and you can enable multilink with the ppp multilink command from the interface configuration mode.

LCP Link Configuration

The **LCP link configuration** process modifies and/or enhances the default characteristics of a PPP connection. This part of the link configuration process manages the link, controls the authentication, and can be used to set link quality. The LCP link configuration process includes the following actions: link establishment, authentication (optional), link-quality determination (optional), Network layer protocol configuration negotiation, and link termination. Each of these link configuration actions is described in the bulleted list below:

- **Link establishment**: PPP must open and configure the PPP connection before any data can be transferred over the link.

- Authentication (optional): CHAP or PAP can be used to verify the identity of the devices that are establishing the connection. CHAP and PAP are discussed in greater detail later in this chapter.

- **Link-quality determination** (optional): Checks the quality of the link and monitors its reliability

- **Network layer protocol configuration negotiation**: Identifies the appropriate Network layer protocol for the connection; the devices negotiate to use a protocol that is common to both.

- **Link termination**: When the call is complete, or the specifications defining the call are no longer met, the call is terminated.

Establishing PPP Communications

There are three phases in the establishing communications process: link establishment, authentication, and Network-layer protocol configuration negotiation. The link establishment phase involves the configuration and testing of the data link. As mentioned earlier, PPP connections may use the information contained in the LCP portion of the PPP packet to configure the link by passing requirements for maximum transmission units and compression.

The second phase of the establishing process is optional. The authentication process can use two authentication types with PPP connections: PPP and CHAP. Most network administrators configure their devices to use CHAP because it is the stronger authentication method of the two. RFC 1994 documents the PAP and CHAP authentication protocols.

PAP uses a simple two-way handshake method to establish the link. In this link, PPP transmits a clear text user name and password across the link between hosts in order to establish the link. The device attempting to establish the link transmits the user name and password, so that the destination host will allow the PPP session. PPP only conducts PAP authentication during initial link establishment.

Compared to PAP, CHAP provides a much more sophisticated authentication process. Like PAP, CHAP provides username and password authentication service during the initial link establishment. However, instead of stopping there, CHAP employs a three-way handshake. Once the link is established, the local router queries the remote host with a packet known as a **challenge**. The challenge is in the form of a unique encryption key. The remote host uses the encryption key to encode the username and password. The router compares the decrypted username and password and looks for a match with its username and password. It then either accepts or drops the connection based on whether the comparison yields a matching username and password.

After the connection is made, CHAP can continue this query process, using a different encryption key each time and using unique and unpredictable intervals. This further ensures that connections are legitimate because it prevents someone from capturing the data packets that are exchanged during the initial authentication process between two authorized systems and then playing those data packets from an unauthorized system in an attempt to gain PPP access to the server.

The router typically controls the authentication process but a **Terminal Access Controller Access Control System (TACACS), RADIUS server,** or third-party authentication server can also be used to centralize management of CHAP authentication and other security features.

PPP is an encapsulation type for serial interface communications. Therefore, to configure a PPP connection, you must access the interface configuration mode for the specific interface you wish to configure. For example, if you want to configure PPP on the first serial interface of the router (S0), you would use the commands shown in Figure 11-3 (assuming that the router was already in enable mode).

```
router#config t
router(config)#int s0
router(config-if)#encap ppp
```

Figure 11-3   Enabling PPP

The third phase of the establishing process is Network layer protocol configuration negotiation. After LCP has finished negotiating the configuration parameters, Network layer protocols can be configured individually by the appropriate NCP. At this point, packets can be sent over the link. The different protocols can be established and terminated at any time.

Configuring PPP Authentication

As mentioned above, using authentication with PPP connections is optional. Therefore, you must specifically configure PPP authentication on each PPP host in order for the host to utilize PPP. You can choose to enable CHAP and/or PAP on your PPP connection, in either order. For example, to set the router to first use CHAP, and then to go to PAP (assuming that CHAP is not available), you would type the command in Figure 11-4.

```
router(config-if)#ppp authentication chap pap
```

Figure 11-4   Enabling both CHAP and PAP authentication

If you entered that command, your local router would request CHAP authentication during the connection, but if the other device did not support CHAP or attempted PAP authentication instead, then PAP would be tried. You could also decide to use just CHAP or just PAP by omitting the undesired method from the command line.

Once you set the authentication type, you must still configure a username and password for the authentication. To do so, you must exit interface configuration mode and enter global configuration mode. Then, type "username" followed by the hostname of the remote router; after that, type "password" followed by the password for that connection. Ensure that each router uses the same password, but uses the other router's hostname after username. The link will go up and down (flapping) until both ends of the point-to-point link are configured correctly. Figure 11-5 illustrates a configuration and the commands required for that configuration to operate using CHAP authentication.

Figure 11-5   Configuring CHAP

If you want to configure the same hostname and password for CHAP authentication on several routers, you can do so via the interface configuration mode prompt. For example, if you wanted to configure the hostname flagstaff and set the password to lumberjack for all routers, you would enter the commands in Figure 11-6 on all routers' PPP interfaces.

```
router(config-if)#ppp chap hostname flagstaff
router(config-if)#ppp chap password lumberjack
```

Figure 11-6   Configuring PPP and CHAP

In this example, the hostname flagstaff sets the alternate CHAP hostname to flagstaff. The password lumberjack part of the command sets the default CHAP password to lumberjack. This type of configuration is easier to implement than the one shown in Figure 11-5, in which you must configure each router with the same password, but with opposite hostnames.

If you are using PAP authentication with Cisco IOS Releases 11.1 or later, you must enable PAP on the interface of the router to receive the PAP request.

Confirming PPP Communications

Once you have completed configuring your PPP interface, you can verify your changes using the show interface command. You must be in privileged EXEC mode in order to view the interfaces. For example, if you want to view your configuration on the Serial 1 interface, type the following:

```
Router#sh int S1
```

ISDN

ISDN is a circuit-switched service provided by telecommunications providers to allow voice, data, video, and audio transmissions over existing digital telephone lines. Circuit switching is preferred for applications using streaming audio and video. This is because the data takes the same route from sender to receiver (unlike packet switching) so time is not required to reorder the packets at the destination. This makes for a smoother delivery of time-sensitive data. ISDN is often used as a lower-cost alternative to Frame Relay or T1 connections, while still offering a higher connection speed than an analog modem. The service is offered at two different levels: Basic Rate Interface (BRI) and Primary Rate Interface (PRI). BRI is typically used in small offices or for home connections, and PRI is used in larger environments because it provides higher bandwidth.

Telecommunications providers offer digital connections via ISDN as channels. BRI connections offer three channels: two at 64 Kbps and one at 16 Kbps. The 64-Kbps channels are known as bearer or B-channels, because they carry the data for the connection. ISDN BRI connections use the 16-Kbps signaling channel or data channel, which is also called a D-channel, to control the communications on the link. The two B-channels can be used together in a process called **bonding** in order to achieve 128 Kbps. If you are using voice with the service, data can be load balanced across both lines or you can talk on the phone, which will use one B-channel, while the data uses the other B-channel. PRI connections offer 23 B-channels and one 64-Kbps D-channel for a total bandwidth of about 1.544 Mbps, which is the same as a T1 line

11

 European ISDN PRI service offers 30 64-Kpbs B-channels and one 64-Kbps D-channel.

In both ISDN BRI and PRI, a single D-channel is used for signaling information, and the B-channels are used to carry the data. Because the control communications are conducted on a channel that is separate from the data transfer, ISDN is said to use **out of band signaling**. In some cases the D-channel can carry data as well as the signaling information. The Data Link layer protocol that manages the signaling exchange on the D-channel is **link access procedure-D (LAPD)**.

ISDN Standards

The ITU maintains several standards on ISDN. These standards are organized into ITU-T groups. The ITU-T groups are organized by three different letter designations: E, I, and Q. Each group is then subdivided into specific protocols, preceded by the group designator. For example, protocols I.430 and I.431 are part of the I-series protocol group. Protocols within each group define a related set of standards. Table 11-1 lists and describes the relationship between the protocol designators and the concepts that they define.

Table 11-1   ISDN protocol series

Protocol Series	Description	Examples
E	Telephone and network standards	E.164 – International telecommunications numbering
I	Methods, terminology, concepts, and interfaces	I.100 – Terminology, structure, and concepts I.300 – Networking recommendations
Q	Signaling and switching standards	Q.921 – Data Link layer LAPD procedures (explained later in this chapter) Q.931 – Network layer functions

ISDN Operations

ISDN can use HDLC (default) or PPP as its WAN protocol. As previously mentioned, it uses the Link Access Procedure-D (LAPD) to pass the signaling messages between the router (or other terminal equipment) and the ISDN switch at the local telco central office. The data travels between routers on the B-channels via HDLC or PPP encapsulation, as shown in Figure 11-7.

Figure 11-7   ISDN operations

Functions and References

ISDN standards use **function groups** and **reference points** to describe the various components that can be utilized in making an ISDN connection. Function groups describe a set of functions that are implemented by a device and software. For example, a terminal adapter (TA) converts network signals to a format appropriate for the ISDN connection. The TA is an example of a function group because it describes a device that provides a set of conversion functions to make ISDN communication possible. The connection between two function groups (including the cabling) is called a reference point. Not all function groups and reference points are required for each ISDN connection. Figure 11-8 shows the variety of different connection types that may exist. You are expected to memorize these components.

Figure 11-8   ISDN function groups and reference points

The function groups shown in the graphic are as follows:

- Terminal adapter: A converter device that allows non-ISDN devices to operate on an ISDN network. For a router that did not have a built-in ISDN interface (TE2), a TA would be a device that converts signals from a standard RS-232 or V.35 interface into ISDN signals.

- **Terminal Equipment 1 (TE1)**: A device that supports ISDN standards and that can be connected directly to an ISDN network connection. For example, ISDN telephones, personal computers, routers with ISDN interfaces, or videophones could function as TE1s.

- **Terminal Equipment 2 (TE2)**: A non-ISDN device, such as an analog phone or modem, or a PC, which requires a TA in order to connect to an ISDN network

- **Network Termination 1 (NT1)**: A small connection box that is attached to ISDN BRI lines. This device provides power for the ISDN service. It terminates the 2-wire connection from the Central Office (CO) and connects to the 4-wire customer network. In the graphic, the CO would be located inside the cloud, which represents the telephone company network.

11

- **Network Termination 2 (NT2):** A device that multiplexes and switches signals between various network devices at the customer site. This type of interface is typically used with PRI lines, when they need to be divided for several functions. For example, some channels may be used for WAN data communications and others for the telephone system and/or video teleconferencing.

 Some function groups can be combined into one device. For example, an NT1 may have a TE1 port and also a TA port for non-ISDN devices (TE2's).

The reference points in Figure 11-8 include the following:

- **U:** The point that defines the demarcation between the user network and the telecommunications provider's ISDN facility. The **U-interface** is the actual two-wire cable, also called the local loop, which connects the customer's equipment to the telecommunications provider. In the U.S., the U interface is supplied on a 2-wire RJ-11 phone jack.

- **R:** The point between non-ISDN equipment (TE2) and the TA. The **R-interface** is the wire or circuit that connects TE2 to the TA.

- **S:** The point between the ISDN customer's TE1 or TA and the network termination (NT1 or NT2). The **S-interface** is a four-wire cable from TE1 or TA to the NT1 or NT2, which is a two-wire termination point.

- **T:** The point between NT1 and NT2, which is also the **T-interface**. This four-wire cable is used to divide the normal telephone company two-wire cable into four wires, which then allows the connection of up to eight ISDN devices.

- **S/T:** When NT2 is not used on a connection that uses NT1, the connection from the router or TA to the NT1 connection is typically called S/T. This is essentially the combination of the S and T reference points. The S/T interface is not typically used in the U.S.

SPID

Many telecommunications providers utilize ISDN switches, which require **Service Profile Identifiers (SPIDs)** for dial-in access. SPIDs are frequently referred to as **ISDN phone numbers** because their functions are similar. SPIDs provide a profile of your equipment to the ISDN switch.

An ISDN device can access each ISDN channel via its SPID number. You can configure the router to utilize a single or multiple SPIDs when making a connection to the ISDN provider. The ISDN provider must assign the SPID numbers for each channel, which is normally an 8- to 14-digit numeric. Then, you can use those numbers to configure your ISDN dialer connections. Most modern ISDN systems now have a feature called **AutoSPID**. This eliminates the need to configure SPID numbers on the router.

You must also define the type of switch that is used at the Central Office to which you are connecting. The commands shown in Figure 11-9 illustrate an ISDN configuration.

```
router(config)#isdn switch-type dms-100
router(config)#interface bri 0
router(config-if)#isdn spid1 52069145231010
router(config-if)#isdn spid2 52069145241010
```

Figure 11-9   ISDN switch configuration

In this figure, the commands illustrate the configuration for a BRI connection over two channels. The switch type will usually be a Northern Telecom DMS-100 or an AT&T 5ess or 4ess. Notice in the first line that the switch type is a DMS-100. You will have to obtain the switch type and the SPID numbers from the ISDN providers. Potential switch types include the following:

- dms-100: Northern Telecom DMS-100 (as described above)
- ni1: National ISDN-1; used in North America
- net3: Net3 switch; used in Europe and the United Kingdom
- ntt: Switch from NTT; used in Japan
- 1tr6: 1TR6 switch; used in Germany
- ts013: TS013 Australian switch
- none: Used when a switch has not been specified

NOTE: In certain circumstances, the switch-type command can be configured in interface configuration mode as well as global configuration mode.

Multilink PPP

RFC 1717 defines multilink PPP, which allows you to combine the individual bandwidth of several modems and/or several ISDN channels to increase the bandwidth of a single connection. Multilink provides load balancing, packet fragmentation and reassembly, and sequencing for packets sent across WAN links. Since multilink is a capability available in PPP connections, it can function over synchronous or asynchronous serial connections, such as analog modems or ISDN channels. The command to enable multilink is:

```
router(config-if)#ppp multilink
```

Each serial interface to be enabled with multilink must also be configured for PPP encapsulation and DDR.

DDR

The **dial-on-demand routing (DDR)** feature that is available on Cisco routers allows you to use bandwidth as needed. This feature can save organizations money on connections because DDR automatically connects and disconnects the line as needed. This is a more economical way to address the need for intermittent WAN access using circuit switching. With DDR, all traffic is classified as either interesting or uninteresting. **Interesting traffic** forces the router to connect to the remote router. Uninteresting traffic will not force the router to connect; however, uninteresting traffic is passed if the line is already active. The dialer-list commands, in conjunction with access-list commands, are used to define what is interesting and what is not.

There are many different and important configuration commands to know for configuring a DDR connection. The following commands, shown in Figure 11-10, define the DDR connection parameters and the connection link.

```
router(config-if)#dial wait-for-carrier time 15
router(config-if)#dialer idle-timeout 300
router(config-if)#dialer load-threshold 50 either
router(config-if)#dialer map ip 192.168.52.1 name FLG speed 56 5205551212
```

Figure 11-10   ISDN settings

The first command tells the dialer to wait no longer than 15 seconds for the ISDN provider to answer during a DDR connection attempt. The second command tells the dialer to hang-up the connection if the connection does not pass any interesting traffic for 300 seconds. The third command tells the dialer to only dial additional lines (assuming that you have configured multiple ISDN channels for the connection) when any channel is transferring at a load value of 50, either inbound or outbound. Load values can range from 1 (not loaded) to 255 (fully loaded) so a load value of 50 would indicate the line being about 20% loaded (50/255). In addition, load-threshold does allow you to specify a percentage load for inbound traffic, outbound traffic, or traffic in either direction. The fourth command maps the dialer to a specific hostname (FLG), IP address (192.168.52.1), speed (56 Kbps), and phone number (5205551212). If you don't configure a speed, the default is assumed to be 64 Kbps.

As previously mentioned, in order to define what type of traffic is considered interesting, you must use dialer-list commands. Sometimes access-list commands are used in conjunction with the dialer-list command. Dialer group commands are used to associate dialer-list commands with the correct interface. The commands in Figure 11-11 illustrate how you can use dialer-list, dialer-group, and access list commands to permit IP traffic on your link, but deny IGRP traffic.

```
router(config-if)#dialer-group 1
router(config-if)#exit
router(config)#dialer-list 1 protocol ip list 110
router(config)#access-list 110 deny igrp any any
router(config)#access-list 110 permit ip any any
```

Figure 11-11   ISDN and access lists

ISDN BRI CONFIGURATION EXAMPLE

Now that you have seen the configuration parameters individually in the sections above, it is useful to consider a sample configuration. Figure 11-12 shows two routers that will be used to create a temporary ISDN BRI connection. The group utilizes up to two channels for IP traffic. The routers will not use a routing protocol because link use is to be minimized for this DDR connection. (The point of DDR is to reduce the money spent on connection time.) In addition, routing updates are unimportant in this config-uration because it is a point-to-point connection.

Figure 11-12   ISDN configuration sample

Note that the routers in the graphic are both using PPP with CHAP authentication. The username has been set for the opposite router in each configuration, and the pass-word is the same so that CHAP will authenticate properly. Each router has the ability to dial the other router. The CLT router is located at the corporate network, which has other connections and uses IGRP to transfer routing tables on that network. However, IGRP is not desired on the ISDN connection, so the CLT router has an access list specifically denying IGRP on the ISDN link.

Further note that both routers do permit all IP traffic on the ISDN link and all IP traffic will be considered interesting or worthy of activating the ISDN link. Multilink is enabled on both routers, and they will dial their additional lines when there is 16% (40/255) or more utilization on the first channel. The link will be terminated if there is no interesting traffic for 600 seconds (10 minutes). The IP routes are configured such that all traffic destined from the corporate network to 192.168.24.0 will be sent to the FLG router. Since the FLG router is a remote branch with no other connections, all traffic that is not specifically destined for 192.168.24.0 will be sent to the CLT router. Notice that each router has its dialer mapped to the IP address of the other router.

Monitoring ISDN

You can use the following commands to view your ISDN configuration, manage the link, and view statistics. All the commands are available via the privileged EXEC mode (enable mode) prompt.

- clear interface: Disconnects all current connections. Use this command if you are having connection problems.

- show dialer: Shows the current dialer status, including the time that the link has been active

- debug dialer: Displays the configuration and operation of the dialer

- debug q921: Shows the call connection establishment and disconnection

- show isdn active: Displays the status of the ISDN connection while the call is in progress

- show isdn status: Gives status information for ISDN connections

- show int bri 0: Shows you the configuration statistics and speed of your ISDN BRI interface

You can also use the show ip route command to view the routing table to ensure that the IP packets are being routed properly on your system. If you have all IP traffic enabled on the link, you can use the ping or telnet command to test the link.

Digital Lines

ISDN is only one type of connection that you can obtain from a telecommunications provider. Other types of digital connections are available. The following list contains some currently available services:

- **T1**: North American, 24-channel digital line capable of supporting data transmissions of up to 1.544 Mbps

- **T1C**: North American, 48-channel digital line capable of supporting data transmissions of up to 3.152 Mbps

- **T2**: North American, 96-channel digital line capable of supporting data transmissions of up to 6.312 Mbps

- **T3**: North American, 672-channel digital line capable of supporting data transmissions of up to 44.376 Mbps

- **T4**: North American, 4032-channel digital line capable of supporting data transmissions of up to 274.176 Mbps

- **E1**: This European 30-channel digital line is capable of supporting data transmissions up to 2.048 Mbps

- **Fractional E1** and **fractional T1**: Some telecommunications providers allow organizations to order fractional T1 or E1 connections. A Fractional T1 or E1 occurs when less than the full bandwidth is available. For example, a Fractional T1 might be a 512-Kbps connection, instead of the full 1.544 Mbps.

- **Digital Subscriber Line (DSL)**: Services that offer high bandwidth over existing copper lines. DSL connections are generically referred to as **xDSL** because there are several different DSL technologies, such as **Asymmetric Digital Subscriber Line (ADSL)**, **High-bit-rate Digital Subscriber Line (HDSL)**, **ISDN Digital Subscriber Line (IDSL)**, **Symmetrical Digital Subscriber Line (SDSL)**, and **Very-high-data-rate Digital Subscriber Line (VDSL)**.

11

CHAPTER SUMMARY

- There are many different WAN connectivity options available for modern networks. These options include digital lines, Frame Relay, and analog modems.

- WAN technologies typically define Data Link and Physical layer standards.

- The Point-to-Point Protocol (PPP) is the most widely used WAN protocol in use today.

- On Cisco routers, PPP is used mainly as a Data Link layer encapsulation method; however, it does provide an interface to the Network layer via specific Network Control Protocols (NCPs).

- PPP provides link establishment, quality determination, Network layer protocol encapsulation, and link termination services.

- PPP is often used over Integrated Digital Service Network (ISDN) connections.

- ISDN is a digital service provided by several telecommunications companies worldwide.

- ISDN was developed as a faster WAN connection to replace analog modems, and as a cheaper alternative to Frame Relay and full T1 connections.

- ISDN service comes in Basic Rate Interface (BRI) and Primary Rate Interface (PRI). BRI offers connections of up to 128 Kbps for data transfer, and PRI offers up to 24 channels in the United States, each with the ability to transfer data at 64 Kbps.

- Connections over ISDN can take advantage of dial-on-demand routing (DDR) and multilink services offered through PPP connections.

- DDR allows the router using an ISDN connection to dial additional channels as needed to support given traffic levels.

- Multilink allows ISDN to utilize multiple channels evenly by spreading the load across those channels.

KEY TERMS

address — The element of the PPP frame represented by the binary sequence 11111111; since PPP is used to create a point-to-point connection, there is no need for PPP to assign an individual address for each host.

AppleTalk Control Protocol (ATCP) — PPP interface protocol for AppleTalk; *See* **Network Control Protocol**.

Asymmetric Digital Subscriber Line (ADSL) — DSL service that provides from 1.536-Mbps to 6.144-Mbps connections in the United States. Outside the U.S. connections are either 2.048 or 4.096 Mbps.

asynchronous character map — The piece of information in the LCP field of the PPP packet that allows PPP to encode its transmission properly for the recipient host.

authentication — The process of verifying the right to complete a connection.

AutoSPID — A feature of modern ISDN systems whereby SPID numbers do not have to be configured on the router.

bonding — Load balancing across the two BRI B-channels to form a 128 Kbps single channel.

challenge — The query packet, or the action of sending the query packet over a CHAP connection, that is used to verify the participants of the PPP connection.

Challenge Handshake Authentication Protocol (CHAP) — PPP authentication protocol that provides better security than PAP in authenticating devices on PPP connections.

compression — Data compression that can be performed on the PPP packet at the source and then uncompressed at the destination.

control — The element of the PPP frame represented by the binary sequence 00000011, which indicates that the transmission of user data will not be sequenced and is to be delivered over a connectionless link.

data — The LCP field is also known as the Data field. This location contains the LCP information and the data that has been encapsulated from the higher layers. The default size of this field is 1500 bytes, but PPP implementations can negotiate a larger size for this field. LCP is explained in greater detail in the following section.

dial-on-demand routing (DDR) — A feature available on Cisco routers that allows you to use bandwidth as needed.

Digital Subscriber Line (DSL) — Telecommunications services that offer high bandwidth over existing copper lines. DSL connections are generically referred to as xDSL because there are several different DSL technologies.

down-when-looped — A Cisco router command that shuts down an interface when looping is detected; used to prevent testing scenarios from causing troubleshooting problems in a production environment.

E1 — European 30-channel digital line capable of supporting up to 2.048-Mbps data transmissions.

flag — Identifies the beginning and ending of the PPP frame.

Frame Check Sequence (FCS) — A mathematical computation placed at the end of the frame that is used to ensure that the frame was not corrupted during transmission.

fractional E1 — A service that offers some number of channels less than the 30 (64-Kbps) digital channels provided by a full E1 connection.

fractional T1 — A service that offers some number of channels less than the 24 (64-Kbps) digital channels provided by a full T1 connection.

function groups — Used in ISDN communication to describe a set of functions that are implemented by a device and its software; a terminal adapter (TA) is a function group.

High-bit-rate Digital Subscriber Line (HDSL) — Symmetric digital communication service capable of 1.536 Mbps in the United States and 2.048 Mbps in Europe.

High-level Data Link Control (HDLC) — A Data Link layer encapsulation protocol that is a superset of the SDLC protocol. HDLC is a WAN protocol that can be used for both point-to-point and multipoint connections.

High-Speed Serial Interface (HSSI) — A type of serial device that was developed by Cisco and T3Plus Network that operates at speeds of up to 52 Mbps over distances of 15 meters.

interesting traffic — Network traffic for which you feel it is worth activating or maintaining an ISDN link that is configured with DDR.

IP Control Protocol (IPCP) — PPP interface protocol for IP; *see* **Network Control Protocol**.

IPX Control Protocol (IPXCP) — PPP interface protocol for IPX; *see* **Network Control Protocol**.

ISDN Digital Subscriber Line (IDSL) — A telecommunications service that makes an ISDN connection into a 128-Kbps DSL connection. Unlike ISDN, IDSL only supports data communications (not analog voice or video).

ISDN phone number — *See* **Service Profile Identifier (SPID)**.

11

LCP link configuration — A process that modifies and/or enhances the default characteristics of a PPP connection; includes the following actions: link establishment, authentication, link-quality determination, Network layer protocol configuration negotiation, and link determination.

link access procedure-D (LAPD) — A Data Link layer WAN protocol adapted from HDLC; used on D-channel over ISDN lines.

Link Control Protocol (LCP) — Used in PPP connections to establish, configure, maintain, and terminate PPP connections.

link establishment — The process of opening and configuring a PPP connection before any data can be transferred over the link.

link-quality determination — The process of checking the quality of a PPP link and monitoring its reliability.

Link Quality Monitoring (LQM) — PPP feature that checks the reliability of the link by monitoring the number of errors, latency between requests, connection retries, and connection failures on the PPP link.

link termination — The process of disconnecting a PPP connection when the call is complete, which is determined by the PPP hosts that made the connection.

loopback command — A Cisco router command that places an interface in a looped back state, which means that all outgoing data will be redirected as incoming data without going out on the network; used for testing purposes.

magic number — Unique numbers added by the router to a packet, which allows it to detect a looped-back link.

maximum receive unit size — The piece of information in the LCP field of the PPP packet that sets the receive buffer size for the LCP connection, typically 1500 bytes.

multilink — Allows multiple transmission devices (such as two modems) to send data over separate physical connections; defined in RFC 1717.

Network Control Protocol (NCP) — Allows PPP to encapsulate multiple protocols including IP, IPX, and AppleTalk. NCPs are functional fields that contain codes that indicate the type of protocol that is encapsulated.

Network layer protocol configuration negotiation — The process of determining a Network layer protocol to use over a PPP connection that is common to both PPP hosts.

Network Termination 1 (NT1) — A small connection box that is attached to ISDN BRI lines. This device terminates the connection from the Central Office (CO).

Network Termination 2 (NT2) — A device that provides switching services for the internal network.

out of band signaling — The practice of controlling an ISDN connection on a channel other than the channel(s) on which data is transferred.

Password Authentication Protocol (PAP) — PPP authentication protocol that provides some security in verifying the identity of devices using PPP connections.

protocol — The element of the PPP frame represented by two bytes used to identify the protocol that is encapsulated.

R — The point between non-ISDN equipment (TE2) and the TA.

RADIUS server — RADIUS is an authentication and accounting server.

reference points — Used in ISDN communications to identify specific connection points along the ISDN connection, including the cables that form those connections; *See* **U** and **U-interface**.

R-interface — The wire or circuit that connects TE2 to the TA.

S — The point between the ISDN customer's TE1 or TA and the network termination, NT1 or NT2.

Service Profile Identifier (SPID) — A reference number assigned to ISDN channels; functions like a phone number.

S-interface — A four-wire cable from TE1 or TA to the NT1 or NT2, which is a two-wire termination point.

S/T — When NT2 is not used on a connection that uses NT1, the connection from the router or TA to the NT1 connection is typically called S/T. This is essentially the combination of the S and T reference points.

Symmetrical Digital Subscriber Line (SDSL) — A symmetric digital communication service that utilizes a combination of HDSL and the regular telephone system.

T — The point between NT1 and NT2, which is also the T-interface; a four-wire cable that is used to divide the normal telephone company two-wire cable into four wires, which then allows you to connect up to eight ISDN devices.

T1 — North American 24-channel digital line capable of supporting up to 1.544-Mbps data transmissions.

T1C — North American 48-channel digital line capable of supporting up to 3.152-Mbps data transmissions.

T2 — North American 96-channel digital line capable of supporting up to 6.312-Mbps data transmissions.

T3 — North American 672-channel digital line capable of supporting up to 44.376-Mbps data transmissions.

T4 — North American 4032-channel digital line capable of supporting up to 274.176-Mbps data transmissions.

Terminal Access Controller Access Control System (TACACS) — An authentication protocol that allows Cisco routers to offload user administration to a central server. TACACS and Extended TAXACS (XTACACS) are defined in RFC 1492.

Terminal Equipment 1 (TE1) — A device that supports ISDN standards and can be connected directly to an ISDN network connection.

Terminal Equipment 2 (TE2) — A non-ISDN device, such as an analog phone or modem, which requires a TA in order to connect to an ISDN network.

T-interface — *See* **T**.

U — The point that defines the demarcation between the user network and the telecommunications provider ISDN facility.

U-interface — The actual two-wire cable, also called the local loop, which connects the customer's equipment to the telecommunications provider.

11

Very-high-data-rate Digital Subscriber Line (VDSL) — A digital subscriber technology that supports 51.84-Mbps connections over unshielded twisted-pair cable.

xDSL — *See* **Digital Subscriber Line**.

REVIEW QUESTIONS

1. What do ISDN protocols that begin with E define?

   a. methods, terminology, concepts, and interfaces

   b. telephone and network standards

   c. encapsulation

   d. signaling and switching

2. The standards defined in the ISDN I.100 protocol cover which of the following?

   a. signaling and switching

   b. telephone and network standards

   c. ISDN addressing

   d. methods, terminology, concepts, and interfaces

3. If you want to use CHAP authentication, which protocol would you employ?

   a. multilink

   b. PAP

   c. Frame Relay

   d. PPP

4. Which of the following is the correct syntax to set the switch type to dms-100? (Choose all that apply.)

   a. router>isdn switch-type dms-100

   b. router#en switch-type dms-100

   c. router(config)#isdn switch-type dms-100

   d. router(config-if)#isdn switch-type dms-100

5. If you are configuring an ISDN connection and want to enable multilink, which of the following is the correct prompt and command?

   a. router(config)#ena multilink

   b. router(config-if)#ppp multilink

   c. router>ppp multilink

   d. router#enable multilink

6. Which of the following is typically used as a cheap alternative to Frame Relay or a T1 connection, but offers better performance than an analog modem?

   a. ISDN BRI

   b. T2

   c. E1

   d. DS5

7. What does the reference point R in ISDN communications indicate?

   a. demarcation point between the user network and the telecommunications company

   b. point between the non–ISDN equipment and the terminal adapter

   c. point between the ISDN customer's TE1 or TA and the network termination NT1

   d. point between NT1 and NT2

8. In ISDN communications, what does the functional group TE2 represent?

   a. terminal adapter

   b. a non–ISDN device

   c. a device often used with ISDN PRI service

   d. connection box that is attached to ISDN BRI lines, which terminates the connection from the CO

9. What is the ISDN indicator for a converter device that allows non–ISDN devices to operate on an ISDN network?

   a. TE2

   b. NT1

   c. U

   d. TA

10. What do ISDN protocols that begin with Q define?

    a. methods, terminology, concepts, and interfaces

    b. telephone and network standards

    c. encapsulation

    d. signaling and switching

11. What does the reference point U in ISDN communications indicate?

    a. a demarcation point between the user network and the telecommunications company

    b. a point between the non–ISDN equipment and the terminal adapter

    c. a point between the ISDN customer's TE1 or TA and the network termination NT1

    d. a point between NT1 and NT2

11

12. In ISDN communications, what does the functional group NT1 represent?

    a. a terminal adapter

    b. a small connection device attached to ISDN BRI lines, which terminates the connection from the CO

    c. a non-ISDN device

    d. device often used with ISDN PRI service, which provides switching services for the internal network

13. What does the reference point S in ISDN communications indicate?

    a. a demarcation point between the user network and the telecommunications company

    b. a point between the non-ISDN equipment and the terminal adapter

    c. a point between the ISDN customer's TE1 or TA and the network termination NT1

    d. a point between NT1 and NT2

14. Which two of the following protocols could be used when establishing a connection over ISDN?

    a. HDLC

    b. PPP

    c. PAP

    d. CHAP

15. What does the reference point T in ISDN communications indicate?

    a. demarcation point between the user network and the telecommunications company

    b. point between the non-ISDN equipment and the terminal adapter

    c. point between the ISDN customer's TE1 or TA and the network termination NT1

    d. point between NT1 and NT2

16. Which portion of a PPP frame indicates the higher layer encapsulated protocol?

    a. Protocol

    b. Address

    c. Control

    d. LCP

17. What is the Data Link layer protocol used on the ISDN D-channel?

    a. LAPD

    b. LAPP

    c. PPP

    d. HDLC

18. What is the default encapsulation type on serial interfaces of Cisco routers?

    a. PPP

    b. HDLC

    c. SDLC

    d. Frame Relay

19. Which of the following is an NCP? (Choose all that apply.)

    a. IPXCP

    b. HDLC

    c. SDLC

    d. ATCP

    e. IPCP

20. PPP was derived from _____.

    a. Frame Relay

    b. HDLC

    c. RBOC

    d. ISDN

21. What is a common reason for looping an interface?

    a. to achieve greater bandwidth

    b. to drop nonessential frames

    c. to increase packet size

    d. testing

22. Which of the following is a unique number that helps devices discover looped interfaces?

    a. MAC

    b. LCP

    c. magic number

    d. bandwidth

23. Which of the following employs the strongest encryption technique?

    a. plain text

    b. PAP

    c. CHAP

    d. clear text

11

24. If you want your router to use CHAP and then PAP authentication, which of the following commands would be correct?

    a. router>ppp au chap pap

    b. router#ppp authentication chap pap

    c. router(config-if)#ppp au pap chap

    d. router(config-if)#ppp au chap pap

    e. router(config)#ppp authentication chap pap

25. Which WAN protocol did PPP replace?

    a. HDLC

    b. SDLC

    c. SLIP

    d. LAPD

CASE PROJECTS

1. Lisa and Jennifer have been asked to handle the WAN setup for a company that has offices in Greensboro and Charlotte, North Carolina. Each office has a few users that must communicate with each other and across the WAN link. All network users utilize a database that is located in Charlotte. They need to connect the two offices via some type of WAN link. The link is not expected to get heavy use, but they do need something better than their 56K modem, which is what they are using now. What kind of questions should they ask about the company's connectivity requirements? What type of information will they need to collect? What equipment might be part of the connectivity solution? How should they configure the connectivity equipment?

2. Dave is an employee of a large dry goods manufacturer in Phoenix, Arizona, but he lives and works 140 miles north of Phoenix in Flagstaff. Currently Dave uses an ISDN BRI connection to connect to the main intranet. Dave also uses one of the BRI channels to routinely transfer files to the main office in Phoenix. The information that Dave transfers to the main office is typically text file order forms, not more than 30K each, and no more than 10 forms per day are usually submitted. However, Dave maintains the company's Web site, which is on his Web server in Flagstaff. Lately, some of the distributors have been complaining that the large product catalogs they require from the company's Web site are downloading quite slowly. In an attempt to keep the distributors happy, Dave is considering ordering a faster connection to the Internet from his telecommunications provider. Assume that you have been sent to help Dave investigate his connectivity options. What information would you collect? Which type of WAN connections would you consider?

3. Your network consulting team has been brought in by XYZ Corporation to solve a WAN connectivity problem. The customer has reported that the ISDN BRI connections it has in three different locations are not functioning properly. The remote office in Lexington, MO, won't connect at all. The router does dial, but the connection is dropped before it ever has a chance to connect. The main office in New York, NY, seems to maintain a connection all the time, even though it is supposed to be dial on demand. The branch office in Los Angeles, CA, doesn't seem to utilize both of its channels no matter how much data is being transmitted across the link. What type of information would you collect from each of these locations? What specific configuration parameters would you be interested in seeing for each location?

11

> **After reading this chapter and completing the exercises, you will be able to:**
> - Understand Frame Relay standards and equipment
> - Describe the role of virtual circuits and performance parameters in Frame Relay
> - Understand the Frame Relay topologies
> - Understand the difference between multipoint and point-to-point configurations
> - Configure and monitor Frame Relay

WAN technologies typically define the Physical and Data Link layer connections. Frame Relay is both a Data Link layer encapsulation type implemented on the router and a Physical service provided by a telecommunications company. In this chapter, you will learn about Frame Relay terms, specifications, and service types. In addition, you will see how to implement and configure Frame Relay connections on Cisco routers.

FRAME RELAY STANDARDS AND EQUIPMENT

Frame Relay is a packet switching and encapsulation technology that functions at the Physical and Data Link layers of the OSI reference model. Frame Relay is a communications technique for sending data over high-speed digital connections operating anywhere from 56 Kbps to 44.736 Mbps or higher. A streamlined version of the older X.25 technology, Frame Relay is more efficient and faster because it does not perform the error checking that was present in X.25. Frame Relay also provides cost-effective access to remote facilities because one site can connect to multiple remote sites using a single connection. The **International Telecommunication Union-Telecommunication Standardization Sector (ITU-T)** and the American National Standards Institute (ANSI) define Frame Relay as a connection between the data terminal equipment (DTE) and the data communications equipment (DCE). DCE is switching equipment, supplied by a telecommunications provider, that serves as a connection to the **public data network (PDN)**. DTE is also known as customer premises equipment (CPE), because it is the equipment that belongs to, and is maintained by, the PDN customer. For example, if you connect your Cisco router to a **Frame Relay switch** (which is provided by the phone company), the Cisco router is the CPE and the Frame Relay switch is the DCE, as shown in Figure 12-1.

Figure 12-1   CPE to DCE connection

The ITU-T was formerly known as the **Consultative Committee on International Telephony and Telegraphy (CCITT)**, which is the primary international organization for fostering cooperative standards for telecommunications equipment and systems.

The physical equipment that is used on a network may vary from one organization to another. For example, some networks may use a separate router and channel service unit/digital service unit (CSU/DSU) to make their WAN connections. In Figure 12-2, you can see a CSU/DSU that is used with a Cisco 2501 router to make the connection. The CSU/DSU is located at the customer location of the digital connection. The unit is used for encoding, filtering, and translating communications to and from the digital line.

Frame Relay Standards and Equipment

Figure 12-2 CSU/DSU and router

Some routers have built-in cards that allow them to make WAN connections. For example, in Figure 12-3, you can see a T1 CSU/DSU card built into the router. The router in the picture is a Cisco 1600 series router. Notice that a T1 line connects directly to the CSU/DSU on the back of the router.

Figure 12-3 CSU/DSU connection

 The order of the acronym—CSU/DSU or DSU/CSU—is unimportant, because both forms refer to the same device. The correct ordering of the three-letter acronyms is a matter of personal preference.

In Frame Relay connections, the network device that connects to the Frame Relay switch is also known as a **Frame Relay access device** (**FRAD**); you may also see this defined as **Frame Relay assembler/disassembler**. The Frame Relay switch is also called the **Frame Relay network device** (**FRND**), which is pronounced "friend." The network administrator typically handles the local connection up to the point that it enters the PDN. Items that are part of the PDN, including the Frame Relay switch, fall under the control and responsibility of the telecommunications provider.

VIRTUAL CIRCUITS

You can use Frame Relay with nearly any serial interface. It operates by multiplexing, which means that it combines multiple data streams onto one physical link. Frame Relay separates each data stream into logical (software-maintained) connections called virtual circuits, which carry the data transferred on the connection. These virtual circuits are multiplexed onto the physical channel. Two types of virtual circuits, switched virtual circuits (SVC) and permanent virtual circuits (PVC), connect Frame Relay ports. SVCs, which are the less common of the two, are controlled by software and are only active while a connection to the WAN is active. The SVC software automatically dials the WAN, establishing and terminating the connection as required to transfer data over the Frame Relay service. PVCs, which are the more common of the two, remain permanently connected to the WAN. The network administrator manually defines the PVC; it remains until the network administrator removes it.

DLCI

Frame Relay connections identify virtual circuits by Data Link Connection Identifier (DLCI) numbers. The DLCI (pronounced *dell-see*) numbers map virtual circuits to layer 3 protocol addresses. For example, a DLCI number associates an IP address with a specific virtual circuit. DLCI numbers are not unique identifiers on the network; instead, they have only local significance, which means they are important only to the local router and Frame Relay switch.

Frame Relay Map

DLCI numbers are mapped, or assigned, to a specific interface. Each router that supports Frame Relay will have a **Frame Relay map**, which is a table that defines the remote interface to which a specific DLCI number is mapped. The definition will contain a DLCI number and an interface identifier, which is typically a remote IP address.

Figure 12-4 shows a sample Frame Relay configuration. RouterA has two serial interfaces configured for Frame Relay. The first serial interface (S0) on RouterA is configured for DLCI 9, in order to form a virtual circuit between itself and RouterB. The second serial interface (S1) is configured for DLCI 12. It refers to a virtual circuit between RouterA and RouterC. The Frame Relay map shows which destination IP addresses are used with which DLCI numbers.

Notice that the **Frame Relay switching table** is configured to map its ports (P0, P1, and P2) to the correct DLCI numbers for the virtual connection. Each switching table entry consists of four elements: the incoming port on the switch, the incoming DLCI number, the outgoing port on the switch, and the outgoing DLCI number. The switching table in this example is simplified; in reality, the switch would be more complex and involve additional Frame Relay switches.

In the example, only the mapping table for RouterA is shown. In reality, however, each router configured for Frame Relay will have its own mapping table. Remember that DLCI numbers are only locally significant, so it would be possible for RouterA and RouterB to use the same DLCI number to specify a virtual circuit.

Figure 12-4   Sample Frame Relay configuration

Subinterfaces

In Figure 12-4, RouterA has two different serial interfaces, each configured for one virtual connection. In early implementations of Frame Relay, each PVC required its own dedicated serial interface. With current technology, however, a single router serial interface can now service multiple PVCs through a single physical serial interface. In order to allow a single serial interface to support multiple PVCs, the IOS divides the interface into logical **subinterfaces**.

By dividing a single physical interface into several logical subinterfaces, the cost of implementing multiple Frame Relay virtual circuits is reduced because only one port is required on the router. Also, the network administrator has to configure and maintain fewer physical connections. You learned in Chapter 9 that decimal numbers following the physical interface identifier reference the subinterfaces defined on Cisco routers. For example, if Serial 0 (S0) had three subinterfaces, they would be referenced as S0.1, S0.2, and S0.3. Sample subinterface configurations are shown later in this chapter.

LMI

Frame Relay engineers designed Local Management Interface (LMI) in 1990 to enhance standard frame relay. The LMI basically extended the functionality of frame relay by:

- Making the DLCIs globally rather than locally significant
- Creating a signaling mechanism between the router and the Frame Relay switch, which could report on the status of the link
- Supporting multicasting

Providing DLCI numbers that are globally rather than just locally significant makes automatic configuration of the Frame Relay map possible (as explained in the following section).

LMI uses **keepalive packets** (sent every 10 seconds by default) to verify the Frame Relay link and to ensure the flow of data. The Frame Relay switch in turn provides the status of all virtual circuits and their respective DLCI numbers to the Frame Relay connectivity device. Each virtual circuit, represented by its DLCI number, can have one of three connection states:

- Active: The connection is working and routers can use it to exchange data
- Inactive: The connection from the local router to the switch is working, but the connection to the remote router is not available
- Deleted: No LMI information is being received from the Frame Relay switch; this can indicate that the connection between the CPE and DCE is not functional

The Frame Relay switch reports this status information to the Frame Relay map on the local router. The status information is used by the Frame Relay connectivity devices to determine whether data can be transmitted over the configured virtual circuits. Without LMI, the Frame Relay map must be built statically in the routers. However, by making the DLCI's globally significant, LMI facilitates dynamic Frame Relay map tables through the use of the Inverse ARP protocol described in the next section.

Inverse ARP

As previously mentioned and illustrated in Figure 12-4, a Frame Relay map includes DLCIs and their corresponding remote IP addresses. In **multipoint** configurations, routers use the protocol Inverse ARP to send a query using the DLCI number to find an IP address. Multipoint and **point-to-point** configurations are discussed later in this chapter. As other routers respond to the Inverse ARP queries, the local router can build its Frame Relay map automatically. In order to maintain the Frame Relay map, routers exchange Inverse ARP messages every 60 seconds, by default.

If the remote router does not support Inverse ARP, the Frame Relay map will have to be maintained statically (built and updated manually by the network administrator). Do not confuse Inverse ARP with Reverse Address Resolution Protocol (RARP); RARP is used primarily on LANs to provide hosts that only have MAC addresses with IP addresses.

Encapsulation Types

In the early days of Frame Relay, vendors and standards organizations worked separately to develop and define LMI. As a result, LMI has several different protocol encapsulation types that it can use for management communications. Different Frame Relay switches, CPE, and Frame Relay connectivity equipment employ or support different types of LMI encapsulation. Cisco routers, for example, support these types of LMI encapsulation:

- cisco: This LMI type was originally defined by four companies: DEC, Nortel, StrataCom, and Cisco. It allows for 992 virtual circuit addresses and uses DLCI 1023 as a management circuit, which transfers link and DLCI status messages. This is the default LMI encapsulation type on Cisco routers.

- ansi: ANSI standard T1.617 Annex-D provides for 976 virtual circuit addresses and uses DLCI 0 as the management circuit.

- q933a: ITU-T Q.933 Annex A, similar to ANSI T1.617 Annex-D, uses DLCI 0 as a management circuit.

Cisco routers (using IOS Release 11.2 or later) can autosense the LMI type used by the Frame Relay switch. If the Frame Relay responds with more than one LMI type, the Cisco router will automatically configure itself to use the last LMI type received. The network administrator can also manually configure the LMI type. This manual configuration is explained later in the chapter.

The basic LMI type has three information elements: report type, keepalive, and PVC status. The report type indicates whether the message is just a keepalive frame or a full status message. The Frame Relay devices send keepalive frames every 5–30 seconds (10 by default) to ensure that the link is still active. Full status messages contain DLCI status in addition to the keepalive information.

As stated, management circuits transfer DLCI status messages. Depending on your Frame Relay provider, these messages may contain all or some of the following pieces of information concerning the status of the virtual circuit:

- New: Used if a new DLCI connection has been configured

- Active: Used to indicate whether the virtual circuit is available for data transfer

- Receiver not ready: Used for flow control to indicate that the virtual circuit is congested; this option is not available in the q933a LMI type

- Minimum bandwidth: Indicates the minimum available bandwidth

- Global addressing: Used to give DLCI global significance, as described earlier

12

- Multicasting: Used to configure a group of destination addresses rather than a single address; the IEEE has reserved DLCI numbers 1019 through 1022 for this purpose; frame Relay devices use multicasting to make DLCI numbers globally significant by advertising them across the Frame Relay network

- Provider-Initiated Status Update: Normally, the Frame Relay switch obtains PVC status information only when the CPE sends a full status message and requests status information for the other DLCI connections; this option allows the provider to initiate a status inquiry

Not all Frame Relay providers support every piece of link status information. All current implementations provide the New and Active information, but support for other information varies by provider.

 Frame Relay does not provide error checking, as do other network protocols such as Synchronous Data Link Control (SDLC). This makes Frame Relay connections more efficient, but it also means that Frame Relay must rely on the upper-layer protocols, such as TCP, to provide error correction.

Split Horizon

Split horizon is a routing technique that reduces the chance of routing loops on a network. A split horizon implementation prevents routing update information received on one physical interface from being rebroadcast to other devices through that same physical interface. People also refer to this rule as **nonbroadcast multiaccess (NBMA)**.

Although split horizon is useful for reducing routing loops, it can cause problems for Frame Relay routing updates. For example, consider a router (RouterA), which is connected to two other routers (RouterB and RouterC) through a single physical interface configured for different virtual circuits, as shown in Figure 12-5. This is a multipoint configuration, which is the default when configuring Frame Relay. Because of split horizon, RouterA would not be able to send router updates received from RouterB to RouterC, and vice versa.

If the network is using IP, split horizon could be disabled on RouterA, which would solve the problem. However, disabling split horizon is not an option for IPX/SPX or AppleTalk. Furthermore, if the network administrator disables split horizon, the chance of getting routing loops on the network will be increased. The best solution is to configure separate point-to-point subinterfaces for each virtual connection, because the individual virtual circuits can be maintained and split horizon can remain on. Routing update information that is received through one subinterface can be propagated to other subinterfaces because they have different logical addresses.

As an example of this use of subinterfaces, examine Figure 12-6. It is the same as Figure 12-5, except that now the division of serial zero (S0) into subinterfaces S0.1 and S0.2 allows a different subnet identifier to be assigned to each virtual circuit. This allows router updates from RouterB to be transmitted to RouterC, and vice versa, because RouterA treats the subinterfaces as physically separate even though they are really only logically separate.

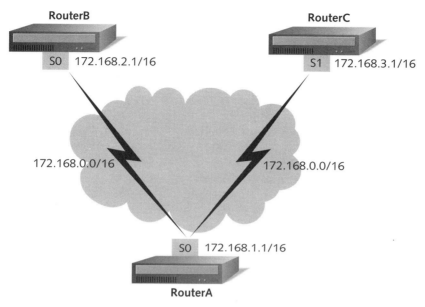

Figure 12-5   Split horizon problem

Figure 12-6   Subinterfaces in use in a point-to-point configuration

The network administrator can configure each subinterface as a point-to-point connection or a multipoint connection. Point-to-point connections allow you to divide a single serial interface into multiple subinterfaces, each supporting a separate virtual connection. The network administrator must configure each subinterface with its own subnet identifier in a point-to-point configuration, as shown in Figure 12-6. In a multipoint configuration, the network administrator can configure a single interface or subinterface to support multiple connections to physical or logical interfaces on other routers. A multipoint configuration is still subject to the split horizon rule, because multiple Frame Relay connections on the same network are connected to a single logical interface. The only benefit to the multipoint configuration is that it allows you to use a single network for all of your routers, as shown in Figure 12-7.

Figure 12-7   Single subinterface configured for multiport connection

Notice that in Figure 12-7, the network uses the same subnet identifier for both virtual circuit connections. Note also that the routers all share the same subnet, identified by their first three octets.

PERFORMANCE PARAMETERS

When organizations contract Frame Relay services from a telecommunications provider such as MCI, Sprint, AT&T, or one of the Regional Bell Operating Companies (RBOCs), the contract specifies parameters by which the connection is expected to function. Terms that appear in the contract may include:

- Access rate: The speed of the line, which indicates transfer rate. Common U.S. access rates are 56 Kps, and 64 and 128 Kbps, which are provided by Integrated Service Digital Network (ISDN) connections; and 1.544 Mbps, which is provided by T1 connections. Access rate is also known as the local access rate.

- Committed information rate (CIR): The minimum transfer rate that the Frame Relay customer negotiates with the Frame Relay service provider. The service provider agrees to always allow the customer to transfer information at no less than the transfer rate specified by the CIR. This is usually lower than the access rate because the transfer rate may exceed the CIR during short bursts.

- Committed Burst Size (CBS): The maximum amount of data bits that the service provider agrees to transfer in a set time period under normal conditions.

- Excess Burst Size (EBS): The amount of excess traffic (over the CBS) that the network will attempt to transfer during a set time period. The network can discard EBS data, if necessary.

- **Oversubscription**: When the sum of the data arriving over all virtual circuits exceeds the access rate, the situation is called oversubscription. This can occur when the CIR is exceeded by burst traffic from the virtual circuits. Oversubscription results in dropped packets. In such a case, the dropped packets must be retransmitted.

12

Congestion

Frame Relay switches attempt to control congestion on the network. When the Frame Relay switch recognizes congestion, it sends a forward explicit congestion notification (FECN) message to the destination router. This message tells the router that congestion was experienced on the virtual circuit. In addition, the switch sends a backward explicit congestion notification (BECN) message to the transmitting, or source, router. The router's reaction to the BECN should be to reduce the amount of traffic it is sending.

A network administrator can configure certain types of traffic at the router as discard eligible (DE). Thus, during times of congestion, the router can discard DE frames in order to provide a higher, more reliable, service to those frames that are not discard eligible.

FRAME FORMAT

Frame Relay devices can utilize different Frame Relay frame formats. Since this course is focused on Cisco devices, this section will focus on the Cisco proprietary Frame Relay frame format, its Frame Relay frame structure, and the Address field of the frame.

Figure 12-8 shows the Frame Relay frame format, the basic frame structure, and an expanded look at the Address field of that structure.

Flag	Address	Ethertype	Data	Frame Check Sequence	Flag
1 byte	2–4 bytes	2 bytes	Variable	2 bytes	1 byte

	8	7	6	5	4	3	2	1
1st byte	DLCI, high-order bits						CR	EAO
2nd byte	DLCI, low-order bits			FECN	BECN	DE	EA1

Figure 12-8   Frame Relay frame format

The Frame Relay frame format has specific parts, as discussed below:

- Flag: An eight-bit binary sequence (01111110) that indicates the start of the data frame

- Address: Two to four bytes that contain several pieces of Frame Relay information

- Ethertype: Identifies the type of higher-layer protocol being encapsulated (IP, IPX, or AppleTalk); this data field is specific to the Cisco proprietary frame format

- Data: A variable length field that contains the information from the higher layers encapsulated in the Frame Relay frame

- FCS: frame check sequence (FCS), or cyclical redundancy check (CRC), a mathematical computation placed at the end of the frame and is used to ensure that the frame was not corrupted during transmission

- Flag: An eight-bit binary sequence (01111110) that indicates the end of the data frame

Although the Address portion of the Frame Relay frame can contain up to four bytes, Figure 12-8 displays only two bytes because that is the most common format. Three- and four-byte addressing varies only slightly from the structure of two-byte addressing. Refer back to Figure 12-8 as you read the descriptions for the bits of the Address field.

- CR: A command or response bit that is used for sending connection management and frame acknowledgement information between stations

- FECN: Setting used to alert receiving devices if the frame experiences congestion

- BECN: Setting used on frames traveling away from the congested area to warn source devices that congestion has occurred on that path

- DE: Discard eligible bit that is used to identify frames that are first to be dropped when the CIR is exceeded; Cisco routers allow you to set the DE bit for a particular virtual connection by DLCI number

- EA: Extension address bits that are used to extend the address field from two bytes to either three or four bytes; it allows you to create additional DLCI numbers; for each EA bit that is turned on, one byte is added to the address field

Although the Frame Relay frame formats vary slightly, the above information provides a thorough description. In addition to variety in Frame Relay formats, there is some variation in the topology that Frame Relay can utilize. In the next section you will explore different Frame Relay topologies.

FRAME RELAY TOPOLOGIES

WAN topologies were discussed in Chapter 5. Frame Relay can use all of the topologies discussed; a peer (point-to-point), star (hub and spoke), partial mesh, or full mesh physical topology. Figure 12-9 depicts the four topologies again for your review.

12

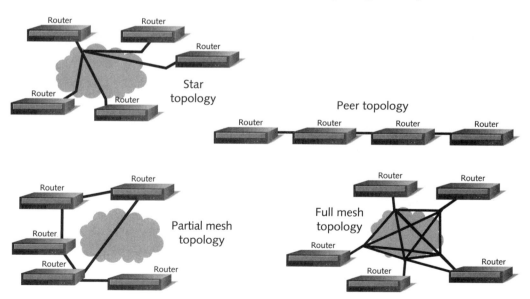

Figure 12-9   WAN topologies

The peer topology is like the bus LAN topology. Nodes are just strung along in a daisy-chained fashion. Very often, there will only be two routers connected. This is the simplest WAN topology, and is the least expensive and easiest to configure. The disadvantage to the peer WAN topology is that a failure between nodes will affect the WAN. There is no redundancy.

The star is the most popular Frame Relay topology. One router functions as a central point, or hub, in a simple hierarchical configuration. All other devices are connected to the central router as spokes would connect to a hub. Typically the network administrator will configure the central router with a single interface that makes a multipoint connection to all other routers. The star is also the least expensive topology because it requires the least number of virtual circuits.

The full mesh is the most expensive topology to implement because each router has a direct connection to every other router. While this offers the most redundancy, it is extremely expensive to implement.

The partial mesh allows redundancy for critical connections while being less expensive than the full mesh. Essentially, any Frame Relay topology that isn't a star or a full mesh is a partial mesh.

FRAME RELAY CONFIGURATION

In this section, you will learn how to configure Frame Relay over serial interfaces, using IP as the Network layer protocol. We will look at several examples beginning with the simplest configuration and moving to successively more complex scenarios.

Basic Multipoint Configuration with Two Routers

We begin with the easiest Frame Relay configuration: a multipoint connection between two routers in which the local and remote routers support LMI and Inverse ARP. In this case, LMI will notify the router about the available DLCI numbers and Inverse ARP will build the Frame Relay map dynamically.

Look at Figure 12-10 and assume that you are responsible for configuring RouterA. RouterA is a Cisco router running IOS version 11.2, so it has the ability to autosense the LMI type. In addition, it automatically receives the DLCI information by querying the network. You only have to configure the serial interface for the correct IP address (129.10.15.1) and the subnet mask (255.255.255.0), and then configure it to support Frame Relay. Assume that the negotiated bandwidth of this connection is 56 Kbps and that you want to use the Routing Information Protocol (RIP) to pass the routing table updates between the routers.

Table 12-1 lists the Cisco router prompts and commands that you will need to complete this configuration.

Figure 12-10   Simple Frame Relay configuration

Table 12-1   Basic router prompts and commands for configuring the multipoint example shown in Figure 12-10

Router prompts this:	You type this:	Description
router>	en	Allows you to enter privileged EXEC (a.k.a. enable) mode. You will be prompted to enter the appropriate password after this command.
router#	config t	Allows you to configure the router from the terminal line
router(config)#	int s1	Tells the router to access interface serial 1 for configuration
router(config-if)#	ip address 129.10.15.1 255.255.255.0	Maps the interface serial 1 to the IP address and subnet mask shown
router(config-if)#	encap fr	Sets the encapsulation for this port to Frame Relay using Cisco (the default). The other option is ietf.
router(config-if)#	ban 56	Sets the bandwidth for this port to 56 Kbps
router(config-if)#	exit	Exits interface configuration mode
router(config)#	router rip	Enables the RIP for routing table updates
router(config-router)#	net 129.10.0.0	Enables RIP on the specified network address

The commands in Table 12-1 successfully configure RouterA for the connection shown in Figure 12-10.

Now, assume that you are the network administrator for RouterB and all the same information applies, except that your router is using IOS release version 11.0, which does not support automatic LMI sensing. To accommodate this new fact, you would have to enter the LMI type and, of course, different IP addresses. Also assume that the LMI type is ansi. With these conditions, the configuration commands for RouterB are shown in Figure 12-11.

```
router#config t
router(config)#int s0
router(config-if)#ip address 129.10.15.2 255.255.255.0
router(config-if)#encap fr
router(config-if)#ban 56
router(config-if)#frame-relay lmi-type ansi
router(config-if)#ex
router(config)# router rip
router(config-router)# net 129.10.0.0
```

Figure 12-11   RouterB configuration

Multipoint Configuration Using a Subinterface

This example configuration requires more work than the last example because we have multiple routers and RouterA is using a subinterface rather than a physical interface. In this case the Frame Relay map will have to be built statically on RouterA. To configure a multipoint subinterface, you map it to multiple remote routers using the same subnet mask, but different DLCI numbers. For example, assume that you are the administrator for RouterA in Figure 12-12 and you want to configure subinterface S1.2, which has IP address 192.168.51.1 and subnet mask 255.255.255.0, to connect over three different virtual connections to the remote Routers B, C, and D.

Figure 12-12   Multipoint subinterface configuration on S1.2

Table 12-2 outlines the steps to configure RouterA.

Table 12-2 Subinterface configuration prompts and commands for RouterA in Figure 12-12

Router prompts this:	You type this:	Description
router#	config t	Allows you to configure the router from the terminal line
router(config)#	int s1	Tells the router to access interface serial 1 for configuration
router(config-if)#	no ip address	When you are configuring a subinterface, you do not want the main interface to have an IP address; this command removes any configured IP address for the S1 interface.
router(config-if)#	encap fr	Sets the encapsulation for this port to Frame Relay using Cisco (the default). The other option is ietf.
router(config-if)#	exit	Exits interface configuration mode
router(config)#	int s1.2 multipoint	Configures subinterface S1.2 for a multi-point connection
router(config-subif)#	ip ad 192.168.51.1 255.255.255.0	Sets S1.2 for the IP address shown
router(config-subif)# Kbps	ban 64	Sets the bandwidth for this port to 64
router(config-subif)#	frame map ip 192.168.51.2 200 b	Maps subinterface to DLCI 200 and enables broadcast routing updates
router(config-subif)#	frame map ip 192.168.51.3 300 b	Maps subinterface to DLCI 300 and enables broadcast routing updates
router(config-subif)#	frame map ip 192.168.51.4 400 b	Maps subinterface to DLCI 400 and enables broadcast routing updates
router(config-subif)#	exit	Leaves subinterface configuration mode
router(config)#	router rip	Enables RIP
router(config-router)#	network 192.168.51.0	Sets RIP to be used on the network

Point-to-Point Configuration Using Subinterfaces

In the example shown in Figure 12-13, we have the same physical star, but our "hub" router will be configured for three separate point-to-point connections to remote routers B, C, and D. Notice there is a different subinterface on RouterA for each remote router connection and the remote routers are all on different subnets. This is the definition of point-to-point. Point-to-point Frame Relay configurations do not support Inverse ARP. In this situation, you will have to configure each subnet separately and use the frame-relay interface-dlci command to associate the dlci numbers with a specific subinterface. The configuration on the remote routers will be much simpler than the one on the hub router. These remote router configurations will resemble the earlier basic multipoint configuration example with two routers. If LMI and Inverse ARP are supported, the remote routers will build their Frame Relay map tables dynamically. The commands to configure RouterA for the point-to-point example shown in Figure 12-13 are shown in Figure 12-14.

Figure 12-13   Point-to-point configuration sample using subinterfaces

```
router(config)#int s1
router(config-if)#no ip address
router(config-if)#en fr
router(config-if)#exit
router(config)#int s1.1 point-to-point
router(config-subif)#ip ad 192.168.51.1 255.255.255.0
router(config-subif)#ban 64
router(config-subif)#frame-relay interface-dlci 200 b
router(config-if)#exit
router(config)#int s1.2 point-to-point
router(config-subif)#ip ad 192.168.52.1 255.255.255.0
router(config-subif)#ban 64
router(config-subif)#frame-relay interface-dlci 300 b
router(config-if)#exit
router(config)#int s1.3 point-to-point
router(config-subif)#ip ad 192.168.53.1 255.255.255.0
router(config-subif)#ban 64
router(config-subif)#frame-relay interface-dlci 400 b
router(config-subif)#exit
router(config)#router rip
router(config-router)#network 192.168.51.0
router(config-router)#network 192.168.52.0
router(config-router)#network 192.168.53.0
```

Figure 12-14   Point-to-point configuration commands

Frame Relay Static Mapping

As shown in Table 12-2 and Figure 12-14, you sometimes have to define the DLCI numbers manually. This is called making a **static address to DLCI Frame Relay map**. You statically configure your DLCI entries in the following situations:

- The remote router doesn't support Inverse ARP

- You need to assign specific subinterfaces to specific DLCI connections

- You want to reduce broadcast traffic

- You are configuring Open Shortest Path First (OSPF) over Frame Relay

Non-Cisco routers use a different Frame Relay encapsulation than Cisco routers do. If you are configuring Cisco routers to connect to other Cisco routers, they will automatically use the cisco Frame Relay encapsulation and you can enable Frame Relay using the encap fr command. If, however, you are connecting a Cisco router to a non-Cisco router, you must specify the "ietf" Frame Relay encapsulation. This is done using the encap fr ietf command.

Keepalive Configuration

By default, keepalive packets are sent out every 10 seconds to the Frame Relay switch. Keepalive packets, as previously described, are used to maintain the connection and inform the router of the connection status. You can change the keepalive period by typing "keepalive" followed by the time in seconds of the keepalive period at the router(config-if)# interface configuration prompt. The keepalive period can be set from as low as zero to as high as 30 seconds. For example, if you want to set the keepalive period to 64 seconds, type "keepalive 64" at the interface configuration prompt.

12

MONITORING FRAME RELAY

You can check your Frame Relay configuration by using show commands. These commands allow you to verify that the commands you entered above produced the desired effect on your router. Figures 12-15, 12-16, 12-17, and 12-18 show the commands and their output.

The serial configuration for each serial interface is available by its interface number (S0, S1, S2, etc.)

The router gives a status report for the interface, the IP address and subnet mask, and DLCI and LMI statistics

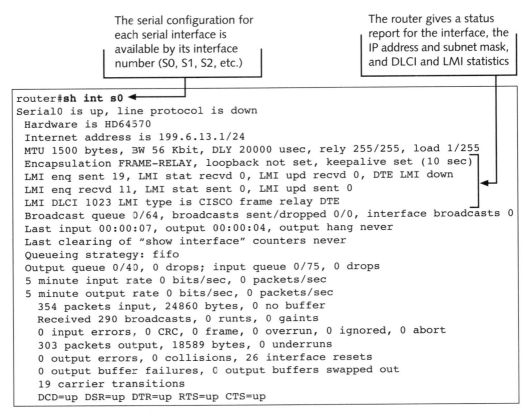

```
router#sh int s0
Serial0 is up, line protocol is down
  Hardware is HD64570
  Internet address is 199.6.13.1/24
  MTU 1500 bytes, BW 56 Kbit, DLY 20000 usec, rely 255/255, load 1/255
  Encapsulation FRAME-RELAY, loopback not set, keepalive set (10 sec)
  LMI enq sent 19, LMI stat recvd 0, LMI upd recvd 0, DTE LMI down
  LMI enq recvd 11, LMI stat sent 0, LMI upd sent 0
  LMI DLCI 1023 LMI type is CISCO frame relay DTE
  Broadcast queue 0/64, broadcasts sent/dropped 0/0, interface broadcasts 0
  Last input 00:00:07, output 00:00:04, output hang never
  Last clearing of "show interface" counters never
  Queueing strategy: fifo
  Output queue 0/40, 0 drops; input queue 0/75, 0 drops
  5 minute input rate 0 bits/sec, 0 packets/sec
  5 minute output rate 0 bits/sec, 0 packets/sec
    354 packets input, 24860 bytes, 0 no buffer
    Received 290 broadcasts, 0 runts, 0 gaints
    0 input errors, 0 CRC, 0 frame, 0 overrun, 0 ignored, 0 abort
    303 packets output, 18589 bytes, 0 underruns
    0 output errors, 0 collisions, 26 interface resets
    0 output buffer failures, 0 output buffers swapped out
    19 carrier transitions
    DCD=up DSR=up DTR=up RTS=up CTS=up
```

Figure 12-15   Show interface command and output

The router tells you the DLCI number and whether the link is active. Other information includes total packet counts for the link and statistics for each FECN, BECN, and DE packet.

This command shows the PVC statistics for each serial interface

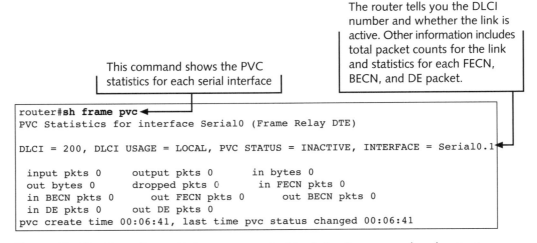

```
router#sh frame pvc
PVC Statistics for interface Serial0 (Frame Relay DTE)

DLCI = 200, DLCI USAGE = LOCAL, PVC STATUS = INACTIVE, INTERFACE = Serial0.1

  input pkts 0      output pkts 0      in bytes 0
  out bytes 0       dropped pkts 0      in FECN pkts 0
  in BECN pkts 0      out FECN pkts 0      out BECN pkts 0
  in DE pkts 0      out DE pkts 0
pvc create time 00:06:41, last time pvc status changed 00:06:41
```

Figure 12-16   Show Frame Relay permanent virtual circuit command and output

This command shows the DLCI-to-Network-layer address mapping for each remote router to which the local device is connected.

```
router#sh frame map◄
Serial0.1 (down): ip 199.6.13.2 dlci 200(0xC8,0x3080), static,
        broadcast,
        CISCO, status defined, inactive
```

Figure 12-17   Show Frame Relay map command and output

This command displays the amount and type of management information that is being transferred over the LMI DLCI connection. It also displays the LMI type used on the interface.

```
router#sh frame lmi◄
LMI Statistics for interface Serial0 (Frame Relay DTE) LMI TYPE = CISCO
 Invalid Unnumbered info 0          Invalid Prot Disc 0
 Invalid dummy Call Ref 0           Invalid Msg Type 0
 Invalid Status Message 0           Invalid Lock Shift 0
 Invalid Information ID 0           Invalid Report IE Len 0
 Invalid Report Request 0           Invalid Keep IE Len 0
 Num Status Enq. Sent 39            Num Status msgs Rcvd 0
 Num Update Status Rcvd 0           Num Status Timeouts 38
```

Figure 12-18   Show Frame Relay Local Management Interface command output

12

CHAPTER SUMMARY

❑ Frame Relay is a flexible WAN technology that can be used to connect two geographically separate LANs.

❑ Frame Relay is both a service and type of encapsulation.

❑ The service parameters must be discussed with the Frame Relay provider (telecommunications company).

❑ Service parameters for Frame Relay include the access rate, Committed Information Rate (CIR), Committed Burst Size (CBS), and Excess Burst Size (EBS).

❑ Frame Relay connections employ virtual circuits that can be either permanent or switched.

❑ Virtual circuit connections across Frame Relay connections are defined by Data Link Connection Identifier (DLCI) numbers.

❑ The DLCI numbers can be associated with remote Network layer addresses; however, they are only locally significant unless the Local Management Interface (LMI) is available.

❑ Most Frame Relay providers support LMI, which allows Frame Relay maps to be dynamically created via Inverse ARP.

❑ Static mappings of DLCI numbers to remote IP addresses can be configured when routers do not support Inverse ARP.

❑ Inverse ARP is on by default for multipoint configurations.

❑ Inverse ARP is not enabled on point-to-point links because there is only one path available.

❑ Frame Relay circuits can be established over serial interfaces or subinterfaces on Cisco routers.

KEY TERMS

Consultative Committee on International Telephony and Telegraphy (CCITT) — The former name of **International Telecommunication Union-Telecommunication Standardization Sector (ITU-T)**.

Frame Relay access device (FRAD) — The device that the Frame Relay customer utilizes to connect to a Frame Relay network; also known as the **Frame Relay assembler/disassembler**.

Frame Relay assembler/disassembler — *See* **Frame Relay access device (FRAD)**.

Frame Relay map — A table that defines the interface to which a specific DLCI number is mapped.

Frame Relay network device (FRND) — The device that the Frame Relay provider supplies as the connection to the Frame Relay network; the acronym FRND is pronounced *friend*.

Frame Relay switch — A telecommunications company device that is used to support Frame Relay connections from customer locations; used to route Frame Relay traffic inside the public data network.

Frame Relay switching table — A table that is maintained on a Frame Relay switch; used to route Frame Relay traffic via virtual circuit DLCI numbers.

International Telecommunication Union-Telecommunication Standardization Sector (ITU-T) — A standards organization based in Europe, but with membership worldwide; involved in telecommunications standardization.

keepalive packets — Data packets sent between devices to confirm that a connection should be maintained between them.

multipoint — The configuration of a single interface or subinterface to use multiple virtual circuits.

nonbroadcast multiaccess (NBMA) — A rule used in Frame Relay that does not allow broadcasts to be sent to multiple locations from a single interface.

oversubscription — When the sum of the data arriving over all virtual circuits exceeds the access rate.

point-to-point — The configuration of one or more interfaces or subinterfaces to connect to multiple virtual circuits. Each circuit will be on its own subnet. Acts like a leased line.

public data network (PDN) — A telecommunications network that connects telephones around the country. These services can be provided by AT&T, Sprint, MCI, and RBOCs.

static address to DLCI Frame Relay map — A Frame Relay map that has been manually created by a network administrator.

subinterface — A logical division of an interface; for example, a single serial interface can be divided into multiple logical subinterfaces.

REVIEW QUESTIONS

1. Which protocol is utilized to automatically build the Frame Relay map along with LMI?

    a. ARP

    b. RARP

    c. Inverse ARP

    d. DLCI

2. In order to make DLCI numbers globally significant, LMI causes routers to issue _____ that advertise the DLCI numbers.

    a. unicasts

    b. keepalives

    c. broadcasts

    d. multicasts

3. When negotiating a data transfer rate for Frame Relay with a telecommunications provider, the rate agreed upon is the _____.

    a. keepalive rate

    b. CIR

    c. EBS

    d. DDR

4. The Address portion of the Frame Relay frame contains which of the following pieces of information? (Choose all that apply.)

    a. DLCI

    b. FECN

    c. flag

    d. BECN

    e. FCS

12

5. The line speed of a Frame Relay connection is known as the _____.

   a. access rate

   b. CBS

   c. EBS

   d. CIR

6. _____ numbers are locally significant in Frame Relay connections and are used to identify specific virtual circuits.

   a. DLCI

   b. PDN

   c. ARP

   d. LMI

7. In order to prevent routing loops, Frame Relay utilizes _____.

   a. loopback attack

   b. split horizon

   c. event horizon

   d. DLCI numbers

8. Frame Relay is more efficient than older WAN encapsulation methods because error correction is handled by _____ in Frame Relay communications.

   a. lower layers

   b. DLCI

   c. LMI

   d. upper layers

9. Frame Relay uses _____ to combine multiple data streams on one connection.

   a. duplexing

   b. simplexing

   c. multiplexing

   d. encoding

10. What is the purpose of keepalive packets?

    a. to reduce data transfer rates

    b. to keep PVCs active

    c. to increase data transfer rates

    d. to negotiate connection speed

11. Which of the following layers do WAN specifications typically define? (Choose all that apply.)

a. Physical

b. Data Link

c. Network

d. Transport

e. Presentation

12. In Frame Relay, what would be considered the DCE?

a. customer's router

b. terminal adapter

c. PPP

d. Frame Relay switch

13. Which of the following was formerly CCITT?

a. ASCII

b. ANSI

c. ITU-T

d. EBCDIC

14. What is another acronym used to describe a Frame Relay switch?

a. FRND

b. FRAD

c. PDN

d. PSTN

15. Which of the following would be a subinterface for Serial 1?

a. S0.1

b. S0.2

c. S1.2

d. S2.1

16. What does LMI stand for?

a. Logical Management Interface

b. Local Management Interface

c. Logical Maintenance Interconnect

d. Logical Maintenance Interface

12

17. What are the three possible connection states for a DLCI? (Choose all that apply.)

    a. interactive

    b. active

    c. inactive

    d. disconnected

    e. deleted

18. Which of the following does not allow broadcasts to be sent to multiple destinations through a single interface?

    a. LMI

    b. subinterfaces

    c. LCP

    d. MBA

    e. NBMA

19. Which of the following is a type of virtual circuit? (Choose all that apply.)

    a. MVC

    b. PVC

    c. SVC

    d. QVC

20. Which of the following are LMI encapsulation types supported by Cisco routers? (Choose all that apply.)

    a. LMI 2

    b. cisco

    c. ansi

    d. v923i

    e. q933a

21. Which of the following is the default LMI encapsulation type for a Cisco router?

    a. LMI 2

    b. cisco

    c. ansi

    d. v923i

    e. q933a

22. What does the router(config-if)#encap fr command do?

    a. sets the enable mode prompt to FR

    b. enables Frame Relay on the first serial interface

    c. sets the encapsulation to Frame Relay

    d. sets the language to French

23. Which of the following commands would show statistics for a virtual circuit?

    a. router>sh frame map

    b. router#sh frame map

    c. router#sh frame pvc

    d. router(config-if)#sh frame pvc

24. What Frame Relay encapsulation must be configured on Cisco routers that are attached to non-Cisco routers?

    a. ietf

    b. cisco

    c. ansi

    d. q933a

25. How often are Frame Relay keepalive packets sent, by default?

    a. every 30 seconds

    b. every 10 seconds

    c. once every hour on the half-hour

    d. once every hour on the hour

    e. once every 30 minutes

12

CASE PROJECTS

1. Big Byte Consulting has hired your company to help them set up Frame Relay to connect several different locations. Their headquarters are in Austin, Texas, and will be connecting PVCs to Dallas, San Antonio, and Houston. You and Jennifer are expected to have a conference call with the network administrators at the other locations to discuss the Frame Relay configuration. What type of information will have to be coordinated among the various locations? What type of information would you require in order to configure your Cisco 2500 series router to support your Frame Relay connection?

2. During the conference call with Big Byte, the subject of multipoint and point-to-point is raised. The Big Byte network team doesn't understand the differences between multipoint and point-to-point connections. How do you explain the differences to Big Byte using their network as an example?

3. Big Byte has configured their Frame Relay network but there are problems. You have been informed that the Frame Relay connection between Austin and Houston is down. Someone has already contacted the phone company and determined that the Frame Relay switches are operating properly. You decide to verify the Frame Relay configuration between the two locations. What type of information would you require? What type of configuration problems might you expect to find? What commands would you use to check the configuration?

13

SWITCHING AND VLANS

After reading this chapter and completing the exercises, you will be able to:

♦ Explain the features and benefits of Fast Ethernet

♦ Describe the guidelines and distance limitations of Fast Ethernet

♦ Define full- and half-duplex Ethernet operations

♦ Distinguish between cut-through, fragment-free, and store-and-forward LAN switching

♦ Define the operation of the Spanning Tree Protocol and its benefits

♦ Describe the benefits of virtual LANs

♦ Understand the purpose of the VLAN trunking protocol (VTP)

In this chapter, you will revisit some of the concepts surrounding Ethernet operations. Specifically, you will learn about Ethernet performance and methods for improving it. Standard and Fast Ethernet will be part of this discussion, as will half- and full-duplex Ethernet operations. The concepts central to LAN switching—such as switch operations, forwarding techniques, and VLANs—will also be explained.

ETHERNET OPERATIONS

As you have learned, **Ethernet** is a **network access method** (or **media access method**) originated by the University of Hawaii, later adopted by Xerox Corporation, and standardized as IEEE 802.3 in the early 1980s. Today, Ethernet is the most pervasive network access method in use and continues to be the most commonly implemented media access method in new LANs. Many companies and individuals are continually working to improve the performance and increase the capabilities of Ethernet technology.

In the following sections, you will revisit the Ethernet access method, discuss Ethernet errors, investigate latency problems, and learn ways in which Ethernet performance can be improved. Becoming comfortable with these concepts will help you troubleshoot and improve the performance of your LAN.

CSMA/CD

Ethernet uses **Carrier Sense Multiple Access with Collision Detection (CSMA/CD)** as its **contention method**. This means that any station connected to a network can transmit anytime there is not already a transmission on the wire. After each transmitted signal, each station must wait a minimum of 9.6 microseconds before transmitting another packet. This is called the **interframe gap**, or **interpacket gap (IPG)**, which provides sufficient spacing between frames so that network interfaces have time to process a packet before receiving another.

Collisions

Even though stations must listen to the wire before sending a transmission, two stations could listen to the wire simultaneously and not sense a **carrier signal**. In such a case, both stations might begin to transmit their data simultaneously. Shortly after the simultaneous transmissions, a collision would occur on the network wire. The stations would detect the collision as their transmitted signals collided with one another.

Once a collision is detected, the first station to detect the collision transmits a 32-bit **jam signal** that tells all other stations not to transmit for a brief period (9.6 microseconds or slightly more). The jam signal is used to ensure that all stations are aware that a collision has occurred. After the first station to detect the collision transmits the jam signal, the two stations that caused the collision use an algorithm to enter a **backoff period**, which causes them not to transmit for a random interval. The backoff period is an attempt to ensure that those two stations do not immediately cause another collision.

Collision Domain

A **collision domain** is the physical area in which a packet collision might occur. You need to understand this concept in order to understand network segmentation, which is essentially the division of collision domains. Repeaters and hubs do not segment the network and therefore do not divide collision domains. Routers, switches, bridges, and **gateways** do segment networks and thus create separate collision domains.

If a station transmits at the same time as another station in the same collision domain, there will be a collision. The 32-bit jam signal that is transmitted when the collision is discovered prevents all stations on that collision domain from transmitting. If the network is segmented, the collision domain is also divided, and the jam signal will only affect those stations that operate within that collision domain. Stations that operate within remote segments (other collision domains) are not subject to the collisions or frame errors that occur on the local segment.

Latency

The time that a signal takes to travel from one point to another point on a network affects the performance of the network. **Latency**, or **propagation delay**, is the length of time that is required to forward, send, or otherwise propagate a data frame. Latency differs depending on the resistance offered by the transmission medium, the number of nodes and, in the case of a connectivity device, the amount of processing that must be done on the packet. For instance, sending a packet across a copper wire does not introduce as much latency as sending a packet across an Ethernet switch.

The amount of time it takes for a packet to be sent from one device and received at another device is called the **transmission time**. The latency of the devices and media between the two hosts affects the transmission time; the more processing a device must perform on a data packet, the higher the latency. The maximum latency for a repeater can be as high as 140 bit times. The maximum propagation delay for an electronic signal to traverse a 100-meter section of Category 5 unshielded twisted-pair (UTP) or shielded twisted-pair (STP) cable is 111.2 bit times.

 A **bit time** is the duration of time to transmit one data bit on a network, which is 100 nanoseconds on a 10-Mbps Ethernet network and 10 nanoseconds on a 100-Mbps Ethernet network.

Table 13-1 illustrates the maximum propagation delays for various media and devices on an Ethernet network. The propagation delays shown illustrate the maximum allowable round-trip delays for cabling and devices on a 100-Mbps Ethernet network.

13

Table 13-1   Propagation delay for Ethernet media and devices

Media or Device	Maximum Propagation Delay (Bit Times)
Two Ethernet stations using two-pair UTP or fiber-optic cable	100
Two Ethernet stations using 100Base-T4	135
1-meter segment of Category 3 or 4 UTP cable	1.14
1-meter segment of Category 5 UTP or STP cable	1.112
10-meter segment of fiber-optic cable	1.0
Class I repeater	140
Class II repeater	92

Repeaters can take anywhere from less than 8 bit times up to 140 bit times to propagate a signal.

Slot time (512 bit times) is an important specification because it limits the physical size of each Ethernet collision domain. Slot time specifies that all collisions should be detected from anywhere in a network in less time than is required to place a 64-byte frame on the network. Slot time is the reason that the IEEE created the **5–4–3 rule**, which limits collision domains to five segments of wire, four repeaters and/or hubs, and three populated hubs between any two stations on a 10-Mbps network. Violating those design parameters could cause network errors. For example, if a station at one end of an Ethernet network didn't receive the jam signal before transmitting a frame on the network, another collision could occur as soon as the jam signal and newly transmitted frame crossed paths. Theoretically, this situation could occur repeatedly and prevent any useful data from being transmitted on the wire.

Ethernet Errors

Different errors and different causes for errors exist on Ethernet networks. Most errors are caused by defective or incorrectly configured equipment. Errors impede the performance of a network and the transmission of useful data. In this section, you will learn about several Ethernet packet errors and their potential causes.

Frame Size Errors

An Ethernet packet sent between two stations should be between 64 bytes and 1518 bytes. Frames that are shorter or longer are, according to Ethernet specifications, considered errors. The following list names and describes several frame size errors that occur on Ethernet networks:

- **Short frame** or **runt**: A frame that is shorter than 64 bytes. A collision, a faulty network adapter, corrupt NIC software drivers, or a repeater fault can cause this error.

- **Long frame**: Also known as a **giant**, a frame that is larger than 1518 bytes. Since 1518 is the largest legal frame size, a long frame is too large to be valid. A collision, a faulty network adapter, an illegal hardware configuration, a transceiver or cable fault, a termination problem, corrupt NIC software drivers, a repeater fault, or noise can cause this error.

- **Jabber**: This is another classification for giant or long frames. This frame is longer than Ethernet standards allow (1518 bytes) and has an incorrect **frame check sequence (FCS)**.

In addition to frame size errors, other packet errors might be seen on an Ethernet network. For example, a **frame check sequence (FCS) error**, which indicates that bits of a frame were corrupted during transmission, can be caused by any of the previously listed errors. An FCS error is detected when the calculation at the end of a packet doesn't conform correctly to the number and sequence of bits in the frame, which means there was some type of bit loss or corruption. An FCS error can be present even if the packet is within the accepted size parameters for Ethernet transmission. If a frame with an FCS error also has an octet missing, it is called an **alignment error**.

Collision Errors

Network administrators should expect collisions to occur on an Ethernet network. However, most administrators consider collision rates above 5% to be high. A large number of devices on a collision domain means a higher chance that there will be a significant number of collisions. Reducing the number of devices per collision domain will usually solve the problem. You can reduce the number of devices per collision domain by segmenting your network with a router, a bridge, or a switch.

13

A transmitting station will attempt to send its packet 16 times before discarding it as a **NIC error**. Thus, a network with a high rate of collisions, which prompts multiple retransmissions, may also have a high rate of NIC errors, and vice versa.

Another Ethernet error related to collisions is called a **late collision**. A late collision occurs when two stations transmit more than 64 bytes of their data frames before detecting a collision. This can occur when there are too many repeaters on a network or when the network cabling is too long. A late collision means that the slot time of 512 bytes has been exceeded.

The only way a station can distinguish between a late and normal collision is by determining that the collision occurred after the first 64 bytes of the frame had been transmitted.

The solution for eliminating late collisions is to determine which part of the Ethernet configuration violates design standards by having too many repeaters or populated segments, or by exceeding maximum cable lengths. Occasionally, a network device malfunction may also cause late collisions. When such problems are located, they must be resolved.

Broadcasts

Stations on a network **broadcast** packets to other stations to make their presence known on the network and to carry out normal network tasks such as IP address-to-MAC address resolution. However, when there is too much broadcast traffic on a segment, utilization increases and network performance in general suffers. People may experience slower file transfers, e-mail access delays, and slower Web access when broadcast traffic is above 10% of the available network bandwidth.

One simple way to reduce broadcast traffic is to reduce the number of services that servers provide on your network and to limit the number of protocols in use on your network. Limiting the number of services will help because each computer that provides a service, such as file sharing, broadcasts its service at a periodic interval over each protocol it has configured. Many operating systems will allow you to bind the service selectively to only a specific protocol, which will reduce broadcast traffic on the network. You can also eliminate unnecessary protocols in order to eliminate broadcast traffic on the network. An example of an unnecessary protocol is the IPX protocol on a server in an IP-only network. In this case, services would be advertised on both IP and IPX, when other stations would only be communicating via IP. IPX advertisements and the use of the IPX protocol is unnecessary in this case because no other stations on the network would be using IPX.

 Network users who share files may be sharing them over multiple protocols. Broadcast messages typically advertise these file-sharing services on each network protocol configured. Therefore, limiting the number of protocols in use on stations that share files can reduce the amount of broadcast traffic on the network.

If a broadcast from one computer causes multiple stations to respond with additional broadcast traffic, it could result in a **broadcast storm**. Broadcast storms will slow down or completely stop network communications, because no other traffic will be able to be transmitted on the network. One of the most common causes of broadcasting is network loops. Loops are created when redundant links between switches and/or bridges exist in the network. The Spanning Tree Protocol, covered in detail later in this chapter, is used to combat the problems caused by these physical loops. A broadcast storm occurs on an Ethernet collision domain when there are 126 or more broadcast packets per second.

Software faults with network card drivers or computer operating systems are the typical causes of broadcast storms. You can use a **protocol analyzer** to locate the device causing the broadcast storm. Once the device is identified, you can correct the configuration error or apply an appropriate software driver update to correct the problem.

Fast Ethernet

When a 10BaseT network is experiencing congestion, upgrading to **Fast Ethernet** can reduce congestion considerably. Fast Ethernet uses the same network access method (CSMA/CD) as common 10BaseT Ethernet, but provides 10 times the data transmission rate—100 Mbps. That means that frames can be transmitted in 90% less time with Fast Ethernet than with standard Ethernet.

When you upgrade from 10BaseT to Fast Ethernet, all the network cards, hubs, and other connectivity devices that are now expected to operate at 100 Mbps must be upgraded. If the 10BaseT network is using Category 5 or higher cable, however, that cable can still be used for Fast Ethernet operations. Also, a 10-Mbps Ethernet NIC can function on a Fast Ethernet network because the Fast Ethernet hub or switch to which the 10-Mbps device attaches will automatically negotiate a 10-Mbps connection. The Fast Ethernet hub will continue to operate at 100 Mbps with the other Fast Ethernet devices. Most modern NICs can operate at either 10 or 100 Mbps. Last, Fast Ethernet devices are also capable of full-duplex operation, which allows them to obtain a transmission rate of 100 Mbps in each direction.

Fast Ethernet, which is defined under the **IEEE 802.3u** standard, has three defined implementations:

13

- **100Base-TX:** Uses two pairs of either Category 5 unshielded twisted-pair (UTP) or shielded twisted-pair (STP); one pair is used for transmit (TX), and the other is used for receive (RX). The maximum segment length is 100 meters; two Class II repeaters and a five-meter patch cable can be used to create a maximum distance of 205 meters between stations, per each collision domain.

- **100Base-T4:** Uses four pairs of either Category 3, 4, or 5 UTP cable; one pair is used for TX, one pair for RX, and two pairs are used as bidirectional data pairs. The maximum segment length is 100 meters; as with 100Base-TX, two Class II repeaters and a five-meter patch cable can be used to create a maximum distance of 205 meters between stations, per each collision domain. Since all four pairs are used, the T4 specification does not support full-duplexing, which is discussed in the next section.

- **100Base-FX:** Uses **multimode fiber-optic (MMF) cable** with one TX and one RX strand per link. The maximum segment length is 412 meters.

IEEE 802.3u specifies two types of repeaters: Class I and Class II. Class I repeaters have higher latency than Class II repeaters, as shown in Table 13-1. When two Class II repeaters are deployed on a twisted-pair network (100Base-TX or 100Base-T4), the specification allows for an additional 5-meter patch cord to connect the repeaters. This patch cord is in addition to the normal 200-meter segment length. This means that the maximum distance between two stations can be up to 205 meters. When repeaters are used on networks with fiber-optic cable (i.e., 100Base-FX), the maximum segment lengths are actually reduced because the repeaters introduce latency. Latency increases the propagation delay, which means that the maximum distance possible between stations must be reduced to ensure that the slot time is maintained.

On a Cisco Catalyst 1900 switch, you can configure the 10BaseT and Fast Ethernet ports via interface configuration mode. The configuration commands follow a similar syntax: *interface Ethernet/fastethernet slot#/port#*. Catalyst 1900 switches only have one slot, which is 0. Also, the only ports that are capable of Fast Ethernet operations are 26 and 27. Ports 1–12 and 25 or 1–24 and 25 (depending on the specific model) are 10-Mbps ports. To enter interface configuration mode for one of the 10-Mbps ports of a switch named Rm410HL, you would use the following commands:

```
Rm410HL#configure terminal
Rm410HL(config)#interface ethernet 0/1
Rm410HL(config-if)#
```

However, if you want to configure one of the Fast Ethernet ports, you would use a slightly different command syntax; substitute the word fastethernet for ethernet:

```
Rm410HL#configure terminal
Rm410HL(config)#interface fastethernet 0/26
Rm410HL(config-if)#
```

To view the configuration of a port, use the show command. The following commands will display the configuration settings for port 1 and port 26:

```
Rm410HL#show interface e0/1
Rm410HL#show interface f0/26
```

Notice that "e" is used to specify 10-Mbps ports and "f" for 100-Mbps ports.

Half- and Full-Duplex Communications

In **half-duplex** communications, devices can send and receive signals, but not at the same time. In **full-duplex** communications, devices can send and receive signals simultaneously. As an analogy of these communication types, consider the walkie-talkie and the telephone. When two people use walkie-talkies, one person must finish speaking before the other can transmit. This is half-duplex communication. When two people communicate over the telephone, both people can speak simultaneously, and both transmissions will be heard at the opposite ends. This is full-duplex communication. Full-duplex is also known just as duplex.

10Base-T, 10Base-F, 100Base-FX, and 100Base-TX Ethernet networks can utilize equipment that supports half- and full-duplex communications. In half-duplex Ethernet communications, when a twisted-pair NIC sends a transmission, the card loops that transmission back from its transmit wire pair onto its receive pair (see Figure 13-1). The card stores the looped-back frame. The transmission is also sent out of the card. The card then compares the looped-back frame to the original frame. If the frame is the same, then there is no collision. If the looped back frame is different from the original frame, then a collision is recorded.

Figure 13-1 Half-duplex Ethernet communications

The transmitted frame travels along the network through the hub to all other stations on the collision domain. Half-duplex NICs cannot transmit and receive simultaneously, so all stations on the collision domain (including the transmitting station) listen to the transmission before sending another.

Full-duplex Ethernet components can send and receive signals at the same time. Full-duplex communications use one set of wires to send and a separate set to receive. Since full-duplex network devices conduct the transmit and receive functions on different wire pairs and do not loop back transmissions as they are sent, collisions cannot occur. Furthermore, full-duplex Ethernet increases the throughput capability between devices because there are two separate communication paths. This means that 10BaseT full-duplex network cards are capable of transferring data at a rate of 10 Mbps in each direction, as compared to half-duplex 10BaseT cards. The benefits of using full duplex are listed below:

- Time is not wasted retransmitting frames, because there are no collisions.

- The full bandwidth is available in both directions because the send and receive functions are separate.

- Stations do not have to wait until other stations complete their transmissions, because there is only one transmitter for each twisted pair.

On a Cisco Catalyst 1900 switch, you can set the duplex capabilities port-by-port. To change the duplex of a switch port, you must enter the interface configuration for the specific port you would like to configure. The following list describes the four different duplex options:

- Auto—The default setting for 100-Mbps Ethernet ports. The switch port is set to determine whether the connected device is full-or half-duplex and configures itself to match.

- Full—This setting forces full-duplex mode on a 10- or 100-Mbps port. Use this if you know that the duplex should be full but auto-negotiate (auto) doesn't seem to be working.

- Full-flow-control—This setting is used for 100BaseTX ports only. As its name implies, it utilizes flow control to ensure that switch buffers don't overflow.

- Half—The default setting for 10-Mbps Ethernet ports, which forces the port to communicate half-duplex.

Assume that you wanted to change port 26 on a Cisco 1900 switch named Rm410HL to full duplex. The commands to complete this operation are as follows:

```
Rm410HL#configure terminal
Rm410HL(config)#interface f0/26
Rm410HL(config-if)#duplex full
```

Networking tools, like the Fluke One-Touch, can determine whether your switch ports are set for full or half duplex. Some operating system tools, such as mii-daig in Linux, allow you to verify full/half-duplex operations. Client network cards can be configured through the system BIOS, operating system, or manufacturer-provided software or hardware.

LAN Segmentation

As mentioned, you can improve the performance of your Ethernet network by reducing the number of stations per collision domain. Typically, network administrators implement bridges, switches, or routers to segment the network and divide the collision domains.

In your previous studies, you learned about using bridges, switches, and routers to segment a network. In this section, you will review the concepts behind segmenting a LAN with bridges and routers.

Segmenting with Bridges

A **bridge** segments a network by filtering traffic at the Data Link layer. It divides a network into two or more segments and only forwards a frame from one segment to another if the frame is a broadcast or has the MAC address of a station on a different segment. Bridges learn MAC addresses by reading the source MAC addresses from frames as the frames are passed across the bridge. As you have already learned, the MAC addresses are contained in the header information inside each packet. If the bridge does not recognize a MAC address, it will forward the frame to all segments except the one it came in on.

The bridge maintains a **bridging table** to keep track of the different hardware addresses on each segment. The bridging table maps each MAC address learned to the port on the bridge that is connected to the segment where that MAC address is located. Bridges increase latency, but since they effectively divide the collision domain, this does not affect slot time.

When you segment a LAN with one or more bridges, remember these points:

- Bridges reduce collisions by segmenting the LAN and filtering traffic based on MAC addresses.

- A bridge does not reduce broadcast or **multicast** traffic.

- A bridge can extend the useful distance of the Ethernet LAN because distance limitations apply to collision domains, and a bridge separates collision domains.

- The bandwidth for the new individual segments is increased because they can operate separately at 10 Mbps or 100 Mbps, depending on the technology.

- Bridges can be used to limit traffic for security purposes by keeping traffic segregated; traffic between two hosts on one side of the bridge will not be propagated to the other side of the bridge.

Segmenting with Routers

A **router** operates at layer 3 of the OSI reference model. It interprets the Network layer protocol and makes forwarding decisions based on the layer 3 address. Routers typically do not propagate broadcast traffic; thus, they reduce network traffic even more than do bridges. Routers maintain routing tables that include the Network layer addresses of different segments. The router forwards packets to the correct router on another segment, based on those Network layer addresses. Since the router has to read the layer 3 address and determine the best path to the destination station, latency is higher than with a bridge or repeater/hub.

Keep in mind that when you segment a LAN with routers, routers will:

- Decrease collisions by filtering traffic;

- Reduce broadcast and multicast traffic by blocking or selectively filtering packets;

13

- Support multiple paths and routes between them;

- Provide increased bandwidth for the newly created segments;

- Increase security by preventing packets between hosts on one side of the router from propagating to the other side of the router;

- Increase the effective distance of the network by creating new collision domains;

- Provide layer 3 routing, packet fragmentation and reassembly, and traffic flow control;

- Provide communications between different technologies such as Ethernet and Token Ring or Ethernet and Frame Relay;

- Have a higher latency than bridges, because routers have more to process; faster processors in the router can reduce some of this latency.

LAN SWITCHING

Although **switches** are similar to bridges in several ways, using a switch on a LAN has a different effect on the way network traffic is propagated. This difference happens because switches do quite a bit more than merely segment the LAN; they truly change the way in which communication is carried out on the LAN.

The remainder of this chapter focuses on the ways in which a switch can affect LAN communications. First, you will learn how a switch segments a LAN. The benefits and drawbacks of using a switch on the LAN will also be described. Then, you will learn how a switch operates and the switching components that are involved. The final section of the chapter will explain how you can use switches to create virtual LANs.

Segmentation with Switches

Bridges and switches are similar—so much so that switches are often called **multiport bridges**. The main difference between a switch and a bridge is that the switch typically connects multiple stations individually, thereby segmenting a LAN into separate ports. A bridge only separates two or more segments and is usually limited to 16 ports. In addition, switches are hardware-controlled whereas bridges are controlled by software. Typically, hubs are connected to the bridge ports, so the workstations connected to the hubs are sharing the bandwidth on that segment. By connecting each port to an individual workstation, switches **microsegment** the network. The bandwidth is not shared as long as each workstation connects to its own switch port. This is called **switched bandwidth**, and it operates differently than the shared bandwidth through hubs.

Consider the illustration shown in Figure 13-2. When Host A sends a unicast to Host D, the switch (which operates at the Data Link layer of the OSI reference model) receives the unicast frame on the port to which Host A is attached, opens the data frame, reads the destination MAC address, and then passes the frame directly to the port to which Host D is attached. Unlike hub operations, the other hosts on the switch will not see the frame. However, when Host B sends a broadcast frame, the switch forwards the frame to all devices attached to the switch. This is similar to how a bridge handles broadcasts. Bridges and switches generally do not create broadcast domains. Figure 13-3 shows the inherent logic structure of this process.

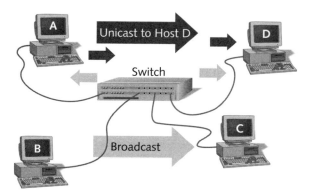

Figure 13-2   Switch packet forwarding actions

Given the number of steps that a switch must perform on each frame, its latency is typically higher than that of a repeater or hub. Although switches do slightly more work than bridges, faster processors and a variety of switching techniques make switches typically faster than bridges. In general, however, you can count on a switch adding approximately 21 microseconds of latency to network communications.

13

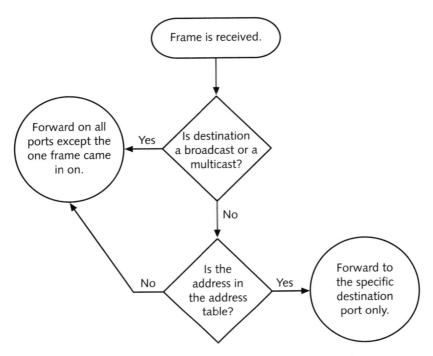

Figure 13-3 Packet forwarding decisions made by a switch

As previously mentioned, since switches microsegment most traffic, there is a better utilization of the available bandwidth. When one host is communicating directly with another host, the hosts can utilize the full bandwidth of the connection. For example, with a 10-Mbps switch on a 10BaseT LAN, the switch can often provide 10-Mbps connections for each host that is attached. If a hub were used instead of a switch, all devices on the collision domain would share the 10-Mbps connection.

Switches provide the following benefits:

- Reduction in network traffic and collisions

- Increase in available bandwidth per station, because stations can communicate in parallel

- Increase in the effective distance of a LAN by dividing it into multiple collision domains

- Increased security, because unicast traffic is sent directly to its destination and not to all other stations on the collision domain

Switch Operations

A switch learns the hardware address of devices to which it is attached by reading the source address of frames as they are transmitted across the switch. The switch matches the source MAC address with the port from which the frame was sent. The MAC-to-switch-port mapping is stored in the switch's **content-addressable memory (CAM)**. The switch refers to the CAM when it is forwarding frames, and it updates the CAM continuously. Each mapping receives a time stamp every time it is referenced. Old entries, which are ones that are not referenced frequently enough, are removed from the CAM.

The switch uses a memory buffer to store frames as it determines to which port(s) a frame will be forwarded. There are two different types of memory buffering that a switch can use: **port-based memory buffering** and **shared memory buffering**. In port-based memory buffering, each port has a certain amount of memory that it can use to store frames. If a port is inactive, then its memory buffer is idle. However, if a port is receiving a high volume of traffic (near network capacity), the traffic may overload its buffer, and other frames may be delayed or require retransmission.

Shared memory buffering offers an advantage over port-based memory buffering in that any port can store frames in the shared memory buffer. The amount of memory that each port uses in the shared memory buffer is dynamically allocated according to the port's activity level and the size of frames transmitted. Shared memory buffering works best when a few ports receive a majority of the traffic. This situation occurs in client/server environments, because the ports to which servers are attached will typically see more activity than the ports to which clients are attached.

Some switches can interconnect network interfaces of different speeds. For example, a switch might have a mix of 10-Mbps and 100-Mbps devices attached. These switches use **asymmetric switching** and, typically, a shared memory buffer. The shared memory buffer allows switches to store packets from the ports operating at higher speeds (100 Mbps) when it is necessary to send that information to ports operating at lower speeds (10 Mbps). Asymmetric switching is also better for client/server environments when the server is configured with a network card that is faster than the network cards of the clients. The switch allows the server's NIC to operate at 100 Mbps and all the clients' NICs to operate at 10 Mbps, if necessary. This allows the server to handle the clients' requests more quickly than if it was limited to 10 Mbps.

Switches that require all attached network interface devices to use the same transmit/receive speed are using **symmetric switching**. For example, a symmetric switch could require all ports to operate at 100 Mbps or maybe at 10 Mbps, but not at a mix of the two speeds.

Securing Switch Ports

There are several degrees of security that you might employ on a switch. First, you can configure a permanent MAC address for a specific port on your switch. This means that

13

only the specified host can connect (physically) to the specified port on the switch. Second, you could define a static MAC address entry into your switching table, which maps a restricted communication path between two ports. For example, port 7 might be configured to send frames only through port 2 via a specific hardware address. Finally, you can configure port security. This stops people from plugging hubs into network connections on your LAN by setting a limit on the number of MAC addresses that can utilize a specific port.

To configure a permanent MAC address on a switch port, the switch must be in global configuration mode. The command follows this syntax: *mac-address-table permanent hwaddress slot#/port#*. Therefore, to set the MAC address 0080c8e81256 to communicate on switch port 7 of your Catalyst 1900 hostname Rm410HL, you would enter the following commands:

```
Rm410HL(config)#mac-address-table permanent
0080.c8e8.1256 e0/7
```

Notice that you must separate the MAC address into three groups separated by dots. Otherwise, the syntax is similar to all the previous switch configuration syntax you have seen.

To configure a static entry, the command follows a similar syntax, but uses *restricted static* in place of *permanent*. However, there is more information required because you are telling the switch to allow communications from a specific port to another specific port with a specific hardware address. For example, to configure port 6 to communicate only with port 12 and specify that all communications should be going to MAC address 0080c8e81259, you would enter:

```
Rm410HL(config)#mac-address-table restricted static
0080.c8e8.1259 e0/6 e0/12
```

If you want to configure port security, the command syntax is quite different. Remember, the purpose of port security is to limit the number of hosts on one switch port. Therefore, you need only set the maximum number of devices that should be allowed to use a port. For example, assume that you have a five-port hub attached to port 10 of your switch. You want to be sure that only those five hosts (already attached) are allowed to utilize switch port 10. In that case, you would enter the following:

```
Rm410HL(config)#interface e/10
Rm410HL(config-if)#port secure max-mac-count 5
```

This would restrict the port to learning five connected MAC addresses. (Keep in mind that when you put a hub with multiple nodes connected to it in a switch port, those users are sharing bandwidth and are not able to take advantage of the switch's switched bandwidth capability.) You can either let the switch learn the MAC addresses of those five hosts on its own (as they communicate) or you can configure the five MAC addresses statically as shown earlier. If the switch learns the address on its own, it is termed a **sticky-learn** by Cisco. This means that the switch, when configured for a maximum limit, will learn that many addresses and configure them automatically as permanent.

Switching Methods

All switches base frame-forwarding decisions on a frame's destination MAC address. However, all switches do not forward frames in the same way. There are three main methods for processing and forwarding frames; cut-through, store-and-forward, and fragment-free. One additional forwarding method was derived from cut-through and store-and-forward. It is called adaptive cut-through. Cisco switches come with a menu system that allows you to choose from the available switch modes, as shown in Figure 13-4 below.

```
Catalyst 2820 - System Configuration
System Revision: 0 Address Capacity: 2048
System UpTime: 2day(s) 21hour(s) 15 minute(s) 4second(s)
-----------Settings-----------
[N] Name of system
[C] Contact name
[L] Location
[S] Switching mode                      FragmentFree
[U] Use of store-and-forward for multicast  Disabled
[A] Action upon address violation       Suspend
[G] Generate alert on address violation   Enabled
[I] Address aging time                  300 seconds
[P] Network Port                        None
[H] Half duplex back pressure (10-mbps ports) Disabled
[E] Enhanced Congestion Control (10 Mbps Ports) Disabled
-------------Actions-------------
[R] Reset system              [F] Reset to factory defaults
----------Related Menus-------------
[B] Broadcast storm control     [X] Exit to Main Menu
Enter Selection:
```

Figure 13-4   Catalyst 2820 switching menu

The figure illustrates the configuration menu for a Cisco Catalyst 2820 switch. Notice that the menu option [S] will allow you to toggle switching modes and that the switch is currently set for fragment-free.

The four switching modes are based on varying levels of latency (delay) and error reduction in forwarding frames. For example, cut-through offers the least latency and least reduction in error propagation, whereas store-and-forward switching offers the best error reduction services, but also the highest latency. Each of these switching methods is described in greater detail in the following sections.

Cut-through

Switches that utilize **cut-through** forwarding start sending a frame immediately after reading the destination MAC address into their buffers. The main benefit of forwarding the frame immediately is a reduction in latency, because the forwarding decision is made almost immediately after the frame is received. For example, the switching decision is made after receiving 14 bytes of a standard Ethernet frame, as shown in Figure 13-5.

Ethernet Frame

7 bytes	1 byte	6 bytes	6 bytes	2 bytes	variable	4 bytes
Preamble	SFD	Destination address	Source address	Length	Data	FCS

Read into switch buffer

Figure 13-5   Portion of packet read into buffer by a cut-through switch

Cisco routers use the term **fast forward** to indicate that a switch is in cut-through mode.

The drawback to forwarding the frame immediately is that there might be errors in the frame, and the switch would be unable to catch those errors because it only reads a small portion of the frame into its buffer. Of course, any errors that occur in the **preamble**, **start frame delimiter (SFD)**, or destination address fields will not be propagated by the switch—unless they are corrupted in such a way as to appear valid, which is highly unlikely.

Store-and-Forward

Store-and-forward switches read the entire frame, no matter how large, into their buffers before forwarding, as shown in Figure 13-6. Because the switch reads the entire frame, it will not forward frames with errors to other ports.

Ethernet Frame

7 bytes	1 byte	6 bytes	6 bytes	2 bytes	variable	4 bytes
Preamble	SFD	Destination address	Source address	Length	Data	FCS

Entire frame read into switch buffer

Figure 13-6   Entire packet read into buffer by a store-and-forward switch

However, because the entire frame is read into the buffer and checked for errors, the store-and-forward method has the highest latency.

Standard bridges typically use the store-and-forward technique.

Fragment-free

Fragment-free switching represents an effort to provide more error-reducing benefits than cut-through switching, while keeping latency lower than does store-and-forward switching. A fragment-free switch reads the first 64 bytes of an Ethernet frame and then begins forwarding it to the appropriate port or ports, as shown in Figure 13-7.

Ethernet Frame

7 bytes	1 byte	6 bytes	6 bytes	2 bytes	variable	4 bytes
Preamble	SFD	Destination address	Source address	Length	Data	FCS

|← 64 bytes read into switch buffer →|

Figure 13-7   Amount of packet read into buffer by a fragment-free switch

By reading the first 64 bytes, the switch will catch the vast majority of Ethernet errors and still provide lower latency than a store-and-forward switch. (Of course, for Ethernet frames that are 64 bytes long, the fragment-free switch is essentially a store-and-forward switch.)

 Fragment-free switches are also known as **modified cut-through** switches.

Adaptive Cut-through

Another variation of the switching techniques described above is the **adaptive cut-through** switch (also known as **error sensing**). For the most part, the adaptive cut-through switch will act as a cut-through switch to provide the lowest latency. However, if a certain level of errors is detected, the switch will change forwarding techniques and act more as a store-and-forward switch. Switches that have this capability are usually the most expensive, but provide the best compromise between error reduction and frame-forwarding speed.

Changing the Switching Mode

If you want to see the type of switching method that your Cisco Catalyst 1900 switch is utilizing, you can issue the show port system command from the enable mode prompt. The default switching type on the 1900 is fragment-free. To change the switching mode to store-and-forward, you would use the following command from global configuration mode:

```
Rm410HL(config)#switching-mode store-and-forward
```

The Catalyst 1900 supports two different modes: fragment-free and store-and-forward. When you change the switching type, you change it for all ports on the switch.

13

Spanning Tree Protocol

In networks that have several switches and/or bridges, there might be **physical path loops**. Physical path loops occur when network devices are connected to one another by two or more physical media links. The physical loops are desirable for network fault tolerance because if one path fails, another will be available. Consider the network shown in Figure 13-8; the four devices (two switches and two bridges) are configured in a physical as well as **logical loop**.

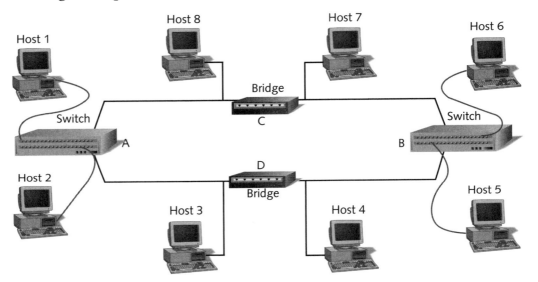

Figure 13-8   Physical loop created on LAN by switches and bridges

Assume that Host 1, which is attached to Switch A, sends out a frame with the destination MAC address of Host 5; there are actually two routes the packet can travel. The packet can be sent from Switch A to Bridge C or Bridge D. From there, it can be sent to Switch B, from which it can be forwarded to Host 5. The benefit of this configuration is that if either Bridge C or Bridge D fails, another path between Switch A and Switch B still exists.

This sample network could have been configured with all switches or all bridges or any combination thereof. The number of switches and/or bridges is not important; the important point is that when switches and/or bridges are interconnected, they might create a physical loop.

The drawback to the configuration is that endless packet looping (when a frame is sent from one device to another, but the final destination is never found) can occur on this network, due to the existence of the physical loop. For example, assume that the MAC address for a station is not in any of the switching or bridging tables on the network. The packet could be forwarded endlessly around the network from bridge to switch to bridge.

The **Spanning Tree Protocol (STP)** was invented by Radia Perlman while she was with Digital Equipment Corporation (now Compaq) in the 1980s. It is a layer 2 link management protocol designed to prevent looping on bridges and switches. The specification for STP is IEEE 802.1d. STP uses the **Spanning Tree Algorithm (STA)** to interrupt the logical loop created by a physical loop in a bridged/switched environment. STP does this by ensuring that certain ports on some of the bridges and/or switches do not forward frames. In this way, a physical loop exists, but a logical loop does not. The benefit derived is that if a device should fail, STP can be used to activate a new logical path over the physical network.

Building a Logical Path

With STP enabled, the switches and bridges on a network use an election process to configure a single logical path. First, a **root bridge (root device)** is selected. Then, the other switches and bridges configure their ports, using the root bridge as a point of reference. STP-enabled devices determine the root bridge via an administratively set priority number; the device with the lowest priority number becomes the root bridge. If the priorities of two or more devices are the same, then the devices will make the decision based on the lowest MAC address.

 When STP-enabled devices are first enabled on a LAN they assume that they are the root device, which begins the election process.

Bridges use STP to transfer the information about each bridge's MAC address and priority number. The messages the devices send to one another are called **bridge protocol data units (BPDU)** or **configuration bridge protocol data units (CBPDU)**. Once the STP devices on the network select a root bridge, each bridge or switch determines which of its own ports offers the best path to the root bridge. The BPDU messages are sent between the root bridge and the best ports on the other devices, which are called **root ports**. The BPDUs transfer status messages about the status of the network. If BPDUs are not received for a certain period of time, the non-root-bridge devices will assume that the root bridge has failed, and a new root bridge will be elected. The devices will then reconfigure their ports on the basis of the paths available to the new root bridge. During this period of reconfiguration, no data traffic is sent or received; only BPDUs are received on the ports.

Once the root bridge is determined and the switches and bridges have calculated their paths to the root bridge, the logical loop is removed by one of the switches or bridges. This switch or bridge will do this by blocking the port that creates the logical loop. This blocking is done by calculating costs for each port in relation to the root bridge and then disabling the port with the highest cost. For example, refer back to Figure 13-8 and assume that Switch A has been elected the root bridge. Switch B would have to block one of its ports to remove the logical loop from the network.

13

Port States

STP will cause the ports on a switch or bridge to settle into a stable state. **Stable states** are the normal operational states of ports when the root bridge is available and all paths are functioning as expected. STP devices use transitory states when the network configuration is undergoing some type of change, such as a root bridge failure. The **transitory states** prevent logical loops during a period of transition from one root bridge to another.

The stable states are as follows:

- **Blocking:** The port is sending and receiving the STP messages (BPDUs), but it is not receiving or forwarding data frames, in order to prevent logical loops in the network.

- **Forwarding:** The port is receiving and forwarding data frames, learning new MAC addresses, and sending and receiving BPDUs. All of the ports on a root bridge are configured for forwarding.

- **Disabled:** The port is disabled and is neither sending or receiving BDPUs nor forwarding or receiving frames.

The transitory states are as follows:

- **Listening:** The port is listening to frames so that a new root can be selected; it is not receiving or forwarding data frames, and it is not learning new MAC addresses.

- **Learning:** The port is learning new MAC addresses based on incoming frames, but it is not yet receiving or forwarding data frames.

STP devices use the transitory states on ports while a new root bridge is being elected. During the listening state, STP devices are configured to receive only the BPDUs that inform them of network status. STP devices use the learning state as a transition once the new root has been selected but all the bridging or switching tables are still being updated. Since the routes may have changed, the old entries must either be timed out or replaced with new entries. Ports on STP-enabled devices move through the different states as indicated below:

- From bridge/switch bootup to blocking

- From blocking to listening (or to disabled)

- From listening to learning (or to disabled)

- From learning to forwarding (or to disabled)

- From forwarding to disabled

In a completely configured and stable STP topology, all ports will be in either the forwarding or blocking state. There will only be one root device (bridge or switch) and all other devices will have one designated root port. All of the root ports on each device and all of the ports on the root bridge will be in the forwarding state.

Topology Changes

When the topology is changed, STP-enabled devices react automatically. If a device in an STP-enabled network stops receiving CBPDUs, then that device will claim to be the root bridge and will begin sending CBPDUs describing itself as such. This begins the rebuilding process, which is the same as the initial building of the STP topology. This event occurs when the root bridge fails or becomes separated from the other devices. Each device claims to be the root bridge for a short period until a new root bridge is elected.

VIRTUAL LANs

A **virtual LAN (VLAN)** is a grouping of network devices that is not restricted to a physical segment or switch. VLANs can be configured on most switches to restructure broadcast domains similarly to the way that bridges, switches, and routers divide collision domains. A **broadcast domain** is a group of network devices that will receive LAN broadcast traffic from each other.

 Since switches and bridges forward broadcast traffic to all ports, by default, they do not separate broadcast domains. Routers are the only devices previously mentioned that both segment the network and divide broadcast domains, because routers do not forward broadcasts by default.

By default, every port on a switch is in VLAN 1. This is the **management** (also known as **default**) **VLAN**, and it cannot be deleted. You can create multiple VLANs on a single switch or even one VLAN across multiple switches; however, the most common configuration is to create multiple VLANs across multiple switches. With the latter configuration, routers must be used to move the traffic between the VLANs. Consider the network configuration shown in Figure 13-9, which does not employ VLANs. Notice that two broadcast domains are created, one on each side of the router.

13

Figure 13-9 Broadcast domains on a LAN

Now consider that same network with VLANs implemented, as shown in Figure 13-10. The broadcast domains can now be further subdivided because of the VLAN configuration. This, of course, is only one way in which VLANs can be used to divide a broadcast domain.

Figure 13-10 Broadcast domains using VLANs

Although VLANs have the capability of separating broadcast domains, as do routers, this does not mean that they segment at layer 3. A VLAN is a layer 2 implementation and does not affect layer 3 logical addressing.

Benefits of VLANs

The benefits of using VLANs center on the concept that the administrator can divide a LAN logically without changing the actual physical configuration. This ability provides the administrator with several benefits:

- It is easier to add and move stations on the LAN.

- It is easier to reconfigure the LAN.

- There is better traffic control.

- There is increased security.

Cisco states that 20 to 40% of the workforce is moved every year. 3Com, another manufacturer of switching equipment, states that 23% of the cost of a network administration team is spent implementing changes and moves. VLANs help to reduce this cost because many changes can be made at the switch. In addition, physical moves do not necessitate the changing of IP addresses and subnets because the VLAN can be made to span multiple switches. Therefore, if a small group is moved to another office, a reconfiguration of the switch to include those ports in the previous VLAN may be all that is required.

In the same way that the VLAN can be used to accommodate a physical change, it can also be used to implement one. For example, assume that a department needs to be divided into two sections, each requiring a separate LAN. Without VLANs, the change may necessitate the physical rewiring of several stations. However, with VLANs available, the change can be made easily by dividing the ports on the switch that connect to the separate sections. Network reconfigurations of this nature are much easier to implement when VLANs are an option.

Since the administrator can set the size of the broadcast domain, the VLAN gives the administrator added control over network traffic. Implementing switching already reduces collision traffic immensely; dividing the broadcast domains further reduces traffic on the wire. In addition, the administrator can decide which stations should be sending broadcast traffic to each other.

Dividing the broadcast domains into logical groups increases security because it is much more difficult for someone to tap a network port and figure out the configuration of the LAN. Thus, the actual physical layout of the LAN is hidden from would-be network spies. Furthermore, the VLAN allows the administrator to make servers behave as if they were distributed throughout the LAN, when in fact they can all be locked up physically in a single central location.

13

As an example of this flexibility, consider Figure 13-11. All the servers are locked in the secured server room, yet they are servicing their individual clients. Notice that even the clients of the different VLANs are not located on the same switches. The figure illustrates the true flexibility of using VLANs, because the logical configuration of the network is quite different from the physical configuration.

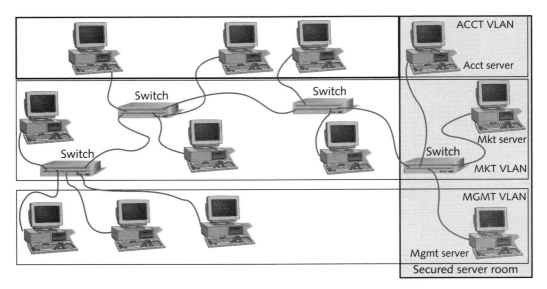

Figure 13-11   Securing servers with VLANs

In addition to allowing for the physical security of mission-critical servers, VLANs can be configured by network administrators to allow membership only for certain devices. Network administrators can do this with the management software included with the switch. The restrictions that can be used are similar to those of a firewall; unwanted users can be flagged or disabled, and administrative alerts can be sent should someone attempt to infiltrate a given VLAN. This type of security is typically implemented by grouping switch ports together according to the type of applications and access privileges required.

Dynamic versus Static VLANs

Depending on the switch and switch management software, VLANs can be configured statically or dynamically. Static VLANs are configured port-by-port, with each port being associated with a particular VLAN. In a static VLAN, the network administrator manually types in the mapping for each port and VLAN.

Dynamic VLAN ports can automatically determine their VLAN configuration. Although they may seem easier to configure than static VLANs, given the description thus far, that is not quite the case. The dynamic VLAN uses a software database of MAC address-to-VLAN mappings that is created manually. This means that the MAC addresses and corresponding

VLANs must be entered and maintained by the network administration team. Instead of saving administrative time, the dynamic VLAN could prove to be more time-consuming than the static VLAN. To its credit, however, the dynamic VLAN does allow the network administration team to keep the entire administrative database in one location. Furthermore, on a dynamic VLAN, it doesn't matter if a cable is moved from one switch port to another, because the VLAN will automatically reconfigure its ports on the basis of the attached workstation's MAC address. This is the real advantage of using dynamic VLAN systems.

VLAN Standardization

Before VLAN was an IEEE standard, early implementations depended on the switch vendor and on a method known as **frame filtering**. Frame filtering was a complex process that involved one table for each VLAN and a master table that was shared by all VLANs. This process allowed for a more sophisticated VLAN separation because frames could be separated into VLANs via MAC address, network-layer protocol type, or application type. The switches would then look up the information and make a forwarding decision based on the table entries.

When creating its VLAN standard, the IEEE did not choose the frame-filtering method. Instead, the **IEEE 802.1q** specification that defines VLANs recommends **frame tagging** (also known as **frame identification**). Frame tagging involves adding a four-byte field to the actual Ethernet frame to identify the VLAN and other pertinent information. The members of the IEEE considered this solution to be more scalable (able to accommodate larger networks) than frame filtering.

Frame tagging makes it easier and more efficient to ship VLAN frames across network backbones because switches on the other side of the backbone can simply read the frame instead of being required to refer back to a frame-filtering table. In this way, the frame-tagging method implemented at layer 2 is similar to routing layer 3 addressing because the identification for each frame is contained within the frame. A tagged frame can be as large as 1522 bytes, whereas a normal Ethernet frame is limited to 1518 bytes. Devices that are not VLAN-aware would see a 1522 byte frame as a long frame (frame larger than normal size) or jabber.

The two most common types of frame tagging (encapsulation) are 802.1q and **Inter-Switch Link (ISL) protocol**. ISL is a Cisco proprietary frame-tagging method that uses a 26-byte header. It only works between Cisco devices. If you need a frame-tagging method that works between Cisco and another vendor, you will have to use 802.1q frame tagging. The Cisco 1900 series switch only supports ISL. The lowest level Cisco router that supports ISL is the 2600 series. Other Cisco switches support additional types of frame tagging, such as **LAN emulation (LANE)** and **IEEE 802.10 (FDDI)**.

13

The additional header with the VLAN addressing information is typically stripped off the frame before it reaches the connected host stations. Otherwise, non-VLAN-aware host stations would see the additional information as a long frame or jabber.

Creating VLANs

Creating VLANs on the Cisco Catalyst 1900 switch using the command line interface is fairly straightforward. You name the VLANs individually via global configuration mode. For example, assume you would like to create three VLANs on your switch (hostname Rm410HL). The three VLANs are production, accounting, and marketing. (There will actually be four VLANs when you are finished, because the default VLAN (VLAN 1) is assumed.) Look at the command sequence below that shows how to create and list VLANs on a Cisco Catalyst 1900:

```
Rm410HL>enable
Rm410HL#configure terminal
Rm410HL(config)#vlan 2 name production
Rm410HL(config)#vlan 3 name accounting
Rm410HL(config)#vlan 4 name marketing
Rm410HL(config)#exit
Rm410HL#show vlan
```

VLAN Name	Status	Ports
1 default	Enabled	1-12, AUI, A, B
2 production	Enabled	
3 accounting	Enabled	
4 marketing	Enabled	

[remaining output cut]

Notice that all ports are still assigned to the default VLAN. Notice also that the Fast Ethernet ports 26 and 27 are displayed as A and B respectively. The next step is to assign switch ports to the new VLANs. Ports can be assigned as static or dynamic. Assigning dynamic VLANs is more complicated and not a requirement for CCNA candidates. The commands to assign ports as static to VLANs are shown below. The commands have to be entered port-by-port because there is no single command to assign multiple switch ports to a VLAN. Assume that you would like to assign port 5 to VLAN 2, port 7 to VLAN 3, and port 9 to VLAN 4.

```
Rm410HL(config)#interface e0/5
Rm410HL(config-if)#vlan-membership static 2
Rm410HL(config-if)#exit
Rm410HL(config)#interface e0/7
Rm410HL(config-if)#vlan-membership static 3
Rm410HL(config-if)#exit
Rm410HL(config)#interface e0/9
Rm410HL(config-if)#vlan-membership static 4
Rm410HL(config-if)#exit
Rm410HL(config)#exit
Rm410HL#show vlan
```

VLAN Name	Status	Ports
1 default	Enabled	1-4, 6, 8, 10-12
2 production	Enabled	5
3 accounting	Enabled	7
4 marketing	Enabled	9

[remaining output cut]

You can use the show vlan [#] command to gather information about a specific VLAN (instead of listing all VLANs). The show vlan-membership command gives a variation of the same output as the show vlan command.

Link Types and Configuration

There are two types of links on Cisco switches, trunk and access links. Trunk links are switch-to-switch or switch-to-router links that can carry traffic from multiple VLANs. Frame tagging is used to keep track of different VLANs between VLAN-aware connectivity devices. Access links are links going to non–VLAN-aware devices such as hubs and individual workstations. These devices have no need to understand VLANs and they operate as if they were on a single broadcast domain.

Trunk links can only be applied to the 100-Mbps (Fast Ethernet) or greater Ethernet ports on a switch. 10-Mbps ports cannot be designated as trunk links. On a Catalyst 1900 switch, the Fast Ethernet ports 26 and 27 are capable of being trunk links. As previously mentioned, port 26 is known as Trunk A and port 27 is Trunk B.

13

There are five different states that you can set for a trunk link, as follows:

- Auto—Configure this interface for trunking only if the connected device is set to on or desirable.
- Desirable—The interface will become a trunk port if the connected device is on, desirable, or auto.
- Nonegotiate—The interface is a trunk interface and will not negotiate that status with any other device.
- Off—The interface is not a trunk interface and will attempt to disable trunking on attached devices.
- On—The interface is a trunk interface and will try to enable trunking on attached devices.

To configure a trunk link on a Catalyst 1900, you must be in the appropriate interface configuration mode. Remember, you only have two possible interfaces: 26 or 27. Assume you have port 26 of your Catalyst 1900 named Rm410HL connected to another switch. You decide that port 26 is your trunk link and you want it to encourage other devices to be trunk links. The commands to complete this operation are as follows:

```
Rm410HL#config term
Rm410HL(config)#int f0/26
Rm410HL(config-if)#trunk on
```

By default, all VLANs are now enabled to be routed over this newly configured trunk link. There is no command to selectively enable VLANs for trunking. However, you can selectively clear a VLAN from a trunk link. For example, let's assume that you don't want packets from VLAN 7 to traverse this link. You would clear VLAN 7 from the trunk using this command:

```
Rm410HL(config-if)#no trunk-vlan 7
```

To verify that this operation was completed successfully, you would use the show trunk command on trunk A with the allowed-vlans option as shown below:

```
Rm410HL#show trunk a allowed-vlans

1-6, 8-1004
```

Notice that every VLAN between 1 and 1004 is listed with the exception of VLAN 7. The VLANs not listed as allowed are excluded from using this trunk link. While the Cisco 1900 switch supports 1005 VLANs, STP can only be used on 64 VLANs simultaneously. By default, STP is enabled on VLANs 1 through 64.

There is a switching table for each VLAN, and there is a root bridge (switch) for each VLAN.

Trunking Protocol

Cisco created the **VLAN trunking protocol (VTP)** to manage all of the configured VLANs that traverse trunks between switches. VTP is a layer 2 messaging protocol that manages all the changes to the VLANs across networks. Any changes made to a VLAN by an administrator (i.e., add, rename, or delete) are automatically propagated by VTP to all VTP-enabled devices.

VTP Domains

VTP devices are organized into domains. Each switch can only be in one **VTP domain** at a time, and all devices that need to share information must be in the same VTP domain. To configure a Catalyst 1900 switch for a VTP domain named hudlogic, you would enter the name of the switch:

```
Rm410HL(config)#VTP domain hudlogic
```

You would have to perform that same command on all of the switches that you expect to share VLAN information. When you make changes to the VTP configuration, you should verify them with the show vtp command from enable mode.

```
Rm410HL(config)#exit
Rm410HL#show VTP
```

 If all of your switches are in the same VLAN, there is no need to configure a VTP domain.

VTP Device Modes

There are three different modes for VTP-enabled devices: server, client, and transparent. Catalyst switches default to server mode, which means that they can add, rename, and delete VLANs and propagate those to the rest of the VTP devices. VTP servers save the VLAN configuration information in NVRAM. You must have at least one **VTP server** in your VTP domain. When a device is placed in **VTP client** mode, it is not allowed to make changes to the VLAN structure, but it can receive, interpret, and propagate changes made by a server. Clients do not save the VTP configuration in NVRAM. **VTP transparent** mode means that a device is not participating in VTP communications other than to forward that information through its configured trunk links.

To configure a Catalyst 1900 switch as a server, client, or transparent mode device, you can enter the appropriate vtp command from global configuration mode. For example, to configure your switch as a client you would enter

```
Rm410HL#config term
Rm410HL(config)#vtp client
```

13

To set the switch back to server mode or to transparent mode, you would type "server" or "transparent" (respectively) instead of "client."

VTP Pruning

There is an option, called **VTP pruning**, which reduces the number of VTP updates that traverse a link. It is off by default on all switches. If you turn VTP pruning on, VTP message broadcasts are only sent through trunk links that must have the information. For example, if a Catalyst 1900 switch with two trunks receives an update concerning VLAN 7 on Trunk A (port 26) it will typically forward that update through Trunk B (port 27), assuming both ports are enabled for trunking.

However, assume that you have removed VLAN 7 from Trunk B. The update would still be forwarded out of Trunk B unless you enabled VTP pruning. VTP pruning can be enabled on a VTP device configured as a server. When you enable VTP pruning on a server, you enable it on every device in the entire domain. The command to enable and disable VTP pruning is straightforward: vtp pruning enable or vtp pruning disable from global configuration mode. For example, to enable VTP pruning on a Catalyst 1900 switch configured as a VTP server, you would use this command:

```
Rm410HL(config)#vtp pruning enable
```

This will prune information as necessary for VLANs 2 through 1005. VLAN 1 is not eligible to be pruned because it is an administrative (and default) VLAN. Therefore, all updates for VLAN 1 will always traverse the switch.

When you add a new switch to a LAN you should be sure to clear all VTP information, so as not to propagate it to the rest of the network. Use the following command:

```
Rm410HL#delete vtp
```

Switch Interface Descriptions

You can configure a name for each port on a switch. This is useful when you begin to define roles for a switch port on a more global basis, such as when you configure VLANs. For example, perhaps you have dedicated port 1 on your switch to serve the production department's VLAN and port 26 on your switch to be a trunk to the next building (#777). You may decide to configure your switch interface descriptions as follows:

```
Rm410HL#configure terminal
Rm410HL(config)#int e0/1
Rm410HL(config-if)#description productionVLAN
Rm410HL(config-if)#int f0/26
Rm410HL(config-if)#description trunkBldg777
```

Nonswitching Hubs and VLANs

When implementing hubs on a network that employs VLANs, you should keep a few important considerations in mind:

- If you insert a hub into a port on the switch and then connect several devices to the hub, all the systems attached to that hub will be in the same VLAN.

- If you must move a single workstation that is attached to a hub with several workstations, you will have to physically attach the device to another hub or switch port in order to change its VLAN assignment.

- The more hosts that are attached to individual switch ports, the greater the microsegmentation and flexibility the VLAN can offer.

Routers and VLANs

Routers can be used with VLANs to increase security and must be used to manage traffic between different VLANs. Typically a separate subinterface is configured on the router for each VLAN supported. In addition, the routers can implement **access lists**, the use of which increases inter-VLAN security. Lastly, the router allows restrictions to be placed on station addresses, application types, and protocol types. Figure 13-12 illustrates how a router might be implemented in a VLAN configuration.

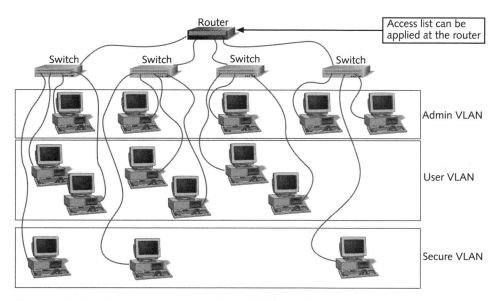

Figure 13-12   Router implemented in a VLAN configuration

The router in Figure 13-12 connects the four switches and routes communications between three different VLAN configurations. An access list on the router can restrict the communications between the separate VLANs. To configure a Cisco router for inter-VLAN communications, several steps are involved. First, enable ISL trunking on the switch port the router is connected to using the trunk on command. Next, assign an IP address to each subinterface on the router that will be associated with a VLAN. Finally, configure ISL encapsulation on the router subinterfaces. The following router commands illustrate how to enable inter-VLAN communications for VLANs 1 and 2 on a Cisco router that supports ISL.

```
Router(config)#interface e0.1
Router(config-if)#ip address 164.106.1.1 255.255.255.0
Router(config-if)#encapsulation isl 1
Router(config-if)#exit
Router(config)#interface e0.2
Router(config-if)#ip address 164.106.2.1 255.255.255.0
Router(config-if)#encapsulation isl 2
```

CHAPTER SUMMARY

◻ Ethernet (CSMA/CD) is a media access method that was developed in the 1960s.

◻ Stations on an Ethernet LAN must listen to the network media before transmitting to ensure that no other station is currently transmitting.

◻ In the event that two stations transmit simultaneously on the same collision domain, there will be a collision.

◻ The transmitting stations must be able to recognize the collision and ensure that other stations know about the collision by transmitting a jam signal. Once the jam signal has cleared the network, other stations can begin transmitting, but the stations that caused the collision must wait for a random backoff period before attempting to transmit again.

◻ The delays caused by collisions on a network can seriously affect performance when collisions are in excess of 5% of the traffic on the collision domain.

◻ One way to reduce the number of collisions that occur on a network is to segment the network with a bridge, switch, or router.

◻ Switches do the most to divide the collision domain and reduce traffic without dividing the broadcast domain. This means that the LAN segment still appears to be a segment when it comes to broadcast and multicast traffic.

◻ However, a switch microsegments unicast traffic by routing frames directly from the incoming port to the destination port. This means that packets sent between two hosts on a LAN segment do not interrupt communication of other hosts on the segment. Switches are therefore able to increase the speed at which communications occur between multiple hosts on the segment.

❏ Another way to increase the speed at which a LAN operates is to upgrade from Ethernet to Fast Ethernet. Moving from Ethernet to Fast Ethernet allows you to increase the speed at which frames are transferred on the wire, thereby increasing the performance of the network.

❏ To fully implement Fast Ethernet, you will have to replace all the hubs, NICs, and any other network interfaces with interfaces that support Fast Ethernet. Several Fast Ethernet devices allow for compatibility between Fast Ethernet and standard Ethernet, but to take full advantage of Fast Ethernet, all components must be upgraded.

❏ Full duplex can also improve Ethernet performance over half-duplex operations because no collisions can occur on a full-duplex LAN.

❏ Full duplex also allows frames to be sent and received simultaneously, which makes a 10-Mbps full-duplex connection seem like two 10-Mbps half-duplex connections.

❏ As with Fast Ethernet, full-duplex operations are only supported by devices designed for this type of communication. This means that the half-duplex devices on a network will have to be completely replaced in order to take advantage of the speed offered by full-duplex operations.

❏ The Spanning Tree Protocol (STP), which is enabled by default on most bridges and switches, allows administrators to create physical loops between bridges and switches without creating logical loops that would create a problem for packet delivery.

❏ Another way to increase the performance, flexibility, and security of a network is to implement VLANs via switches.

❏ VLANs are separate broadcast domains that are not limited by physical configurations. Instead, a VLAN is a logical broadcast domain implemented via one or more switches.

❏ Performance benefits associated with VLANs are derived from limiting the amount of broadcast traffic that would naturally pass through a switch without filtration. The enhanced flexibility to assign any port on any switch to a particular VLAN makes moving, adding, and changing network configurations easier.

❏ Since on a VLAN broadcast traffic can be limited to a specific group of computers, security is also enhanced by making it more difficult for eavesdropping systems to learn the configuration of a network. In addition, the microsegmentation of unicast traffic makes it even more difficult to intercept useful data passed between two hosts.

❏ VLAN information is communicated to switches using the VLAN trunking protocol (VTP).

13

KEY TERMS

100Base-FX — A Fast Ethernet implementation over multimode fiber-optic (MMF) cabling. The maximum segment length is 412 meters.

100Base-T4 — A 100-Mbps Fast Ethernet implementation that uses four pairs of either Category 3, 4, or 5 UTP cable. The maximum segment length is 100 meters.

100Base-TX — A Fast Ethernet implementation that uses two pairs of either Category 5 unshielded twisted-pair (UTP) or shielded twisted-pair (STP). 100Base-TX operates at 100 Mbps with a maximum segment distance of 100 meters.

5-4-3 rule — The networking rule that stipulates that between stations on a 10-Mbps half-duplex LAN, there can be no more than 5 wire segments connected, the maximum number of repeaters or hubs between the segments is 4, and the maximum number of populated hubs is 3.

access list — A list of criteria to which all packets are compared.

adaptive cut-through — A method of switching whereby the switch uses the cut-through technique unless network errors reach a certain threshold; then, it automatically switches to store-and-forward switching until the error rate returns to an acceptable level. Also known as **error sensing**.

alignment error — A frame that has both an FCS error and an entire octet missing from the frame.

asymmetric switching — A type of LAN switching that allows for multiple speeds of network communication; a switch that supports both 10-Mbps and 100-Mbps communications is an example of asymmetric switching.

backoff period — A random interval used by devices that have caused a collision on an Ethernet network during which the devices cannot send, to prevent them from causing another collision immediately after the one they have just caused.

bit time — The duration of time to transmit one data bit on a network, which is 100 nanoseconds on a 10-Mbps Ethernet network or 10 nanoseconds on a 100-Mbps Ethernet network.

blocking — A port state on a switch that indicates that the port is receiving and sending BPDUs, but is not receiving and forwarding data frames in order to prevent logical loops in the network.

bridge — A device that segments a network at the Data Link layer by filtering traffic based on the MAC address.

bridge protocol data unit (BPDU) — An STP management message used to transfer status information about the Spanning Tree configuration of a switched and/or bridged network. Also known as **configuration bridge protocol data unit (CBPDU)**.

bridging table — A table maintained on a bridge that maps MAC addresses to the bridge port through which they can be accessed.

broadcast — A frame that is addressed to all stations on the broadcast domain. The destination MAC address is set to FFFFFFFFFFFF so that all local stations will process the packet.

broadcast domain — A logical or physical group of devices that will receive broadcast traffic from each other on a LAN.

broadcast storm — An error condition in which broadcast traffic is above 126 packets per second and network communications are impeded. This is typically the result of a software configuration error or programming error.

Carrier Sense Multiple Access with Collision Detection (CSMA/CD) — An Ethernet networking method defined by IEEE standard 802.3, which states that an Ethernet station must first listen before transmitting on a network. Any station can transmit as long as there are no transmissions active on the network. If two stations transmit simultaneously, a collision will occur, and those stations must detect the collision and reset themselves.

carrier signal — A transmitted electromagnetic pulse or wave on the network wire that indicates that a transmission is in progress.

collision domain — The area on a network in which collision can occur; a section of network that is not separated by routers, switches, or bridges.

configuration bridge protocol data unit (CBPDU) — *See* **bridge protocol data unit (BPDU)**.

content-addressable memory (CAM) — A memory location on a switch that contains the MAC address-to-switch port mapping information, which the switch uses to forward frames to the appropriate destination.

contention method — The method by which computers on a network must share the available capacity of the network wire with other computers.

cut-through — A switching technique in which an Ethernet frame is forwarded immediately after the destination address is deciphered. This method offers the lowest latency, but does not reduce packet errors.

default VLAN — The default configuration of every port on a switch. Same as VLAN 1.

disabled — A port state on a switch that indicates that the port is neither receiving BPDUs nor forwarding frames.

error sensing — *See* **adaptive cut-through**.

Ethernet — *See* **Carrier Sense Multiple Access with Collision Detection (CSMA/CD)**.

Fast Ethernet — Defined in IEEE 802.3u; any of the following 100-Mbps Ethernet LAN technologies: 100Base-T4, 100Base-TX, 100Base-FX.

fast forward — Indicates that a switch is in cut-through mode.

forwarding — The state of a port on a switch or bridge that indicates that it will learn MAC addresses and forward frames out that port.

fragment free — A method of switching whereby the switch reads the first 64 bytes of the incoming frame before forwarding it to the destination port(s).

frame check sequence (FCS) — A calculation based on the size of a transmitted data frame that verifies whether it was received intact.

frame check sequence (FCS) error — An error that occurs when the calculation in the FCS field indicates that a frame was not received intact.

13

frame filtering — A technique used on early VLAN implementations that employed the use of multiple switching tables.

frame identification — *See* **frame tagging**.

frame tagging — A method of VLAN identification endorsed by the IEEE 802.1q specification that calls for an additional four-byte field in the VLAN frame after the source and destination addresses in the data packet. Also known as **frame identification**.

full-duplex — A connection that allows communication in two directions at once; common telephone connections are typically full-duplex because people can talk and listen at the same time.

gateway — A combination of software and hardware that translates between different protocol suites.

giant — *See* **long frame**.

half-duplex — A connection that allows communication in two directions, but not simultaneously; the circuit can be used for sending or receiving bits in only one direction at a time.

IEEE 802.10 (FDDI) — A frame-tagging method used to identify VLANs trunked across Fiber Distributed Data Interfaces (FDDI).

IEEE 802.1q — The IEEE standard that defines VLAN implementations and recommends frame tagging as the way in which switches should identify VLANs. Used by Cisco switches for compatability with non-Cisco switches.

IEEE 802.3u — The IEEE standard that defines Fast Ethernet implementations, including 100Base-T4, 100Base-TX, and 100Base-FX.

interframe gap — The time required between the transmission of data frames on the network: 9.6 microseconds.

interpacket gap (IPG) — *See* **interframe gap**.

Inter-Switch Link (ISL) protocol — A frame-tagging method for VLANs proprietary to Cisco devices. Uses a 26-byte header.

jabber — A frame that is longer than the 1518 bytes acceptable for transmission between stations and that also has an FCS error.

jam signal — A 32-bit signal that is sent by the first station to detect a collision on an Ethernet network; ensures that all other stations are aware of the collision.

LAN Emulation (LANE) — A frame-tagging method used for VLANs on Asynchronous Transfer Mode (ATM) devices.

late collision — A situation that occurs when two stations transmit more than 64 bytes of their frames before detecting a collision.

latency — The lag or delay that a device or part of the network media causes; for example, fiber-optic cable delays a transmitted signal 1 bit time every 10 meters.

learning — A transitory state on a bridge or switch port that indicates it is trying to learn new MAC addresses and correct its bridge table before forwarding frames on the network; used to prevent loops during the election of a new root bridge.

listening — A transitory state on a bridge or switch port that is used during the election of a new root bridge; the port does not learn MAC addresses nor does it forward data frames when in this state.

logical loop — A situation that occurs when a packet can be routed in an endless loop around a network because bridging tables and/or routing tables reference each other as the destination for a given address.

long frame — An Ethernet frame that is over the 1518 bytes acceptable for transmission between stations.

management VLAN — The default configuration of every port on a switch. Same as VLAN1.

media access method — *See* **network access method**.

microsegmentation — Increasing the number of collision domains without increasing the number of subnets.

modified cut-through — *See* **fragment free**.

multicast — A frame that is addressed to a group of systems; typically used in radio- or television-style broadcasting on the network.

multimode fiber-optic (MMF) cable — Fiber-optic cabling that allows for multiple simultaneous light transmissions.

multiport bridge — Another name for a switch.

network access method — The process by which network interface cards and devices communicate data on a network; an example is CSMA/CD. Also known as **media access method**.

NIC error — An error that indicates that a NIC is unable to transmit/receive a packet.

physical path loops — A loop that occurs when network devices are connected to one another by two or more physical media links.

port-based memory buffering — A memory buffer on a switch assigned by port, equally; doesn't allow for dynamic allocation of buffer space according to the activity level of a port.

preamble — Binary timing information that precedes an Ethernet frame; used by the receiving station to synchronize its clock circuits so the frame can be received correctly.

propagation delay — *See* **latency**.

protocol analyzer — A hardware or software device that can capture and analyze network packets and that is used to analyze traffic flow and packet errors, and to track network problems.

root bridge — The bridge or switch that is designated the point of reference (point of origin) in STP operations. Also known as a root device.

root device — *See* **root bridge**.

root port — The communications port on a non-root bridge device that is used for BPDU communication between itself and the root bridge.

router — A device that segments a network at the Network layer by filtering on logical addresses. Creates networks or subnetworks.

13

runt — *See* **short frame**.

shared memory buffering — Dynamic memory buffer that is shared by all switch ports and allocated according to the needs of the ports; ports that have more activity and/or larger frames to process are allowed to utilize more memory buffer space.

short frame — A frame that is smaller than the 64-byte minimum frame transmission size required by Ethernet.

slot time — 512 bit times, which should be slightly longer than the time it takes to transmit a 64-byte frame on an Ethernet wire.

Spanning Tree Algorithm (STA) — The algorithm used by STP to ensure that logical loops are not created in the presence of physical loops on a network.

Spanning Tree Protocol (STP) — The Data Link layer protocol used by switches and bridges to prevent logical loops in a network, even though physical loops may exist.

stable state — The normal operational states of ports when the root bridge is available and all paths are functioning as expected.

start frame delimiter (SFD) — The one-octet binary pattern (10101011) that indicates that the preamble is over and that the following information should be considered the actual data frame.

sticky-learn — A term used when a switch automatically learns MAC addresses during communications and configures them as permanent due to a limit set by an administrator on the number of MAC addresses that can use a particular port.

store-and-forward — A switching method in which the entire transmitted frame is read into a switch's buffer before being forwarded by the switch. This method offers the greatest error reduction, but the highest latency. *See* **cut-through and adaptive cut-through**.

switch — A device that connects devices on a LAN and segments collision domains by port.

switched bandwidth — A switching technique whereby the total network bandwidth is dedicated to each unicast transmission, even if there are multiple unicast transmissions through the switch at the same time. Unicast traffic between devices on a switch do not share the total bandwidth of the network.

symmetric switching — A type of LAN switching that requires all devices to be operating at the same speed; it does not allow for a mix of 10-Mbps and 100-Mbps communications.

transitory state — The operational states of ports that prevent logical loops during a period of transition from one root bridge to another.

transmission time — The time it takes for a transmission to go from the source host to the destination host.

unicast — A frame that is sent/addressed to a single destination host; compare to multicast and broadcast.

virtual LAN (VLAN) — A logical broadcast domain on a LAN, created by one or more switches, that is not constrained by the physical configuration.

VLAN Trunking Protocol (VTP) — A Data Link layer protocol used to track VLAN membership changes across trunk links between VTP-enabled devices.

VTP client — A VTP device that receives and shares VTP information, but one that does not add, modify, or delete information and does not store the VTP database in NVRAM.

VTP domain — A group of VTP-enabled devices configured under one name to share VLAN information.

VTP pruning — An option configured for an entire VTP domain that prohibits the forwarding of VTP updates about VLANs disabled on specific trunk links.

VTP server — A VTP device that is capable of adding, modifying, sending, and deleting VTP configuration information.

VTP transparent — A device that does not participate in receiving or managing VTP domains, but will forward VTP information through its trunk ports.

REVIEW QUESTIONS

1. The IEEE standard 802.1q recommends which type of VLAN identification method?

   a. frame filtering

   b. frame tagging

   c. frame segmenting

   d. frame sequencing

2. Which of the following types of switching methods reads the first 64 bytes of a frame before forwarding it?

   a. store-and-forward

   b. cut-through

   c. fragment-free

   d. adaptive

3. The _____ provides sufficient spacing between frames so that network interfaces have time to process a packet before receiving another.

   a. interframe gap

   b. jam signal

   c. backoff period

   d. latency

4. Which devices look at a MAC address when making their forwarding decision? (Choose all that apply.)

   a. switch

   b. repeater

   c. bridge

   d. router

13

5. Which of the following network media provides the lowest latency?

   a. STP

   b. Category 3 UTP

   c. Category 4 UTP

   d. Category 5 UTP

   e. Fiber-optic cable

6. Which of the following correctly describes microsegmentation?

   a. Creating additional segments with passive hubs

   b. Creating additional segments with routers

   c. Creating additional segments with fewer users per segment via layer 2

   d. Limiting network segments to no more than 10 users

7. Which of the following Ethernet errors describes a packet that has a bad FCS and is over 1518 bytes?

   a. runt

   b. short

   c. jabber

   d. bad FCS frame

8. When two Ethernet stations are able to send more than 64 bytes of their data frames before detecting a collision, this is called a _____.

   a. jabber

   b. jam signal

   c. slot time

   d. late collision

9. The minimum size of an Ethernet frame should be _____ bytes.

   a. 32

   b. 64

   c. 512

   d. 1518

10. Collisions and Ethernet errors typically occur within the first _____ bytes of an Ethernet frame, which is why fragment-free switching catches most Ethernet errors.

    a. 64

    b. 512

    c. 1024

    d. 1518

11. Which of the following describes a method of Ethernet networking that does not have collisions?

   a. Fast Ethernet

   b. 100-Mbps Ethernet

   c. Full-duplex Ethernet

   d. Half-duplex Ethernet

12. Which of the following switching types has the highest latency?

   a. store-and-forward

   b. cut-through

   c. adaptive

   d. fragment-free

13. If a broadcast from one computer causes multiple stations to respond with additional broadcast traffic, and the level of broadcast traffic goes above 126 broadcasts per second, the situation is deemed a(n) _____.

   a. broadcast storm

   b. transmission overload

   c. excessive burst

   d. jabber

14. Which of the following fall under the heading of Fast Ethernet? (Choose all that apply.)

   a. 10BaseT

   b. 100Base-T4

   c. 10BaseF

   d. 100Base-TX

   e. 100Base-FX

15. Which of the following are reasons that a bridge port would be placed in the forwarding state? (Choose all correct answers.)

   a. The port is on the root bridge.

   b. The port is connected to multiple bridges.

   c. The port is the root port.

   d. The port is non-operational.

16. Which of the following are able to divide a collision domain? (Choose all that apply.)

   a. switch

   b. bridge

   c. router

   d. hub

13

17. Which of the following allows you to reorganize broadcast domains no matter what the physical configuration dictates?

    a. router

    b. VLAN

    c. bridge

    d. switch

18. If you attach a hub with five stations into a switch port that is configured for VLANs, how many different VLANs will the devices on the hubs be in?

    a. Five

    b. Three

    c. Two

    d. One

19. Which of the following are advantages of VLANs? (Choose all that apply.)

    a. VLANs make relocating devices easier.

    b. Separate VLANs do not require routers.

    c. VLANs increase effective bandwidth utilization.

    d. VLANs restructure broadcast domains.

20. Which of the following is a benefit that routers provide on the VLAN to increase security?

    a. Dividing broadcast domains

    b. Dividing collision domains

    c. Allowing for the creation of access lists

    d. Bridging the IP to IPX layer 3 protocol gap

21. When collisions are above 5%, you should consider:

    a. segmenting the LAN.

    b. increasing traffic on the LAN.

    c. monitoring traffic on the LAN.

    d. adding hubs to the LAN.

22. Which of the following are advantages that Cisco switches can provide over hubs? (Choose all that apply.)

    a. Separating collision domains

    b. Increased bandwidth for individual users

    c. Reduced latency

    d. Concurrent frame forwarding

23. Which of the following are true of half-duplex operation on a CSMA/CD network? (Choose all that apply.)

    a. The transmitting NIC loops back its transmission.

    b. The NIC listens to the media before transmitting.

    c. The transmitting NIC compares the original frame with the looped-back frame to determine whether there was a collision.

    d. Collisions are not possible in a half-duplex Ethernet.

24. The _____ switching method begins forwarding the incoming frame immediately after reading the destination address.

    a. cut-through

    b. store-and-forward

    c. adaptive

    d. fragment-free

25. Which of the following are VTP modes of operation? (Choose all that apply.)

    a. client

    b. server

    c. transparent

    d. blocking

CASE PROJECTS

1. Your network administration consulting team at Winslow Networks has been assigned to a new project. Your client has requested that you optimize their LAN. Before you can begin making recommendations, what type of performance statistics should your team collect, at a minimum? What other information would be useful?

2. A local company has decided to upgrade its LAN configuration from a configuration with five hubs and a single router to one that implements 10 switches. The switches the company is planning to buy have many more ports than necessary to support each segment. However, the company wants to divide the 10 different departments into separate entities. The company is planning on using routers between each switch, thereby dividing the broadcast domains between the switches. What other options for configuring its network should the company consider? Moe has suggested foregoing the routers and using VLANs to divide the departments. What do you think?

3. The Flagstone Corporation has purchased a Cisco 1900 series switch and wants you to configure it. What kind of interface is available for configuration? What are the default settings on the switch? Does the switch support VLANs?

13

APPENDIX

A

CCNA CERTIFICATION
OBJECTIVES

This appendix maps the Cisco CCNA certification objectives with the book chapter in which these objectives are covered. There are eight categories of objectives assigned by Cisco. These categories are:

- ◆ Bridging/Switching
- ◆ OSI Reference Model & Layered Communications
- ◆ Network Protocols
- ◆ Routing
- ◆ WAN Protocols
- ◆ Network Management
- ◆ LAN Design
- ◆ Cisco Basics, IOS & Network Basics

The following tables, Tables A-1 through A-8, map the objectives of each category to a specific chapter. Primary references to each objective are in bold type in the tables.

Table A-1   Bridging/Switching

Objective	Chapter: Section
Name and describe two switching methods.	**Chapter 13: LAN Switching**
Distinguish between cut-through and store-and-forward LAN switching.	**Chapter 13: LAN Switching**
Describe the operation of the Spanning Tree Protocol and its benefits.	**Chapter 13: LAN Switching**
Describe the benefits of virtual LANs.	**Chapter 13: Virtual LANs**

Table A-2   OSI Reference Model & Layered Communications

Objective	Chapter: Section
Describe data link and network addresses and identify key differences between them.	**Chapter 1: Understanding the OSI Model**
Define and describe the function of the MAC address.	**Chapter 1: Understanding the OSI Model**
List the key internetworking functions for the OSI Network layer.	**Chapter 1: Understanding the OSI Model**
Identify at least three reasons why the industry uses a layered model.	**Chapter 1: Understanding the OSI Model**
Describe the two parts of network addressing; then identify the parts in specific protocol address examples.	Chapter 1: Understanding the OSI Model **Chapter 3: IP Addressing**
Define and explain the five conversion steps of data encapsulation.	**Chapter 1: Understanding the OSI Model**
Describe connection-oriented network service and connectionless network service, and identify their key differences.	**Chapter 1: Understanding the OSI Model** Chapter 3: Overview of the TCP/IP Protocol Suite
Identify the parts in specific protocol address examples.	Chapter 1: Understanding the OSI Model **Chapter 3: IP Addressing** Chapter 9: IPX/SPX Addressing
Describe the advantages of LAN segmentation.	**Chapter 2: Network Segmentation**
Describe LAN segmentation using bridges.	**Chapter 2: Bridges**
Describe LAN segmentation using routers.	**Chapter 2: Routers**
Describe LAN segmentation using switches.	**Chapter 2: Switches**
Describe the benefits of network segmentation with bridges.	**Chapter 2: Bridges**
Describe the benefits of network segmentation with routers.	**Chapter 2: Routers**
Describe the benefits of network segmentation with switches.	**Chapter 2: Switches**

Table A-3   Network Protocols

Objective	Chapter: Section
Describe the different classes of IP addresses (and subnetting).	Chapter 3: IP Addressing
Identify the functions of the TCP/IP network-layer protocol.	Chapter 3: Overview of the TCP/IP Protocol Suite
Identify the functions performed by ICMP.	Chapter 3: Overview of the TCP/IP Protocol Suite
Configure IP addresses.	Chapter 7: IP on the Router; IP on the Switch
Verify IP addresses.	Chapter 7: IP Connectivity
List the required IPX address and encapsulation type.	Chapter 9: IPX/SPX Data Link Layer Frame Types; IPX/SPX Addressing

Table A-4   Routing

Objective	Chapter: Section
Define flow control and describe the three basic methods used in networking.	Chapter 3: Overview of the TCP/IP Protocol Suite
Add the RIP routing protocol to your configuration.	Chapter 8: Routing Information Protocol
Add the IGRP routing protocol to your configuration.	Chapter 8: Interior Gateway Routing Protocol

Table A-5   WAN Protocols

Objective	Chapter: Section
Recognize key Frame Relay terms and features.	Chapter 12: All Sections
List commands to configure Frame Relay LMIs, maps, and subinterfaces.	Chapter 12: Frame Configuration
List commands to monitor Frame Relay operation in the router.	Chapter 12: Monitoring Frame Relay
State a relevant use and context for ISDN networking.	Chapter 11: ISDN
Identify ISDN protocols, function groups, reference points, and channels.	Chapter 11: ISDN
Identify PPP operations to encapsulate WAN data on Cisco routers.	Chapter 11: PPP

Table A-6   Network Management

Objective	Chapter: Section
Configure standard access lists to filter IP traffic.	Chapter 10: Standard IP Access Lists
Configure extended access lists to filter IP traffic.	Chapter 10: Extended IP Access Lists
Monitor and verify selected access list operations on the router.	Chapter 10: Standard IP Access Lists; Extended IP Access Lists

Table A-7   LAN Design

Objective	Chapter: Section
Describe full- and half-duplex Ethernet operation.	Chapter 13: Ethernet Operations
Describe network congestion problems in Ethernet networks.	Chapter 13: Ethernet Operations
Describe the features and benefits of Fast Ethernet.	Chapter 13: Ethernet Operations
Describe the guidelines and distance limitations of Fast Ethernet.	Chapter 13: Ethernet Operations

Table A-8   Cisco Basics, IOS & Network Basics

Objective	Chapter: Section
Examine router elements.	Chapter 6: Router Components
Manage configuration files from the privilege EXEC mode.	Chapter 6: Cisco Router User Interface
Control router passwords, identification, and banner.	Chapter 6: Cisco Router User Interface
Identify the main Cisco IOS software commands for router	Chapter 6: Cisco Router User Interface
Log in to a router in both user and privilege modes.	Chapter 6: Cisco Router User Interface
Check an initial configuration using the setup command.	Chapter 6: Cisco Router User Interface
Use the context-sensitive help facility.	Chapter 6: Cisco Router User Interface
Use the command history and editing features.	Chapter 6: Cisco Router User Interface
List the commands to load Cisco IOS software from: Flash memory, a TFTP server, or ROM.	Chapter 7: Router Setup and Startup
Prepare to backup, upgrade, and load a backup Cisco IOS software image.	Chapter 7: Router Setup and Startup
List problems that each routing type encounters when dealing with topology changes, and describe techniques to reduce the number of these problems.	Chapter 8: Routing Protocols Chapter 13:LAN Switching
Prepare the initial configuration of your router and enable IP.	Chapter 7: IP on the Router

B

ADDITIONAL RESOURCES

This appendix contains additional sources for information on subjects covered in this course.

INTERNET RESOURCES

Internet resources are invaluable for obtaining information on the latest news, technology, and standards. The Internet and Web resources listed in this section are divided into different categories, as follows:

- Standards organizations
- Technology reference
- Networking overviews and tutorials
- Technical forums
- Cisco routers
- Exam preparation resources

Standards Organizations

The following are sites for organizations that provide networking standards discussed in this course:

- American National Standards Institute: *http://www.ansi.org/*
- Electronic Industries Alliance: *http://www.eia.org*
- Telecommunications Industry Association: *http://www.tiaonline.org*
- Institute of Electrical and Electronics Engineers (IEEE): *http://www.ieee.org/*
- Internet Engineering Task Force (IETF): *http://www.ietf.org/*
- International Telecommunication Union (ITU): *http://www.itu.int/*
- International Organization for Standardization (ISO): *http://www.iso.ch/*
- International Electrotechnical Commission (IEC): *http://www.iec.ch/*
- Optimized Engineering Corporation Compendium: *http://www.optimized.com/COMPENDI/*
- World Wide Web Consortium (W3C): *http://www.w3.org/*

- RFC Editor: *http://www.rfc-editor.org/*
- Computer and Communications Standards: *http://www.cmpcmm.com/cc/standards.html*
- Underwriters Laboratories (UL): *http://www.ul.com*

Technology Reference

These Web sites have online definitions for computer and networking terminology:

- Babel: Glossary of Computer Oriented Abbreviations and Acronyms: *http://www.geocities.com/ikind_babel/babel/babel.html*
- Federal Standard 1037C: Glossary of Telecommunications Terms: *http://glossary.its.bldrdoc.gov/fs-1037/*
- Webopedia: *http://www.pcwebopaedia.com/*
- Whatis.com: *http://www.whatis.com*

Networking Overviews and Tutorials

An introduction to various networking concepts is provided on the following Web sites:

- Alliance Datacom's Frame Relay tutorial list: *http://www.alliancedatacom.com/frame-relay-tutorials.htm*
- Charles Spurgeon's Ethernet Web Site: *http://www.ethermanage.com/ethernet/ethernet.html*
- Interoperability Lab Tutorials: *http://www.iol.unh.edu/training/*
- Optimized Engineering Corporation: *http://www.optimized.com/*

Technical Forums

The following sites contain technical information, discussions, and links to information covered in this course:

- Frame Relay Forum: *http://www.frforum.com/*
- Open Group: *http://www.opengroup.org/*
- Protocols.com: *http://www.protocols.com*

Cisco Routers

The following locations have information specific to Cisco routers:

- Cisco: *http://www.cisco.com*
  - Cisco product documentation list: *http://www.cisco.com/univercd/cc/td/doc/product/*

B

- Cisco command reference documents by subject: *http://www.cisco.com/univercd/cc/td/doc/product/software/ios100/rpcr/index.htm*

■ Cisco routing tutorial: *http://www.alliancedatacom.com/cisco-routing-tutorial.htm*

Exam Preparation Resources

The following Web sites contain information and technical papers concerning the CCNA exam:

■ CCPrep.com: *http://www.ccprep.com*

■ CertNotes: *http://www.certnotes.com*

■ Cramsession: *http://www.cramsession.com*

■ Transcender: *http://www.transcender.com*

■ CertIndex: *http://www.certindex.com*

■ Boson Software: *http://www.boson.com*

■ CICPREP: *http://www.cicprep.com*

C

A NETWORKING PROFESSIONAL'S TOOLKIT

Throughout this book, you have learned about the many tools you may use while implementing, analyzing, and troubleshooting a network. Although information on networking devices or software packages is readily available, it is not always easy to find details about the tools used by networking professionals. This appendix provides pictures of networking tools, some familiar and some probably unfamiliar, along with their proper names and uses. You can often find these tools together in toolkits with carrying cases. Toolkit providers include Aven Tools, Black Box, Curtis, Paladin, and Siemon.

Figure C-1 A networking professional's toolkit

Many of the tools used by networking professionals are similar or identical to tools used by electricians. Tools pictured in the following figures fall into this category.

Figure C-2 Soldering iron, solder, and solder wick; used for repairing connections

C

Figure C-3   Pliers; used for bending cable or components or working in tight spaces

Figure C-4   Screwdriver with several different head types; used for installing and uninstalling components

Figure C-5 Hex keyset; used for removing computer covers or components

Figure C-6 Pocket flashlights; used to illuminate the interior of devices

Figure C-7 Wire cutters

Figure C-8 Precision knife

Other tools used by networking professionals are unique to computer repair or telephony technicians. Tools pictured in the following figures fall into this category.

Figure C-9 Cable preparation tool, including wire stripper and cutter; used for preparing cable for termination

Figure C-10 Crimp tools; used for crimping wires into terminators

C

Figure C-11   Punch-down block tool; used for crimping wires into punch-down blocks

Figure C-12   Cable testing tools; used for verifying cable integrity

Figure C-13   Cable ties; used for holding bundles of cables together

Figure C-14   Magnetic extractor; used for retrieving small components

Figure C-15   Extractors; used for retrieving small components

Figure C-16   Tweezers; used for holding and maneuvering small components

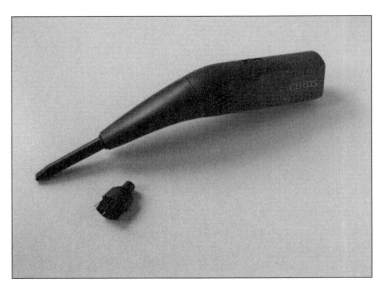

Figure C-17   Antistatic vacuum; used for cleaning electronic devices

D

COMMAND SUMMARY

This appendix lists the commands presented in this course. You should review these commands before you attempt the CCNA certification examination. The router commands in this section are organized into the following categories:

- ◆ Identification and navigation
- ◆ Passwords
- ◆ Router Startup configuration
- ◆ Examining the router
- ◆ Interface configuration
- ◆ IP-related commands
- ◆ IPX commands
- ◆ Access list configuration and status commands
- ◆ WAN configuration
- ◆ VLAN configuration

The tables in the following sections list the mode, command syntax, and description of each command. The mode column is abbreviated so that you can see the router/switch configuration mode that you must be in to properly execute the command. The following list illustrates the symbols used in the command tables:

- >: Symbolizes user mode where the command prompt looks like hostname>

- #: Symbolizes privileged mode, or enable mode, in which the command prompt looks like hostname#

- GC: Indicates global configuration mode, in which the command prompt looks like hostname(config)#

- IF: Indicates interface configuration mode, in which the command prompt looks like hostname(config-if)#

- CL: Indicates line configuration mode, in which the command prompt looks like hostname(config-line)#

- CR: Indicates router configuration mode, in which the command prompt looks like hostname(config-router)#

- CS: Indicates subinterface mode, in which the command prompt looks like hostname(config-subif)#

- NA: Indicates that the mode is not significant for this command

If multiple symbols are listed in the mode field, the command will work with all modes listed.

 This is not a comprehensive guide to all commands and options with which you can configure a router; such a guide would be too large for this appendix. This is an abridged guide that summarizes only the commands covered in this course. If you would like to see a larger list of Cisco commands, visit the Cisco Web site at *http://www.cisco.com/univercd/cc/td/doc/product/software/ios100/rpcr/index.htm*.

IDENTIFICATION AND NAVIGATION

The commands shown in the following table are basic navigation commands for the router. These commands allow you to change the router into different configuration modes and even set the identity and clock of the router.

Table D-1   Identification and navigation commands

Mode	Command Syntax	Description
>	enable	Allows you to access privileged mode from user mode
#	disable	Returns prompt to user mode from privileged mode

Table D-1   Identification and navigation commands (continued)

Mode	Command Syntax	Description
#	configure terminal	Allows you to access global configuration mode
GC	line console 0	Allows you to configure the console line that is used to access the router; often used to set a console line password; see Table D2
GC	line vty *[#]*	Allows you to access line configuration mode for virtual terminal lines; typing "line vty 0 4" affects all five virtual terminal lines at the same time; typing a single number (0–4) allows configuration of the virtual terminal number that you entered
GC	interface *[interface type and number]*	Allows you to access interface configuration mode; requires that you enter the type and number of the interface after the command; to configure the first Ethernet interface on your router, type "interface ethernet 0"
GC	interface *[subinterface type and number]*	Allows you to enter subinterface configuration mode; when creating an interface with Frame Relay with this command, add point-to-point or multipoint to this command
GC	router *[routing protocol or static]*	Allows you to enter router configuration mode; requires that you specify the name of a routing protocol or indicate static (to indicate a manually configured routing table); to enable RIP routing, for example, type "router rip"
GC	hostname *[name]*	Allows you to set the hostname for your router; requires that you enter the name after the hostname command; for example, to name your router "clyde", you would type "hostname clyde"
GC	banner motd *[banner end character]*	Allows you to set the "message of the day" banner; to use this command, type "banner motd" followed by the single character that you want to end the message; for example, if you type banner motd @, the router prompt will move to the next line, and everything you type following that will be your banner message, until you enter the @ character, which indicates that you are finished typing your banner message; to see your message, reboot the router
NA	ctrl+z	Returns you to enable mode; do not press the plus key; press Ctrl+Z
#	clock set *[hh:mm:ss month day year]*	Used to set the time and date on the router

D

Table D-1   Identification and navigation commands (continued)

Mode	Command Syntax	Description
#	reload *[in hh:mm]* *[month day	day month]*	Reboots the router; setting a time delay or month and day for the reboot is optional
NA	exit	Logs you out from the > or # prompt; from other prompts, command takes you back one level; for example, typing exit at the router(config-if)# prompt takes you back to the router(config)# prompt
NA	CTRL ^	Allows you to abort a command in progress; executed by pressing Ctrl+Shift+6
> #	quit	Logs you out of the router

PASSWORDS

The commands shown in the following table allow you to configure passwords for your router. Do not forget the passwords that you configure; you will need them when you want to access your router in the future.

Table D-2   Commands for configuring passwords

Mode	Command Syntax	Description
GC	enable password *[password]*	Allows you to set the privileged mode password, which is used to enter privileged mode
GC	enable secret *[password]*	Allows you to set the encrypted privileged mode password; overrides the enable password when configured
CL	login *[Enter]* password *[password]*	Allows you to set a line password; requires that you first type "login", press the Return or Enter key, then type "password" followed by the password you would like to set

ROUTER/SWITCH GENERAL & STARTUP CONFIGURATION

The commands listed in this section are vital to configuring and managing the configuration of the router or switch. These commands cover saving, copying, and replacing the contents of the IOS and the device's configuration file.

Table D-3 Startup and running configuration commands

Mode	Command Syntax	Description
#	hostname *[hostname]*	Configures the hostname of a router or switch
#	copy running-config startup-config	Copies the router running configuration to the NVRAM on the router; saves configuration changes you make while the router is running, so that they are implemented next time the router is restarted
#	copy startup-config running-config	Copies the router startup configuration from NVRAM to the running configuration. Does not replace the running configuration.
#	copy tftp flash	Copies a router IOS file from a TFTP server to flash memory
#	copy flash tftp	Copies a router IOS file from flash memory to a TFTP server
#	copy tftp startup-config	Copies the router configuration file from a TFTP server to the startup configuration in NVRAM on the router
#	copy startup-config tftp	Copies the router startup configuration in NVRAM to a TFTP server
#	erase flash	Erases the flash memory on the router
#	erase startup-config	Erases the router startup configuration from NVRAM
#	delete nvram	Erases the switch configuration
#	copy *tftp://tftp ip address/ IOS image/opcode*	Copies an IOS image to a switch from a TFTP server
#	copy nvram *tftp: //tftp ip addressname*	Copies the configuration of a switch to a TFTP server
#	copy *tftp://tftp ip address/ name* nvram	Copies the configuration stored on a TFTP server to the switch
GC	mac-address-table permanent *[mac#] [slot/#]*	Maps a permanent MAC address to a switch port
GC	switching-mode *[mode]*	Configures the switching mode (fast forward, fragment-free, or store-and-forward)

D

EXAMINING THE ROUTER & SWITCH

The following list of commands allows you to examine router & switch configuration, components, resources, and other statistics. These commands are useful for checking the device's performance and troubleshooting configuration problems.

Table D-4   Commands for examining components and configuration

Mode	Command Syntax	Description
> #	show clock	Displays the time and date
> #	show processes	Displays CPU utilization information
> #	show interface ethernet *[#]*	Shows statistics and configuration information for the Ethernet interface that is listed; requires that you enter the number of the interface after the command
> #	show interface serial *[#]*	Shows statistics and configuration information for the serial interface that is listed; requires that you enter the number of the interface after the command
> #	show interfaces	Lists configuration and statistics for all interfaces configured on the router
> #	show protocol	Shows the protocols configured on the system and indicates which interfaces are using them
> #	show history	Displays the last 10 commands executed
> #	show flash	Shows the flash file(s), size, name, and the amount of flash memory used, total, and available
> #	show cdp neighbor	Shows a list of Cisco devices that are directly attached to this device
> #	show cdp neighbor detail	Adds IP address information to output obtained from show cdp neighbor command
#	show running-config	Displays the currently running router configuration file
#	show startup-config	Displays the router startup configuration maintained in NVRAM
#	show mac-address-table	Displays the MAC address table of a switch
#	show port system	Displays the switching mode of a switch
> #	show version	Displays version information for the router/switch. On a router this includes the startup register setting, the router series number, how long the router has been up and running, and the IOS version number

INTERFACE CONFIGURATION

Interfaces are an important part of the router, and the next table lists those that are specific to interface configuration. Table D-9 lists additional interface configuration commands, as related to WAN configuration.

Table D-5 Interface configuration commands

Mode	Command Syntax	Description
GC	interface serial *[#]*	Allows you to configure the specific serial interface that you identify
GC	interface ethernet *[#]*	Allows you to configure the specific Ethernet interface on a router that you specify
GC	interface ethernet *[slot/#]*	On a switch, you enter the slot number and the port number to configure an interface
GC	interface fastethernet *[slot/#]*	On a switch, FastEthernet interfaces and slots must be specified when configuring
IF	encapsulation *[encapsulation type]*	Allows you to set the encapsulation type for your interface
GC	cdp run	Allows you to enable the Cisco Discovery Protocol on a device
GC	no cdp run	Allows you to disable the Cisco Discovery Protocol on a device
IF	cdp enable	Allows you to enable the Cisco Discovery Protocol on an interface
IF	no cdp enable	Allows you to disable the Cisco Discovery Protocol on an interface
IF	description *[description]*	Allows you to configure a description for an interface
IF	duplex *[mode]*	Sets the duplex type on a 10Mbps Ethernet interface (auto, full, full-flow-control, half)
IF	no shutdown	Tells the router or switch to not shutdown the interface; leave enabled
IF	loopback	Allows you to configure the interface for loopback that is used for testing purposes; information transmitted out that interface will be immediately returned on the receive circuit of that same interface
GC	interface *[interface #.subinterface #]*	Creates and/or accesses a subinterface; for example, to create a subinterface #1 off of S1, type "interface s1.1"

IP COMMANDS

The commands in the following table are related to the configuration, control, and troubleshooting of TCP/IP. They cover configuring an IP address and subnet mask, in addition to configuring routing protocols.

Table D-6   IP-related commands

Mode	Command Syntax	Description
IF	ip address [ip address][mask]	Sets the IP address and subnet mask for an interface on a router
GC	ip address [ip address][mask]	Sets the IP address and the subnet mask for an interface on a switch
GC	ip default-gateway [ip address]	Sets the default gateway for an interface on a switch
#	show ip	Shows the IP address configuration of a switch
IF CS	ip unnumbered [interface or logical interface]	Allows you to establish that the interface is to support the IP protocol, but not be assigned an IP address
GC	router rip	Enables RIP routing and accesses router configuration mode
GC	router igrp [autonomous system number]	Enables IGRP routing and accesses router configuration mode; requires that you enter an autonomous system number
CR	network [major network number]	Used after router rip and router igrp to indicate network number
GC	no ip routing	Disables IP routing on the router
GC	ip routing	Enables IP routing on the router
#	debug ip rip	Enables RIP debugging, which allows you to monitor RIP updates
#	debug ip igrp [transaction or events]	Enables IGRP transactions and/or event monitoring
#	no debug all	Disables all debugging activities
#	debug all	Enables all debugging options
#	undebug all	Disables all debugging activities
> #	show ip route	Displays the router's routing table
> #	ping [ip address I hostname]	Allows you to verify that a host is reachable either by IP address or host name
> #	telnet [ip address]	Allows the user to start a telnet session with a telnet server
> #	show ip protocol	Shows statistics for the IP protocol, such as routing protocol information, timers, networks serviced, and gateway information
> #	show ip interface [interface type and number]	Shows statistics for interfaces configured for IP; adding the specific interface type and number is optional; if you only type "show ip interface", all interfaces configured with IP will be shown

IPX COMMANDS

The following table illustrates how to configure IPX on the router with configuration, troubleshooting, and routing commands. To learn how to configure IPX access lists, see Table D-8.

Table D-7   IPX commands

Mode	Command Syntax	Description
IF CS	ipx network *[network number]* encapsulation *[frame type]*	Sets the IPX network address and frame type for the router's Ethernet interface
GC	ipx routing	Enables IPX routing on the router
GC	no ipx routing	Disables IPX routing on the router
#	show ipx route	Shows the IPX routing table
#	show ipx interface	Shows statistics for interfaces using IPX
#	show ipx traffic	Shows IPX sent and received packet statistics
#	debug ipx routing activity	Enables routing activity debugging
#	no debug ipx routing activity	Disables routing activity debugging

ACCESS LISTS

Access lists allow you to control the types of packets that are allowed to traverse the router. The following table illustrates the commands for both IPX and IP access list creation and configuration.

Table D-8   Access list configuration and status commands

Mode	Command Syntax	Description
GC	access-list *[list #]* *[permit	deny]* *[ip address]* *[mask]*	Creates a standard IP access list
GC	access-list *[list #]* *[permit	deny]* *[protocol]* *[source IP address]* *[source wildcard mask]* *[destination IP address]* *[destination wildcard mask]* *[operator]* *[port]* *[log]*	Creates an extended IP access list
GC	no access-list *[list #]*	Removes the access list indicated
IF	ip access-group *[list number]* *[in	out]*	Applies IP access list to interface
IF	no ip access-group *[list #]* *[in	out]*	Removes an IP access list from the interface
IF	ipx access-group *[list number]* *[in	out]*	Applies IPX access list to interface

D

Table D-8   Access list configuration and status commands (continued)

Mode	Command Syntax	Description
IF	no ipx access-group *[list #] [in	out]*	Removes an IPX access list from the interface
GC	access-list *[list #] [permit	deny] [source network/node address] [destination network/ node address]*	Creates a standard IPX access list
GC	access-list *[list#] [permit	deny] [protocol] [source network/ node] [socket] [destination network/node] [socket]*	Creates an extended IPX access list
GC	access-list *[list #] [permit	deny] [source network/node] [service-type]*	Creates a SAP filter
IF CS	ipx input-sap-filter *[list #]*	Applies input SAP filter to interface
IF CS	ipx output-sap-filter *[list #]*	Applies output SAP filter to interface
#	show ip access-lists	Shows all IP access lists
#	show access-list *[list #]*	Allows you to review all access lists; you can enter the access list number you would like to view instead of reviewing all

WAN CONFIGURATION

The following commands cover the WAN configuration techniques mentioned in this course. These commands allow you to configure ISDN, PPP, and Frame Relay interfaces.

Table D-9   WAN configuration commands

Mode	Command Syntax	Description
IF CS	bandwidth *[bandwidth]*	Sets the bandwidth allowed on the serial interface in kilobits per second
IF	clock rate *[clock rate]*	Sets the clock rate in bits per second for a serial interface
IF CS	encapsulation *[WAN protocol]*	Sets the encapsulation type for a serial interface; common options are PPP, Frame Relay, and HDLC; for example, to set the interface to PPP encapsulation, type "encapsulation ppp"

Table D-9   WAN configuration commands (continued)

Mode	Command Syntax	Description
IF CS	ppp authentication [chap | pap]	Sets the authentication type for ppp encapsulation; can be chap or pap; if both pap and chap are used, the order in which they are entered on the command line is the order in which they will be used
IF CS	frame-relay interface-dlci [dlci #]	Configures a DLCI number for a serial interface using Frame Relay encapsulation
IF CS	frame-relay lmi-type [lmi-type]	Sets the LMI type for a Frame Relay interface; options are cisco, q933i, and ansi
#	show frame-relay lmi	Allows you to view configuration and interface statistics concerning your Frame Relay interfaces using LMI; also shows LMI type
#	show frame-relay map	Displays the Frame Relay map
GC	isdn switch-type [switch identifier]	Sets the ISDN switch type to which the router will be configured to communicate
GC	isdn spid [spid channel designation] [SPID #]	Sets the Service Profile Identifier (SPID) for each ISDN channel

D

VLAN CONFIGURATION

The following commands cover the VLAN configuration techniques mentioned in this course. These commands work only on VLAN-enabled devices and assume configuration via a Cisco Catalyst 1900.

Table D-10   VLAN configuration commands

Mode	Command Syntax	Description
#	show vlan	Shows the VLAN configuration of the switch
#	show vlan-membership	Shows VLAN assignments by port number
#	show trunk [A/B] allowed-vlans	Shows the allowed VLANs on the selected trunk
#	delete vtp	Deletes the vtp configuration on the selected device
GC	vtp password [word]	Sets the VTP password for a domain
GC	vtp server	Sets the current device as a vtp server
GC	vtp client	Configures the current device as a vtp client
GC	vtp transparent	Sets the current device in vtp transparent mode
GC	vtp domain	Sets the vtp domain name
GC	vtp pruning [enable/disable]	Enables or disables VTP pruning

Table D-10   VLAN configuration commands (continued)

Mode	Command Syntax	Description
GC	vlan *[#]* name *[name]*	Configures the name of the specified VLAN number
IF	no trunk-vlan *[#]*	Disables the VLAN number from being able to traverse the trunk port
IF	trunk on	Configures VLAN trunking on the selected port
IF	vlan-membership static *[#]*	Configures the VLAN membership for the selected port

Glossary

10Base2 — An Ethernet standard that specifies a 10-Mbps baseband transmission over thin Ethernet (RG-58); the maximum transmission distance of any single segment is 185 meters, which is represented by the number two at the end of the specification.

10Base5 — An Ethernet standard that indicates a 10-Mbps baseband transmission over a maximum segment length of 500 meters; the type of cable used in this standard is called thick Ethernet, or thicknet, and uses RG-8 coaxial cable.

10BaseT — An Ethernet standard that specifies a 10-Mbps baseband transmission over twisted-pair cabling; the maximum segment length is 100 meters.

100BaseT — An Ethernet standard that provides a 100-Mbps baseband transfer rate over twisted-pair cabling. Also called Fast Ethernet.

100Base-T4 — A 100-Mbps Fast Ethernet implementation that uses four pairs of either Category 3, 4, or 5 UTP cable. The maximum segment length is 100 meters.

100Base-TX — A Fast Ethernet implementation that uses two pairs of either Category 5 unshielded twisted-pair (UTP) or shielded twisted-pair (STP). 100Base-TX operates at 100 Mbps with a maximum segment distance of 100 meters.

100Base-FX — A Fast Ethernet implementation over multimode fiber-optic (MMF) cabling. The maximum segment length is 412 meters.

5-4-3 rule — The rule that stipulates that between stations on a LAN, there can be no more than five network segments connected, the maximum number of repeaters between the segments is four, and the maximum number of segments with stations on them is three.

802.2 — A standard of the IEEE that specifies the subdivision of the Logical Link Control sublayer from the Media Access Control (MAC) sublayer. These sublayers are part of the OSI Data Link layer.

802.3 — The IEEE standard that defines CSMA/CD or Ethernet networking.

802.5 — The IEEE standard that defines Token Ring networking.

802.11 — The IEEE standard that defines wireless LANs.

access layer — The layer in the three-layer network model that provides users access to the network. This is the layer in which end systems are connected to the network.

access list — A list of criteria to which all packets are compared.

access lists — Permit or deny statements that filter traffic based on criteria such as source address, destination address, and protocol type.

access method — The rules that determine which station can send data and how collisions are managed. The two most popular access methods are CSMA/CD and token-passing. Access method is also known as logical topology.

Access Rate — The speed of the line that indicates transfer rate; common U.S. access rates are 64 Kbps and 128 Kbps, provided by Integrated Service Digital Network (ISDN) connections, and 1.544 Mbps, provided by T1 connections.

active hub — A device that connects multiple nodes and/or networks, is connected to external power, and repeats and regenerates signals on a network.

active monitor — The computer in a Token Ring network that is powered on first and that manages the beaconing process.

adaptive cut-through — A method of switching whereby the switch uses the cut-through technique unless network errors reach a certain threshold; then, it automatically switches to store-and-forward switching until the error rate returns to an acceptable level. Also known as error sensing.

address — The element of the PPP frame represented by the binary sequence 11111111; since PPP is used to create a point-to-point connection, there is no need for PPP to assign an individual address for each host.

Address Resolution Protocol (ARP) — A protocol that works at the Internetwork layer of the TCP/IP networking model; resolves a known IP address to an unknown MAC address, which is the final leg of communication between the source and destination.

administration system — The centralized management component that collects and analyzes the information from the managers in a network-management system, such as SNMP or CMIP.

administrative distance — A value used to determine the reliability/desirability of a particular routing table update.

Advanced Data Communication Control Procedures (ADCCP) — The ANSI standard for HDLC.

Advanced Research Projects Agency (ARPA) — The government organization operating in the Department of Defense (DOD) that was responsible for the creation and proliferation of the Internet and the TCP/IP protocol suite.

Advanced Research Projects Agency Network (ARPANET) — The original name of the Internet.

agent — The client software part of the management tool in a network-management system, such as SNMP or CMIP; responsible for collecting the information that is used by the management system; resides on each network device.

alignment error — A frame that has both an FCS error and an entire octet missing from the frame.

alternating current (AC) — Type of current that is delivered to homes and office buildings. It changes polarity cyclically as it is manufactured by power plants.

American National Standards Institute (ANSI) — The organization that guides the process of standardization by ensuring that consensus, openness, and due process are maintained during the development process. ANSI is responsible for the FDDI standard.

American Standard Code for Information Interchange (ASCII) — A standardized method for formatting binary information and text for communications and printer control. The acronym ASCII is pronounced "ask-ee."

amplifier — A device used to boost analog signals on a broadband network.

analog — A method of signal transmission on broadband networks.

any — A keyword used to represent all hosts or networks; replaces 0.0.0.0 255.255.255.255 in an access list.

AppleTalk Control Protocol (ATCP) — PPP interface protocol for AppleTalk; *See* **Network Control Protocol**.

Application layer — The seventh layer of the OSI model, which is responsible for requesting network services and for providing services to applications. Also, the TCP/IP layer that corresponds to the Application, Presentation, and Session layers of the OSI model.

ARP reply — A reply sent by the device that discovers its own IP address in the IP header of the ARP request frame and includes the requested MAC address.

ARP request — A process used to obtain the correct mapping when a source computer cannot locate a MAC address for a known IP address in its ARP table.

ARP table — A table used by a network device that contains MAC to IP address mappings.

Asymmetric Digital Subscriber Line (ADSL) — DSL service that provides from 1.536-Mbps to 6.144-Mbps connections in the United States. Outside the U.S. connections are either 2.048 or 4.096 Mbps.

asymmetric switching — A type of LAN switching that allows for multiple speeds of network communication; a switch that supports both 10-Mbps and 100-Mbps communications is an example of asymmetric switching.

asynchronous — Asynchronous communications rely on start and stop bits to define the end-points of a transmission; timing mechanisms are not needed to maintain clock synchronization between the source and destination.

Asynchronous character map — The piece of information in the LCP field of the PPP packet that allows PPP to encode its transmission properly for the recipient host.

asynchronous serial — Serial connections that are employed in most modems connected to residential phone lines.

Asynchronous Transfer Mode (ATM) — A networking implementation for both high-speed LAN and WAN connectivity.

attachment unit interface (AUI) port — A 15-pin physical connector interface between a computer's network interface card (NIC) and an Ethernet network that uses 10Base5 ("thicknet") coaxial cable. On 10Base5 Ethernet, the NIC uses the AUI to connect to a transceiver cable that in turn taps into the main cable.

attenuation — The natural degradation of a transmitted signal over distance.

authentication — The process of verifying the right to complete a connection.

autonomous system (AS) — A group of routers under the control of a single administration.

AutoSPID — A feature of modern ISDN systems whereby SPID numbers do not have to be configured on the router.

AUX line password — A password used to access the router through the AUX port.

AUX port — *See* **auxiliary port (AUX)**.

auxiliary port (AUX) — A secondary port that allows connection to a modem that will be used for direct access to the router for configuration.

B-channel (bearer channels) — An ISDN channel used to carry data; two or more B-channels, each supporting 64 Kbps, are provided with ISDN service.

backbone — Cabling used to connect wiring hubs in an extended star topology; typically, 62.5/125-micron multimode cable is used for this connection; however, 100-ohm UTP, 150-ohm STP, and single-mode fiber can also be used to connect wiring closets to wiring closets, wiring closets to the POP, and wiring closets between buildings; sometimes called vertical cable.

backoff algorithm — A mathematical calculation performed by computers after a collision occurs on a CSMA/CD network, which forces machines to wait a random amount of time before resending the destroyed packet. A backoff algorithm is run by computers to set the length of time for the backoff period.

backoff period — A random interval used by devices that have caused a collision on an Ethernet network during which the devices cannot send, to prevent them from causing another collision immediately after the one they have just caused.

Backward Explicit Congestion Notification (BECN) — When congestion is recognized, the Frame Relay switch sends a BECN message to the source router; should reduce the amount of traffic that is sent by the router.

bandwidth — The available capacity of the network. The greater the network bandwidth, the greater the speed in data transfer.

barrel connector — Used in coaxial networks; connects one coaxial cable segment to another, effectively forming a single cable.

baseband — A digital signal used in network transmissions where a single carrier frequency is used to transmit the signal.

Basic Rate Interface (BRI) — An ISDN service that provides two B-channels for data transfers up to 128 Kbps and one D-channel to control the communications.

beaconing — A fault-detection method implemented in Token Ring networks where stations broadcast packets to other stations on the ring in an attempt to find a break in the wire or a faulty interface.

bit stream — The stream of bits, or data, that flows between a source (transmitter) and a destination (receiver); can be communicated by synchronous or asynchronous methods.

bit time — The duration of time to transmit one data bit on a network, which is 100 nanoseconds on a 10-Mbps Ethernet network or 10 nanoseconds on a 100-Mbps Ethernet network.

blocking — A port state on a switch that indicates that the port is receiving and sending BPDUs, but is not receiving and forwarding data frames in order to prevent logical loops in the network.

BMP — A Windows Bitmap (BMP) file, a graphical image type used with Microsoft Windows applications.

BNC — A hardware connector for coaxial cable that has a cylindrical shell with two small knobs that allow it to be locked into place when twisted. Depending on the source, the letters BNC are said to stand for Bayonet Navy Connector, British Naval Connector, Bayonet Neill Concelman, or Bayonet Nut Connector. See also barrel connector.

bonding — Load balancing across the two BRI B-channels to form a 128 Kbps single channel.

bootstrap — A small program used to load a much larger program. In the case of a router or switch, the bootstrap program loads the IOS.

Border Gateway Protocol (BGP) — An exterior gateway protocol used to route between multiple autonomous systems.

bridge — A device that segments a network at the Data Link layer by filtering traffic based on the MAC address.

bridge protocol data unit (BPDU) — An STP management message used to transfer status information about the Spanning Tree configuration of a switched and/or bridged network. Also known as configuration bridge protocol data unit (CBPDU).

bridging table — A table maintained on a bridge that maps MAC addresses to the bridge port through which they can be accessed.

broadcast — A frame that is addressed to all stations on the broadcast domain. The destination MAC address is set to FFFFFFFFFFFF so that all local stations will process the packet.

broadcast domain — A logical or physical group of devices that will receive broadcast traffic from each other on a LAN.

broadcast storm — An error condition in which broadcast traffic is above 126 packets per second and network communications are impeded. This is typically the result of a software configuration error or programming error.

brouter — A device that functions as a bridge for nonroutable protocols and a router for routable protocols. The brouter operates at both the Data Link and Network layers.

buffer — A portion of memory used to store information that is being sent or created too fast for a system to process.

buffering — A way in which devices on a network are able to handle packet flows that exceed their processing capabilities. Packets are stored in a buffer until the system can process them.

bus — In the physical sense, a network topology where computers are daisy-chained together on the same coaxial cable segment; in the logical sense, refers to the CSMA/CD access method that sends data frames to all other stations simultaneously.

bus/star — A physical bus and physical star can be combined to form a star/bus or bus/star physical topology; hubs that have connectors for coaxial cable as well as twisted-pair wiring are used to form these types of networks. When different topologies are applied to a network, it is often called a mixed-media network.

cancellation — The desirable situation in which magnetic fields generated by two different wires carrying electronic signals cancel out the others; cancellation provides limited protection from crosstalk and external interference.

capacitance — A naturally occurring opposition to voltage changes in a wire used for electronic signal transmission.

Carrier Sense Multiple Access/Collision Avoidance (CSMA/CA) — The network access method used by wireless LANs as outlined in IEEE 802.11. Nodes must first listen to a channel before transmitting. If the channel is busy, nodes configure a random backoff time to wait before transmitting.

Carrier Sense Multiple Access with Collision Detection (CSMA/CD) — An Ethernet networking method defined by IEEE standard 802.3, which states that an Ethernet station must first listen before transmitting on a network. Any station can transmit as long as there are no transmissions active on the network. If two stations transmit simultaneously, a collision will occur, and those stations must detect the collision and reset themselves.

carrier signal — A transmitted electromagnetic pulse or wave on the network wire that indicates that a transmission is in progress.

CAT 1 — Category 1 unshielded twisted-pair (Cat 1 UTP) is a voice-grade only communication medium that should not be used as network media.

CAT 2 — Category 2 unshielded twisted-pair (Cat 2 UTP) is a voice- or data-grade medium that is rarely used in modern networks but that does have the rating to transmit up to 4 Mbps.

CAT 3 — Category 3 unshielded twisted-pair (Cat 3 UTP) is a voice- or data-grade medium that can transmit at 10 Mbps and that supports 10BaseT networking.

CAT 4 — Category 4 unshielded twisted-pair (Cat 4 UTP) supports voice or data and is capable of a 16-Mbps transmission rate.

CAT 5 — Category 5 unshielded twisted-pair (Cat 5 UTP) is the most popular installation medium today; this media type supports 100-Mbps transmission rates, but new standards attempt to achieve 1000 Mbps over CAT 5 cabling.

catchment area — The area serviced; for example, the area serviced by a wiring closet is the catchment area of that wiring closet.

Central Office (CO) switch — The telecommunications company location that is part of the PSTN or toll network; point of entry to the toll network from the demarc.

challenge — The query packet, or the action of sending the query packet over a CHAP connection, that is used to verify the participants of the PPP connection.

Challenge Handshake Authentication Protocol (CHAP) — PPP authentication protocol that provides better security than PAP in authenticating devices on PPP connections.

channel service unit/data service unit (CSU/DSU) — A telecommunications company device that provides connectivity between the WAN service provider network and the customer's LAN.

cheapernet — A reference to RG-58 thin Ethernet cable.

circuit — A path in which electrical current can flow.

Cisco Discovery Protocol (CDP) — A Cisco proprietary Data Link layer protocol that shares configuration information between Cisco devices that are locally connected.

Cisco Internetwork Operating System (IOS) — A router operating system that provides a command-line interface, which allows network operators to check the status of the router and allows network administrators to manage and configure the router.

Classless Inter-Domain Routing (CIDR) — The notation method that specifies the subnet mask following an IP address as the number of masked bits. For example, the IP address 192.168.1.1 with subnet mask 255.255.240.0 could be represented by 192.168.1.1/20 because the subnet mask 255.255.240.0 represents the masking of 20 bits.

client — A computer that operates on a network and that requests and uses the services of other computers on the network, but that does not necessarily provide any services to other computers.

client/server — A type of networking in which a few dedicated computers, called servers, share files, printers, disk drives, and other resources with a group of client computers.

collision domain — In Ethernet networking, a single segment on a network. Any station on the same physical segment or separated by a repeater is in the same collision domain. Bridges, routers, and switches (depending on how they are configured) can separate collision domains.

command executive — The user interface that interprets commands and is provided by the Cisco IOS (a.k.a. the EXEC).

Committed Burst Size (CBS) — The maximum amount of data bits that the service provider agrees to transfer in a set period under normal conditions.

Committed Information Rate (CIR) — The minimum average transfer rate of the Frame Relay circuit; usually lower than the access rate because the transfer rate may exceed the CIR during short bursts.

Common Management Information Protocol (CMIP) — A standard developed by the International Organization for Standardization (ISO) to provide a method for monitoring and managing network resources.

compression — Data compression that can be performed on the PPP packet at the source and then uncompressed at the destination.

concentrator — A term used to describe a hub.

conductor — Material with low resistance to electron flow.

configuration bridge protocol data unit (CBPDU) — See **bridge protocol data unit (BPDU)**.

configuration register — A feature in Cisco routers that is stored in NVRAM and allows the administrator to control several boot functions.

congestion avoidance — A method by which a system on the network can reduce the flow of packets on a network by sending a message request to the sender to reduce the rate at which they are being transmitted.

connection-oriented — Network communications that require acknowledgment. On the OSI reference model, the decision to use connection-oriented communications is made at the Transport layer.

connectionless — Network communications that do not require acknowledgment. On the OSI reference model, the decision to use connectionless communications is made at the Transport layer.

console — A physical connection on the back of the router to which you can connect a rollover cable to attach to a PC for router configuration (a.k.a. console port).

console password — The password that is used to access the router through the console port.

console port — See **console**.

Consultative Committee on International Telephony and Telegraphy (CCITT) — The former name of International Telecommunication Union - Telecommunication Standardization Sector (ITU-T).

content-addressable memory (CAM) — A memory location on a switch that contains the MAC address-to-switch port mapping information, which the switch uses to forward frames to the appropriate destination.

contention — The condition that occurs when computers on a network must share the available capacity of the network wire with other computers.

contention method — The method by which computers on a network must share the available capacity of the network wire with other computers.

context-sensitive Help — Help with the syntax of commands for the router that is based on the current router mode and prompt, as well as any part of a command that is typed.

control — The element of the PPP frame represented by the binary sequence 00000011, which indicates that the transmission of user data will not be sequenced and is to be delivered over a connectionless link.

convergence — The point at which all routers on a network share a similar view of the network.

core layer — The layer that provides fast WAN connectivity for large network designs using the three-layer network model.

count-to-infinity — A routing loop whereby packets bounce infinitely around an internetwork.

counters — Detailed statistics kept by a router about data passing across its interface.

cross-connect jumpers — Cables used to connect networking devices inside a wiring closet; a type of patch cable or cord.

crosstalk — Signal bleed from one cable to another; this type of error usually occurs in poorly wired media.

customer premises equipment (CPE) — Equipment under the customer's control; also known as customer-provided equipment, depending on the publication.

cut-through — A switching technique in which an Ethernet frame is forwarded immediately after the destination address is deciphered. This method offers the lowest latency, but does not reduce packet errors.

cyclic redundancy check (CRC) — The process that ensures that data was not corrupted during transmission. This is accomplished by comparing CRC calculations before and after transmission.

D-channel (data channel) — The control channel used in ISDN communications; can be 16 to 64 Kbps.

data — The LCP field is also known as the Data field. This location contains the LCP information and the data that has been encapsulated from the higher layers. The default size of this field is 1500 bytes, but PPP implementations can negotiate a larger size for this field.

data circuit-terminating equipment (DCE) — Typically, the telecommunications-provided device on the customer side that allows the customer to connect to the WAN; often, a CSU/DSU, but can also be a modem or TA.

Data Link Connection Identifier (DLCI) — Pronounced *dell-see*, information in a Frame Relay connection that is configured on the router and used to identify which path leads to a specific Network Layer address (i.e., IP address). The DLCI is only locally significant, meaning that it can, and usually does, change on each Physical Link.

Data Link layer — The second layer of the OSI protocol stack, which defines the rules for sending and receiving information across the network media. It encodes and frames data for transmission and provides error detection and control. This layer has two parts: LLC and MAC.

data terminal equipment (DTE) — A customer device that is used to connect to the telecommunications company equipment. This device is typically a router, but it can also be a computer or other type of terminal.

datagram — A message or packet that is sent across a network and that does not require acknowledgment by the destination station.

data communication equipment (DCE) — Equipment that performs some type of signal conversion between the terminal device and the transmission facility. Usually the DCE is part of the telco provider's equipment.

default gateway — The address that a host or IP device sends a packet to when it does not have a record of where to send the packet. TCP/IP clients send packets to the default gateway when the destination host is not on their subnet. The default gateway is usually an interface on a router.

default route — A static route that directs all traffic not specified anywhere else in the routing table to a particular route. Same as quad zero route.

default VLAN — The default configuration of every port on a switch. Same as VLAN 1.

defining a maximum — A technique used with distance-vector routing protocols to prevent packets from bouncing infinitely throughout an internetwork.

demarc — Location that is the responsibility of the telecommunications provider and that connects to the nearest telephone company office.

demarcation — *See* **demarc**.

destination unreachable — An ICMP message sent back to the source host when a gateway cannot deliver an IP datagram.

dial-on-demand routing (DDR) — A feature available on Cisco routers that allows you to use bandwidth as needed.

Digital Subscriber Line (DSL) — Telecommunications services that offer high bandwidth over existing copper lines. DSL connections are generically referred to as xDSL because there are several different DSL technologies.

directed broadcasts — Broadcasts sent to specific segments. For example, a broadcast on segment 192.168.1.0 would be 192.168.1.255.

disabled — A port state on a switch that indicates that the port is neither receiving BPDUs nor forwarding frames.

Discard-Eligible (DE) — During times of congestion, DE frames are discarded in order to provide a higher, more reliable service to those frames that are not discard-eligible.

diskless workstation — Workstations configured to download their operating systems from a central server. These workstations typically do not have a hard drive.

distance-vector routing protocol — A routing protocol that functions by broadcasting the entire routing table periodically to all connected neighbors; examples include RIP and IGRP.

distribution layer — Provides the backbone for a network; this layer is used in the three-layer network model to allow for access and protocol control and to increase security on the network.

Domain Name System (DNS) — A hierarchical naming service that is used on the Internet and IP networks to provide host name to IP address resolution.

down-when-looped — A Cisco router command that shuts down an interface when looping is detected; used to prevent testing scenarios from causing troubleshooting problems in a production environment.

dynamic NAT — A type of network address translation in which the valid external IP addresses to be mapped to internal addresses are floating or not-fixed. The NAT router can then dynamically assign any of the available external addresses to any of the hosts on the internal network.

dynamic random access memory (DRAM) — *See* **random access memory (RAM)**.

dynamic routing protocol — A protocol that builds the routing table automatically. Examples include RIP and IGRP.

E1 — European 30-channel digital line capable of supporting up to 2.048-Mbps data transmissions.

echo request/reply — The most commonly used ICMP message. ICMP echo request/reply messages are used to check the availability of a remote host, the devices along a network path (intermediate gateways), and to verify the installation of the TCP/IP protocol on the local source host.

EIA/TIA — *See* **Electronic Industries Alliance** and **Telecommunication Industry Association**.

EIA/TIA-568 — Defines and describes operational parameters for various grades of unshielded twisted-pair cabling.

EIA/TIA-568A — A wiring method used to indicate which colors are assigned to which pin for UTP cable.

EIA/TIA-568B — A wiring method used to indicate which colors are assigned to which pin for UTP cable.

EIA/TIA-569 — Describes various network media configurations, such as those for horizontal pathways, entrance facilities, wiring closets, equipment rooms, and workstations.

electromagnetic interference (EMI) — Electronic noise that disrupts signals on cables. This noise is frequently caused by motors and generators, but can also be caused by sunspots and other natural EMI-producing phenomenon.

Electronic Industries Alliance (EIA) — The organization that provides standards that define how cabling should be configured on a network; often, these standards are done as a joint operation with the TIA.

enable mode — Another name for the privileged EXEC mode. The enable or enable secret password must be entered in order to access this mode.

enable mode prompt — The prompt that indicates operation in privileged EXEC or enable mode. It has two elements: the host name of the router and the pound (#) symbol.

enable password — The password that protects enable mode in the event that the enable secret password has been removed.

enable secret password — An MD5 encrypted password that is not visible when viewing the system configuration; supersedes the enable password.

encapsulation — A process that occurs during transmission through the protocol stack in which data from the higher layers is wrapped in a protocol header and/or trailer; common frame types are 802.3, 802.2, and Ethernet_II.

end system — The location and/or set of controls that the user can manipulate to interact with a computer or a network.

eNetWare Core Protocol (NCP) — Upper-layer protocol that handles most of the client/server interaction on a Novell NetWare network.

Enhanced Interior Gateway Routing Protocol (EIGRP) — A proprietary Cisco distance-vector protocol developed to overcome some of the limitations associated with distance-vector protocols. EIGRP is considered a hybrid routing protocol.

error sensing — *See* **adaptive cut-through**.

established — A keyword that requires traffic to have originated inside the trusted network.

Ethernet — A standard networking architecture that defines the physical layout, lengths, and types of media that can be used. There are many variations of Ethernet but most use the CSMA/CD network access method.

Excess Burst Size (EBS) — The amount of excess traffic (over the CBS) that the network will attempt to transfer during a set period; can be discarded by the network, if necessary.

EXEC — *See* **command executive**.

expectational acknowledgment — A TCP acknowledgment process in which the acknowledgment number refers to the sequence number expected next. If the expected sequence is not received within an expected time interval, a retransmission is requested.

Extended Binary Coded Decimal Interchange Code (EBCDIC) — A standardized formatting method for both binary and text files for communications and printer control. IBM developed EBCDIC. The acronym EBCDIC is pronounced "eb-see-dick."

extended IP access lists — IP access lists that filter traffic by source IP address, destination IP address, protocol type, and port number.

extended IPX access lists — IPX access lists that filter traffic based on source and destination IPX nodes or networks, IPX protocol type, and IPX socket number.

extended mode ping — When you type the word "ping" at the privileged EXEC prompt, and then press the Return or Enter key, you will be presented with ping options. Extended mode ping options include the destination address of the ping, the protocol, repeat count, and datagram size.

Exterior Gateway Protocol (EGP) — A gateway protocol used to route between multiple autonomous systems.

Fast Ethernet — Defined in IEEE 802.3u; any of the following 100-Mbps Ethernet LAN technologies: 100Base-T4, 100Base-TX, 100Base-FX.

fast forward — Indicates that a switch is in cut-through mode.

Fiber Distributed Data Interface (FDDI) — Describes the general specifications for the use, installation, configuration, and limitations of fiber-optic networking; pronounced "fiddy;" this standard is the responsibility of ANSI.

fiber-optic cable — A type of cable that conducts light signals through glass or plastic to generate network signals. Fiber-optic cable allows for transmission rates of 100 megabits per second or greater. It is impervious to electromagnetic interference because it sends eight signals rather than elective signals along the cable.

File Transfer Protocol (FTP) — A part of the TCP/IP protocol suite that provides reliable file transfers across the Internet or other TCP/IP networks. FTP uses TCP to transfer files.

flag — A field placed at the beginning and end of an HDLC and PPP frame to mark the beginning and end of the frame.

flash memory — Erasable, programmable, read-only memory (EPROM). The content of flash memory is maintained when the router is rebooted. Flash memory contains the working copy of the Cisco IOS and it is the component that initializes the IOS for normal router operations.

floods — The process of broadcasting packets onto a network.

flooded broadcasts — A broadcast for any subnet that uses the IP address 255.255.255.255. Routers do not pass flooded broadcasts.

flush interval — The time at which a route is totally removed from the routing table.

Forward Explicit Congestion Notification (FECN) — Message sent to the destination router on a frame relay circuit that tells the router that congestion was experienced on the virtual circuit.

forwarding — The state of a port on a switch or bridge that indicates that it will learn MAC addresses and forward frames out that port.

fractional E1 — A service that offers some number of channels less than the 30 (64-Kbps) digital channels provided by a full E1 connection.

fractional T1 — A service that offers some number of channels less than the 24 (64-Kbps) digital channels provided by a full T1 connection.

fragment free — A method of switching whereby the switch reads the first 64 bytes of the incoming frame before forwarding it to the destination port(s).

frame — A segment of data. The words "frame" and "data packet" are often used interchangeably, although technically a frame is found at layer 2 of the OSI model and a packet is found at layer 3.

Frame Check Sequence (FCS) — A mathematical computation placed at the end of the frame that is used to ensure that the frame was not corrupted during transmission.

frame check sequence (FCS) error — An error that occurs when the calculation in the FCS field indicates that a frame was not received intact.

frame filtering — A technique used on early VLAN implementations that employed the use of multiple switching tables.

frame identification — See **frame tagging**.

Frame Relay — A Data Link layer protocol that relies on high-speed, reliable connections; can operate between 56 Kbps and 45 Mbps over a WAN connection.

Frame Relay access device (FRAD) — The device that the Frame Relay customer utilizes to connect to a Frame Relay network; also known as the Frame Relay assembler/disassembler.

Frame Relay assembler/disassembler — *See* **Frame Relay access device (FRAD)**.

Frame Relay map — A table that defines the interface to which a specific DLCI number is mapped.

Frame Relay network device (FRND) — The device that the Frame Relay provider supplies as the connection to the Frame Relay network; the acronym FRND is pronounced "friend."

Frame Relay switch — A telecommunications company device that is used to support Frame Relay connections from customer locations; used to route Frame Relay traffic inside the public data network.

Frame Relay switching table — A table that is maintained on a Frame Relay switch; used to route Frame Relay traffic via virtual circuit DLCI numbers.

frame tagging — A method of VLAN identification endorsed by the IEEE 802.1q specification that calls for an additional four-byte field in the VLAN frame after the source and destination addresses in the data packet. Also known as frame identification.

full-duplex — A connection that allows communication in two directions at once; common telephone connections are typically full-duplex because people can talk and listen at the same time.

function groups — Used in ISDN communication to describe a set of functions that are implemented by a device and its software; a terminal adapter (TA) is a function group.

gateway — A combination of hardware and software that translates between different protocols on a network.

Get Nearest Server (GNS) — A SAP request sent by clients; attempts to locate the nearest NetWare server.

giant — *See* **long frame**.

Gigabit Ethernet — New 802.3 standard that allows 1-Gbps transmission, usually across fiber-optic cable.

global configuration mode — A router mode that allows manipulation of most of the router's generic settings. The prompt for global configuration mode is router(config)#.

half-duplex — A connection that allows communication in two directions, but not simultaneously; the circuit can be used for sending or receiving bits in one direction at a time only.

hexadecimal — A numbering method that relies on a base of 16. Hexadecimal digits can be 0, 1, 2, 3, 4, 5, 6, 7, 8, 9, A, B, C, D, E, or F.

hierarchical design — In network design methodology, a network that is structured in a layered hierarchical fashion, such as the one-layer, two-layer, and three-layer network models; the opposite would be a mesh design.

High-bit-rate Digital Subscriber Line (HDSL) — Symmetric digital communication service capable of 1.536 Mbps in the United States and 2.048 Mbps in Europe.

High-level Data Link Control (HDLC) — A Data Link layer encapsulation protocol that is a superset of the SDLC protocol. HDLC is a WAN protocol that can be used for both point-to-point and multipoint connections.

High-Speed Serial Interface (HSSI) — A type of serial device that was developed by Cisco and T3Plus Network that operates at speeds of up to 52 Mbps over distances of 15 meters.

hold-down timers — A technique used to stop routing loops in which updates from an inferior source are not allowed for a certain interval. Used by routers to stabilize routing tables and to prevent erroneous routing table updates.

hop count — A count of the number of routers a packet must pass through in order to reach a destination network.

horizontal cabling — Media that connects workstations and wiring closets.

host — A keyword for an extended IP list that specifies that an address should have a wildcard mask of 0.0.0.0.

hub — An active or passive device that connects network segments. Passive hubs are connection points; active hubs repeat and regenerate signals.

Hypertext Transfer Protocol (HTTP) — A protocol used for communications on the World Wide Web. Web servers are HTTP servers.

ICMP flood — A large quantity of ICMP echo requests sent to a target device by a malicious person or program in an attempt to crash or greatly reduce the performance of the target device.

IEEE 802 — Standard that focuses on the Physical and Data Link layers of the OSI model; developed in February 1980.

IEEE 802.1q — The IEEE standard that defines VLAN implementations and recommends frame tagging as the way in which switches should identify VLANs. Used by Cisco switches for compatability with non-Cisco switches.

IEEE 802.10 (FDDI) — A frame-tagging method used to identify VLANs trunked across Fiber Distributed Data Interfaces (FDDI).

IEEE 802.3u — The IEEE standard that defines Fast Ethernet implementations, including 100Base-T4, 100Base-TX, and 100Base-FX.

impedance — Measure of the total opposition to electron flow, changes in current, and changes in voltage in cable; causes attenuation.

implicit deny any — Blocks all packets that do not meet the requirements of the access list. Exists at the end of all lists.

inbound — A direction parameter used when applying an access list. Direction is into the router.

inductance — Opposition to the changes of electrical current in a wire.

information request/reply — ICMP messages that are typically used to determine the subnet mask used by the destination. This message allows a host to determine the number of the network it is on.

infrared — Invisible light at the upper end of the electromagnetic spectrum. It is used in some types of computer networking, especially for data transfers between laptop and desktop systems. It is one of the wireless technologies defined in IEEE 802.11. This technology requires line-of-sight between the transmitter and receiver. It is low power but cannot be intercepted.

initial sequence number (ISN) — Sequence numbers that allow communicating hosts to synchronize their communications in a TCP three-way handshake. When the communication is initiated, two hosts communicating over TCP will synchronize their initial sequence numbers.

Institute of Electrical and Electronics Engineers (IEEE) — A technical professional society that fosters national and international standards.

Integrated Services Digital Network (ISDN) — A service provided by most major telecommunication carriers, such as AT&T, Sprint, and the RBOCs; operates over existing phone lines and transfers both voice and data.

Inter-Switch Link (ISL) protocol — A frame-tagging method for VLANs proprietary to Cisco devices. Uses a 26-byte header.

interesting traffic — Network traffic for which you feel it is worth activating or maintaining an ISDN link that is configured with DDR.

interface configuration mode — A router mode that allows you to configure the Ethernet and serial interfaces. The prompt for this mode is router(config-if)#.

interframe gap — The time required between the transmission of data frames on the network: 9.6 microseconds.

Interior Gateway Protocol (IGP) — A gateway protocol used to route within one autonomous system.

Interior Gateway Routing Protocol (IGRP) — A proprietary Cisco distance-vector routing protocol that uses delay and bandwidth as its default metrics.

Intermediate Distribution Facility (IDF) —
Dependent upon the MDF in a star topology;
another wiring closet used to support devices on
a network.

**International Organization for Standardization
(ISO)** — A multi-industry association that
attempts to standardize and define items that
increase communication and compatibility in many
different industries.

**International Telecommunication Union -
Telecommunication Standardization Sector
(ITU-T)** — A standards organization based in
Europe, but with membership worldwide;
involved in telecommunications standardization.

**Internet Assigned Numbers Authority
(IANA)** — The regulatory agency responsible for
subdividing and administering the address hierarchy
used on the Internet.

Internet Control Message Protocol (ICMP) —
A protocol in the TCP/IP protocol suite at the
Internetwork layer. ICMP messages control and
manage IP protocol communications.

Internet Engineering Task Force (IETF) —
Organization that defines Internet operating protocols; defines the serial line protocols PPP and SLIP.

**Internet Network Information Center
(InterNIC)** — The main regulatory agency of the
Internet. It is responsible for administrative tasks
involving the Internet and individuals and/or public or private organizations.

Internet Protocol (IP) — The Network layer
(Internetwork layer) protocol that is responsible for
addressing, which allows IP to be routed.

internetwork — A large network comprised of
smaller interconnected networks.

Internetwork layer — The layer of TCP/IP that is
equivalent to the Network layer of the OSI model.

Internetwork Packet Exchange (IPX) —
Predominantly a layer 3 protocol used by the
IPX/SPX protocol stack for routing packets along
the shortest path in an IPX internetwork.

**Internetwork Packet Exchange/Sequence
Packet Exchange (IPX/SPX)** — A routed pro-
tocol stack developed by Novell for use with the
NetWare network operating system.

interpacket gap (IPG) — *See* **interframe gap.**

inverse mask — *See* **wildcard mask.**

IP address — A 32-bit binary address used on
TCP/IP networks; consists of a host portion and a
network portion.

IP addressing — The act of assigning (unique) IP
addresses to devices on the network.

IP Control Protocol (IPCP) — PPP interface protocol for IP; *see* **Network Control Protocol.**

IPX Control Protocol (IPXCP) — PPP interface
protocol for IPX; *see* **Network Control
Protocol.**

IPX SAP filters — Access lists that filter SAP traffic
on a network.

IPX/SPX addresses — Eighty-bit addresses consisting of a 32-bit network portion and a 48-bit
node portion; the network administrator arbitrarily assigns the network portion; the MAC
address of the node makes up the node portion
of the address; addresses normally appear in
hexadecimal format.

ISDN Digital Subscriber Line (IDSL) — A
telecommunications service that makes an ISDN
connection into a 128-Kbps DSL connection.
Unlike ISDN, IDSL only supports data communications (not analog voice or video).

ISDN modem — A modem used in ISDN communications that must be installed at ISDN subscriber
locations.

ISDN phone number — *See* **Service Profile
Identifier (SPID).**

jabber — A frame that is longer than the 1518 bytes
acceptable for transmission between stations and
that also has an FCS error.

jam signal — A 32-bit signal sent by the first station to detect a collision on an Ethernet network
that ensures that all other stations are aware of
the collision.

keepalive frames — Data frames sent between two hosts to ensure that the connection between those hosts remains open.

keepalive packets — Data packets sent between devices to confirm that a connection should be maintained between them.

LAN Emulation (LANE) — A frame-tagging method used for VLANs on Asynchronous Transfer Mode (ATM) devices.

late collision — A situation that occurs when two stations transmit more than 64 bytes of their frames before detecting a collision.

latency — A delay on a network caused by a variety of factors, including the addition of devices.

LCP link configuration — A process that modifies and/or enhances the default characteristics of a PPP connection; includes the following actions: link establishment, authentication, link-quality determination, Network layer protocol configuration negotiation, and link determination.

learning — A transitory state on a bridge or switch port that indicates it is trying to learn new MAC addresses and correct its bridge table before forwarding frames on the network; used to prevent loops during the election of a new root bridge.

line configuration mode — A router mode that allows you to configure the virtual terminals, console, and AUX lines that let you access the router. The prompt for this mode is router(config-line)#.

Link Access Procedure Balanced (LAPB) — A derivative of the HDLC WAN protocol; adapted to provide WAN services over X.25 networks.

Link Access Procedure D-channel (LAPD) — A Data Link layer WAN protocol adapted from HDLC; used on D-channel over ISDN lines.

Link Control Protocol (LCP) — Used in PPP connections to establish, configure, maintain, and terminate PPP connections.

link establishment — The process of opening and configuring a PPP connection before any data can be transferred over the link.

Link Quality Monitoring (LQM) — PPP feature that checks the reliability of the link by monitoring the number of errors, latency between requests, connection retries, and connection failures on the PPP link.

link termination — The process of disconnecting a PPP connection when the call is complete, which is determined by the PPP hosts that made the connection.

link-quality determination — The process of checking the quality of a PPP link and monitoring its reliability.

link-state — A routing protocol that uses cost when calculating the best path between two points. It considers items such as network traffic, router congestion, bandwidth, reliability, and other factors that could affect network performance.

link-state advertisement (LSA) — A routing information packet used by link-state routing protocols to advertise their local network link information to neighbor routers in an internetwork.

link-state packets (LSP) — Packets used to send out link-state advertisements.

link-state routing protocols — Routing protocols that function via link-state advertisements using link-state packets to inform all routers on the internetwork of route tables. OSPF is the most common link-state routing protocol.

listening — A transitory state on a bridge or switch port that is used during the election of a new root bridge; the port does not learn MAC addresses nor does it forward data frames when in this state.

load balancing — The ability of a router to distribute packets among multiple same cost paths.

local area network (LAN) — A group of computers and other devices typically connected by a cable. Is normally located in a single geographic region such as a building or floor in a building.

local loop — The connection between the demarcation and the telephone company (WAN service provider) office.

Local Management Interface (LMI) — A standard signaling mechanism between the CPE and the Frame Relay connection; can provide the network server with a local or global DLCI; can provide keep-alive and status information to the Frame Relay connection.

logical addresses — Layer 3 addresses (also referred to as Network layer addresses) that allow routed protocols to determine which network a particular host is on.

Logical Link Control (LLC) layer — A sublayer of the Data Link layer that forms the connection between the other software in the protocol stack and the networking hardware (such as the NIC and the cables).

logical loop — A situation that occurs when a packet can be routed in an endless loop around a network because bridging tables and/or routing tables reference each other as the destination for a given address.

logical topology — Describes the way a signal travels in a network, which is a function of the access method; the logical topology is usually a bus or a ring.

long frame — An Ethernet frame that is over the 1518 bytes acceptable for transmission between stations, but that is smaller than 6000 bytes. Also known as a giant.

loopback — The TCP/IP Class A address 127.x.x.x that is reserved for diagnostic purposes. This address allows you to check if TCP/IP has been properly installed on the system. (Specifically, the IP address 127.0.0.1 is the address usually given as the loopback.)

loopback command — A Cisco router command that places an interface in a looped back state, which means that all outgoing data will be redirected as incoming data without going out on the network; used for testing purposes.

magic number — Unique numbers added by the router to a packet, which allows it to detect a looped-back link.

Main Distribution Facility (MDF) — The central wiring closet in an extended star topology; typically, an MDF houses the POP, patch panel, and network-interconnection devices (bridges, routers, switches, repeaters, and concentrators).

Management Information Base (MIB) — A central repository of network statistics used by SNMP and CMIP; allows management protocols to maintain network statistics; can be modified to control workstations and other network devices.

management VLAN — The default configuration of every port on a switch. Same as VLAN1.

manager — A centralized software component that is used to manage the network in a network management system, such as SNMP or CMIP.

maximum receive unit size — The piece of information in the LCP field of the PPP packet that sets the receive buffer size for the LCP connection, typically 1500 bytes.

MD5 algorithm — An algorithm used to encrypt an enable secret password. It has no known reversal.

media — The cable, glass, or telephone lines that host the signal from one computer to another on a network.

Media Access Control (MAC) layer — A sublayer of the Data Link layer that defines the hardware address of the physical network interface. In addition, it discards corrupted packets and identifies which packets were directed to the local system.

media access method — *See* **network access method**.

mesh design — In network design methodology, a network that has no organized structure; the opposite would be a hierarchical design.

metric — A value used to define the suitability or desirability of a particular route.

metropolitan area network (MAN) — An intermediate specification that defines networks confined to a fairly restricted geographic area, such as a campus, town, or city. These private networks span multiple geographically separate locations that are near to one another.

microsegmentation — The type of segmentation that occurs through the use of virtual circuits between switches and nodes. Each connection enjoys the total bandwidth. Bandwidth is not shared as it is through hubs.

mixed media — When different physical topologies are applied to a network, it is often called a mixed media network; for example, the bus and star topologies can be combined to form a star/bus or bus/star physical topology.

modified cut-through — *See* **fragment free**.

multicast — A frame that is addressed to a group of systems; typically used in radio- or television-style broadcasting on the network.

multicast address — A special subdivision of IP categories reserved for data streaming. Multicast addresses are used to send information to groups of computers. The range for multicasting addresses is 224.0.0.0 to 239.255.255.255.

multilink — Allows multiple transmission devices (such as two modems) to send data over separate physical connections; defined in RFC 1717.

multimode fiber-optic (MMF) cable — Fiber-optic cabling that allows for multiple simultaneous light transmissions.

multiplexed — Combining different traffic streams onto a single physical medium. The traffic is separated (demultiplexed) at the receiving end.

multipoint — The configuration of a single interface or subinterface to use multiple virtual circuits.

multiport bridge — Another name for a switch.

Multistation Access Unit (MAU) — The central device in a Token Ring architecture; forces the signal to be transmitted in a logical ring topology.

named access list — Access list that uses names instead of number ranges.

near end crosstalk (NEXT) — A measure of crosstalk performed at the location nearest the cable tester; the cable tester injects a signal of varying frequencies on a wire and measures signal bleed between other pairs of wires.

nearest active downstream neighbor (NADN) — The station on a Token Ring network that, during normal operations, receives the token from its nearest active upstream neighbor (NAUN).

nearest active upstream neighbor (NAUN) — The station on a Token Ring network that, during normal operations, passes the token to its NADN.

NetWare Core Protocol (NCP) — Upper-layer protocol that handles most of the client/sever interaction on a Novell NetWare network.

NetWare Link State Protocol (NLSP) — Layer 3 link state routing protocol built into the IPX/SPX protocol stack.

network — Two or more computers connected by some type of media and using a common protocol to communicate.

network access method — The process by which network interface cards and devices communicate data on a network; an example is CSMA/CD. Also known as media access method.

Network Address Translation (NAT) — A method for using a router to separate an internal network from an external network (usually the Internet), which is defined in RFC 3022. Internal hosts with private or unregistered IP addresses can effectively utilize one or more public registered IP addresses to communicate with external systems.

network analyzer — A device that can collect and analyze information obtained by monitoring network traffic; may be able to query and manage network devices; also called protocol analyzer.

network architecture — A network's physical and logical topology, including its physical structure or layout, the media used, the network access method, and the standards and protocols employed.

Network Control Protocol (NCP) — A functional field that contains codes that indicate the type of protocol that is encapsulated; allows PPP to encapsulate multiple protocols including IP, IPX, and AppleTalk.

Network File System (NFS) — A file system associated with the UNIX operating system that allows for network communications between hosts.

network interface card (NIC) — A hardware device that transmits and receives electronic signals on a network.

Network Interface layer — In TCP/IP, the layer that is equivalent to the Physical and Data Link layers of the OSI model.

Network layer — The third layer of the OSI conceptual networking model, which allows communications to be routed on a network. It provides a logical address for computers on a network.

Network layer protocol configuration negotiation — The process of determining a Network layer protocol to use over a PPP connection that is common to both PPP hosts.

network monitor — A program that collects information by monitoring network traffic; typically, does not have the advanced features of analysis and device management common to network analyzers.

network operating system (NOS) — Operating software that has networking components built into its structure.

Network Termination 1 (NT1) — A small connection box that is attached to ISDN BRI lines. This device terminates the connection from the Central Office (CO).

Network Termination 2 (NT2) — A device that provides switching services for the internal network.

NIC error — An error that indicates that a NIC is unable to transmit/receive a packet.

node — A connection point or junction on the network. A node can be a terminal or computer connected to the network.

nonbroadcast multiaccess (NBMA) — A rule used in Frame Relay that does not allow broadcasts to be sent to multiple locations from a single interface.

nonroutable protocols — Protocols that do not contain Network layer addressing and therefore cannot pass between multiple networks.

nonvolatile random access memory (NVRAM) — A special type of RAM that is not cleared when the router is rebooted. NVRAM is where the startup configuration file for the router is stored.

one-layer network model — Includes WAN connectivity equipment and organizes a network so that it can be easily adapted to the two- and three-layer design models in the future.

Open Shortest Path First (OSPF) — A link-state routing protocol based upon open (nonproprietary) standards.

Open Systems Interconnection (OSI) — A seven-layer reference model created by the International Organization for Standardization (ISO) to define and separate networking hardware and software into distinct layers and functions. This model makes it easy for developers and manufacturers to ensure that their networking implementations are compatible with other implementations in the industry.

oscillations — Undesirable, irregular signals (noise) riding on top of the desired signal.

out-of-band signaling — The practice of controlling an ISDN connection on a channel other than the channel(s) on which data is transferred.

outbound — A direction parameter used when applying an access list. Direction is out of the router.

overlapping — A type of NAT used when an organization wants to connect to the Internet, but its internal addressing scheme is registered to another entity. Instead of renumbering the internal network, the organization uses NAT to translate its private addressing scheme to the address that it was assigned by the InterNIC or its IP.

overloading — A type of NAT that allows multiple internal hosts to utilize one or more external IP addresses. The NAT router uses a table to keep track of the IP addresses and ports of each host, dynamically mapping each internal socket to a valid external socket.

oversubscription — When the sum of the data arriving over all virtual circuits exceeds the access rate.

packet — A group of data that is transmitted across a network.

Packet Internet Groper (ping) — A troubleshooting utility that verifies that a remote host is currently running and accessible.

parameter problem — An ICMP message sent whenever incorrect datagram header information is received. The message identifies the octet in the datagram that caused the problem.

partial masking — When an octet in a wildcard mask contains a mix of binary 1's and 0's.

passive hub — A device that connects network segments, but does not perform signal regeneration.

Password Authentication Protocol (PAP) — PPP authentication protocol that provides some security in verifying the identity of devices using PPP connections.

patch cable — *See* **patch cord**.

patch cord — Cables used to terminate communication circuits in a wiring closet or between a workstation and a telecommunications outlet. *See* **cross-connect jumpers**.

patch panel — A device that includes ports and pin locations used to connect devices in a wiring closet to devices on the network; acts as a switchboard for the network.

peer communication — The method of communication among the levels of the OSI model in which each protocol in the OSI protocol stack encodes its own protocol data unit into the network hierarchy, so that it can communicate with the equivalent layer on the destination computer.

peer-to-peer networks — Small networks, normally consisting of fewer than 10 computers, in which each computer can give and receive network services.

permanent virtual circuit (PVC) — A connection to the WAN that is established by the network administrator at the customer location; not expected to be terminated and therefore remains active.

physical address — Also called the MAC address. It is burned into the network interface card (NIC) during the manufacturing process.

Physical layer — The first layer of the OSI conceptual networking model, which defines the physical media and electronic transmission methods used in networking.

physical path loops — A loop that occurs when network devices are connected to one another by two or more physical media links.

physical ring — *See* **ring**.

plenum — A space or enclosure in which air or gas is at a higher pressure than that of the outside atmosphere; a rating for network cable that specifies that the cable does not give off a toxic gas when burned.

Point of Presence (POP) — The point of interconnection between the telephone company and the building, floor, or company.

point-to-point — The configuration of one or more interfaces or subinterfaces to connect to multiple virtual circuits. Each circuit will be on its own subnet. Acts like a leased line.

Point-to-Point Protocol (PPP) — An Internet standard WAN protocol defined in RFCs 2153 and 1661; used to provide router-to-router, host-to-router, and host-to-host WAN connections.

policy-based connectivity — A method that the network administrator uses to control access. The network administrator creates policies, such as "no video streaming is allowed at site 1," then implements them on the network, using equipment such as routers and switches.

port — A connection point, usually for network cable, on a device such as a hub, bridge, switch, or router.

port address translation (PAT) — A process used in overloading that allows multiple internal, unregistered IP addresses to use a single external registered address.

port forwarding — A method for sending packets from an external host system through a firewall or NAT router to an internal device. In this way, the internal device IP address is hidden from the external network and yet the internal device can still service requests from the external network.

port-based memory buffering — A memory buffer on a switch assigned by port, equally; doesn't allow for dynamic allocation of buffer space according to the activity level of a port.

Post Office Protocol version 3 (POP3) — A protocol used by client machines, which allows users to check their e-mail boxes on an e-mail server.

power-on self test (POST) — A diagnostic program in ROM that runs when the router is powered on. POST checks hardware availability.

preamble — Binary timing information that precedes an Ethernet frame; used by the receiving station to synchronize its clock circuits so the frame can be received correctly.

Presentation layer — The sixth layer of the OSI network model, responsible for data formatting and encryption.

Primary Rate Interface (PRI) — An ISDN service that provides 23 B-channels for data transfers up to 1.544 Mbps and one D-channel for controlling communications.

privileged EXEC mode — A router mode used to configure the router.

propagation delay — *See* **latency**.

protocol — A definition of rules for communication between two or more computers. Computers must have a common protocol (or a translator) in order to communicate. Also, the element of the PPP frame represented by two bytes used to identify the protocol that is encapsulated.

protocol analyzer — A hardware or software device that can capture and analyze network packets and that is used to analyze traffic flow and packet errors, and to track network problems. Also, *see* **network analyzer**.

protocol data unit (PDU) — Information added to a data packet by the layers of the protocol stack. It can be header or trailer information that is attached to the data packet prior to transmission.

public data network (PDN) — A telecommunications network that connects telephones around the country. These services can be provided by AT&T, Sprint, MCI, and RBOCs.

Public Switched Telephone Network (PSTN) — A telecommunications network that connects telephones around the country.

punch tool — Used to punch down cable at the patch panel or RJ-45 wall jack; completes the connection while simultaneously removing excess wire.

quad zero route — *See* **default route**.

R — The point between non-ISDN equipment (TE2) and the TA.

R-interface — The wire or circuit that connects TE2 to the TA.

radio frequency interference (RFI) — Electronic signal interference caused by radio transmissions.

RADIUS server — RADIUS is an authentication and accounting server.

random access memory (RAM) — Memory that stores the working copy of the router configuration. This configuration is erased if the router is rebooted, unless it is saved to the startup configuration.

read-only memory (ROM) — Memory that contains the necessary routines to boot the system and check its hardware. It also contains a limited version of the Cisco IOS for use only when the primary copies of the IOS in flash memory or on a TFTP server are accidentally lost.

redirect — An ICMP message sent to source hosts requesting that they change routes since the one they chose was not optimal. This packet is used to update a source host's internal routing table.

reference points — Used in ISDN communications to identify specific connection points along the ISDN connection, including the cable that form those connections; See **U and U-interface**.

Registered Jack (RJ) — A type of telecommunications connector that is used for twisted-pair cabling.

remote login application (rlogin) — A utility that allows remote computers to connect to other computers or devices.

Remote Procedure Call (RPC) — A method used to establish communications between computer systems at the Session layer.

repeater — A device that repeats or boosts a network signal along network wire. It reduces signal degradation and increases the maximum usable length of network cable.

Requests for Comments (RFC) — A group of Internet-related documents maintained by the InterNIC that specify Internet protocols and standards.

reset packet (RST) — A packet indicating that the receiver should delete the TCP connection without further interaction.

resistance — Opposition to the flow of electrons in a wire.

Reverse Address Resolution Protocol (RARP) — A protocol used to resolve the client's unknown IP address to the client's MAC address for the final leg of communication between an IP source and destination. RARP clients broadcast a request for their IP address. A RARP server has a table of IP to MAC mappings and responds to the client with a RARP reply.

RG-8 — A type of thick coaxial cable that meets the 10Base5 Ethernet specification.

RG-58 — A type of thin coaxial cable that meets the 10Base2 Ethernet specification.

ring — A physical topology in which computers or other devices are connected in a circle or ring.

RJ-45 to DB-9 — A connector that ships with the router to enable connection to a PC with a DB-9 com port to the router console port.

RJ-45 to DB-25 — A connector that ships with the router to enable connection to a PC with a DB-25 com port to the router console port.

RJ-45 to RJ-45 rollover cable — A cable that connects the console port on the back of the router to an RJ-45 to DB-9 or RJ-45 to DB-25 connector on the back of a PC. This cable ships with the router.

ROM Monitor — A bootstrap program that runs during the power-on self-test and checks basic operations of hardware, including CPU, memory, and interfaces.

ROM Monitor mode — A router mode that allows you to configure your router manually in the event that there is no valid IOS file in your flash memory.

root bridge — The bridge or switch that is designated the point of reference (point of origin) in STP operations. Also known as a root device.

root device — See **root bridge**.

root port — The communications port on a non-root-bridge device that is used for BPDU communication between itself and the root bridge.

routed protocol — A protocol that contains enough OSI Network layer information that its packets can be routed from a source to a remote destination on an internetwork.

router — A device that connects multiple segments, subdivides a network, filters broadcast traffic, and maintains a routing table. A router uses the logical address to move data packets from point to point.

router# — See **enable mode prompt**.

router> — See **user EXEC mode**.

router configuration mode — A router mode that allows you to enable routing protocols such as RIP and IGRP. The prompt for router configuration mode is router(config-router)#.

routing by rumor — The learning of routes through second-hand information, and not directly from the router experiencing the change. Routing by rumor is characteristic of distance-vector routing protocols.

Routing Information Protocol (RIP) — A distance-vector routing protocol that uses hop count as its only metric.

routing loops — A network state in which packets are continually forwarded from one router to another in an attempt to find the destination network.

routing protocols — Protocols used by routers to define and exchange routing table information in an internetwork.

routing table — A table used by a router to determine which of its interfaces is connected to the destination network.

runt — *See* **short frame**.

RXBoot mode — A configuration mode that can be entered when changes to a system make it impossible to boot from the flash memory and a valid IOS image cannot be located.

S — The point between the ISDN customer's TE1 or TA and the network termination, NT1 or NT2.

S-interface — A four-wire cable from TE1 or TA to the NT1 or NT2, which is a two-wire termination point.

S/T — When NT2 is not used on a connection that uses NT1, the connection from the router or TA to the NT1 connection is typically called S/T. This is essentially the combination of the S and T reference points.

segment (noun) — A section of a network that has been subdivided by routers, switches, or bridges.

segment (verb) — To subdivide a network with a networking device, such as a bridge, switch, or router.

segmentation — The process of breaking a network into smaller broadcast or collision domains.

Sequenced Packet Exchange (SPX) — Layer 4 connection-oriented protocol used to provide guaranteed delivery services to IPX.

Serial Line Internet Protocol (SLIP) — A protocol that was originally used for IP connections over serial lines. It was replaced by the more efficient and versatile PPP.

server — A computer that shares resources with other devices on a network.

Service Access Point (SAP) — A protocol located in the Logical Link Control layer; defines how data can be passed up to higher layers.

Service Advertisement Protocol (SAP) — Upper-layer protocol used by IPX/SPX servers to advertise available services; also used by clients to discover what services are available on the local segment.

Service Profile Identifier (SPID) — A reference number assigned to ISDN channels; functions like a phone number.

Session layer — The fifth layer of the OSI model, which controls the connection between two computers sharing data. It maintains, defines, and recovers connections that are established between two computers.

shared memory buffering — Dynamic memory buffer that is shared by all switch ports and allocated according to the needs of the ports; ports that have more activity and/or larger frames to process are allowed to utilize more memory buffer space.

shielded twisted-pair (STP) — Describes a type of cabling in which pairs of wires are twisted around one another inside a wire bundle; the wire bundle is then shielded by a foil coating, which protects it from external interference.

short frame — A frame that is smaller than the 64-byte minimum frame transmission size required by Ethernet.

Shortest Path First (SPF) algorithm — A complex algorithm used by link-state routing protocols to determine the best path in an internetwork.

signal injector — Puts traffic on a wire so that a cable tester can measure attenuation and crosstalk.

signal reference ground — Zero-volt reference point on a computer cabinet or chassis; incoming signals are measured against this ground to determine if they are a "one" or a "zero."

Simple Mail Transfer Protocol (SMTP) — The main protocol that transfers electronic mail on the Internet between e-mail servers.

Simple Network Management Protocol (SNMP) — A protocol that provides network administrators the ability to centrally control and monitor the network.

simplex — A circuit that is unidirectional is called simplex because data can only be transmitted in one direction.

sliding windows — A feature of TCP used to control the flow of communications between two hosts. The size of the TCP sliding window regulates how often acknowledgments will be sent to the transmitting host from the receiving host.

slot time — 512 bit times, which should be slightly longer than the time it takes to transmit a 64-byte frame on an Ethernet wire.

source quench — An ICMP message request to reduce the rate at which the sender is transmitting packets to the destination. This message is used for flow control, when packets arrive too fast (the receiving host runs out of buffer space for the message), or if the system is near capacity (network is congested).

Spanning Tree Algorithm (STA) — The algorithm used by STP to ensure that logical loops are not created in the presence of physical loops on a network.

Spanning Tree Protocol (STP) — The Data Link layer protocol used by switches and bridges to prevent logical loops in a network, even though physical loops may exist.

split horizon — A technique used by routers to prevent routing loops. In short, a router will not send an update for a route via an interface from which it originally received knowledge of that route.

split horizon with poison reverse — A split horizon in which the router responds to attempts to update a route with an update that marks the route in contention as unreachable.

spread spectrum — One of the wireless technologies defined in IEEE 802.11. This technology involves radio frequency transmission with the deliberate spreading of the signal over different frequencies.

stable state — The normal operational states of ports when the root bridge is available and all paths are functioning as expected.

standard IP access lists — Filter traffic based on source IP address.

standard IPX access lists — Filter traffic based on source and destination IPX nodes or networks.

star — Most popular physical topology in which computers are connected to a central device, usually a hub or a MAU.

star-bus — A network architecture that utilizes a physical star topology with a logical bus topology.

star-ring — A network architecture that utilizes a physical star topology with a logical ring topology.

start frame delimiter (SFD) — The one-octet binary pattern (10101011) that indicates that the preamble is over and that the following information should be considered the actual data frame.

static address-to-DLCI Frame Relay map — A Frame Relay map that has been manually created by a network administrator.

static NAT — A type of network address translation (NAT) that allows for a one-to-one mapping of internal to external addresses. One internal address is mapped to one specific external address.

static routes — A route manually added by a network administrator to the routing table of a router.

statistical multiplexing — A method for transmitting several types of data simultaneously across a single line; bandwidth is dynamically allocated to the virtual circuits on a packet-by-packet basis.

sticky-learn — A term used when a switch automatically learns MAC addresses during communications and configures them as permanent due to a limit set by an administrator on the number of MAC addresses that can use a particular port.

storage area network (SAN) — A subsystem of networked storage devices physically separate from the servers.

store-and-forward — A switching method in which the entire transmitted frame is read into a switch's buffer before being forwarded by the switch. This method offers the greatest error reduction, but the highest latency. *See* **cut-through** and **adaptive cut-through**.

Structured Query Language (SQL) — A computer language used to query, manipulate, and communicate with databases.

stub network — A network with only one route to the Internet.

stub router — A router that is last in a chain of routers. There is only one path for all hosts connected to this router to get to the outside world.

subinterface — A logical division of an interface; for example, a single serial interface can be divided into multiple logical subinterfaces.

subnet — A portion of a network that has been separated out from the main network by using a different subnet mask.

subnet mask — A required component for all IP hosts used in combination with an IP address to determine to which subnet the local host belongs. The local host uses this information to determine if the destination is local or remote to the source. Based on this information, the source will either broadcast information on the local network or send the packet to the default gateway for delivery to a remote network.

subnetting — The act of subdividing a network logically with subnet masks.

subnetwork — A portion of the network created by manipulating a network address and breaking it down into smaller parts.

switch — A device used between nodes on a network or between networks to create virtual circuits between two points. A switch increases bandwidth by isolating traffic between two points.

switched bandwidth — A switching technique whereby the total network bandwidth is dedicated to each unicast transmission even if there are multiple unicast transmissions through the switch at the same time. Unicast traffic between devices on a switch do not share the total bandwidth of the network.

switched virtual circuit (SVC) — A temporary virtual circuit created when a network device calls the WAN to establish a connection; is terminated when the connection is terminated.

symmetric switching — A type of LAN switching that requires all devices to be operating at the same speed; it does not allow for a mix of 10-Mbps and 100-Mbps communications.

Symmetrical Digital Subscriber Line (SDSL) — A symmetric digital communication service that utilizes a combination of HDSL and the regular telephone system.

synchronous — Communications that rely on a clock. The clock of the source and destination must be synchronized so that the destination can pick up and interpret the transmitted frames correctly.

Synchronous Data Link Control (SDLC) — A protocol that was developed by IBM in the 1970s to allow IBM host systems to communicate over WAN connections; can be used for point-to-point or point-to-multipoint connections between remote devices and a central mainframe.

synchronous serial — The type of serial connection used with ISDN lines.

System Configuration Dialog — An automated setup routine that runs if you type "setup" from privileged EXEC mode or if the router is started/restarted without a configuration file.

T — The point between NT1 and NT2, which is also the T-interface; a four-wire cable that is used to divide the normal telephone company two-wire cable into four wires, which then allows you to connect up to eight ISDN devices.

T-connector — Used with coaxial cabling to connect a workstation NIC to a coaxial network.

T-interface — *See* **T**.

T1 — North American 24-channel leased digital line capable of supporting up to 1.544-Mbps data and voice transmissions.

T1C — North American 48-channel digital line capable of supporting up to 3.152-Mbps data transmissions.

T2 — North American 96-channel digital line capable of supporting up to 6.312-Mbps data transmissions.

T3 — North American 672-channel digital line capable of supporting up to 44.376-Mbps data transmissions.

T4 — North American 4032-channel digital line capable of supporting up to 274.176-Mbps data transmissions.

TCP/IP — *See* **TCP** and **IP**.

Telecommunications Industry Association (TIA) — Provides standards that define how cabling should be configured on a network; often, these standards are done as a joint operation with the EIA.

Terminal Access Controller Access Control System (TACACS) — An authentication protocol that allows Cisco routers to offload user administration to a central server. TACACS and Extended TAXACS (XTACACS) are defined in RFC 1492.

terminal adapter (TA) — An adapter that allows non-ISDN terminals to operate on ISDN lines.

terminal emulation protocol (telnet) — A connection-oriented, Application layer utility that allows TCP/IP clients to login to a remote system and operate on that system as if the connection between the two were local.

Terminal Equipment 1 (TE1) — A device that supports ISDN standards and can be connected directly to an ISDN network connection.

Terminal Equipment 2 (TE2) — A non-ISDN device, such as an analog phone or modem, which requires a TA in order to connect to an ISDN network.

terminator — A device used at the end of a coaxial segment to absorb a signal and prevent it from reflecting back along the wire.

thick Ethernet — *See* **thicknet**.

thicknet — An Ethernet networking standard that employs RG-8 coaxial cabling; a thicknet network can have segments of up to 500 meters and provides a 10-Mbps baseband transmission rate.

thin Ethernet — *See* **thinnet**.

thinnet — An Ethernet networking standard that employs RG-58 coaxial cabling; the specification includes a 10-Mbps baseband transmission rate and up to 185-meter segments.

three-layer network model — Divides a network into three connectivity layers: core, distribution, and access.

three-way handshake — The method used by TCP to negotiate a reliable connection between two hosts on a network. This process involves the exchange of three data packets before the communication process begins.

throughput — The observed transfer rate of a network; transfer rate is affected by device latency, network traffic, and capacity of source and destination to send and receive traffic.

ticks — 1/18-second time counts used to determine the desirability of a particular route.

Time Division Multiplexing (TDM) — A method for transmitting several types of data simultaneously across a single line; each path (circuit) has dedicated bandwidth allocated to that particular circuit for the duration of the call; less efficient than statistical division multiplexing.

time exceeded — An ICMP message sent whenever a packet's time-to-live (hop count) reaches zero and the datagram is dropped.

time-to-live (TTL) — The number of hops (routers) that a packet can make before it is discarded. The router discards a packet when its TTL is zero, which prevents a packet from looping endlessly around the network. Routers normally decrement the packet TTL by one before passing the packet to the next router.

time-domain reflectometer (TDR) — Cable tester that can detect the overall length of a cable or the distance to a cable break or opening by measuring the distance to where the signal is reflected anytime the wiring is open.

timestamp request/reply — ICMP messages that are used to synchronize clocks by requesting the destination machine's current time of day value, which is given in milliseconds since midnight Universal Time.

Token Ring — A networking method developed by IBM that organizes the network into a physical or logical ring. The token is a logical device and, because stations may only broadcast on the network when they have the token, traffic does not collide.

Token-passing — A network access method that employs the use of a data token to enable a computer to transmit information.

toll network — A section of a WAN that is owned by a telecommunications provider; a monthly billed connection or a per-minute billed connection for the customer.

topology — The physical or logical structure of an internetwork.

trace — A utility that uses ICMP messages to determine the path between a source and destination host. Trace can discover all of the hops (routers) along the path between two points.

transceiver — A device that converts a data signal into an electronic signal for transmission; designed to attach to a specific type of wiring or network media; transceivers for thinnet and UTP are on the NIC; transceivers for thicknet are usually attached to a vampire tap on the cable itself.

transformer — Device that steps voltage up or down where the hot lead originates and the neutral wire is grounded.

transitory state — The operational states of ports that prevent logical loops during a period of transition from one root bridge to another.

Transmission Control Protocol (TCP) — The protocol that guarantees the delivery of a packet by sending an acknowledgment for each window of data received. This protocol operates at the Transport layer and sends its data encapsulated in the IP protocol. TCP communications are also known as connection-oriented because TCP negotiates a communication path between hosts on the network.

Transmission Control Protocol/Internet Protocol (TCP/IP) — Routed protocol stack developed in the late 1960s for use on the precursor to the Internet; protocol stack of the modern-day Internet.

transmission time — The time it takes for a transmission to go from the source host to the destination host.

Transport layer — The fourth layer of the OSI reference model, which segments and reassembles data frames. It also provides for connection-oriented and connectionless communications. Also, the TCP/IP layer that maps directly to the OSI model Transport layer.

triggered updates — Occur due to network topology changes, not periodic route table advertisements.

Trivial File Transfer Protocol (TFTP) — A file transfer utility used on the Internet. TFTP uses UDP to transfer files and is therefore less reliable than FTP, which uses TCP in transferring files.

Trivial File Transfer Protocol (TFTP) server — A computer that provides TFTP services and can be used to maintain the IOS and configuration file of a Cisco router.

two-layer network model — Divides a network into two connectivity layers: core and access.

U — The point that defines the demarcation between the user network and the telecommunications provider ISDN facility.

U-interface — The actual two-wire cable, also called the local loop, which connects the customer's equipment to the telecommunications provider.

unicast — A frame that is sent/addressed to a single destination host; compare to multicast and broadcast.

Universal Time Code (UTC) — Based on the time in the city of Greenwich in the United Kingdom. All other time zones are either plus or minus hours of the clocks in Greenwich.

unshielded twisted-pair (UTP) — A type of cabling in which pairs of wires are twisted around one another inside a wire bundle.

User Datagram Protocol (UDP) — The protocol that operates at the Transport Layer and transports data unreliably over IP. This is sometimes known as connectionless communication because the messages are sent without expectation of acknowledgment. There is no connection negotiation process as in TCP. The packets that are sent by UDP are also known as datagrams. Since UDP does not negotiate a connection, it is faster than TCP.

user EXEC mode — A router mode that allows a network operator to check router status, see if the interfaces are operational, and review several of the router settings.

user mode — *See* **user EXEC mode**.

vertical cabling — *See* **backbone**.

Very-high-data-rate Digital Subscriber Line (VDSL) — A digital subscriber technology that supports 51.84-Mbps connections over unshielded twisted-pair cable.

virtual circuit — A private connection between two points created by a switch that allows the two points to use the entire available bandwidth between them without contention.

virtual LAN (VLAN) — A logical broadcast domain on a LAN, created by one or more switches, that is not constrained by the physical configuration.

virtual terminal password — A password that is used to access the router over a telnet connection.

virtual terminals (VTY) — Terminals provided with each Cisco router that can be used by telnet sessions to configure the router.

VLAN Trunking Protocol (VTP) — A Data Link layer protocol used to track VLAN membership changes across trunk links between VTP-enabled devices.

volatile — Contents of memory that are lost when the power is turned off. RAM is an example of volatile memory.

VTP client — A VTP device that receives and shares VTP information, but one that does not add, modify, or delete information and does not store the VTP database in NVRAM.

VTP domain — A group of VTP-enabled devices configured under one name to share VLAN information.

VTP pruning — An option configured for an entire VTP domain that prohibits the forwarding of VTP updates about VLANs disabled on specific trunk links.

VTP server — A VTP device that is capable of adding, modifying, sending, and deleting VTP configuration information.

VTP transparent — A device that does not participate in receiving or managing VTP domains, but will forward VTP information through its trunk ports.

WAV — An audio file format used with Microsoft Windows applications.

Well Known Ports — TCP and UDP ports from 0 through 1023 on which client applications expect to find common Internet services.

wide area network (WAN) — A network that spans two or more geographically diverse locations and typically uses public telecommunications carriers in order to connect its individual segments.

wildcard mask — Applied to IP addresses to determine if an access list line will act upon a packet. Zeros are placed in positions deemed significant, and ones are placed in nonsignificant positions.

wire map — A function that displays the connections of UTP wiring from point to point; used to see if the connectors were properly wired.

wireless — Communications that are not conducted over physical wires or cables. These communications can include infrared, radio, and other types of transmissions that are sent through the air between two or more locations.

wiring closet — A central junction point, usually located in a separate room, used for interconnecting various network devices.

X-Windows — A standard graphical user interface (GUI) used on UNIX systems.

xDSL — *See* **Digital Subscriber Line**.

Index

Special Characters

^ (caret), 196

> (greater-than symbol), 192, 194, 207

(pound sign), 194, 202, 205–206

? (question mark), 192, 193

[] (square brackets), 317

A

AC (alternating current) signal noise, 128–129

access layer, 138, 140, 147

access list(s)

  activity, logging, 328

  counters, 334–335

  described, 311–312, 343, 440

  displaying, 322–323, 325–326, 337, 340, 342

  established parameter and, 333–334, 344

  examples, 321–333, 335–342

  extended IP, 327–335

  extended IPX, 337–340

  monitoring, 334–335, 337, 339–340, 342

  named, 342

  removing, 315, 324, 333, 337

  routers and, 312–316, 318, 321–328, 333, 337, 340–342

  rules, 314–317

  standard IP, 317–327, 333, 334

  standard IPX, 335–337

  troubleshooting, 313–314, 334

  VLANs and, 437

wildcard masks and, 317–320, 322, 328, 329

access methods. *See also* CSMA/CD (Carrier Sense Multiple Access with Collision Detection)

  defined, 104, 133–134

  Ethernet, 406–414

access rates. *See also* bandwidth

  described, 177

  design considerations and, 117–121

  Frame Relay and, 167, 387

ACK (acknowledgement), 12, 54–56

active

  hubs, 29

  monitor, 135

  state, 382

adaptive cut-through switches, 423

ADCCP (Advanced Data Communication Control Procedures), 163

Add/Remove Programs applet, 180

Address field, 387–389

Address Resolution Protocol. *See* ARP (Address Resolution Protocol)

administration system, 143, 147

administrative distance

  changing, 271–272

  described, 261–262, 273

  IGRP and, 267

ADSL (Asymmetric Digital Subscriber Line), 365

Advanced Data Communication Control Procedures (ADCCP). *See* ADCCP (Advanced Data Communication Control Procedures)

Advanced Research Projects Agency. *See* ARPA (Advanced Research Projects Agency)

Advanced Research Projects Agency Network. *See* ARPANET (Advanced Research Projects Agency Network)

agents, defined, 143, 147

alignment errors, 409, 440

algorithms, 31, 196, 214, 257, 258, 425

American National Standards Institute. *See* ANSI (American National Standards Institute)

American Registry of Internet Numbers. *See* ARIN (American Registry of Internet Numbers)

American Standard Code for Information Interchange. *See* ASCII (American Standard Code for Information Interchange)

American Telephone & Telegraph. *See* AT&T (American Telephone & Telegraph)

amplifiers, 28, 38

analog networks, 28

AND operation, 71–72, 80

ANSI (American National Standards Institute), 136, 147, 160, 378, 383

any keyword, 322, 343